Clinical Intelligence in Medical Malpractice

A Practical Framework for Evaluating Negligence, Causation, Wrongful Death, and Damages

By Michelle Carroll

Lexcura Summit
Gainesville, Florida

I0874388

Dedication

For the patients and families whose lives cannot be fully understood from the medical record alone.

Preface

Why This Book Was Written

Medical-malpractice cases are rarely difficult because counsel lacks records. They are difficult because the records do not arrive with an explanation of what mattered.

A file may contain thousands of pages of hospital documentation, office notes, laboratory reports, imaging interpretations, policies, medication records, and expert opinions. Every page may appear relevant. Yet the questions that determine whether the case should proceed can remain unresolved.

What was happening to the patient before the disputed care? When did the clinical picture change? What information was available to the responsible professional? What did that information reasonably mean at the time? What treatment remained available, and what difference would it probably have made?

Those questions are clinical before they become legal.

Attorneys are trained to identify disputed facts, test testimony, apply legal standards, and build persuasive arguments. They are not expected to practice medicine. They do, however, need enough command of the medical course to know what their experts are assuming, where the record is incomplete, which disagreement actually matters, and whether the proposed theory fits the patient.

That need is what led to this book.

In reviewing medical-malpractice, wrongful-death, and healthcare-negligence matters, I repeatedly saw cases become committed to a theory before the patient's course had been reconstructed. A severe outcome created understandable urgency. One troubling note or delayed response appeared to explain everything that followed. An expert identified a departure, and the case began moving before anyone had established whether the proposed treatment remained available or whether it probably would have changed the outcome.

I also saw the opposite problem. Patients with age, disability, chronic disease, or limited life expectancy were sometimes treated as though nothing meaningful remained to be lost. Their baseline was reduced to a diagnosis list. Their retained independence, relationships, decision-making, comfort, or expected survival disappeared from the analysis.

Both errors arise when the outcome begins controlling the medicine.

The Clinical Intelligence framework is intended to prevent that. It begins with the integrity of the evidence and the patient's actual baseline. It then examines objective evidence, reconstructs the clinically material timeline, identifies the relevant professional and institutional obligations, defines the treatment opportunity, tests competing causes, and measures the additional injury the disputed care probably produced.

The framework does not assume that the case belongs to the plaintiff or the defense.

A careful review may strengthen the original claim. It may narrow the actionable period, reduce the number of defendants, or change the injury from complete prevention to increased severity. It may reveal an institutional failure where the case initially appeared to concern one individual. It may support resolution. It may strengthen the defense. It may show that the matter should not proceed.

Each can be the proper result.

The purpose is not to produce more criticism. It is to produce a more reliable explanation.

This book is written for attorneys who already understand litigation. It does not attempt to teach civil procedure, evidence, or the basic elements of negligence. Its focus is the clinical foundation beneath those legal questions.

The chapters move through the work in the order counsel commonly encounters it: initial assessment, record completeness, baseline, objective evidence, timeline, workflow, standard of care, causation, damages, expert selection, discovery, deposition, valuation, mediation, and trial. The later chapters apply the framework to realistic case patterns involving stroke, postoperative deterioration, infection, medication error, abnormal-result follow-up, nursing-facility wounds, and difficult defense evaluations.

Those applications are important because medical analysis cannot remain abstract. The meaning of delay depends on the disease. The value of an earlier intervention depends on eligibility, timing, available resources, and patient condition. The significance of a missed result depends on what the result showed and what timely action would have produced. The effect of an injury depends on the life the patient was living before it occurred.

The same framework must therefore lead to different conclusions in different patients.

Clinical Intelligence is not a substitute for qualified expert testimony. It is the disciplined work that allows counsel to identify the right experts, ask better questions, recognize unsupported assumptions, and bring the separate opinions into one coherent case.

The framework is most useful when it eventually disappears.

A mediator should not hear counsel recite a model. A jury should not be asked to follow a checklist. They should understand the patient's course: who the patient was, what changed, when the obligation arose, what response remained available, and what difference the disputed care made.

That understanding must come before advocacy.

Once it does, advocacy becomes more focused, more credible, and more difficult to defeat.

Copyright Page

Clinical Intelligence in Medical Malpractice
A Practical Framework for Evaluating Negligence, Causation, Wrongful Death, and Damages

Published by Lexcura Summit
Gainesville, Florida

First edition, 2026

The information contained in this book is provided for educational and professional-development purposes only. It is not legal advice, medical advice, or a substitute for the independent judgment of qualified legal counsel, licensed healthcare professionals, or retained experts.

Medical-malpractice, wrongful-death, and healthcare-negligence matters are fact-specific and jurisdiction-dependent. Standards of care, evidentiary requirements, procedural rules, and legal doctrines vary by jurisdiction and may change over time. Readers should consult applicable law, current professional guidance, and appropriately qualified experts before relying on any analysis in a particular matter.

The case examples in this book are intended to illustrate clinical and litigation principles. Identifying details have been altered, combined, or fictionalized where necessary to protect confidentiality. Any resemblance to a specific patient, clinician, institution, claim, or proceeding is coincidental unless expressly stated otherwise.

References to professional standards, clinical practices, policies, guidelines, or medical literature should be evaluated in the context of the time, location, specialty, patient population, and circumstances involved.

Lexcura Summit and the author make no representation or warranty concerning the outcome of any case, claim, investigation, negotiation, mediation, or trial.

ISBN: 979-8-952094-06-2

Printed in the United States of America

Contents

Introduction 1

Acknowledgments 11

PART I - Foundations of Clinical Intelligence 12

Chapter 1 - Why Medical Cases Fail Despite Serious Injuries 13

Chapter 2 - The Clinical Intelligence Model 31

Chapter 3 - The First Attorney Assessment 51

PART II - Building the Clinical Record 66

Chapter 4 - Building the Preliminary Clinical Theory 67

Chapter 5 - Determining Whether the Medical Record Is Complete 84

Chapter 6 - Establishing the Patient's True Baseline 108

Chapter 7 - Imaging and Objective Evidence Analysis 129

Chapter 8 - Reconstructing the Clinically Material Timeline 147

Chapter 9 - Reconstructing Communication and Clinical Workflow 166

PART III - Standard of Care, Responsibility, and Causation 189

Chapter 10 - Identifying the Patient-Specific Standard of Care 190

Chapter 11 - Distinguishing Reasonable Clinical Judgment From Departure 207

Chapter 12 - Identifying Individual and Institutional Responsibility 224

Chapter 13 - Using Policies, Regulations, Guidelines, and Protocols Correctly 244

Chapter 14 - Separating Breach From Causation 263

Chapter 15 - Identifying the Treatment or Rescue Opportunity 281

Chapter 16 - Reconstructing the Probable Alternative Course 301

Chapter 17 - Testing Competing Causes 321

Chapter 18 - Wrongful Death, Accelerated Death, and Lost Survival 345

Chapter 19 - Distinguishing New Injury, Aggravation, Acceleration, and Increased Severity 369

PART IV - Damages, Experts, and Litigation Strategy 394

Chapter 20 - Functional Damages and the Patient's Changed Life 395

Contents

Chapter 21 - Future Care, Life-Care Planning, and Economic Loss 423

Chapter 22 - Selecting and Directing the Correct Experts 449

Chapter 23 - Using Clinical Intelligence in Discovery 475

Chapter 24 - Preparing Clinically Effective Depositions 497

Chapter 25 - Evaluating the Strength of the Opposing Medical Theory 521

Chapter 26 - Classifying the Case After Clinical Review 543

Chapter 27 - Deciding Whether to Proceed, Narrow, Redirect, Resolve, or Stop 561

Chapter 28 - Settlement Valuation Through Clinical Risk 575

Chapter 29 - Presenting the Clinical Theory in Mediation and Trial 591

PART V - Applied Case Analysis 610

Chapter 30 - Delayed Stroke Diagnosis After Repeated Emergency Encounters 611

Chapter 31 - Postoperative Deterioration and Failure to Rescue 629

Chapter 32 - Missed Infection and Wrongful Death in a Medically Fragile Patient 646

Chapter 33 - Medication Error, Monitoring Failure, and Multistage Responsibility 663

Chapter 34 - Institutional Failure to Communicate or Follow Up an Abnormal Result 681

Chapter 35 - Nursing-Facility Decline, Wound Progression, and Amputation 697

Chapter 36 - When the Model Shows the Case Should Not Proceed 714

Chapter 37 - When the Model Strengthens the Defense 727

PART VI - Judgment, Conclusion, and Practice Tools 744

Chapter 38 - Understanding Before Advocacy 745

Conclusion - The Case the Medicine Can Support 758

Appendix A - The Clinical Intelligence Case-Review Framework 763

Contents

Appendix B - Preliminary Medical-Malpractice Case Assessment 770

Appendix C - Questions for Expert Review 773

Appendix D - Clinical Intelligence in Relation to Established Frameworks 776

Introduction

Understanding the Medicine Before Building the Case

Medical-malpractice, wrongful-death, and healthcare-negligence matters rarely arrive in a form that permits an immediate judgment. They usually arrive as a story of serious harm.

A patient entered the hospital walking and left unable to care for himself. A mother deteriorated after delivery. A child returned for care several times before a serious diagnosis was made. A surgical patient worsened overnight while the chart continued to describe the recovery as expected. An abnormal result was reported, but no one acted on it. A nursing-facility resident developed a wound, infection, or decline that the family believes should have been prevented.

By the time the matter reaches counsel, the outcome is already known. The family may have spent months, sometimes years, trying to understand it. Later clinicians may have said what they believe should have happened. The records may contain language that appears incriminating. One missed test, delayed call, discharge decision, or unexplained gap in care may seem to account for everything that followed. Sometimes it does. Often, the connection is not that simple.

The first task is not to decide whether the injury is serious. That is usually apparent. Nor is it to identify something that could have been done differently. In a complicated medical course, another test, consultation, period of observation, or treatment can almost always be imagined after the outcome is known.

The harder work is determining what was happening to the patient before the disputed care, what information became available, what that information reasonably meant at the time, what response the situation required, what treatment opportunity remained, and what difference another course probably would have made.

Until those questions are answered, counsel has an allegation and an outcome, but not yet a reliable clinical theory.

That distinction becomes difficult to maintain when the injury is severe. Once postoperative bleeding has been confirmed, every earlier change in blood pressure can begin to look like an obvious warning. Once a stroke is diagnosed, a prior complaint of dizziness can appear unmistakably neurological. Once meningitis is found, an earlier fever, irritability, or loss of appetite may seem diagnostic.

Later evidence may reveal what was happening biologically. It does not automatically establish what was reasonably recognizable earlier.

The disease may have been present before a clinician had enough information to identify it. A complication may have begun before the findings required intervention. An abnormality may be visible during retrospective imaging review without having been sufficiently apparent to make the original interpretation unreasonable.

Counsel is asked to examine the past. The medicine has to be examined without pretending the future was already known.

Cases often lose their footing when that discipline is abandoned. Some are built around an error that did not cause the injury being claimed. Others assume that earlier treatment would have produced a favorable result without identifying the treatment, whether the patient remained eligible for it, how quickly it could have occurred, or what benefit was probable.

The opposite mistake is just as serious. An elderly, disabled, or medically fragile patient may be treated as though nothing meaningful remained to be lost. Yet a person can carry several serious diagnoses and remain independent, cognitively intact, employed, responsible for a household, or central to a family. Even where cure was no longer possible, negligent care may have accelerated death, increased the severity of injury, removed a treatment option, prolonged suffering, or caused greater dependence.

The patient's prior condition matters. It does not erase the patient.

A sound review therefore begins with who the patient was before the event and what changed afterward. That inquiry usually requires more than reading the designated medical record from beginning to end.

Healthcare is documented across systems that do not always travel together. The physician's note may appear in one platform, the medication record in another, imaging in a separate archive, and secure communications in a system omitted from the ordinary production. A referral may be visible without evidence that the appointment occurred. A result may appear in an inbox without showing whether anyone opened it. A medication order may not establish what the patient received. A signed note may not show what the clinician knew when the decision was made.

The production can be enormous and still omit the evidence that controls the case.

This becomes particularly important when timing is disputed. Medical records contain several kinds of time. Symptoms begin and are reported later. A clinician examines the patient and signs the note hours afterward. A test is ordered, performed, interpreted, finalized, routed, acknowledged, and acted upon at different moments. Medication may be prescribed promptly and administered late. A nurse may recognize deterioration before documenting it. A consultant may give advice that is implemented only after another delay.

A chronology can place every entry in order and still fail to explain the patient's course.

The important interval is the period during which the patient's condition changed, that change became reasonably significant, the plan should have changed, and treatment continued to offer a meaningful benefit.

That interval may be much shorter than the period first alleged. A postoperative case may initially appear to involve twelve hours of neglect. Closer review may show that the first eight hours were consistent with ordinary recovery and that the real concern arose during the final four, when tachycardia persisted, urine output fell, pain increased, blood pressure declined, and the response to fluid did not hold.

A delayed-diagnosis case may appear to involve several missed encounters. The evidence may show that the condition became reasonably recognizable only at the second or third presentation.

Narrowing the case in that way is not a retreat. It is often the first indication that the theory is becoming clinically accurate.

The same discipline belongs in causation. A professional departure and a causal injury are separate conclusions. A result may have been missed without changing prognosis. A patient may have been discharged after an incomplete reassessment and later deteriorated from a process that developed after leaving. A complication may have been recognized too slowly, while the additional delay prolonged hospitalization without causing the permanent disability being alleged. Those possibilities should not be assumed. They have to be tested.

The treatment opportunity must be described as an actual clinical course. What would appropriate care have involved? Would the patient have been admitted, transferred, imaged, operated upon, medicated, or observed longer? How soon could that have happened? Was the patient a candidate? What risks or contraindications existed? How much injury had already occurred, and what benefit remained probable?

"Earlier treatment" is not enough.

The alternative course must be reconstructed with the same care as the course that occurred. It may include further delay, treatment risks, residual impairment, prolonged recovery, or injury that could not have been avoided despite reasonable care.

The question is not whether counsel can imagine a better result. It is whether a materially better result was probable.

The answer is often narrower than the theory formed at intake. The patient may have sustained some neurological injury but probably would have retained speech or independent mobility. A limb may not have been fully salvageable, but a lower amputation may have been avoided. A patient with cancer may not have been assured a cure, but may have lost earlier-stage treatment and meaningful survival. A medically fragile resident may not have returned to perfect health, but may have survived an acute infection or avoided a far more difficult final course. The injury should be stated at the level the medicine supports.

That judgment affects far more than credibility at trial. It determines which experts are needed, which records should be pursued, how discovery is directed, what damages can be supported, how the case is valued, and what counsel can responsibly tell the client.

An overstated theory sends every later part of the case in the wrong direction. A life-care planner may project services that do not match the causal opinion. An economist may calculate a work life the patient probably would not have had. A wrongful-death claim may assume ordinary life expectancy when the medical evidence supports a shorter period of lost survival.

Sophisticated legal work cannot repair an imprecise clinical foundation.

The Clinical Intelligence Model is intended to provide counsel with a disciplined way to understand that foundation before the case becomes committed to a theory the evidence cannot carry. It does not replace legal judgment or the qualified experts whose opinions will be required.

The review begins with the integrity of the evidence because no conclusion is stronger than the material beneath it. It establishes baseline because causation and damages depend on knowing what existed before the event. It examines objective evidence and reconstructs the clinical course because the narrative chart does not always show what was happening or when it became important. It considers professional and institutional responsibility because healthcare is delivered through both individual judgment and operational systems. It then examines the treatment opportunity, the probable alternative course, and the additional injury that can fairly be attributed. The final decision remains counsel's.

As the evidence develops, the case may become stronger. It may narrow to one encounter, one defendant, or one injury. It may move from technical negligence to failure to rescue, from individual fault to institutional responsibility, or from complete prevention to increased severity. A departure may be established while causation remains too uncertain to proceed. A troubling record may ultimately support the defense.

A useful framework has to permit each of those results. Its value does not lie in finding liability. It lies in making the reason for the conclusion visible.

The cases discussed throughout this book involve different patients, ages, diseases, and care settings. A birth-injury matter will not contain the same evidence as a delayed cancer diagnosis. A young adult with stroke will not have the same baseline or treatment opportunity as a frail nursing-facility resident. Medication toxicity in pregnancy may involve separate causal questions for the mother and child. A postoperative complication may begin during reasonable care and become actionable only when rescue is delayed.

The clinical questions remain recognizable even though the answers change with the patient.

This book is written for attorneys who already understand litigation. It does not reduce medical cases to a checklist or repeat the basic proposition that an adverse outcome does not establish negligence. Its focus is the point at which clinical understanding changes legal strategy: determining whether the record is genuinely complete, reconstructing baseline and the material course, interpreting objective evidence in context, identifying where responsibility rested, defining the treatment opportunity, testing competing causes, and matching damages to the additional loss the evidence supports.

The later case applications show what happens when those questions are answered honestly. Some cases become stronger. Some narrow or change direction. Some should not proceed. That is not inconsistency. It is the purpose of the work.

The outcome brings the case to counsel's attention. The client's account begins the inquiry. The records and experts develop the evidence.

Before advocacy begins, someone has to understand what happened to the patient.

A Note About the Case Examples

The case examples in this book are presented to illustrate clinical and litigation analysis. They are not intended as reports of identifiable patients, professionals, institutions, claims, or proceedings.

Details may have been altered, combined, generalized, or fictionalized to protect confidentiality and to focus attention on the analytical principles being discussed. The examples should not be read as establishing the standard of care for every patient, facility, specialty, or jurisdiction.

Each medical-malpractice matter must be evaluated according to its own record, applicable law, relevant professional standards, available resources, and qualified expert testimony.

Acknowledgments

This book grew from years of examining difficult medical records, reconstructing patient courses, and working with attorneys who understood that the strongest advocacy begins with an honest assessment of the medicine.

I am grateful to the attorneys, physicians, nurses, clinical professionals, and consultants whose questions and insights helped refine the Clinical Intelligence framework. Their willingness to examine difficult facts, reconsider early assumptions, and remain focused on the patient strengthened both the method and this book.

I also acknowledge the patients and families whose experiences reveal how much can be lost when a medical record is read without understanding the life behind it. Their stories are the reason this work matters.

Finally, I am grateful to my family for their encouragement, patience, and belief in this project.

PART I

FOUNDATIONS OF CLINICAL INTELLIGENCE

Chapters 1–3

CHAPTER ONE

Why Medical Cases Fail Despite Serious Injuries

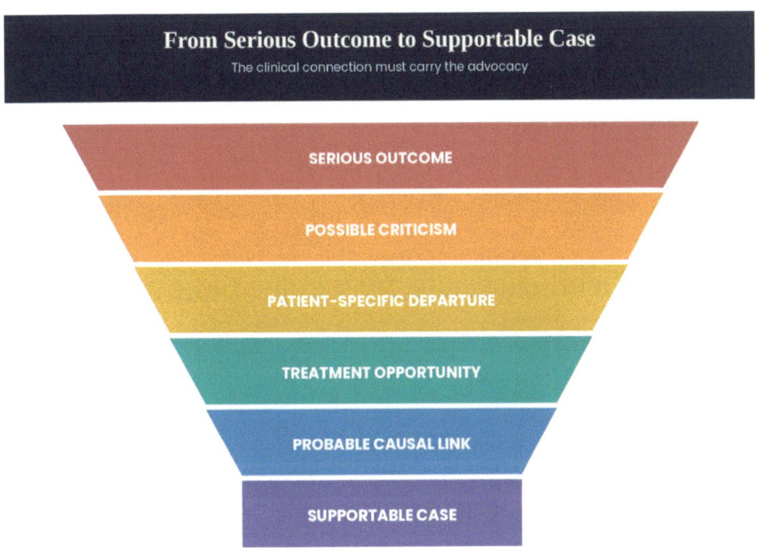

A serious medical injury can make a case feel established before the medicine has been understood.

The patient died. A child sustained permanent neurological injury. Someone entered the hospital living independently and returned home dependent on others.

A postoperative complication led to weeks in intensive care. A delayed diagnosis changed the treatment that remained available.

The scale of the harm naturally draws attention to the care that came before it. That is also where the first analytical danger appears.

A devastating outcome can create the impression that the care must contain an equally serious failure. Sometimes it does. In other cases, the outcome was driven largely by the underlying disease, by a complication that can occur despite reasonable care, or by an injury that had already become irreversible before the disputed decision was made.

The difficult cases are not separated by whether something terrible happened. They are separated by whether the evidence provides a clinically coherent explanation of why it happened and what reasonable care probably would have changed.

Experienced attorneys already know that injury does not establish negligence and negligence does not establish causation. The difficulty is holding those principles steady when the client's account is compelling, the record is incomplete, the medicine is unfamiliar, and one troubling entry appears to confirm the theory formed at intake.

A case can gather momentum quickly under those conditions. The family identifies the moment everything changed. A later physician says the diagnosis should have been made sooner. The chart contains an abnormal result, a delayed consultation, an unexplained discharge, or a note that seems inconsistent with the patient's condition. An expert offers an early indication that the care can be criticized. Each development appears to support the same conclusion.

By the time contrary evidence emerges, the case may already have a settled narrative, multiple defendants, retained experts, projected damages, and a client who understandably believes the central question has been answered. That is one reason medical cases fail late.

They do not fail for lack of effort. They fail after extensive record collection, expert review, discovery, motion practice, and expense. The weakness was present earlier, but the case was never organized in a way that exposed it.

The first question often asked is whether the care could have been better. In most cases, the answer is yes.

Another test could have been ordered. A specialist could have been consulted. The patient could have been observed longer. Documentation could have been clearer. A nurse could have escalated concern more forcefully. A physician could have chosen the more cautious course. A hospital could have designed a more reliable process.

Healthcare is full of available alternatives. The existence of one does not establish that the approach taken fell outside the range of reasonable practice.

Even when the care did fall outside that range, another question remains: what did the difference cause? That is where many apparently strong cases become unstable.

An abnormal result may have been overlooked, while timely follow-up still would not have changed the stage of disease. A patient may have been discharged after an incomplete reassessment and later deteriorated from a process that developed after leaving. A surgeon may have been slow to recognize a complication, while the additional delay prolonged hospitalization without causing the permanent impairment alleged. A referral system may have failed after the patient had already passed the point at which treatment was likely to help.

Those possibilities should not be accepted without investigation. They illustrate why a clear departure and a serious injury do not complete the same analysis. The reverse error can be just as damaging.

A patient may have been elderly, medically complex, disabled, or living with advanced disease. Those facts affect treatment eligibility, recovery, life expectancy, and damages. They do not answer whether the patient suffered an additional loss.

A person with several chronic illnesses may still have been living independently. A nursing-facility resident may have required substantial assistance while remaining alert, communicative, comfortable, and closely connected to family. A patient with cancer may have had limited life expectancy and still lost meaningful survival.

A child with developmental limitations may have sustained a new injury that altered an already complicated course.

Medical fragility is not a defense by itself. It may explain why the patient was vulnerable, but it may also explain why delayed treatment or inadequate monitoring carried greater consequences.

The patient's pre-event condition must be understood rather than reduced to a problem list. Otherwise, the plaintiff may attribute prior limitations to the disputed care, while the defense treats those same limitations as though nothing remained to be lost.

Both positions become less credible once the actual patient comes into view.

Another early weakness lies in the way the case is first described. Clients usually bring facts and conclusions together because they have lived through the outcome and are trying to make sense of it.

"They ignored the infection."

"The radiologist missed the cancer."

"They sent her home while she was having a stroke."

"The facility let the wound become infected."

"The surgeon caused the bleeding."

Any of those statements may prove substantially correct. Each may also combine several clinical questions that have to be separated before the theory can be trusted.

In an infection case, counsel still needs to determine whether the infection was present during the earlier encounter, whether it was clinically recognizable, what signs were available, what treatment would have followed, and whether that treatment probably would have changed the outcome.

In a delayed-cancer case, the original imaging must be reviewed. Was the study technically adequate? Was the lesion visible? Was it a finding a reasonable reader should have recognized at the time, or did its significance become apparent only after later progression? What treatment would earlier detection realistically have made available?

A stroke case requires the same discipline. The condition may already have been developing during the first visit, but that does not establish that the symptoms required stroke treatment at that point. Counsel still needs to know whether the patient was eligible for intervention, when the relevant findings became recognizable, and how much injury had already occurred.

A nursing-facility wound may have been preventable, but immobility, vascular disease, malnutrition, and poor healing may also have made some degree of injury likely. The stronger causal question may be whether delayed escalation made the wound deeper, more infected, or more likely to require amputation.

The client should not be expected to answer those questions. The client's account begins the investigation. It does not complete the medical analysis.

Family members often know facts the chart does not contain. They may have seen confusion, weakness, pain, reduced responsiveness, or loss of function that was poorly documented. They may understand the patient's prior independence better than any clinician involved in the disputed event. They may remember telephone calls, conversations, or instructions that never entered the record.

That evidence can be essential, but it still has to be considered beside the contemporaneous documentation, objective findings, later clinical course, and qualified expert interpretation. The family knows the patient and the consequence. The clinical pathway between earlier care and later injury must be established independently.

A second source of failure is the assumption that a large production is a complete production.

Medical cases often arrive with thousands of pages. The records may be indexed, placed in chronological order, and divided by provider. The file may include physician notes, nursing entries, laboratory reports, medication lists, discharge summaries, billing records, and consultant documentation. It looks complete because it is large. The evidence that decides the case may still be missing.

The original imaging may not have been produced with the written reports. The electronic record may omit the routing history showing where an abnormal result went. Medication-administration data may differ from the physician's order. Secure messages, call logs, staffing records, device downloads, pharmacy information, pathology material, fetal-monitoring data, ambulance records, referral platforms, and records from other facilities may exist outside the ordinary chart.

In a missed-result case, the report may be less important than the path it followed after finalization. In a medication case, the prescription may not establish the dose the patient received. In a deterioration case, a progress note entered later may not show what the clinician knew when the decision was made. In a transfer case, the sending hospital's chart may not contain the communication record maintained by the receiving facility or transport service.

The record request has to follow the clinical problem rather than the institution's standard production. Otherwise, counsel may spend months organizing the wrong evidence.

Time creates a related problem because the medical record does not contain one type of timestamp.

A symptom begins and is reported later. A nurse notices a change and documents it after completing care. A physician examines the patient before entering the note. A test is ordered, performed, interpreted, finalized, transmitted, acknowledged, and acted upon at different times. Medication is ordered promptly and administered later. A consultation occurs by telephone, while the formal note is signed hours afterward. Those differences can determine the case.

The chart may make a response appear prompt because the order and note were entered near the time treatment occurred, while audit data shows that the critical information had been available much earlier. The reverse can also happen. A late-signed note may create the appearance of delay even though the examination or communication occurred promptly.

A chronology that merely arranges entries by timestamp can therefore be accurate and clinically misleading.

The useful timeline asks when the patient's condition changed, when the change became reasonably recognizable, when the plan should have changed, and how long effective treatment remained available. That interval is often narrower than the initial allegation.

A patient may have remained in the hospital for twelve hours before emergency surgery. The case may not concern all twelve. The early period may have been consistent with reasonable observation. The actionable period may begin only when treatment failed, new findings appeared, or the patient's course no longer fit the working diagnosis.

Delayed-diagnosis cases present the same issue in another form. Disease may have existed biologically long before it became clinically detectable. The fact that the diagnosis was eventually made does not mean it should have been identified at every earlier encounter.

Counsel has to locate the point at which the available evidence changed the professional obligation. That may be the first visit, the second visit, the return of a test result, the failure of treatment, the patient's return, or the moment a reassuring explanation stopped fitting the course.

Cases become stronger when that transition is identified honestly. They become weaker when every earlier encounter is criticized because the final diagnosis is now known.

Hindsight cannot be removed from retrospective review, but it does not have to control the analysis.

Later evidence may show that infection was developing, ischemia was progressing, bleeding had begun, or cancer was already present. It does not automatically establish that the earlier presentation required a different response.

A specialist may later identify a subtle abnormality on an old image. The existence of the abnormality and the reasonableness of the original interpretation remain separate questions.

A later stroke diagnosis may explain the biological meaning of earlier dizziness. It does not establish that dizziness alone required stroke treatment. A later diagnosis of sepsis may show that infection was already developing without identifying the point at which the earlier pattern required hospital transfer.

Professional conduct must be evaluated through the information available at the time. Causation must still be evaluated through what was actually happening in the patient. The work requires both perspectives.

Policies, protocols, and guidelines can create another kind of premature certainty. They may be highly relevant. They can define result-notification procedures, escalation pathways, medication safeguards, staffing responsibilities, referral processes, and monitoring requirements. They may show that an institution recognized a particular risk and adopted a method intended to control it.

A deviation may matter. It does not decide the case without context.

Counsel still needs to determine whether the policy applied to the patient and setting, which role it governed, whether it was in effect at the time, what risk it addressed, and whether the deviation represented the failure of a real safeguard or merely a technical difference in practice. It is also necessary to ask whether another equivalent process was used and whether the departure affected treatment or outcome.

Guidelines require the same care. A recommendation may describe accepted or preferred practice without defining what reasonable care required in every patient. Contraindications, competing risks, resource limitations, and presentations outside the studied population may affect its application.

A guideline is useful when connected to the actual decision. It becomes misleading when a general recommendation is treated as though it resolves a patient-specific dispute. Expert support can produce the same false confidence.

A favorable opinion may be necessary to proceed. Its existence does not establish the strength of its foundation.

Counsel needs to know what the expert reviewed, which facts were assumed, what contrary evidence was considered, and whether the opinion answers the question the litigation actually presents.

An expert may say earlier treatment would have improved the outcome without identifying what treatment would have been given, when it could have begun, whether the patient was eligible, or how much improvement was probable. A specialist may describe the care that would have been ideal at a tertiary center while overlooking the reasonable options available to a generalist in a smaller facility. An imaging expert may identify an abnormality without being qualified to say how treatment would have changed the later neurological course. A standard-of-care expert may establish that escalation was required and remain unable to determine whether rescue was still possible.

The opinion may not be wrong. It may simply be incomplete for the legal and medical question counsel needs to answer.

A viable case depends on alignment. The factual record, timeline, objective evidence, standard-of-care analysis, causation opinion, and damages theory must describe the same patient moving through the same course.

When they do not, the weakness can remain hidden for a long time.

The standard-of-care expert may place the required intervention at noon while the causation expert assumes treatment could have begun at nine. The rehabilitation expert may predict meaningful recovery while the life-care planner projects the current level of dependence for life. The damages analysis may assume the patient was fully independent while prior records show substantial assistance before the event. A wrongful-death theory may assume cure while the oncology opinion supports only improved prognosis or prolonged survival.

Each professional may have produced competent work. Together, they may have produced several different cases.

Those inconsistencies should be found within the team before opposing counsel finds them.

The strongest competing medical explanation must also be taken seriously. It is not simply an argument to defeat. It is an account the preferred theory must be able to answer.

The defense may contend that the disease was advanced, the injury unavoidable, the presentation too late, or treatment contraindicated. The plaintiff may answer that those positions overstate prior illness, ignore progression, or fail to account for additional injury caused by delay.

The useful question is not which explanation is more favorable. It is which one accounts for the full record with fewer unsupported assumptions.

A sound plaintiff theory can acknowledge pre-existing disease and still identify the additional loss. A sound defense can acknowledge an imperfect process and explain why it did not alter the outcome.

Several causes may coexist. Underlying disease may have created the initial risk while delayed treatment increased the severity. A surgical complication may have been unavoidable while the response to it was not. A patient may have had limited life expectancy and still have lost meaningful survival.

Cases become unstable when those facts are forced into an all-or-nothing structure the medicine does not support.

This is particularly common in wrongful-death matters. The real question is seldom whether the patient would have lived indefinitely. It may be whether death would have been prevented at that time, whether survival would have been prolonged, whether the patient would have remained eligible for treatment, or whether the final course would have been less painful and medically burdensome.

Those distinctions affect liability, damages, valuation, and client expectations. They also determine whether the theory will survive serious expert review.

The pressure to preserve a theory grows after the case has been accepted. The firm has invested time and money. Pleadings may contain broad allegations. Experts have been retained. The client believes the case is moving forward. New evidence is then measured by whether it supports or threatens the existing position. That is a dangerous point in the case.

Earlier records may show that part of the claimed disability predated the event. Original imaging may eliminate an alleged miss. Audit data may establish that a result was received earlier than the printed chart suggested. A treatment expert may conclude that the meaningful opportunity had already closed. Deposition testimony may move responsibility from one participant to another. The theory has to remain capable of changing.

Revision is not evidence that the original analysis failed. It shows that the case remains tied to the record.

Sometimes the case becomes stronger. A vague allegation becomes a clearly timed failure to respond while the patient remained salvageable. A presumed technical complication becomes a well-supported failure-to-rescue case. A problem first attributed to one clinician becomes an institutional breakdown in which no one had reliable ownership.

Sometimes the case becomes narrower. The evidence may support increased severity rather than complete prevention. One defendant may remain central while others should be removed. A wrongful-death claim may become one of accelerated death or lost survival. Sometimes the investigation shows that the case should end.

A catastrophic injury may be real without supporting liability. The condition may not have been reasonably detectable. The care may have remained within the acceptable professional range. The proposed treatment may have been unavailable, contraindicated, or unlikely to change the result. The injury may already have been complete.

That conclusion is difficult for clients and often difficult for counsel. It does not mean the investigation failed. It means the investigation answered the question before litigation created additional expense and expectation.

Clinical review is not intended to produce caution for its own sake. Its purpose is to make the legal position proportionate to the medical evidence.

A devastating outcome may support no viable claim. A less dramatic injury may support a strong one. A broad allegation may become a narrow and persuasive theory. A patient with serious prior disease may still have sustained a clearly identifiable additional loss.

The case cannot be measured by emotional force, record volume, or the number of possible criticisms.

It has to be measured by the quality of the clinical connection: what was happening to the patient, when the professional obligation changed, what response remained available, what probably would have happened under reasonable care, and what portion of the final injury belongs to the difference.

Until that connection is established, the matter may be serious, troubling, and worthy of investigation. It is not yet ready to carry the weight of advocacy.

"Until that connection is established, the matter may be serious, troubling, and worthy of investigation. It is not yet ready to carry the weight of advocacy."

CHAPTER TWO

The Clinical Intelligence Model

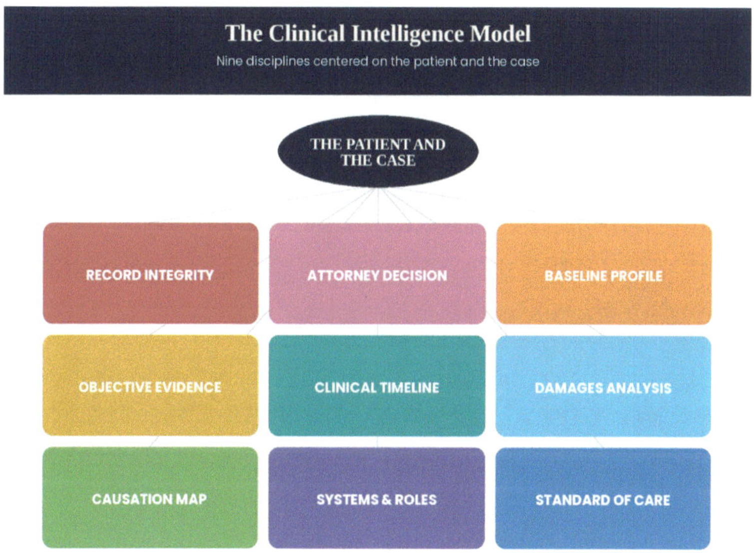

By the time a medical case reaches meaningful review, counsel usually has more information than clarity.

There may be hospital records, office notes, imaging reports, laboratory data, family accounts, policies, deposition testimony, expert impressions, and a chronology prepared by someone who has done exactly what was asked. The file may be organized, indexed, and summarized, yet the questions that determine the case can still be unresolved.

What was happening to this patient? When did the condition become clinically important? What information was available at the time, and what did it reasonably mean? What response did the situation require? Would another course probably have changed the outcome? What part of the eventual injury, death, or loss can fairly be attributed to the disputed care?

Those questions belong to the same case, but they are not interchangeable. Each requires different evidence and a different kind of clinical judgment. The Clinical Intelligence Model organizes that work so counsel can move from the records to a coherent account of the patient rather than from the outcome directly to a legal theory.

The model consists of Record Integrity, Baseline Profiling, Objective Evidence Analysis, Clinical Timeline Reconstruction, Standard-of-Care Analysis, Institutional and System Analysis, Causation Mapping, Damages Analysis, and the Attorney Decision.

That order matters, although the work is rarely perfectly linear. Conclusions should be tested in both directions. A causation opinion should send counsel back to the objective evidence and timeline to confirm that the treatment opportunity existed when the alleged departure occurred. A substantial damages claim should be checked against the patient's baseline. An institutional theory should be compared with the evidence showing how responsibility and information actually moved through the organization.

The model is not a checklist in which one section is completed and forgotten. Each part affects the next, and later evidence may require counsel to revisit an earlier conclusion. Its purpose is not to produce an automatic answer. It is to keep the answer tied to the medical evidence.

Record Integrity

Record Integrity comes first because every later conclusion depends on the evidence beneath it.

This is not simply a matter of confirming that authorizations were sent and each named provider produced a chart. Administrative completion and clinical completeness are different things. Counsel may possess the entire designated medical record and still be missing the evidence that decides the case.

Original imaging may not accompany the written report. Audit information may be stored in a separate electronic system. Secure messages may not appear in the printed chart. The medication record may distinguish what was ordered from what was administered. Telephone logs, referral platforms, staffing assignments, monitoring data, pharmacy records, device downloads, pathology material, fetal-monitoring strips, and records from another facility may require separate requests.

The practical question is not whether the production is large. It is whether the production contains the evidence needed to answer the disputed clinical issue.

Consider an abnormal imaging result that was never acted upon. The report may appear in the chart with a finalization time, but that alone does not show when it became available to the responsible professional, how it was routed, whether anyone opened it, who owned the follow-up, or what happened when the ordinary process failed.

When interpretation is disputed, the original images and report will be central. When receipt is disputed, routing and acknowledgment data may matter more. When the case concerns institutional responsibility, the coverage rules and ownership process may become decisive. The record needed depends on the question being asked.

Record Integrity also concerns the reliability and meaning of what has been produced. Medical records are not neutral transcripts of everything that occurred. They are working documents created during care and for billing, compliance, communication, and continuity. Entries may be copied forward, entered late, templated, corrected, or based partly on information supplied by someone else.

That does not make the record inherently unreliable. It means the record has to be interpreted.

A note signed at four may describe an examination performed at noon. A medication order may appear promptly even though administration occurred much later. A discharge summary may state that symptoms resolved while the final nursing note records continuing confusion. A later consultant may describe the earlier condition more dramatically than anyone did at the time.

Counsel needs to know which source is closest to the event, which entry reflects direct observation, and which facts remain disputed. Record Integrity is not clerical preparation performed before the real work begins. It is part of the analysis.

Baseline Profiling

Once the evidentiary foundation is reasonably secure, the next task is to understand who the patient was before the disputed event.

Baseline includes diagnosis, but it is not a diagnosis list. It is the patient's condition, function, prognosis, treatment burden, and care needs before the event against which the claimed injury must be measured.

What did the diagnoses mean in the patient's life? Could the patient walk independently, work, drive, manage medication and finances, care for children or a spouse, live alone, attend school, communicate normally, or participate in community life? Was there already pain, weakness, cognitive decline, or another limitation now being attributed to the disputed care?

A patient may have extensive medical complexity and retain meaningful independence. Another may have a shorter problem list and substantial functional impairment. Baseline must remain patient-specific.

The relevant evidence changes across the lifespan. For an infant, prenatal development, birth condition, feeding, growth, neurological findings, and early milestones may matter. For a child, the focus may include language, mobility, school performance, behavior, and developmental progress. In adolescence, education, athletics, mental health, emerging independence, and vocational direction may become important. For an adult, employment, parenting, household function, driving, and financial responsibility often provide the clearest picture. In an older patient, cognition, mobility, independent living, social participation, and caregiving roles may reveal far more than the diagnoses listed in the chart.

Baseline is especially important in wrongful-death cases. The issue is not simply the patient's age or the number of chronic conditions. Counsel needs to understand the survival, treatment course, function, and meaningful activity that probably remained.

A patient with advanced disease may still have expected additional survival, further treatment, or time at home. A frail patient may still have been comfortable, communicative, and closely connected to family before an avoidable deterioration.

A reliable baseline prevents overstatement from either side. It prevents the plaintiff from assigning every later limitation to the defendant, and it prevents the defense from treating prior illness as though nothing remained to be lost.

Objective Evidence Analysis

The next step is to examine the evidence that can anchor the clinical account.

Objective evidence includes imaging, laboratory trends, pathology, monitoring data, medication records, operative findings, device information, autopsy findings, physical measurements, and the patient's response to treatment. These sources often clarify events that the narrative chart describes incompletely or inconsistently.

Their value is not that they are immune from interpretation. Their value is that they establish boundaries.

A laboratory value may matter because it changed sharply from the patient's baseline, not because it crossed the printed reference range. Imaging may show progression between two points. A medication record may establish that treatment was ordered but never given. Monitoring data may reveal deterioration that progress notes did not capture. Pathology may support an injury mechanism that was not understood during the patient's life.

Objective evidence may strengthen the apparent theory, narrow it, or point elsewhere.

It also has limits. A later image may show a large abnormality without proving the finding was visible earlier. A laboratory value may have been chronically abnormal. Monitor artifact may resemble a clinical event. An autopsy may establish the cause of death while leaving unresolved when the process became detectable or treatable.

The important question is not simply what the objective evidence shows. It is what that evidence contributes to mechanism, recognizability, timing, treatment opportunity, and loss.

Clinical Timeline Reconstruction

Once the objective evidence has been examined, counsel can reconstruct the clinically meaningful timeline.

A chronology places events in date and time order. A clinical timeline explains how the patient's condition evolved and identifies the point at which that evolution should have changed care.

Medical records contain several forms of time. Symptoms begin and are reported later. The patient is examined before the note is entered. A test is ordered, performed, interpreted, finalized, communicated, and acted upon at different moments. Treatment may be ordered promptly and administered later. Reassessment may occur without immediate documentation. Those times frequently do not align.

The clinical timeline asks when the patient changed, when that change became reasonably recognizable, when the existing plan no longer fit, and how long meaningful treatment remained available.

Suppose a postoperative patient deteriorates during a twelve-hour period. The first allegation may describe twelve hours of failure to rescue. Review may show that the first eight hours were consistent with expected recovery, while the final four included persistent tachycardia, falling urine output, increasing pain, hypotension, and altered mental status.

Those hours do not carry the same clinical significance. The case turns on the period during which the findings stopped behaving like routine postoperative recovery and began to require escalation.

The same principle applies in delayed-diagnosis cases. A disease may have been present biologically before it was clinically detectable. The fact that the diagnosis was eventually made does not establish that every earlier encounter represented a missed opportunity.

The timeline should identify the point at which the available facts changed the professional obligation. It should also distinguish disease time from recognition time, and recognition time from treatment time.

A condition may become recognizable at one point while the most effective treatment remains available only briefly. In another case, treatment may remain possible for days while the probability of benefit gradually declines.

Without that temporal structure, delay remains an accusation rather than a causal analysis.

Standard-of-Care Analysis

Standard-of-care analysis should not begin with ideal practice. The question is what this professional or institution was reasonably required to do in this setting, with the information available at the time.

That inquiry depends on role, specialty, resources, urgency, clinical presentation, and patient-specific risk.

An emergency physician does not have the same role as a neurologist. A bedside nurse does not have the same responsibilities as a radiologist, pharmacist, surgeon, hospitalist, or facility administrator. A rural emergency department may not have the same immediate resources as a tertiary center, but it may still be required to stabilize the patient, obtain consultation, arrange transfer, or escalate care.

The professional obligation must be defined precisely enough to test. What information was available? What significance did it reasonably carry? Which options remained within the accepted range? Was a particular response required, and what occurred instead?

That is more useful than asking whether the care could have been better.

Medicine frequently permits several reasonable approaches. A later preference for another course does not establish a departure.

It is also important to distinguish a judgment issue from a process failure. A clinician may reasonably choose one accepted treatment over another or adopt a working diagnosis while continuing to watch for alternatives. Those are matters of clinical judgment.

A different problem arises when required work never occurs: a significant result is not reviewed, a deteriorating patient is not reassessed, a material change is not communicated, medication monitoring is not performed, or necessary follow-up is never arranged.

The evidentiary path will differ. A judgment case may depend heavily on expert testimony about the range of reasonable practice. A process case may be supported by evidence showing that essential work simply never reached completion.

Both still require patient-specific analysis, and both still require causation.

Institutional and System Analysis

Medical cases are often framed initially around the person whose name appears in the chart. The actual failure may be distributed across a system.

A result may enter a shared inbox without clear ownership. Nursing escalation may fail because the chain of command is poorly understood. A referral may be placed without anyone tracking it to completion. A medication safeguard may fail during prescribing, verification, dispensing, administration, or monitoring. Transfer may be delayed because responsibility moves between departments without one person retaining control.

Counsel needs to understand how care was supposed to move through the organization and how it actually moved.

That does not mean every adverse outcome should become an institutional claim. It means individual conduct cannot always be evaluated fairly without understanding the process in which the person was working.

A clinician may have acted reasonably within a defective system. An institution may have had a sound policy that was not followed. A staff member may have departed from a workflow that otherwise would have protected the patient. Several smaller failures may have combined to produce an outcome that no single act adequately explains.

The useful inquiry follows ownership and movement. Who controlled the task? How was information transmitted? What safeguard was intended to detect failure? What occurred when the ordinary process broke down? Did supervision, staffing, or available resources matter? Did the operational failure affect the timing or quality of the patient's care?

Those questions help identify the proper defendants, discovery, and experts. They also keep a policy from becoming a substitute for proof. A policy matters because of the work it required, the risk it addressed, and what happened to the patient when the process failed.

A technical deviation does not establish liability merely because it can be identified.

Causation Mapping

Causation Mapping asks the question that often decides whether the case can proceed: what difference did the alleged failure probably make?

That question must remain separate from standard of care. A professional may have acted unreasonably without causing additional injury. A patient may have suffered severe harm even though the care remained within the accepted range. An institutional process may have failed without altering treatment or prognosis.

Causation begins with the underlying disease or injury mechanism. The alleged departure is then placed within that biological course.

What treatment or rescue remained available? Was the patient eligible? How quickly could it realistically have been provided? What probability of benefit existed? What would the likely course have been under reasonable care? Which other factors contributed, and what additional harm belongs to the disputed difference?

This prevents causation from being reduced to sequence. The fact that negligence preceded an injury does not establish that it caused the injury.

A delayed result may precede diagnosis without changing the stage of disease. A missed escalation may occur after the condition has already become irreversible. A surgical complication may cause injury without having been negligently created. Treatment may be delayed while the same outcome remains probable because the disease was already too advanced.

Causation therefore requires a supported alternative course: what probably would have happened under appropriate care.

Medicine often cannot provide certainty. It must still provide more than the statement that earlier care might have helped.

The treatment opportunity should be defined in practical terms. What intervention would have been provided, and when? What benefit could reasonably be expected? What contraindications or risks applied? How was this patient likely to respond? Which part of the final injury had already occurred, and which part remained preventable?

The answer may support complete prevention. More often, it may support something narrower: reduced severity, preserved function, delayed progression, prolonged survival, avoidance of additional treatment, or less suffering.

The causal conclusion should be proportionate to the evidence.

That becomes especially important when several causes coexist. Underlying disease may have created the original danger while delayed care worsened the result. A complication may have been unavoidable while the response increased the injury. A patient may have had limited life expectancy and still have lost meaningful survival.

Causation does not require one cause to eliminate every other cause. It requires the disputed care to have made a legally and medically material difference at the level the evidence supports.

Damages Analysis

Damages Analysis defines that difference in the patient's life.

It should not begin with a list of post-event diagnoses or expenses. It should begin with baseline and the causal conclusion.

What injury is new? What prior condition was aggravated? What decline was accelerated? What function was lost? What treatment became necessary? Which care needs increased? Was survival shortened? What additional suffering occurred?

This is where the medical work must align with vocational, economic, life-care, and wrongful-death analysis.

A patient who required some assistance before the event may require substantially more afterward. The loss lies in that increase. A child with a prior developmental condition may sustain a separate neurological injury that changes the expected course. A patient with cancer may lose an earlier treatment opportunity or period of survival rather than a guaranteed cure. An older adult may lose independence, mobility, communication, comfort, or the ability to remain at home.

Damages should reflect the causal role supported by the evidence. Overstatement can undermine an otherwise persuasive liability case. At the same time, understating the patient's prior function can allow a real loss to disappear behind age, diagnosis, or comorbidity.

The proper comparison is between the course reasonably expected without the alleged failure and the course that actually followed.

The Attorney Decision

The final component is the Attorney Decision.

The model does not make that decision. It organizes the clinical evidence so counsel can exercise legal judgment with a clearer understanding of the case.

By the end of the review, the important questions should be answerable. Is the evidentiary record sufficient? Is the baseline reliable? Do the objective evidence and timeline support the same clinical course? Can the disputed professional obligation be defined? Is there evidence of individual or institutional departure? Did a meaningful treatment opportunity remain? Does causation rise above possibility? Have the strongest competing explanations been addressed? Do the damages match the causal conclusion? Different answers will lead to different decisions.

The case may remain supportable as first alleged. It may require focused additional evidence. It may narrow to another encounter, defendant, or injury. It may support a departure without supporting causation. The evidence may support aggravation or accelerated decline rather than complete prevention. The matter may be appropriate for resolution, ready for trial, or not supportable at all.

The model permits each of those outcomes because it does not force the evidence toward a predetermined result.

It also gives the litigation team a common clinical foundation. Counsel, clinical reviewers, experts, economists, life-care planners, and other professionals should not be working from different versions of the patient, the timeline, or the causal theory.

That does not blur professional roles. The attorney owns the legal decision. The qualified expert owns the specialized medical opinion. Clinical analysis connects the evidence to the questions each must answer.

Nor is the model intended to delay necessary legal action while the file is examined exhaustively. Records may need to be preserved. Limitations periods must be protected. Preliminary experts may need to be consulted. A pleading may have to be filed before every medical issue is resolved.

Preliminary conclusions are often necessary. They should remain provisional.

At intake, the available information may support a plausible theory. Initial records may make the theory more specific. Original imaging, audit data, earlier medical records, expert review, or discovery may change it again.

The model should remain active as the case develops, but that does not mean repeating the entire analysis after every document or deposition. It means returning to the part affected by the new evidence and asking whether the larger theory has changed.

A prior record may alter baseline and damages. Imaging review may alter timing and causation. Deposition testimony may change responsibility. A treatment expert may reshape the alternative course.

The framework remains stable so the analysis does not become driven by the preferred outcome. The case remains capable of change because the evidence continues to develop.

The chapters that follow examine these components in the order counsel commonly encounters them. The questions will remain recognizable. What counts as reliable evidence, a reasonable response, an available treatment opportunity, or an attributable loss will change with the patient and the medicine.

That is what the model is intended to reveal: what the complete clinical evidence permits counsel to say, and what decision should follow.

"That is what the model is intended to reveal: what the complete clinical evidence permits counsel to say, and what decision should follow."

CHAPTER THREE

The First Attorney Assessment

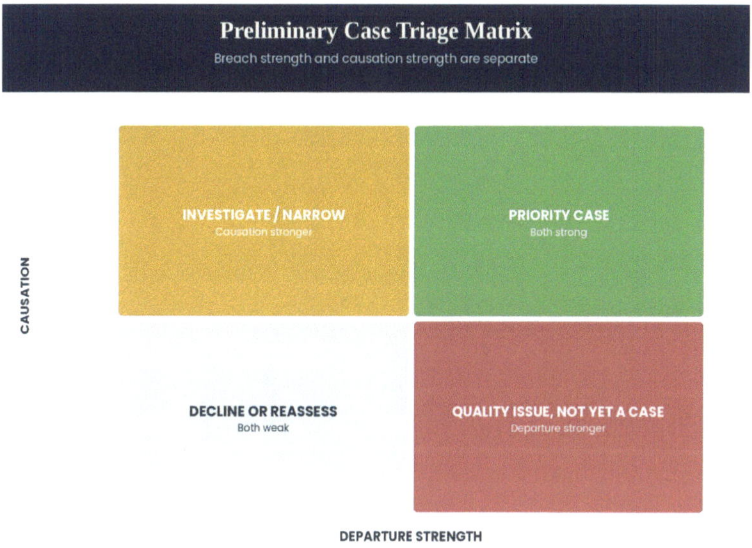

The first assessment of a medical case is almost never made with a complete record.

You may have a client interview, a discharge summary, several office notes, a death certificate, a handful of laboratory reports, and the family's understanding of what occurred. Sometimes there is more. Often there is much less. The original imaging may not yet be available. Earlier records may be missing. The treatment options and their probable effect may not be understood. You may not even know which experts will ultimately be needed. Even so, decisions have to be made.

The statute of limitations may be running. Records may need to be preserved. The client needs some direction, and the firm has to decide whether the matter justifies further investigation and expense.

That first decision influences everything that follows. It affects the records you request, the clinicians and systems you examine, the experts you approach, and the facts that receive early attention. It also begins to shape the client's expectations.

The purpose of the first assessment is not to decide the entire case. It is to determine whether there is a clinically plausible reason to investigate further and what evidence will be needed before a responsible conclusion can be reached. Those are not the same question.

A matter may justify investigation without yet supporting a claim. It may contain a troubling event but no clear causal injury. It may involve a devastating outcome with very little evidence of professional departure. It may also appear weak at intake because the available records omit the evidence that later explains what happened.

The first assessment has to remain open to each of those possibilities.

Begin With the Client's Account

The client's account is the natural place to begin.

The patient or family will usually describe the event directly:

"They failed to diagnose the stroke."

"They discharged him while he was septic."

"They never told us about the abnormal scan."

"The medication dose was wrong."

"She kept getting worse, and no one did anything."

That account matters. It tells you what the family observed, what they were told, where they believe the course changed, and why they sought legal advice. It may also contain information that is not clearly documented.

A family member may remember that the patient stopped speaking normally, could no longer walk, became unusually confused, or repeatedly complained about a symptom that appears only once in the chart. The family may understand the patient's prior level of independence far better than any one clinician involved in the event.

At the same time, the account has usually taken shape after the outcome was known. The family may have received later explanations from treating physicians, other clinicians, friends, or sources they found independently. The eventual diagnosis may now influence the way every earlier symptom is understood.

That does not make the client's account unreliable. It means you need to separate what was observed at the time from what was concluded later.

What did the family personally see? What did the patient report then? What were they told by the healthcare professionals? Which conclusions developed only after the diagnosis or injury became known?

That separation is useful because observations can be compared with contemporaneous documentation and objective evidence. Conclusions will require further clinical support.

Identify the Event the Client Believes Caused the Harm

The client's explanation often includes more than one possible event.

A patient may have visited the emergency department twice, been discharged both times, returned in severe distress, and then undergone emergency treatment. The family may understandably view the entire sequence as one prolonged failure.

Your first assessment should separate the possible decision points.

Was the concern the first discharge, the second examination, a result that returned after discharge, the response when the patient came back, or a delay after admission?

The same distinction matters in postoperative cases. The injury may have begun during surgery, while the supportable allegation concerns what happened afterward. A complication may not have been preventable, but the failure to recognize and respond to deterioration may have increased the harm.

In a delayed-diagnosis case, the relevant issue may not be every earlier visit. It may be the first encounter at which the symptoms, examination, imaging, or laboratory results created a materially different obligation.

At the beginning, you may not know which event controls the case. You should at least know which events need to be examined separately.

Understand the Outcome Without Assuming Its Cause

The first assessment also needs to establish what happened to the patient after the disputed care.

That may sound obvious, but the final diagnosis and the legally attributable injury are not always the same thing.

A patient may ultimately have been diagnosed with a stroke, while the claim concerns the additional neurological loss caused by delayed treatment. A patient may have developed postoperative bleeding, while the disputed injury involves the consequences of delayed rescue rather than the bleeding itself. A patient may have died from infection, while the supportable theory concerns accelerated death rather than complete prevention. The outcome therefore needs to be described carefully.

What condition was eventually diagnosed? What treatment followed? What permanent impairment, additional treatment, increased care need, or loss of survival is alleged? How much of that outcome may already have existed before the disputed event?

At this stage, the answers may remain incomplete. The important point is not to let the severity of the result substitute for a causation analysis that has not yet been performed.

Establish a Preliminary Baseline

A complete baseline will require records and, in many cases, collateral evidence. The initial assessment still needs a practical understanding of who the patient was before the event.

Was the patient living independently, working, driving, attending school, or caring for another person? Could the patient manage medication and finances? Was home-health or nursing assistance already required? Was the patient undergoing treatment for a serious disease? Were symptoms similar to the claimed injury already present? This preliminary baseline affects both viability and record collection.

When the claimed injury is loss of mobility, earlier primary-care and rehabilitation records may be necessary. When the case concerns cognitive decline, prior neurological, educational, or functional evidence may matter. In a wrongful-death case, the patient's pre-event prognosis and treatment course may be central.

Baseline should not be used at intake to discount a matter merely because the patient was older, ill, or disabled. Prior limitations should not be ignored simply because the later injury is severe.

The initial question is straightforward: who was this patient before the event, and what appears to have changed?

Determine What Evidence Is Actually Available

A small intake packet creates obvious uncertainty. A large production can conceal it.

The first review should identify what is present, what is absent, and what cannot yet be determined from the material provided.

Do you have the original imaging or only the reports? Are the medication-administration records included? Are the earlier records necessary to establish baseline available? Is the full hospital chart present, including nursing flowsheets and consultant notes? Do you have the records from the next facility? Is there evidence showing how an abnormal result was routed, received, or acknowledged?

The objective at this stage is not to prepare every final record request. It is to recognize when an apparent weakness in the case may actually be an evidentiary gap.

The chart may show that an abnormal study was finalized without showing whether the result reached anyone responsible for acting on it. A medication order may appear without evidence of when the drug was administered. A progress note may suggest a timely response while the underlying vital-sign, monitoring, and communication records are missing.

You should not assume that the absent evidence will support the client's position. You should know when that evidence is necessary before the matter can be judged fairly.

Locate the Preliminary Clinical Question

Potential medical cases often arrive under legal labels: failure to diagnose, failure to monitor, negligent surgery, medication error, or failure to rescue.

Those labels may describe the general category. They do not yet identify the clinical question that needs to be investigated.

The clinical question should focus on the decision that appears to matter.

Did the patient's symptoms and examination during the second emergency visit require neurological imaging or consultation?

Did the postoperative pattern require escalation before the patient became unstable?

Did the abnormal imaging result create a follow-up obligation, and who was responsible for completing it?

Did the medication dose, impaired clearance, or failure to monitor create the injury?

Was the nursing-facility resident's deterioration sufficiently different from baseline to require urgent provider reassessment or transfer?

The wording will change as the evidence develops. At intake, the question only needs to be specific enough to direct the next step.

Separate the Possible Departure From the Possible Injury

Even at this early stage, breach and causation should not be allowed to merge.

The available material may suggest that something was handled poorly. That does not establish that another course probably would have produced a different outcome.

If an abnormal result was not communicated, what treatment would timely communication have produced? If the patient should have been admitted, what would have happened during the admission? If a specialist should have been consulted, what would that specialist probably have recommended? If treatment was delayed, was the patient still eligible, and what benefit remained?

You may not yet have reliable answers. Asking the questions tells you whether the case contains a plausible treatment or rescue opportunity that deserves focused investigation.

A matter with no apparent alternative treatment pathway may require an early causation consultation before the firm commits substantial resources. A case with a clearly identifiable treatment opportunity may justify prompt preservation and record development even though the standard-of-care analysis remains incomplete.

Consider the Strongest Contrary Explanation

The first assessment should not be an effort to defeat the client's account. It should identify the explanation most likely to challenge it.

Was the disease already too advanced to treat? Were the symptoms too nonspecific to require another response? Was the complication recognized and unavoidable? Did the patient decline the recommended evaluation? Was the abnormality not reasonably visible on the earlier study? Would the same outcome probably have occurred despite timely intervention?

A contrary explanation does not end the inquiry merely because it is medically possible. It tells you where the investigation must be strongest.

When the likely defense is that the patient presented too late, the timeline and treatment window require immediate attention. When severe pre-existing disease is likely to be emphasized, prior function and prognosis should be investigated early. When a complication is described as unavoidable, the review should separate the occurrence of the complication from the response after it developed.

The first assessment becomes more dependable when the likely defense is considered before the case has gathered momentum.

Decide What the Case Requires Next

The result of the first assessment is not limited to accept or decline.

Some matters can be declined because the available facts do not suggest a plausible departure, treatment opportunity, or attributable injury. Others justify a limited investigation before a final decision. That may involve one focused set of records, original imaging, a preliminary specialist review, or clarification of the patient's prior condition.

Some matters require immediate action because evidence may be lost or a filing deadline is approaching. A smaller number may already contain enough information to justify broader development, although those conclusions should still remain provisional.

Whatever the decision, it should identify what remains unresolved and why the answer matters.

A useful assessment may conclude that the case cannot be evaluated until the original imaging is reviewed. It may find that standard of care appears supportable but causation requires a treatment specialist. It may identify substantial overlap between the claimed injury and the patient's prior condition, making baseline records necessary before damages can be assessed. Those are not incomplete conclusions. They are directions for the investigation.

Manage Expectations at the Beginning

The language used with the client during this stage matters.

The seriousness of the injury should be acknowledged without suggesting that liability has already been established. A decision to obtain additional records or consult an expert should not be described as acceptance of the claim unless that decision has actually been made.

Medical cases often change as the records and qualified opinions develop. The relevant encounter may narrow. A suspected individual error may become an institutional issue. A theory of complete prevention may become one of increased severity or shortened survival. The evidence may ultimately show that the matter should not proceed.

That possibility is easier to explain when the investigation has been described accurately from the beginning.

Counsel does not need to communicate every clinical uncertainty during the first meeting. The client should understand that a serious outcome deserves careful attention, while the legal conclusion will depend on what the complete evidence shows about the care, the remaining treatment opportunity, and the cause of the loss.

The Product of the First Assessment

By the end of the initial assessment, counsel should have a working understanding of the patient before the event, the care or decision being questioned, the condition eventually diagnosed, the injury or loss alleged, the principal evidentiary gaps, the apparent treatment or rescue opportunity, the strongest competing explanation, and the next investigation required. This is not the final theory.

It is the point at which the matter becomes sufficiently defined to build one.

The next step is to turn that initial understanding into a preliminary clinical theory: a working account of what may have happened, where the important decision appears to have occurred, and what another response might have changed.

"The next step is to turn that initial understanding into a preliminary clinical theory: a working account of what may have happened, where the important decision appears to have occurred, and what another response might have changed."

"I am not trying to decide whether malpractice occurred. I am trying to understand what the case may actually be."

PART II

BUILDING THE CLINICAL RECORD

Chapters 4–9

CHAPTER FOUR

Building the Preliminary Clinical Theory

When I first begin working through a medical case with counsel, I am not trying to decide whether malpractice occurred. I am trying to understand what the case may actually be.

Those are different tasks. When they are confused too early, the rest of the investigation can become distorted.

The family may describe a missed diagnosis, a delayed response, or a negligent procedure. Their account may be entirely understandable and may ultimately prove substantially correct. At the beginning, however, we usually have a serious outcome, an incomplete medical story, and an explanation formed after everyone already knows how the case ended.

The preliminary clinical theory gives counsel a disciplined place to begin without requiring the firm to defend the first explanation that came through the door.

It is not a pleading, an expert opinion, or the final theory of liability. It is a working account of what may have happened to this patient, where the clinically important decision appears to have occurred, and what difference another response might have made.

That account needs to be specific enough to guide the investigation while remaining open to correction as the evidence develops.

A theory such as "failure to diagnose," "failure to monitor," "negligent surgery," or "failure to rescue" is too broad to do much useful work. Those phrases describe categories of cases. They do not identify the encounter that mattered, the findings that changed the professional obligation, the response that should have followed, or the injury that may have resulted.

A theory that becomes fixed too early creates the opposite problem. Once the matter is described as a missed stroke, a preventable death, or a surgical injury, counsel may begin reading every new record through that conclusion. Supporting facts stand out. Contrary facts start to look like obstacles. Before long, the investigation is directed toward preserving the theory rather than determining whether it is right.

What you need at this stage is a clear, provisional explanation that can be tested.

I usually begin with the patient's condition rather than the defendant's alleged fault. What brought the patient into care? What was happening clinically? What changed? When did that change become important? What response followed, and what happened afterward?

Responsibility is considered after the clinical process is understood.

That order matters because the person whose name appears most prominently in the chart is not always the person or entity responsible for the failure. A family may focus on the physician who discharged the patient when the real problem involved a result-routing system, an uncommunicated nursing concern, or a consultation that was requested but never completed. A surgeon may be blamed for causing a complication when the supportable issue concerns the later failure to recognize and respond to it. A radiologist may be accused of missing a finding even though the image was interpreted reasonably and the real failure was that recommended follow-up never occurred.

The clinical process should therefore be reconstructed before responsibility is assigned.

In most cases, that process is not one isolated act. A symptom is reported. Someone evaluates it. A test is ordered. The result becomes available. Someone interprets or receives it. A decision is made. Treatment begins, is delayed, or never occurs. The patient is reassessed, or is not. The condition improves, remains unchanged, or deteriorates.

The preliminary theory should help identify where that sequence may have broken and whether the break mattered.

Not every irregularity matters in the same way. A note may have been signed late without delaying care. A policy may have been followed imperfectly while the intended safeguard still worked. A consultation may have occurred later than ideal after the meaningful treatment opportunity had already closed. A test may not have been ordered because the patient did not yet have findings that reasonably required it.

The object is not to collect everything that might have been handled differently. It is to identify the failure that may have changed the patient's course.

This is where many medical cases become unnecessarily broad. A severe outcome creates pressure to include every questionable decision, every possible defendant, and every criticism an expert may be willing to offer. Expansion can feel protective. In practice, it often obscures the case.

Five marginal criticisms do not necessarily create a stronger case than one clinically consequential failure. Frequently, the broader case is weaker. The important facts become harder to see. Experts begin answering different questions. Discovery expands without becoming more focused. Opposing counsel can attack the overstated portions and use them to undermine the credible part.

A sound preliminary theory gives the matter a clinical center.

Consider a postoperative patient who later develops overwhelming infection and dies. The early chart may contain several concerns. The prophylactic antibiotic may have been given later than preferred. The wound description may be incomplete. A physician may not have personally examined the patient during one interval. Laboratory testing may not have been repeated as early as possible. Transfer to intensive care may have occurred only after substantial deterioration.

A theory could be built around every one of those points. Before doing that, I would want to know when the patient's course changed from expected postoperative recovery to a pattern requiring urgent reassessment and escalation.

The early pain, mild fever, and fatigue may have remained within the expected range. Later, the patient may have developed persistent tachycardia, falling urine output, worsening hypotension, increasing confusion, and failure to respond to fluids. That later interval may be the center of the case.

Once that interval is identified, the other facts can be evaluated according to whether they contributed to the failure to recognize and respond. The delayed antibiotic may matter. The nursing documentation may matter. The physician's availability and transfer process may matter. Their significance comes from their relationship to the clinically consequential breakdown, not merely from the fact that each can be criticized. That is the difference between a list of concerns and a theory.

The theory must also separate the patient's underlying condition from the injury allegedly caused by the care. Those are often not the same thing.

A patient may suffer a stroke because of vascular disease. The claim may be that delayed diagnosis increased the amount of permanent brain injury.

A patient may develop an infection despite reasonable preventive care. The claim may be that delayed recognition allowed the infection to progress to shock, organ failure, or death.

A patient may experience a recognized surgical complication. The allegation may concern the response rather than the occurrence of the complication.

A child may have a congenital disorder that no one caused. The claim may be that failure to recognize it deprived the child of an earlier treatment opportunity and worsened the developmental course.

The preliminary theory should identify what the alleged negligence may have caused, not simply what happened afterward.

This is especially important in wrongful-death cases because death can dominate the analysis from the outset. Sometimes the evidence will support that the defendant caused the death. In other cases, the more accurate question is whether earlier treatment probably would have prevented death at that time, prolonged meaningful survival, preserved eligibility for treatment, avoided a more painful course, or reduced the severity of the final deterioration.

Those are different theories. They require different evidence, experts, and approaches to damages.

A patient with advanced cancer may not have had a realistic prospect of cure when an earlier abnormality should have been investigated. The evidence may still show that delayed diagnosis allowed progression, eliminated a treatment option, or shortened survival. That may be a substantial case, but it should not be presented as complete prevention of death unless the medicine supports that conclusion.

The preliminary theory must leave room for that degree of precision.

Timing deserves the same care. In medical litigation, the relevant delay is rarely measured simply from the first symptom to the final outcome. The clinically important interval usually begins when the condition became reasonably recognizable and ends when meaningful intervention was no longer available or when appropriate care finally occurred. Those points may be different from the dates that first attract attention.

A family may describe a two-day delay because the patient was seen twice before the diagnosis was made.

The first encounter may have involved vague symptoms, a normal examination, and apparent improvement. The second may have included new weakness, difficulty speaking, and an inability to walk normally. The supportable theory may concern the second encounter rather than both.

That narrowing does not weaken the case. It may strengthen it because the allegation now follows the actual clinical change.

The reverse can also occur. The printed chart may suggest that a result was handled promptly because a note was signed shortly before treatment began. Audit evidence may later show that the result had been available for hours and remained unacknowledged. The material delay may therefore be longer than the ordinary record suggests.

This is why the theory must remain provisional. At the outset, you may know the apparent sequence without knowing the true clinical timeline.

The same caution applies to the treatment opportunity. A theory is not complete simply because it identifies what should have been done differently. Counsel also needs a plausible account of what that different care could have accomplished.

It is not enough to say that a test, consultation, admission, transfer, or treatment should have occurred earlier. You need to know what diagnosis probably would have followed, what treatment would have been available, whether the patient was eligible, and what benefit could reasonably have been expected at that point.

At the beginning, those answers may not yet be available. You should at least know that the case depends on obtaining them.

That separates a meaningful causation theory from the broad statement that earlier care would have been better. Earlier care often would have been better. The litigation question is whether it probably would have made a material difference for this patient. The words “for this patient” matter.

A treatment does not offer the same benefit to everyone. Age, disease stage, comorbidities, contraindications, treatment tolerance, prior function, and biological response all affect the likely result. Medical literature may describe what a treatment can accomplish within a particular population. The case still requires patient-specific reasoning.

One therapy may be effective in many patients while offering little benefit to someone whose disease was already advanced. Another may carry only a partial probability of success and still represent a meaningful lost opportunity. The preliminary theory should reflect what can reasonably be said without pretending the uncertainty has already been resolved.

Baseline enters the theory for the same reason. You cannot identify the additional harm without some understanding of who the patient was before the event.

That does not mean the complete baseline must be established before a preliminary theory can be developed. It does mean the theory cannot casually assume that every post-event limitation is new.

If the patient already needed help with bathing and dressing, the alleged loss may concern the increased level of assistance now required. If the patient had prior cognitive impairment, the injury may be an additional loss of communication, recognition, or independence. If the patient had severe chronic disease, the wrongful-death theory may involve accelerated death or lost survival rather than ordinary life expectancy.

At the same time, if the patient remained independent despite numerous diagnoses, that independence must remain visible. It should not disappear simply because the problem list is long.

A clinically sound theory is built around the actual patient, not the average patient and not the patient most convenient to the claim.

The strongest competing explanation should also be identified early. It does not have to be resolved before the investigation is complete, but it should be understood.

The condition may already have been irreversible. The presentation may have been too nonspecific to require another response. The patient may have declined the recommended evaluation. The proposed treatment may have been contraindicated. The complication may have occurred despite reasonable care. Another disease may explain both the symptoms and the outcome. The injury may have developed suddenly after the disputed encounter. Part of the claimed loss may belong to the patient's baseline.

A theory that cannot confront the strongest alternative explanation is not reliable enough to guide major litigation decisions.

I would rather know the strongest defense at the beginning than after the firm has spent heavily developing a theory that cannot answer it.

Consider a patient diagnosed with metastatic cancer eight months after an earlier scan showed a small abnormality. The preliminary concern may be that the abnormality should have been recognized and investigated, allowing diagnosis before the disease spread.

That is a plausible theory. The strongest competing explanation may be that the cancer was already systemic or biologically aggressive when the earlier scan was taken, so earlier diagnosis would not have produced cure or materially prolonged survival. That dispute tells counsel what the case requires.

You need the original imaging, not merely a later report describing it. You need to determine whether the abnormality was reasonably visible, understand the natural history of that particular cancer, estimate its probable stage at the earlier time, and identify what treatment would then have been available and what effect it likely would have had.

The final theory may support cure. It may support prolonged survival, delayed progression, or preservation of a treatment option. It may show no material difference.

The preliminary theory should open that inquiry rather than decide the answer before the evidence exists.

It should also make expert selection more precise. “Please review for malpractice” is not a useful request in a complex case. It asks one person to move from a large record to a broad legal conclusion without separating the clinical issues.

A developed working theory allows counsel to ask better questions. Was the abnormality visible on the earlier image? Would a reasonable radiologist have recommended further evaluation? What stage was the disease probably in at that point? What treatment would have been available, and what effect would it likely have had on progression or survival?

Those questions may require more than one specialty. The radiologist may address visibility and interpretation. The oncologist may address stage, treatment, and prognosis. Neither should be asked casually to answer the entire case merely because each understands part of it.

The same is true in a system case. A clinical expert may explain the significance of the abnormal result. Another professional may be needed to address responsibility for follow-up. Institutional evidence may show how the result moved through the electronic system. A causation expert may then explain what the delay changed.

The preliminary theory reveals those divisions. It identifies not only what the case may be, but what professional work will be required to test it.

At this stage, I also want to know what evidence could materially weaken or disprove the theory.

That question becomes uncomfortable only when the purpose of the investigation has shifted from understanding to confirmation.

Original imaging may show that the finding was not visible. Audit data may establish that the result was reviewed promptly. Earlier records may show that the claimed impairment was longstanding. The proposed treatment may have been unavailable or contraindicated. Pathology may reveal a disease process so aggressive that earlier intervention probably would not have altered the course. The patient may have declined the recommended evaluation. A later event may better explain the injury.

Identifying those possibilities does not damage the case. It gives the investigation integrity and helps counsel decide the order in which resources should be used.

Some questions must be answered before substantial expense is incurred. Others can wait. When one piece of evidence could eliminate the central causal theory, it should be pursued early.

The preliminary theory is therefore more than a summary. It is a decision tool. It explains what the available evidence suggests, where the uncertainty lies, what could change the analysis, and what should happen next.

The written version need not be long. A few developed paragraphs can usually capture the working theory. They should identify who the patient was before the event, which clinical change appears to matter, when it may have become recognizable, what response may have been required, what occurred instead, which treatment opportunity may have been lost, what additional harm is being investigated, which competing explanation must be tested, and what evidence remains necessary. That is enough to align the litigation team.

Without a shared theory, different versions of the same case begin to develop. One expert assumes the injury began before admission. Another assumes it occurred hours later. The damages team relies on a baseline the clinical review has already questioned. Discovery continues against a defendant whose role no longer appears central. The complaint preserves allegations the evidence has quietly abandoned.

A visible working theory helps prevent those inconsistencies from becoming embedded.

It should also be revised openly. When new evidence changes the case, the theory should change with it. An earlier record may alter baseline. Original imaging may change the apparent time of injury. A deposition may show that another person owned the decision. A causation expert may conclude that earlier treatment would have reduced severity but not prevented the injury. A system audit may reveal that an apparent individual failure was institutional.

When that happens, counsel should be able to explain what changed, why it matters, and what should happen next. That is not instability. It is disciplined development.

By the time the preliminary theory has done its work, you should be able to explain the matter without reciting every chart entry and without reducing it to a slogan. You should be able to describe the patient before the event, the clinical change that appears to matter, when it may have become recognizable, the response that may have been required, what occurred instead, the treatment opportunity that may have been lost, the additional harm under investigation, the strongest competing explanation, and the evidence still needed.

That gives the case direction without pretending the record is complete. It focuses resources, makes expert review more precise, and exposes weak assumptions while there is still time to address them.

The preliminary clinical theory is the bridge between the client's account and the fully developed case. It should be clear enough to test, flexible enough to change, and tied throughout to the same practical question: what happened to this patient, what should have happened differently, and what material difference does the evidence support?

"It should be clear enough to test, flexible enough to change, and tied throughout to the same practical question: what happened to this patient, what should have happened differently, and what material difference does the evidence support?"

CHAPTER FIVE

Determining Whether the Medical Record Is Complete

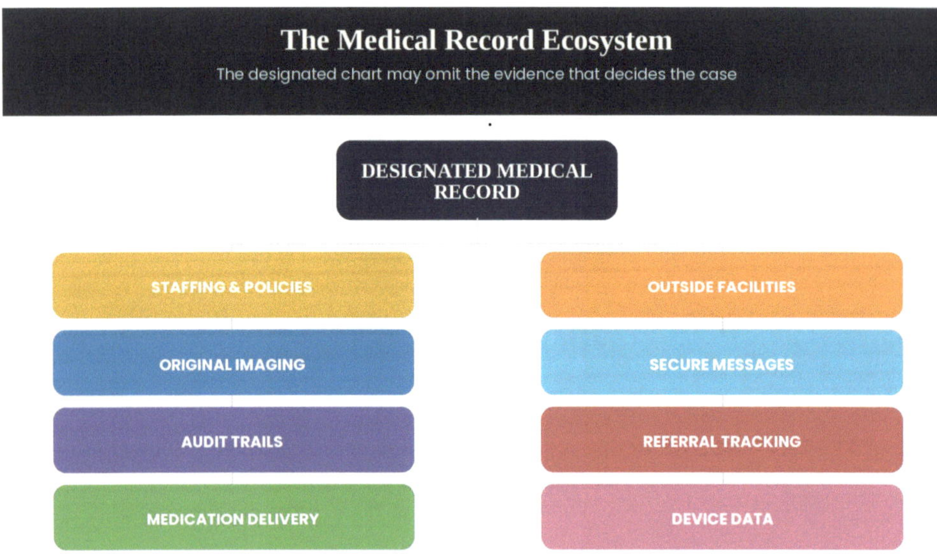

When a medical case first arrives, the record often looks more complete than it is.

There may be thousands of pages. The hospital production may include physician and nursing notes, orders, laboratory reports, medication records, consultations, operative reports, discharge summaries, and billing documents. Outside providers may have sent their office records. The file may already be indexed, arranged chronologically, and summarized.

From an administrative standpoint, it can appear that everyone responded and the collection is finished.

That does not necessarily mean you have the evidence needed to evaluate the case.

The first distinction I make with counsel is between a record that is complete as a production and one that is complete for the clinical question. A facility may produce what it calls the designated medical record while omitting original imaging, the electronic history of a result, communications outside the formal chart, device data that captured deterioration, or staffing information showing who was responsible at a critical time.

The size of the file tells you very little about whether it is clinically complete. What matters is whether it contains the evidence needed to understand what happened.

That changes the way the collection should be approached. Instead of asking only whether every provider has responded, counsel should begin with what the working theory requires the evidence to prove or disprove.

If the dispute concerns a radiological finding, the written report may not be enough. If the issue is whether a critical result was communicated, the result itself will not show who received it or when. In a delayed-medication case, the order may show what was intended while the administration record shows what reached the patient. In a failure-to-rescue case, a progress note signed later may tell you far less than contemporaneous vital signs, monitor data, nursing observations, escalation calls, and response times. The clinical issue tells you what evidence matters.

This is one reason the preliminary clinical theory comes before the full record analysis. Once you have a working understanding of the disputed event, you can ask whether the production permits you to test it.

A request for the complete medical record is necessary, but it is rarely sufficient in a complex malpractice, wrongful-death, or healthcare-negligence case. The evidence usually needs to be pursued in layers, with each layer tied to an unresolved question.

Suppose the case concerns an abnormal imaging result that was not acted upon. The ordinary chart may show that the study was performed, interpreted, and finalized. It may contain a physician note saying the result was reviewed, or it may contain no follow-up at all. Neither circumstance necessarily tells the full story.

The original images may be needed to determine whether the abnormality was reasonably visible. Preliminary and final reports may show whether the interpretation changed. Routing data may reveal where the result went after it was signed. Acknowledgment records may show whether anyone opened it. Telephone or secure-message records may establish whether direct communication was attempted. The institution's workflow may identify who was responsible when the ordering clinician was unavailable. Scheduling or referral information may show that follow-up began but never reached completion.

Each source answers a different question. Together, they reconstruct the process.

Without that evidence, the file may support an impression without supporting a conclusion. The absence of a follow-up note may look like proof that no one reviewed the result when the communication was recorded elsewhere. The presence of a result in an inbox may look like proof of receipt even though it was delivered to a pooled account with no clear owner. A note stating that the patient was informed may appear conclusive until the underlying call record shows that no one answered.

The record does not interpret itself. Before drawing conclusions from it, you need to know whether you are seeing the full evidentiary pathway.

I approach completeness by asking which systems touched the patient's care.

Healthcare is rarely documented in one continuous chart. The physician note may be in one platform, the medication history in another, imaging in a separate archive, monitor information in a device system, and secure communications in an application that does not print with the conventional record. A referral may have been entered into a tracking platform that never appears in the office note. An ambulance will have its own record. A nursing facility may use separate wound-care software. A laboratory may retain correction histories and communication logs outside the report produced to counsel.

The request has to follow the care rather than the provider's standard production package.

That becomes particularly important when the case turns on time. The most consequential question is often not whether something occurred, but when. The conventional chart can obscure that because it contains several timestamps, and those timestamps do not all describe the same event.

A note may show when it was signed rather than when the patient was examined. An order may show when it was entered rather than when the decision was made. A result may show when it was finalized rather than when preliminary information became available. A medication entry may reflect when the dose was documented rather than when it was given. A telephone note may summarize a conversation that took place hours earlier.

When reasonable and delayed care are separated by minutes or hours, those distinctions can decide the case.

I would not assume that a timestamp proves the underlying clinical event until I understand what the field represents. In an electronic record, time may refer to order entry, specimen collection, performance, verification, posting, acknowledgment, administration, or documentation. The same screen may display several of those values without making the differences obvious.

Audit information may help. It can show when a note was created, copied, edited, opened, or signed. It may show when a result entered an inbox, when a user accessed it, or whether an entry was changed after the event.

Audit data should not be requested automatically in every case. When the theory depends on who knew what and when, however, it may be more probative than the face of the chart.

The same is true of metadata associated with imaging, monitors, and devices. An imaging report may have been finalized at three, although the study was available for review at 2:12. A monitor may have recorded episodes never transcribed into a nursing note. An infusion pump may show that medication was paused, delayed, or delivered at a rate different from the order. A ventilator log may identify deterioration that the narrative chart describes only generally.

Objective data can clarify the sequence only when counsel knows it exists and obtains it in a usable form.

A clinically complete record must also include enough of the patient's history before the disputed event.

The records from the provider accused of negligence often receive most of the attention because that is where the event occurred. Prior records may be just as important. They establish baseline and may show whether a laboratory abnormality was new or chronic, whether neurological complaints had occurred before, whether the patient already had functional limitations, or whether an imaging finding predated the event.

They may reveal a prior diagnosis, treatment recommendation, refusal, missed appointment, or risk factor that affects causation. They may also show that the patient was functioning far better than the later problem list suggests.

The relevant time period depends on the dispute. A sudden neurological injury may require several years of earlier medical and functional records. A delayed cancer diagnosis may require previous imaging and screening history. A birth-injury matter may involve prenatal, maternal, fetal, labor, placental, and neonatal records. A nursing-facility case may require hospital, rehabilitation, wound, nutritional, vascular, and home-care records predating admission.

There is no universal number of years that makes baseline complete. The appropriate range depends on the condition, alleged mechanism, and damages theory.

Nor should counsel limit the collection to medical records when the baseline is primarily functional. School records may matter in pediatric and adolescent cases. Employment records may show what an adult was actually doing before the event. Home-health assessments may describe independence more accurately than office notes. Therapy records may establish prior mobility, cognition, or speech. Family testimony may become important when ordinary daily function was never documented clinically.

The goal is not to collect everything that exists. It is to obtain enough reliable evidence to describe the patient before and after the event without speculation.

There is also an important difference between evidence that is missing and evidence that never existed.

A note may be absent because it was not produced. It may exist in another system. The event may have occurred but never been documented. Or it may not have occurred at all. Those possibilities should not be treated as equivalent.

Before drawing an inference from silence, I want to understand the documentation process. Was the action ordinarily charted? Where would it appear? Was the system working at the time? Did this professional ordinarily document that type of communication? Is there another source that would confirm or contradict it?

The absence of a note may become meaningful, especially when the event was important and documentation would normally be expected. It should not become automatic proof without examination of the surrounding record.

Copied and templated material creates a related problem. Electronic records often carry diagnoses, examination findings, and plans forward from earlier notes. A document may look detailed while containing very little new observation. Language that appears contemporaneous may have been imported from another entry. Normal findings may remain in a template even when the surrounding chart suggests the examination was limited.

That does not mean copied material should be discarded. It means you need to distinguish what the clinician actually observed from what the system reproduced.

Repeated notes should be compared. Identical language over several days may be clinically accurate, or it may indicate carry-forward documentation. A change within an otherwise copied section may reveal when someone actually reassessed the patient. A note entered after deterioration may describe earlier findings through the lens of the later diagnosis.

The purpose is not to criticize documentation style. It is to determine how much evidentiary weight an entry can carry.

Late entries and amendments require the same restraint. A late note may be entirely legitimate. Clinicians often document after urgent care has been completed. An amendment may correct an error or add information that was inadvertently omitted. Timing alone does not establish impropriety.

What matters is what changed, why it changed, and whether the revised account is supported elsewhere.

When a note created after the adverse outcome introduces a critical finding absent from contemporaneous nursing records, orders, monitoring data, or witness accounts, the discrepancy deserves attention. When the late entry simply formalizes a consultation or procedure reflected throughout the chart, it may remain reliable despite its timing.

A complete review does not equate irregular documentation with negligence. It identifies where documentation affects confidence in the clinical reconstruction.

Medication records are another area in which apparent completeness can be deceptive. The physician's order is only one part of the medication process. Depending on the case, counsel may need the order history, pharmacy verification, dispensing record, medication-administration record, infusion data, barcode scanning history, reconciliation documents, and monitoring results.

An antibiotic may have been ordered at the proper time and administered much later. A medication may have been charted as given and then held, stopped, or returned. A dose may have been administered despite worsening renal function or another contraindication. A home medication may have disappeared during transfer between facilities.

When the case involves medication error or delayed treatment, the relevant question is not merely what the plan said. It is what reached the patient, at what dose, by which route, at what time, and with what monitoring.

Communication evidence requires similar depth because the medical chart often contains a summary of a communication rather than the communication itself.

A note may say that a physician was notified without showing what information was conveyed, whether the urgency was understood, what response was given, or whether the patient was reassessed. A consultant may say that a recommendation was communicated while the receiving clinician's note reflects a different understanding. A discharge summary may state that follow-up was arranged while scheduling records show no appointment was made.

Telephone logs, paging records, secure messages, handoff tools, transfer-center records, and referral systems may therefore become important. Their relevance depends on the disputed pathway.

In a failure-to-rescue case, I want to know how concern moved from bedside staff to the responsible clinician, whether the escalation chain was used, what response followed, and whether an unresolved concern crossed a shift change.

In a result-follow-up case, I want to know who owned the task, how the system signaled noncompletion, and what happened when the ordinary process failed.

Institutional records become important when responsibility may extend beyond one individual. Policies, job descriptions, staffing schedules, workflow documents, committee material, incident reports, and training records may help explain how the system was intended to operate.

They should be requested thoughtfully. A demand for every policy in the institution may produce a large volume of marginal material. A request tied to the clinical pathway is far more useful.

When the dispute concerns an abnormal test result, the relevant materials may address routing, acknowledgment, patient notification, follow-up ownership, unresolved-result queues, and coverage when the ordering professional is absent. When the issue is deterioration, the useful records may concern rapid-response criteria, escalation chains, staffing assignments, handoff practices, and monitoring expectations.

The request should follow the theory, but it must remain capable of changing as the theory changes.

A case that initially appears to involve an individual may become a system case after the ordinary chart is reviewed. The reverse can also happen. A policy may initially look defective while operational evidence shows that the safeguard was sound and one person departed from it.

The level of responsibility should not be decided before the evidence shows how the process actually worked.

Incident reports and internal reviews require particular care because their availability and discoverability depend on applicable law and the nature of the document. Clinically, those materials may identify the event, the institution's understanding of the process, or changes made afterward. Whether they can be obtained or used is a legal decision for counsel.

That division should remain clear. Clinical Intelligence identifies why a category of evidence may matter. Counsel decides whether it is discoverable, admissible, privileged, or strategically appropriate to pursue.

The same applies to peer-review material, quality files, credentialing records, and protected patient-safety work.

Clinical relevance does not answer the legal question of access.

In obstetrical and neonatal cases, completeness requires another level of coordination because maternal and fetal records may be separated even though the clinical course was continuous. The maternal chart, fetal-monitoring tracings, labor flowsheets, medication records, operative and anesthesia records, cord gases, placental pathology, neonatal resuscitation records, intensive-care documentation, imaging, and later developmental assessments may all contribute.

A missing segment of a tracing can matter. So can the quality of the archived tracing, its annotations, clock synchronization, and the relationship between fetal events and maternal interventions. A printed summary is not an adequate substitute for the full tracing when timing and interpretation are disputed.

The same principle applies in other settings. A pediatric case may require growth charts, immunization history, developmental records, parental communications, school notes, and records from several urgent-care or emergency visits. An adolescent behavioral-health matter may involve emergency care, outpatient treatment, school communication, family reports, medication history, and safety planning. A nursing-facility case may require wound photographs, repositioning records, nutrition data, weight trends, staffing evidence, therapy notes, hospital transfers, and vascular assessments.

The analytical framework remains stable. What constitutes a complete record changes with the clinical problem.

Photographs and video deserve attention because they often sit outside the formal production. Family photographs may document pre-event function, wound progression, swelling, gait, speech, or appearance. Facility photographs may show the evolution of a wound. Surveillance footage may establish mobility, supervision, or timing in a fall case. Home video may be relevant to developmental or neurological change.

These sources need context. A photograph can be powerful without being self-explanatory. You need to know when it was taken, by whom, under what circumstances, and whether it accurately represents the condition being described. The same image may support different interpretations depending on its timing.

Original files may also contain metadata that a screenshot or printed copy does not preserve. When visual evidence matters, preservation should be addressed early.

Autopsy and pathology evidence may also fall outside the ordinary record. In a wrongful-death case, the death certificate is usually only the starting point. The autopsy report, photographs, toxicology, histology, specimen inventory, and underlying pathology material may affect the cause and timing of death. Surgical pathology or cytology slides may be needed in a delayed-diagnosis matter. Placental material may be central to a birth-injury case.

The report tells you what someone concluded. The underlying material allows the conclusion to be tested.

That does not mean every case requires every original source. Proportionality matters. The question is whether the disputed issue depends on an interpretation that cannot be evaluated from the report alone.

When original imaging is not material, reviewing it may add very little. When the case turns on whether a finding was visible, the report is inadequate. When a pathology diagnosis is undisputed, the slides may not be necessary. When diagnosis, stage, or timing is contested, they may be essential.

The objective is not maximal collection. It is sufficient collection for reliable decision-making.

Absolute completeness is rarely possible. Device data may no longer exist. A verbal communication may never have been recorded. A facility may no longer retain archived material. A witness may not remember what happened.

The analysis does not require certainty before it can begin. It requires counsel to identify what is missing and understand how the absence affects the conclusion.

I find it useful to separate missing material into three practical groups.

Some evidence is essential. Without it, the central theory cannot be tested responsibly. Original imaging in a missed-imaging case may fall into that category, as may the records needed to determine whether the patient was eligible for the treatment on which causation depends.

Other evidence is important but not indispensable. It may strengthen or clarify the analysis, although the issue can be addressed through another reliable source. A missing secure message may matter less when both participants documented the communication contemporaneously and immediate action followed.

A third group is peripheral. The material may be interesting without changing the decision. Pursuing it can consume substantial time and expense while adding little clinical value.

Counsel needs to know which category applies. The question is not whether every gap can be filled. It is whether a particular gap prevents the team from answering a material question.

The gaps themselves should remain visible. Saying generally that the record is incomplete tells the team very little.

It is more useful to say that the original imaging has not been obtained, so the reasonableness of the first interpretation cannot yet be assessed. Or that the medication-administration record is absent, so the actual treatment time remains uncertain. Or that prior functional records are unavailable, so the degree of new impairment cannot yet be separated from baseline. Specific gaps lead to specific action.

They also permit more honest communication with the client and the expert. An expert should know which records are absent and which assumptions remain provisional. Otherwise, a preliminary opinion may harden around a factual foundation that later changes.

I would be especially careful with summaries prepared before the collection is complete. A chronology or medical summary can be extremely useful, but once written, it tends to become the accepted version of events. Later records may be added without changing the original narrative.

The summary should therefore reveal its sources and limitations. Material facts should be traceable. Disputed facts should remain disputed. Missing periods should be identified. The difference between the event and its documentation should be preserved.

A summary that smooths the chart into one coherent story can create false confidence. Medical records are often inconsistent. Some inconsistencies are noise. Others are central to the case. The reviewer should not resolve them silently.

Suppose the physician's note says the patient's confusion resolved before discharge while the nursing record describes continued disorientation. The summary should not simply choose one account. It should identify the discrepancy and determine what other evidence might help resolve it, such as reassessment documentation, family testimony, video, the later presentation, or deposition testimony.

The same applies when the client's account conflicts with the chart. The client should not automatically be discounted because the record is silent, and the chart should not automatically be rejected because the client remembers the event differently.

The conflict should be evaluated according to the reliability of each source and the circumstances in which it was created.

Medical records are important evidence. They are not necessarily the whole story.

There is also a danger in treating the provider's label for the production as authoritative. A production may be certified as complete while excluding material held by another department or vendor. The certification may accurately mean that the designated chart was produced. It does not necessarily mean that every source relevant to the patient's care was included.

When the case warrants it, counsel should ask practical questions. Which electronic systems were used? Were images stored separately? How were messages exchanged? Where were telephone calls recorded? Did the unit use paper flowsheets in addition to electronic documentation? Were device logs retained? Did an outside vendor manage referrals, monitoring, pharmacy, or laboratory services?

Those are not fishing questions when tied to the clinical theory. They identify where the evidence may be located.

The production should also be checked for continuity. Missing records are not always obvious. Encounter numbers may skip. A progress note may refer to a consultation that is absent. A discharge summary may mention a study not included in the production. Medication changes may appear without an order. A later entry may refer to a conversation or event that cannot be found elsewhere. Those internal references often reveal what is missing.

Billing information can occasionally identify services absent from the clinical production, although it should not be treated as proof that the service occurred exactly as coded. Claims data may identify an encounter, test, or provider that leads to another source. Appointment logs may reveal canceled or missed follow-up. Transfer records may identify another facility or transport service whose chart is needed.

The value lies in using one source to test the completeness of another.

In a complex case, the record map should be expected to evolve. At first, you identify the obvious providers and encounters. As the clinical pathway becomes clearer, new custodians emerge. A reference to outside imaging leads to another facility. A transfer note identifies an ambulance service. A medication history leads to a pharmacy. A postoperative complication leads to rehabilitation records that establish the actual injury.

collection should follow those connections until the material questions can be answered.

There is a point, however, when further collection stops improving the analysis. That point is not reached when every conceivable document has been obtained. It is reached when the relevant evidence is sufficiently reliable to support the next attorney decision and the remaining gaps are understood.

The next decision may be to obtain expert review, conduct focused discovery, revise the theory, value the case, or decline it. The level of completeness required will not be the same at every stage.

An intake decision can be made on less information than a final causation opinion. A preliminary expert consultation can proceed while some records remain outstanding, provided the limitations are clear. A settlement recommendation or trial position requires a firmer foundation.

Completeness is contextual. The practical question is always: complete enough for which decision?

That prevents two opposite errors. The first is moving too quickly because the file looks substantial. The second is postponing every decision while pursuing a perfect record that will never exist.

Clinical Intelligence does not demand perfection. It demands visibility. Counsel should know what has been obtained, what remains missing, why the missing evidence matters, and whether the current foundation is strong enough for the decision at hand.

By the end of this stage, you should be able to do more than say that the records have been collected. You should be able to explain how the evidence supports the clinical reconstruction.

You should know whether original source material has been obtained where interpretation is disputed. You should understand whether the relevant timestamps describe the clinical event or merely its documentation. You should know whether communication and workflow evidence exists outside the ordinary chart, whether prior records are sufficient to establish baseline, which inconsistencies remain unresolved, and which missing items could materially change the theory.

Most importantly, you should know whether the record allows counsel to ask the next question responsibly.

The volume of the file will not answer that, nor will the fact that every provider responded.

A record is clinically complete when it permits the team to reconstruct the patient's relevant condition, follow the disputed information or decision through the care process, test the competing explanations, and identify the limits of what can presently be concluded.

Until then, the file may be administratively organized and still clinically unfinished.

"Until then, the file may be administratively organized and still clinically unfinished."

CHAPTER SIX

Establishing the Patient's True Baseline

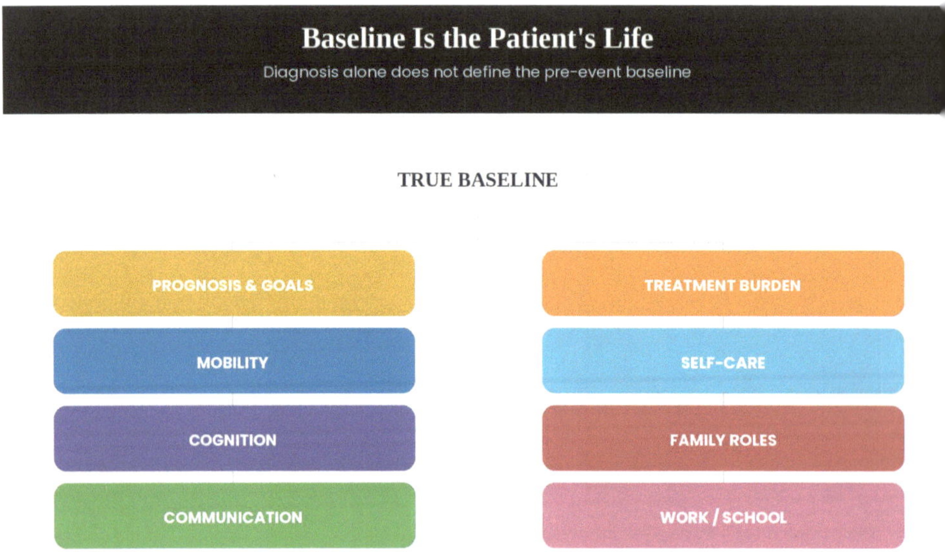

Before we can say what the patient lost, we have to know who the patient was.

That sounds straightforward, but baseline is often reduced to a problem list, a few diagnoses, and perhaps a sentence saying the patient was "independent" or "medically complex." That is rarely enough.

A diagnosis tells us that a condition existed. It does not necessarily tell us how the condition affected daily life, what treatment it required, whether it was stable, or what course could reasonably have been expected without the event under review.

Baseline is the point from which the case is measured. It affects causation, damages, prognosis, life expectancy, future care, employment loss, household loss, and the credibility of the position presented to the other side. When baseline is wrong, the injury is likely to be misunderstood as well.

A patient may have several chronic diseases and still live independently, work, drive, travel, care for family members, and manage every aspect of daily life. Another may have relatively few diagnoses and already depend heavily on others.

The number of conditions in the chart does not tell us which patient we are dealing with. The question is what those conditions meant before the disputed event.

When I work through baseline with counsel, I am not looking for a polished biography. I am looking for a reliable comparison.

What was the patient's medical condition? What could the patient do? What help was already required? Which symptoms were already present? What treatment was ongoing? Was the patient stable, improving, or declining? After the event, what changed? The comparison should be as concrete as the evidence allows.

"Independent before the event" may mean that the patient lived alone, drove, cooked, shopped, managed medication, paid bills, climbed stairs, and attended appointments without help. It may also mean only that the patient performed personal care within a supervised setting.

The word has value only when we know what it describes.

The same is true of labels such as active, functional, frail, disabled, or cognitively impaired. A person described as frail may still have been mentally sharp, socially engaged, and able to walk throughout the home. Someone described as ambulatory may have needed a walker, frequent rest, and another person nearby. A patient with cognitive impairment may have had mild memory difficulty while retaining judgment, recognition, conversation, and the ability to make ordinary decisions.

Baseline has to be built from the patient's actual life.

That usually requires more than one source. Medical records matter, but office notes tend to focus on the reason for the visit. They may list diagnoses and medications while saying very little about function. A cardiology note may say heart failure was stable without mentioning that the patient continued to work. A primary-care note may document arthritis without showing whether it limited walking. A problem list may carry the word dementia forward for years without describing the patient's current cognition.

Other records may be more revealing. Physical-therapy notes can show mobility, endurance, balance, and assistive-device use. Occupational-therapy records may describe dressing, bathing, meal preparation, and household activity. Home-health assessments may show what the patient could do alone and where assistance was needed. School records can establish a child's academic and developmental course. Employment records may document attendance, duties, physical demands, and earnings. Photographs, videos, calendars, messages, and family testimony may show how the patient actually lived.

No single source should be treated as complete merely because it appears formal.

Baseline is usually reconstructed by comparing records created for different purposes.

The family's account is often essential. Family members know whether the patient was driving, cooking, walking the dog, caring for grandchildren, managing a business, attending religious services, or requiring help each morning.

Their memories should still be tested against contemporaneous evidence. A family may minimize earlier limitations because everyone is focused on the later loss. Years after the event, the post-injury condition may also have become so familiar that prior impairment is remembered as worse than it was.

That does not make the family unreliable. It means their account should be evaluated in the same way as the chart.

The strongest baseline usually appears when several sources align. Medical records show stable disease. Therapy notes establish independent mobility. Employment records show regular work. Family members describe the same daily activities.

When the sources do not align, the inconsistency should remain visible until it can be explained.

Suppose the family describes the patient as completely independent, while home-health records show daily help with bathing, medication, and meals. The baseline is not "independent" simply because the family uses the word.

At the same time, home-health services do not necessarily mean that the patient lacked meaningful autonomy. The patient may have required limited support while continuing to make decisions, move around the home, communicate normally, and participate actively in family life.

The legal and clinical significance lies in the detail.

That detail becomes particularly important when the defense relies on age or comorbidity. A seventy-nine-year-old patient with diabetes, hypertension, chronic kidney disease, and arthritis may sound medically fragile when those diagnoses are listed together. If the evidence also shows that the patient lived alone, drove, shopped, managed finances, and cared for a spouse, the baseline tells a fuller story.

The chronic conditions remain relevant. They may affect healing, prognosis, treatment eligibility, physiological reserve, and life expectancy. They do not establish that the patient had little function or little to lose.

The plaintiff can make the opposite mistake by treating medical complexity as though it had no effect. A patient with severe vascular disease, chronic wounds, and renal impairment may have faced a substantial risk of amputation regardless of the disputed delay. A patient with advanced cancer may have had limited survival even with earlier diagnosis. Someone with progressive neurological disease may already have been declining.

Baseline should not idealize the patient. It should show where the patient actually stood.

That is why the period reviewed matters. It should be long enough to reveal the patient's course rather than capture one unusually good or unusually poor moment.

A patient may appear highly dependent during a brief hospitalization and later return to a much better level at home. Another may seem stable during occasional office visits while therapy, home-health, and family records show gradual decline. A note saying that the patient was "doing well" may mean only that the condition had not changed, not that no impairment existed.

We need enough history to determine whether the baseline was stable, improving, or deteriorating.

That can materially change causation. If the patient was already declining rapidly from advanced disease, the event may have accelerated an established course. If the condition had been stable for years, a sudden post-event loss is easier to distinguish. If the patient was recovering from an earlier injury, the right comparison may not be the distant pre-injury state or the worst point in rehabilitation. It may be the trajectory the patient was following immediately before the event.

Baseline is not always a single fixed point. Sometimes it is a course.

That is particularly true in delayed-diagnosis cases. The patient's condition at the missed opportunity may differ from the condition when the diagnosis was finally made. Disease may have progressed during the interval.

In a cancer case, baseline includes more than daily function. It may include probable disease stage, treatment options, performance status, organ function, and ability to tolerate therapy. A patient may have been working and active while harboring an undiagnosed malignancy.

Both facts can be true. The disease existed, but the patient had not yet experienced the later progression, treatment burden, or loss of survival.

The analysis depends on what earlier diagnosis probably would have changed, not on pretending the disease was absent.

Postoperative and failure-to-rescue cases may require baseline to be defined at more than one level. There is the patient's condition before surgery, the expected condition immediately afterward, and the condition just before the alleged deterioration was missed.

A patient recovering from major surgery is not expected to look as well as before admission. Pain, fatigue, reduced mobility, and temporary laboratory changes may be ordinary. The question is whether the patient remained within that expected range or developed a pattern suggesting complication.

If we compare the patient only with the preoperative condition, every postoperative symptom may look alarming. If we compare the patient only with postoperative patients generally, we may miss an important departure from this patient's own early course. Baseline has to fit the clinical question.

The same applies in nursing-facility cases. A resident may enter with limited mobility, cognitive impairment, poor nutrition, vascular disease, and a high risk of skin injury. That starting point matters when assessing whether a wound was preventable and whether later decline can be attributed to the facility. Risk, however, is not the same as outcome.

The resident may have entered with intact skin and no infection. The person may have been able to transfer with assistance, eat with supervision, report discomfort, and participate in activities. If the resident later develops a deep wound, sepsis, hospitalization, and profound decline, prior vulnerability does not explain every part of what followed.

The analysis has to separate what was already present from what was added.

That often produces a description more careful than either side initially prefers. The plaintiff may want to say the resident was doing well. The defense may want to say the resident was frail and medically compromised. Both may be partly correct.

A clinically useful baseline might be that the resident had severe chronic disease and required assistance with mobility and personal care, but had intact skin, stable nutrition, meaningful communication, and no active infection. That identifies the actual change under review.

Pediatric baseline requires a different approach because the child is still developing. We are not comparing a stable adult level of function with a later loss. We are trying to understand the developmental course before the event and the course that probably would have followed.

For an infant or young child, growth, feeding, motor development, language, social interaction, behavior, and milestone progression may be central. The child may not yet have reached the age at which a particular ability normally develops. In that setting, the injury may involve a lost developmental opportunity or a divergence from the expected trajectory rather than the loss of an already acquired skill.

The analysis becomes more difficult when the child already had developmental delay, prematurity, a genetic condition, or a congenital abnormality. The disputed event may have caused a new neurological injury, aggravated the existing condition, or made it substantially harder for the child to reach expected milestones.

The baseline should not erase earlier concerns. It should not allow them to absorb a distinct later injury either.

School and therapy records are often valuable because they show function over time. They may document attention, language, mobility, behavior, academic performance, and support needs. For an adolescent, the evidence may also include athletics, employment, driving, social independence, and plans for education or vocational training.

Damages involving a young person will inevitably involve some projection. Baseline gives that projection an evidentiary foundation.

A healthy teenager who attended school, played sports, worked part time, and was preparing for college had a different expected course from an adolescent who already required substantial educational and medical support. That does not mean the second child has less value. It means the additional loss is different. The model measures change, not human worth.

Maternal and obstetrical cases may require baseline to be considered in two related but separate ways. The mother has her own health, function, pregnancy course, and risk factors. The fetus has a developing clinical condition shaped by maternal health, placental function, growth, infection, labor, and delivery.

A maternal wrongful-death case may involve a woman who entered pregnancy with chronic disease but was functioning well and expected to survive. The existence of pregnancy-related risk does not answer whether a later hemorrhage, infection, embolism, or hypertensive emergency was preventable.

In a birth-injury case, the fetal baseline may include prenatal growth, anatomy, movement, testing, and evidence of pre-existing injury or placental compromise. The newborn's condition after delivery is part of the outcome being explained, not the starting point.

Prenatal and placental evidence may show that injury began before labor, during labor, or after delivery. It may establish that the fetus already faced substantial risk, or it may show normal development before a time-sensitive event.

Baseline does not resolve causation by itself, but it establishes what causation can reasonably mean.

In adult catastrophic-injury cases, pre-event function is often the most visible part of baseline, although physiological reserve matters as well. Two patients may perform the same daily activities and still have very different capacities to recover.

A young adult without major disease may have substantial rehabilitation potential after a neurological event. An older patient with significant heart, lung, and renal disease may have much less reserve. That affects prognosis and future care. It should not be used to assume that the older patient lacked a meaningful pre-event life.

We need both parts: what the patient could do and which vulnerabilities shaped the likely course.

Medication and treatment cases show how baseline can affect liability as well as damages. A drug injury cannot be evaluated without understanding renal function, liver function, prior medication use, allergies, interactions, body weight, and relevant laboratory trends.

What appears to be an acute abnormality may have been chronic. What looks like a routine dose may have been inappropriate for this patient's physiology.

If renal function was already impaired, reasonable care may have required dose adjustment or closer monitoring. If the impairment developed after treatment began, the timing of the change may become central. A laboratory trend can serve as both baseline evidence and evidence of deterioration.

This is why baseline should not be treated as a separate compartment. It supports causation and damages, but it may also shape the standard of care. Prior condition affects foreseeable risks, monitoring needs, available treatment, and how quickly change should have been recognized.

Counsel should remain alert to records that appear peripheral but alter that context. A history of falls may matter in a hospital-fall case. Earlier confusion may affect a claim involving neurological decline. Prior difficulty healing may matter in a surgical or facility case. Previous treatment intolerance may affect the alternative course in a delayed-diagnosis matter.

Pre-existing conditions do not defeat the claim. They define the patient-specific questions the claim must answer.

Medical baseline should also be separated from legal attribution. The fact that a condition existed before the event does not mean every later consequence belongs to it. The analysis still has to determine whether the event caused a new injury, aggravated the condition, accelerated progression, or increased the required level of care.

A patient with arthritis may already have walked slowly but remained independent. After a neurological injury, the patient may require a wheelchair and complete assistance. Arthritis belongs in the baseline. It does not account for the new dependence.

A person with mild cognitive impairment may have needed reminders while still recognizing family, participating in decisions, and living at home. After hypoxic injury, that patient may no longer communicate or perform basic tasks. The prior impairment matters. It does not erase the change.

A patient with metastatic cancer may already have had limited life expectancy. If a treatment error causes earlier death or prolonged avoidable suffering, the cancer affects the measure of the loss without eliminating it.

A careful baseline allows those distinctions to be explained to experts, mediators, judges, and juries.

It also protects credibility. An exaggerated baseline is easy to attack. If the plaintiff presents the patient as entirely independent and the defense produces records showing substantial prior assistance, the damage can spread beyond the disputed function and undermine the larger theory.

The defense faces the same risk. Describing someone as elderly and frail without addressing evidence of independent living, employment, or caregiving can make the position appear dismissive. Age and diagnosis are not substitutes for evidence.

The strongest presentation usually acknowledges the full baseline, including facts that complicate the preferred position.

A plaintiff may explain that the patient had diabetes, chronic kidney disease, and reduced endurance but lived alone, drove, and required no help with personal care. The event did not take the patient from perfect health to disability. It created a new level of dependence.

A defense may acknowledge that the patient remained active in the community while maintaining that the underlying cancer was already advanced, treatment options were limited, and earlier diagnosis probably would not have produced cure. The remaining question may be whether some period of survival or treatment opportunity was lost.

Those positions are credible because neither asks the evidence to deny what is inconvenient.

Experts need the same honest baseline. Their opinions about causation, prognosis, and future care can be no stronger than the comparison they are given.

This becomes especially important when several experts are involved. The standard-of-care expert may focus on the encounter. The causation expert may examine disease progression. A rehabilitation expert may assess function. A life-care planner may project future needs. An economist may calculate financial loss.

If each begins with a different baseline, the case will contain internal contradictions even if every expert is individually competent.

One expert may assume the patient was working full time while another understands that employment had already ended. A life-care plan may treat all attendant care as new while earlier records show some assistance was already in place. An economist may project earnings through an age the medical prognosis does not support. Those inconsistencies should be resolved before opinions are finalized.

A controlled baseline summary can help, provided it remains traceable to the source material. It should describe the relevant diagnoses, treatment, function, cognition, independence, employment, living arrangement, care needs, and prognosis. Important inconsistencies should be identified rather than smoothed away.

The summary does not need to be long. It needs to be accurate.

For a complex adult case, it might explain that the patient had chronic heart and kidney disease, used a cane outside the home, and received help with heavy housekeeping, but lived independently, drove locally, managed medication and finances, and handled personal care without assistance. That paragraph provides more litigation value than a two-page diagnosis list.

For a child, the baseline might state that language and social development were age appropriate, with mild gross-motor delay, before the event caused broader neurological impairment.

For a nursing-facility resident, it might explain that the resident needed help with transfers and bathing and had poor vascular health and reduced appetite, but had intact skin, no active infection, meaningful conversation, and regular family involvement.

Baseline should be written so that the later change becomes understandable.

There will be cases in which baseline remains uncertain. Records may be sparse. The patient may have had limited access to care. Family accounts may conflict. The relevant period may have occurred years earlier. A child may have been too young for the expected future course to be predicted confidently.

Uncertainty should be stated rather than filled with assumption.

We may be able to establish that the patient walked without knowing the exact distance. We may know that the patient lived at home without knowing how much informal help was provided. We may know that a child was progressing developmentally without being able to predict the eventual educational level.

Baseline does not have to be perfect to be useful. We need to know which conclusions are secure and which remain provisional.

That distinction affects the strength with which damages can be presented. A well-documented loss of employment may be stated confidently. A projected vocational path for a young child requires more qualification. Loss of independence may be clear even when the exact amount of prior assistance is disputed. The analysis should match the evidence.

Baseline also begins to merge with the probable alternative course when the patient's condition was already changing before the alleged negligence.

Suppose an older adult with progressive weakness is admitted after several falls and later suffers a major injury when an acute neurological condition is not recognized. The immediate baseline already includes decline. The relevant question is not whether the patient would have returned to the level of function enjoyed several years earlier. It is what course was reasonably expected from the condition as it existed when the failure occurred.

Likewise, a patient receiving cancer treatment may already have fatigue, weight loss, and reduced work capacity before a medication error causes additional organ injury. Damages must separate the expected effects of the cancer and treatment from the new consequences of the error.

At that point, the comparison is no longer simply before and after. It is the likely course without the event compared with the course that actually occurred.

That analysis may show that the patient would have required some future care regardless, while the event increased its amount, intensity, or duration. It may show expected gradual decline followed instead by abrupt dependence. It may show that death was likely within a limited period but occurred sooner and through a more difficult course. The injury lies in the difference between those paths.

That is why baseline cannot be postponed until the damages phase. It should influence intake, record collection, expert selection, causation, discovery, valuation, and communication with the client from the beginning.

Baseline is not a sympathetic biography added to humanize the case. It is clinical evidence.

Nor is it a device for diminishing someone whose life was already limited. A person does not have to be healthy, employed, or entirely independent to sustain a serious additional loss. The inquiry is what this patient had, what this patient could do, and what this patient lost.

By the end of the baseline analysis, counsel should be able to describe the patient without exaggeration and without allowing the diagnoses to take over the person.

You should know which conditions existed, how they affected function, what care was already required, whether the course was stable or changing, what prognosis existed, and what evidence supports those conclusions. You should also know what remains uncertain and whether that uncertainty affects causation, damages, or both.

Most importantly, you should be able to state the change the case is actually about.

The event may have caused a wholly new disability. It may have aggravated an existing condition, accelerated decline, increased dependence, shortened survival, or added suffering to an already difficult course.

Once the baseline is clear, the case becomes more precise. We are no longer asking what happened to a patient described only by age, diagnosis, or outcome. We are asking what happened to this patient, from this starting point, and what difference the evidence supports.

"We are asking what happened to this patient, from this starting point, and what difference the evidence supports."

CHAPTER SEVEN

Imaging and Objective Evidence Analysis

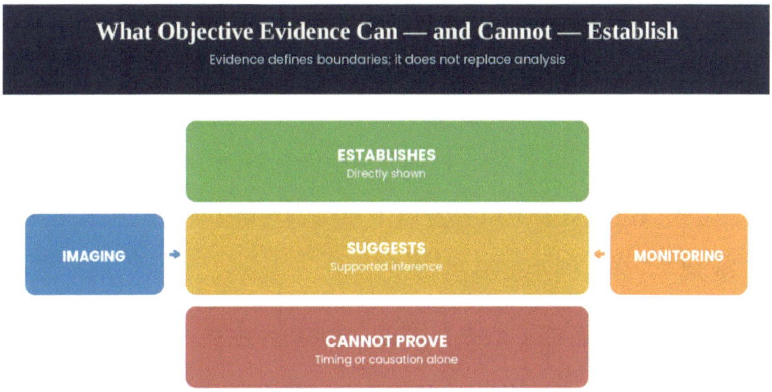

Imaging and objective evidence often determine whether a medical case begins to take shape or starts to lose it.

Until that evidence is examined, much of the case may depend on narrative. The patient reported pain. A family member noticed confusion. A nurse described a change. A physician documented improvement. A later clinician believed the condition must have been present earlier.

Those accounts matter, but each is affected by memory, perspective, documentation practices, and knowledge of what happened next.

Objective evidence gives us another route into the case. It may show the location and extent of an injury, the progression of disease, the timing of a complication, the presence of another explanation, or the patient's response to treatment. It may confirm that the condition changed when the chart says it did, reveal that the change began earlier, or show that a finding described as acute was longstanding.

It may also expose a gap between what was ordered and what actually occurred.

For counsel, that can be enormously useful. It can also be misleading when the evidence is treated as though it explains its own legal significance.

A scan does not determine whether the standard of care was breached. A laboratory value does not identify the point at which the response should have changed. A monitor tracing does not establish that a clinician saw or understood what it recorded. Pathology may show which disease was present without establishing when it became reasonably diagnosable. An autopsy may identify the mechanism of death while leaving unresolved whether the disputed care changed the outcome.

Objective evidence can anchor the analysis. It is neither self-interpreting nor self-proving.

When counsel first sees a striking image or a severely abnormal laboratory value, it is natural to treat it as the fact that explains the case. Sometimes it does. More often, it answers only part of the question.

A later scan may show a large stroke. That does not establish when the stroke began, whether symptoms during an earlier encounter were caused by it, or whether treatment remained available at the relevant time.

A pathology report may confirm an aggressive cancer without telling us whether an earlier image should have been interpreted differently or whether earlier diagnosis probably would have changed survival.

A markedly abnormal laboratory value may prove severe deterioration at one moment without showing when the process first became clinically recognizable.

We therefore need to distinguish what the evidence establishes, what it suggests, and what still requires qualified interpretation.

That work begins with obtaining the original source whenever the dispute depends on interpretation.

A written imaging report tells us what the original reader concluded. It does not allow another qualified specialist to determine whether the study was technically adequate, whether a finding was visible, whether it was acute or chronic, or whether the original interpretation remained within the reasonable professional range.

When the allegation is that a radiologist missed a hemorrhage, mass, fracture, vascular occlusion, or another abnormality, the images themselves are central. The report cannot substitute for them.

The same is true when the defense relies on an earlier study as normal. A later reviewer may conclude that the study was truly negative, technically limited, equivocal, or already showed the beginning of the condition.

Retrospective visibility and contemporaneous negligence are not the same conclusion.

Once the later diagnosis is known, a subtle abnormality on an earlier study may become much easier to see. The later image directs the reviewer to the exact location. Knowledge of the outcome may give significance to something that appeared nonspecific at the time.

That does not make the later interpretation wrong. It means the relevant inquiry remains whether a reasonable reader, working from the original study, the information then supplied, and the original degree of visibility, should have identified the finding.

A subtle abnormality may have been present without supporting a departure. In another case, a study called negative may contain a clinically significant finding that should reasonably have been recognized.

The fact that someone sees the finding now does not answer whether it was reasonably recognizable then.

Technical quality matters just as much. A study may be unable to answer the clinical question it was expected to answer. Contrast timing, image sequences, patient movement, field of view, slice thickness, projection, and equipment quality may all limit what can be seen.

Sometimes that limitation supports the original interpretation. In other cases, it raises a different issue: whether the proper study was ordered or whether additional imaging was required.

A negative study is meaningful only within the limits of what that study could reliably detect.

For that reason, I would resist saying simply that "the imaging was negative." I would want to know which modality was used, why the study was ordered, which conditions it could reasonably identify, which limitations were present, and whether the result fit the patient's presentation.

A noncontrast head CT may be appropriate for one emergency question and inadequate for another. A plain radiograph may exclude one kind of injury while leaving soft-tissue or vascular disease unresolved. An early study may not reveal a process that becomes visible later. An abnormality may be present but too subtle to characterize without further testing. Those distinctions affect liability and causation.

Imaging may establish that disease existed without showing that it could have been detected through the study performed. It may demonstrate that a lesion was chronic and undermine an allegation that the disputed event caused it. It may show progression between two points and help define when the patient's condition worsened.

Serial studies are often more useful than a single image because one study shows anatomy at one moment while a series shows change.

In a neurological case, serial imaging may reveal expansion of a hemorrhage, increasing edema, new infarction, or progression from an early subtle finding to an obvious injury. In an infection case, repeated studies may show development of an abscess, worsening infiltrates, increasing fluid, or tissue destruction. In an oncology matter, the sequence may help establish growth, spread, or progression from localized to advanced disease.

The images still have to be aligned with the clinical course. Counsel needs to know which symptoms existed at each point, what treatment occurred between the studies, and whether the change shown on imaging corresponds to the alleged delay.

A worsening later image may support progression. It does not prove that different care would have prevented it. That conclusion belongs to causation.

Laboratory evidence presents a similar problem. Lawyers are often drawn to the most abnormal number in the chart. Clinically, the trend may matter far more than the isolated value.

A creatinine of 2.0 may represent serious acute kidney injury in one patient and a stable chronic baseline in another. A low hemoglobin may be unchanged from prior testing. A lactate may begin only modestly elevated and rise rapidly during deterioration. A patient with severe infection may have a normal white-cell count.

The reference range tells us whether the result falls outside a general interval. It does not tell us what the result meant for this patient.

We need the earlier values, the direction and rate of change, the clinical context, and the treatment occurring at the time.

This is where baseline and objective evidence meet. A result may be important not merely because it is abnormal, but because it departs from what was ordinary or expected for that patient.

Trends may also reveal deterioration before the narrative record acknowledges it. Falling platelets, worsening renal function, progressive acidosis, declining hemoglobin, increasing inflammatory markers, or abnormal coagulation may show a process developing before the notes describe it clearly.

The first abnormal result does not necessarily establish the moment when the condition should have been recognized. The trend helps identify when separate findings became a clinically meaningful pattern.

One mildly abnormal result may not require a change in management. Several related abnormalities moving in the same direction, particularly when they align with symptoms and vital signs, may create a very different picture.

Objective evidence is most useful when integrated rather than viewed in isolation.

Tachycardia can have many explanations. Persistent tachycardia combined with falling blood pressure, reduced urine output, increasing respiratory rate, confusion, and worsening laboratory findings may describe a patient becoming unstable.

No single fact necessarily carries the case. The pattern may.

Monitoring data can reveal that pattern more accurately than narrative notes. Continuous cardiac monitoring, pulse oximetry, blood-pressure recordings, fetal monitoring, glucose data, ventilator measurements, intracranial-pressure recordings, and other device-generated information may show changes over time that a note compresses into one sentence.

A nurse may chart that the patient was stable overnight while the monitor shows repeated episodes of hypoxia, tachycardia, or hypotension. The same data may show that those episodes were brief, associated with movement, or caused by artifact. The raw evidence still requires interpretation.

Sensors disconnect. Movement creates artifact. Values may be imported incorrectly. Automated alerts may reflect poor signal quality rather than a true clinical event.

The relevant question is not simply whether an abnormal number appeared. It is whether the data represented a real change, whether the treating professionals had access to it in a useful form, and whether it required a response.

That last point matters because objective information can exist in a system without being clinically available.

A device may store retrospective data that was never displayed at the bedside. A monitor may record a change no one reviewed. A laboratory result may be technically available but never routed to the responsible clinician.

The existence of information and a professional's access to it are different questions.

That distinction becomes central in result-management cases. A laboratory or imaging abnormality may have been generated promptly. The dispute may concern when it became available, where it went, who was expected to review it, and what happened afterward. The result itself is one source. The electronic pathway is another.

Medication records present the same kind of separation. The order shows what the clinician intended. The medication-administration record shows what was charted as given. Pharmacy records may show verification and dispensing. Infusion-pump data may show what was actually delivered. Those records do not always agree.

Medication may be ordered on time and administered late. It may be recorded as given but stopped shortly afterward. The dose may be changed in one section of the chart and remain unchanged elsewhere. An infusion may run at the wrong rate despite a correct order.

When the case depends on treatment timing, toxicity, or failure to respond, counsel needs the evidence showing what actually reached the patient.

An order is not treatment, and a plan is not implementation.

That distinction can materially change the theory. The chart may suggest that antibiotics were provided within an acceptable period because the order was entered promptly. The administration record may show a substantial delay. A clinician may document that fluids were started, while pump data shows that far less volume was delivered than intended. A reversal agent may have been ordered but unavailable on the unit.

Objective evidence moves the case from what was planned to what actually occurred.

Pathology requires a different analysis. It can confirm diagnosis, classify disease, identify tissue injury, and sometimes help explain mechanism or duration. In cancer matters, it may define the type and biological aggressiveness of the disease. In obstetrical cases, placental pathology may reveal chronic compromise, infection, inflammation, vascular injury, or evidence of an acute event. In surgical cases, tissue findings may help explain infection, necrosis, or organ damage.

The report may be sufficient when diagnosis is undisputed. When grade, stage, timing, or even the diagnosis itself is central, the underlying slides or specimens may require independent review.

As with imaging, later review must be framed carefully. A pathologist may identify features consistent with a chronic process without being able to give a precise onset. Pathology may establish that a condition existed before the disputed care without showing that it was clinically detectable. The evidence should not be pushed beyond what the discipline can support.

Autopsy evidence is often treated as definitive because it follows death and may identify the cause. It can be extraordinarily important, particularly when the diagnosis during life was uncertain. It may reveal pulmonary embolism, hemorrhage, infection, medication toxicity, airway obstruction, organ injury, or another mechanism that was not recognized.

An autopsy may tell us what caused death. It may not tell us whether earlier care would have prevented it. That still depends on timing, treatment opportunity, eligibility, and probable benefit.

The medical cause of death and the legally attributable loss are related but not always identical. A patient may die from an embolism. The case may still turn on whether the earlier presentation required investigation, whether treatment remained available, and whether that treatment probably would have changed the outcome.

An autopsy may also identify several contributing conditions. That does not establish that the alleged negligence played no role. It means causation must account for their interaction.

Objective evidence often exposes competing explanations that the narrative theory has overlooked.

A scan may show old infarcts inconsistent with a claim that all cognitive impairment began after the disputed event. Prior imaging may show that a structural abnormality was already present. Laboratory history may establish chronic organ dysfunction. Pathology may reveal an aggressive disease process that limits the likely benefit of earlier treatment.

Those findings may narrow the case. They may also strengthen it by identifying the additional injury more accurately.

If imaging shows substantial pre-existing disease together with a clear new injury, the case no longer depends on claiming that the patient had no prior impairment. It can identify what changed.

If pathology shows that cure was unlikely but treatment probably would have prolonged survival, the theory may shift from complete prevention to lost time. Objective evidence forces that kind of precision.

It also helps identify which questions belong to which experts. A radiologist may explain what an image shows and whether the original interpretation was reasonable. A neurologist may address the clinical significance of the finding and the likely effect of treatment. A pathologist may describe disease characteristics. An oncologist may explain treatment and prognosis.

Familiarity with one part of the evidence does not qualify an expert to answer every question arising from it.

This matters because objective evidence can create an illusion of certainty. A scan appears concrete. A laboratory value has a number. A pathology report may use definitive language. The litigation team may assume the case has become simpler. Often, it has become more specific rather than simpler.

An image may establish that a hemorrhage existed at a particular time. Counsel may still need to determine when it began, whether it was visible earlier, which symptoms it caused, and what intervention could have changed the injury.

A laboratory trend may show worsening organ failure while leaving unresolved when the pattern required escalation and whether the patient remained salvageable.

Objective evidence narrows uncertainty. It does not always eliminate it.

Another practical distinction is between biological timing and clinical timing.

A disease may begin before it can be detected. A tumor may exist microscopically before it is visible on imaging. A clot may form before symptoms appear. An infection may be developing before it produces a recognizable pattern. A fetal injury may begin before monitoring reflects a change.

The fact that a process was biologically present does not establish that it should have been diagnosed or treated at that point.

Clinical timing asks when the information available to the treating professionals should reasonably have changed care.

That is the bridge from objective evidence to the timeline. Before reconstructing the sequence, we need to understand what imaging, laboratory data, pathology, monitoring, medication, and treatment records tell us about the patient at each stage.

We should also be careful with the word objective. It does not mean free from interpretation.

Images are interpreted. Laboratory results depend on proper collection, handling, calibration, and context. Monitor data may contain artifact. Pathology depends on sampling and professional judgment. Device records may be incomplete or difficult to align with chart time.

These sources may be more stable than recollection or narrative description, but their reliability still has to be assessed.

Was the sample collected properly? Was the study complete? Were timestamps synchronized? Does the device identify the correct patient? Was the image affected by technical limitation? Does the report reflect the final or preliminary interpretation? Was the abnormal result repeated or confirmed?

The purpose of those questions is practical. We need to know how much weight the evidence can bear.

Counsel does not need to become a radiologist, pathologist, or laboratory specialist. Counsel does need to understand what the source establishes, what professional interpretation remains necessary, and how the conclusion connects with the case theory.

Objective evidence should also be summarized in a way that preserves change over time. A list of abnormal results is usually less useful than an explanation of the trend and its clinical meaning.

Instead of listing tachycardia, abnormal creatinine, low urine output, and rising lactate separately, the analysis may explain that the patient developed progressive circulatory and organ dysfunction over a defined interval.

Instead of repeating several imaging reports, it should explain what changed anatomically and when.

That synthesis prepares the timeline by identifying the clinical markers that may define the beginning of the material period.

The source evidence must remain traceable. A synthesis is useful only if counsel and the experts can return to the actual study, result, or recording. Important findings should not exist solely in someone else's summary.

This becomes particularly important when experts disagree. The dispute may concern what the image shows, whether the study was adequate, whether a trend was clinically meaningful, or whether the evidence establishes timing.

One expert may see an abnormality and another may not. Both may agree that it is present but disagree about whether it was reasonably visible at the relevant time. The disagreement may concern neither existence nor visibility, but the clinical significance or causal effect of the finding. Those are different disputes and should be kept separate.

At the end of the objective-evidence analysis, counsel should know what anchors the case and what remains inferential.

You may know that a hemorrhage was present by a particular time, that oxygenation declined progressively, that medication was not administered when ordered, that disease was advanced at diagnosis, or that a lesion existed on an earlier image.

You may not yet know when the condition became reasonably recognizable, when the professional obligation changed, or whether intervention would have altered the outcome. Those questions belong to the next stages of the analysis.

That is why imaging and objective evidence come before the timeline. First identify the markers of the patient's condition. Then place them in sequence and determine when the course became clinically consequential.

Without objective evidence, a timeline may become little more than a chronology of notes. With it, the timeline can reconstruct the patient's actual clinical course.

"Without objective evidence, a timeline may become little more than a chronology of notes. With it, the timeline can reconstruct the patient's actual clinical course."

CHAPTER EIGHT

Reconstructing the Clinically Material Timeline

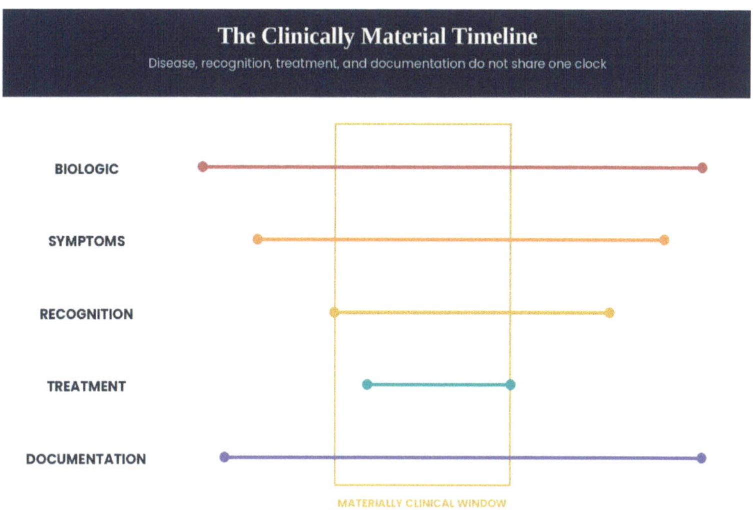

Once the objective evidence has been examined, the timeline serves a different purpose.

We are no longer arranging records according to when they were written. We are trying to understand how the patient's condition changed, when that change became clinically important, and when the opportunity for effective intervention began to narrow.

That distinction is central to almost every malpractice, wrongful-death, or healthcare-negligence case involving delay.

A chronology can tell us that the patient arrived at 9:10, was examined at 9:35, had blood drawn at 10:05, underwent imaging at 11:20, received medication at 12:10, and deteriorated at two. It does not tell us whether the patient was already unstable at 9:35, whether the laboratory pattern became concerning at 10:45, whether the imaging should have changed the plan at 11:50, or whether meaningful treatment remained available at noon.

The clinically material timeline is intended to answer those questions.

When I work through a timeline with counsel, I am looking for the point at which the patient's course moved from one that could reasonably be observed, treated, or discharged to one requiring a different response. Sometimes that point is obvious. More often, it emerges through a pattern.

Pain, fever, weakness, dizziness, or shortness of breath do not always signal an immediate emergency. Their meaning changes when they persist, worsen, combine with new findings, fail to respond to treatment, or no longer fit the working diagnosis.

A useful timeline shows progression, not merely elapsed time.

By this stage, we have already examined baseline and objective evidence. We know which findings were new, which abnormalities were chronic, what the imaging showed, and which laboratory or monitoring trends may mark deterioration. The timeline places those findings in sequence and asks what they meant as the course developed.

The first difficulty is that the medical record does not contain one reliable clock. It contains several.

A symptom may begin at home and be reported hours later. A nurse may observe a change and document it after completing care. A physician may examine the patient at noon and sign the note at four. A test may be ordered, performed, interpreted, finalized, and communicated at different times. Medication may be ordered promptly and administered later. A consultant may give advice by telephone before entering a formal note. Those times are related, but they are not interchangeable.

The signature time of a note is not necessarily the time of the examination. The order time is not the administration time. The final report time may not be the moment a preliminary interpretation became available. A later chart entry may describe an earlier event.

When the theory depends on delay measured in minutes or hours, those distinctions can determine the case.

I would not rely on document order alone. Wherever possible, the timeline should distinguish the clinical event from its documentation.

Suppose a physician note signed at 6:20 says the patient was examined at three and appeared stable. A nursing entry at 3:15 describes confusion and falling blood pressure. A later note says the physician was notified at 3:30.

The signature time does not establish whether the physician knew about the deterioration during the earlier examination.

The physician may have examined the patient before the condition changed. The deterioration may already have been present but overlooked. The documentation may be too sparse to establish the sequence reliably.

Each possibility produces a different analysis, and the timeline should preserve that uncertainty.

Audit information, medication-administration data, monitor records, and communication logs may clarify what the conventional chart leaves unresolved. They also require interpretation. A user opening a record does not prove that a particular finding was seen. A paging log may show that a message was sent without revealing what it said or whether it was understood. The timeline should distinguish established facts from reasonable inference.

I find it useful to think of the clinical course in phases rather than as one uninterrupted stream.

There is the patient's condition on presentation. An initial working diagnosis and plan follow. The patient may then enter a period of stability, treatment, or observation. The course may change through new symptoms, worsening vital signs, abnormal results, failure to improve, or a finding that no longer fits the original explanation.

That change may lead to reassessment and escalation. It may instead be missed, delayed, or interpreted as part of the expected course.

The patient eventually reaches an outcome: improvement, transfer, emergency intervention, permanent injury, or death.

The important question is where the course crossed from one phase into another. That transition is often the real beginning of the case.

Consider a postoperative patient who develops pain, low-grade fever, and fatigue. During the first hours after surgery, those findings may be expected. If the patient remains hemodynamically stable, maintains urine output, responds to medication, and shows no worsening abdominal or neurological signs, observation may be reasonable.

Later, the patient develops persistent tachycardia, increasing pain, reduced urine output, falling blood pressure, and confusion. The broad categories of symptoms may appear similar, but the pattern now carries a different clinical meaning.

The timeline should not describe the whole postoperative period as one undifferentiated delay. It should identify when the findings moved outside the expected range and escalation became necessary.

That may reduce an allegation of twelve hours of inaction to a more supportable four-hour failure-to-rescue interval.

Some attorneys worry that narrowing the timeline weakens the case. In practice, it often strengthens it. A precise interval can be defended because it is tied to a recognizable clinical change. It tells the standard-of-care expert which decision to evaluate, identifies the communications and staffing relevant to discovery, and tells the causation expert when the treatment opportunity must be assessed.

A broad delay may sound serious while remaining clinically vague. A defined interval shows when the obligation changed. The same reasoning applies to repeated encounters.

A patient may visit urgent care, an emergency department, or a physician's office several times before a diagnosis is made. Once the final diagnosis is known, every earlier encounter can look like a missed opportunity. A careful reconstruction may show otherwise.

The first encounter may involve mild, nonspecific symptoms, reassuring vital signs, a normal examination, and improvement with treatment. The second may involve persistent symptoms without objective change. The third may include focal weakness, altered mental status, abnormal laboratory findings, or failure to improve.

The supportable theory may concern only the later encounter.

Every visit should not be forced into the same allegation merely because the disease was biologically present throughout. The important question is when the presentation became sufficiently recognizable to require a different evaluation or treatment.

Disease onset, clinical detectability, and professional recognizability are separate points in time.

A tumor may exist before it can be seen. A clot may form before symptoms appear. An infection may develop before the patient shows a pattern requiring escalation. A stroke may begin before focal findings emerge. The timeline has to respect those distinctions.

This is especially important in delayed-diagnosis cases because the date of eventual diagnosis tends to dominate the narrative. Counsel may be tempted to measure the delay from the first symptom or earliest study to the final diagnosis. That period may be useful descriptively, but it may not represent the clinically material delay.

The relevant interval begins when the condition should reasonably have been recognized or investigated. It ends when the missed opportunity was corrected or when the probable benefit of correction became materially reduced. Those endpoints need evidentiary support.

In a cancer case, an earlier abnormality may have required follow-up within a defined period rather than immediate diagnosis. The material delay may begin when that follow-up should have occurred, not when the original study was performed. It may end when progression changed the available treatment or prognosis.

In a stroke matter, the interval may begin when neurological findings became apparent and end when the treatment window closed or the injury became largely irreversible.

In an infection case, the interval may begin when symptoms, vital signs, laboratory changes, and response to treatment combined into a pattern requiring escalation. It may end when organ failure had progressed to the point that earlier treatment was no longer likely to prevent death. The timeline therefore becomes inseparable from the treatment opportunity.

A delay matters causally only while something useful could still have been done. That boundary is not always exact. Treatment benefit often declines over time rather than disappearing at one moment.

An intervention may offer substantial benefit at one point, less benefit several hours later, remain technically possible after that, and become largely futile by the time it occurs. The timeline should not treat the entire period as clinically equivalent.

The patient changes. The treatment opportunity changes. The professional obligation may change more than once.

A patient may initially require observation, later require additional testing, and then require consultation, transfer, or emergency treatment. The reasonableness of each decision depends on what was known at that point. The timeline should preserve those decision points.

At each material stage, the analysis should identify what was known, what remained unknown, what could reasonably be inferred, which options were available, and what response followed.

That does not mean every minor event belongs in the final timeline. The purpose is not to create the longest possible chronology. It is to identify the events that changed the clinical meaning of the case. A useful timeline is selective without becoming incomplete.

It should include the patient's starting condition, material symptoms, objective changes, important results, reassessments, communications, decisions, treatments, responses, and the point of deterioration or injury. Routine entries that do not affect the theory need not receive equal weight.

That selectivity has to remain disciplined. Facts should not disappear because they complicate the preferred position.

If the patient improved temporarily, that matters. If vital signs normalized, that matters. If a neurological examination was normal, that matters. If the patient refused testing or left before the evaluation was complete, that matters.

The timeline should not be written as a plaintiff's or defense argument. It should reconstruct the course accurately enough for either position to be tested against it.

The most reliable timelines often display uncertainty rather than conceal it.

Suppose one note says the patient's confusion resolved while another describes continued disorientation. The timeline should not quietly select one account. It should identify the conflict and consider what might help resolve it: later examinations, family observations, video, medication effects, or the patient's condition on return.

A conflict in the record is not always something to edit away. It may be the central issue.

The same applies when later testimony differs from the contemporaneous chart. Later recollection may be accurate where documentation was sparse. It may also be influenced by the known outcome or by customary practice rather than actual memory. The timeline should preserve the source and timing of each account.

This becomes important in deposition. A witness may say, “I would have reassessed the patient,” or “We always call the physician in that situation.” That is not the same as evidence that the action occurred in this case.

The inquiry concerns what happened to this patient and what the evidence can establish.

Age and care setting affect the kinds of facts that carry the timeline.

In a pediatric matter, parental observations may be unusually important because a young child cannot describe symptoms reliably. The sequence may depend on feeding, responsiveness, movement, crying, play, or sleep. A parent may report that the child was “not acting right” before objective findings became dramatic.

That statement should not be dismissed as too vague to matter. It should be considered alongside age, development, vital signs, examination, hydration, and the later course. Sometimes the parent’s observation is the earliest meaningful sign of deterioration. In other cases, it remains nonspecific until objective change appears.

The timeline helps show when it became clinically important.

In an obstetrical case, the sequence may involve maternal symptoms, fetal-monitoring patterns, medication administration, cervical change, interventions, operative decisions, and delivery. Timing may depend on clocks that were not perfectly synchronized across the fetal monitor, anesthesia record, operating-room log, and neonatal documentation.

A difference of several minutes matters only if the timestamps are reliable.

The analysis must separate what the tracing showed, when the team could reasonably interpret it, which intervention remained available, and whether the fetus was still likely to benefit from earlier delivery.

In an older or medically fragile patient, the timeline may need to distinguish chronic fluctuation from acute change. A resident with dementia may have intermittent confusion at baseline. The material change may be a new degree of lethargy, inability to eat, fever, or reduced interaction. A patient with chronic lung disease may ordinarily have low oxygen values and then develop a new, sustained decline.

Baseline gives those changes meaning. Without it, a chronic abnormality may be overstated or an acute departure may be missed.

Communication belongs in the timeline when it affected care, not merely because a message existed.

A nurse may notify a physician of a change. The timeline should show what information was communicated, when it was conveyed, what response followed, and whether the patient was reassessed.

A radiologist may issue an important result. Counsel needs to know when it became available, how it was routed, whether direct communication occurred, and what happened next.

A transfer may be ordered but delayed because no bed is available. A consultation may be requested but never completed. A family member may call repeatedly about worsening symptoms and receive reassurance based on an earlier assessment.

The clinically material timeline follows information as well as the patient.

A result that exists but never reaches the responsible decision-maker cannot affect care. A concern that is communicated but misunderstood presents a different problem. A recommendation that is received but not implemented presents another. The timeline should make those transitions visible.

The patient's response to treatment is another important marker. Failure to improve can be as significant as an abnormal finding at presentation.

A working diagnosis may be reasonable initially. The obligation changes when the patient does not respond as expected.

A patient treated for dehydration may remain tachycardic and confused despite fluids. A child treated for a presumed viral illness may return with persistent fever and reduced responsiveness. A postoperative patient may continue to worsen despite routine pain control and observation.

The absence of expected improvement belongs in the timeline because it may identify when the original plan became inadequate.

This is one place where hindsight is often mishandled. The later diagnosis may make the initial plan seem unreasonable from the beginning, when the plan became unreasonable only after the patient failed to follow the expected course.

A careful timeline protects both sides from that distortion.

It may show that the initial judgment was reasonable and the later response was not. It may also show that the patient remained consistent with the original diagnosis until a sudden event occurred that could not reasonably have been anticipated.

Timeline reconstruction is not only a plaintiff's tool. It may support the defense just as clearly.

The evidence may show that the condition developed after discharge, that the treatment window had already closed, or that the response followed promptly after the first meaningful sign. A long period between presentation and outcome may contain no clinically actionable delay.

The length of time and the significance of time are not the same thing.

I would avoid phrases such as "hours of delay" unless the evidence supports that the entire period was clinically consequential. It is more credible to say that the patient remained within an acceptable observational course until a defined change, after which escalation did not occur for three hours. That is a precise allegation. It can be tested.

The timeline should also identify when the evidence is too uncertain to support an exact conclusion.

A patient may be found unresponsive after an unwitnessed interval. A fetal tracing may contain gaps. A neurological event may develop overnight without adequate documentation. A nursing-facility record may contain only sparse observations before transfer.

In those circumstances, the timeline should define the range the evidence supports.

We may be able to say that deterioration occurred between the last reliable normal observation and the first documented abnormal state. Monitor data, treatment response, or witness testimony may narrow the interval.

We should not invent an exact time because precision would make the theory easier to present.

False precision is particularly dangerous in causation. An expert opinion may depend on whether injury began before or after a treatment window closed. When the evidence supports only a range, the expert must address that range honestly.

Counsel should know whether the theory remains supportable throughout the plausible interval or depends on selecting the most favorable moment within it. Those are very different levels of litigation risk.

A developed timeline usually contains several kinds of evidence, but they should be integrated rather than separated into unrelated categories.

Symptoms show what the patient experienced. Vital signs and laboratory trends show physiological change. Imaging and pathology show anatomy and disease progression. Communications show how information moved. Orders and administration records show what was intended and what happened. Reassessments show whether the plan changed with the patient. The timeline becomes clinically meaningful when those sources are read together.

Any single source may mislead. A physician note may describe improvement while vital signs show continued instability. The family may report worsening confusion while medication records show recent administration of a sedating drug. A laboratory trend may look newly concerning until earlier records establish that the values were chronic. Integration gives the sequence meaning.

By the end of this stage, counsel should be able to identify the patient's critical interval: the period during which the clinical picture became sufficiently concerning to require another response while meaningful intervention remained available.

There may be more than one interval. A case may contain an initial diagnostic opportunity, a later rescue opportunity, and an even later failure to communicate prognosis or treatment choices. The theory should identify which period is legally and causally important.

The final timeline should not become a warehouse of dates. It should reconstruct the course well enough to ask the legal questions at the correct moments.

What was happening to the patient? What information was available? What did it mean at the time? Which response was reasonable? What happened next? How long did a meaningful opportunity remain?

Once that sequence is clear, standard-of-care analysis becomes far more precise. We are no longer asking whether care might have been better in general. We are asking what a particular professional or institution was required to do at a particular point in this patient's course, using the information then available.

That is the difference between a chronology and a clinical theory of time.

"That is the difference between a chronology and a clinical theory of time."

CHAPTER NINE

Reconstructing Communication and Clinical Workflow

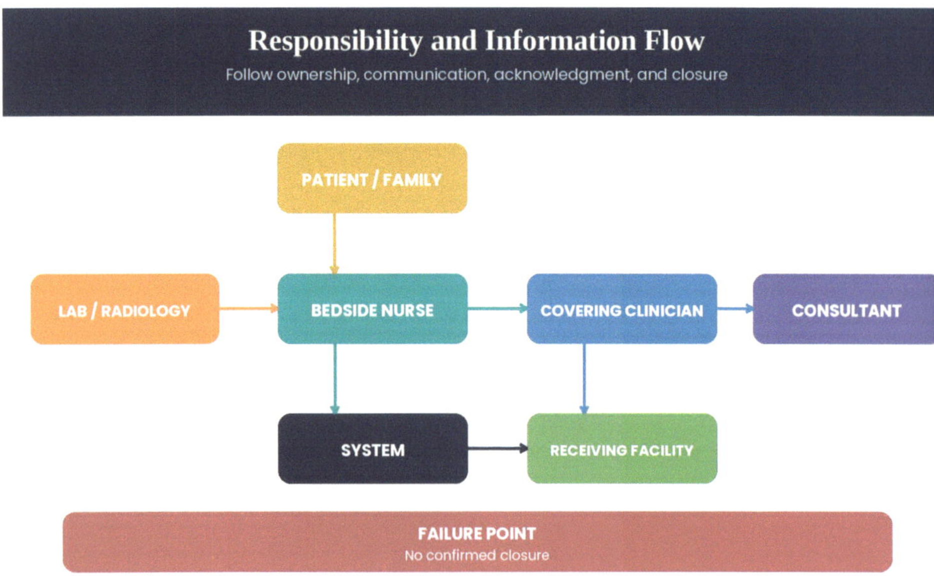

Some medical cases initially appear to concern one bad decision. Once the record is reconstructed, the more important issue is often how information moved through the healthcare system—or failed to move at all.

A result was generated but never reached the person responsible for acting on it. A nurse recognized deterioration and reported it, but the urgency was not understood. A consultant made a recommendation that disappeared during a shift change. A referral was placed but never scheduled. A patient was discharged with instructions that depended on follow-up no one actually owned. A medication order was correct, but the process failed during verification, dispensing, administration, or monitoring.

These cases are difficult because the chart usually records pieces of the process rather than the process itself.

One note says the physician was notified. Another describes the patient as stable. A later entry refers to a recommendation that cannot be found in the contemporaneous record. The discharge summary says follow-up was arranged, but no appointment appears. The imaging report contains an alert, yet the chart does not show who received it.

Several people may have completed their individual tasks, and the patient may still have fallen through the space between them.

To understand what occurred, we need to reconstruct workflow rather than simply review documentation.

Workflow is the path through which information, decisions, and responsibility move. It includes who observes the patient, who receives a finding, who interprets it, who decides what should happen, who carries out that decision, who confirms that the work was completed, and who assumes responsibility when the first process fails.

That sequence matters because healthcare is rarely delivered by one person working alone.

Even a straightforward encounter may involve several handoffs. One clinician orders a test. Another department performs it. A specialist interprets it. The result is delivered electronically. Someone covering for the ordering clinician reviews it. Staff communicate with the patient, and another office eventually converts the recommendation into treatment or follow-up.

When one step is unclear, incomplete, or unowned, a result may exist without producing care.

That is why the absence of action does not necessarily tell us where the failure occurred.

Suppose imaging identifies a suspicious pulmonary nodule. The radiologist describes it and recommends follow-up. Months later, the patient is diagnosed with advanced lung cancer. The initial theory may be that the ordering physician ignored the report.

That may be correct. Before reaching that conclusion, I would want to know what happened from the moment the report was finalized.

Did it go directly to the ordering clinician or into a shared inbox? Was that clinician still responsible for the patient? Did someone else cover the inbox? How was the finding categorized? Did the system require acknowledgment? Was an alert generated when no one responded? Was the recommendation displayed in the part of the report routinely reviewed? Did staff try to contact the patient? Was a follow-up order entered but never scheduled?

The clinical significance of the finding is only part of the case. Workflow tells us how that significance should have become action.

Without reconstructing the pathway, counsel may identify the wrong defendant, request the wrong evidence, or ask an expert to criticize someone who did not control the failed process.

The same issue appears in deterioration cases. A bedside nurse may be the first person to recognize that the patient is changing. The record may show a call to the physician, but the words "physician notified" tell us very little. We need to know what was reported.

Was one low blood-pressure reading mentioned, or was the full pattern of worsening hypotension, tachycardia, confusion, reduced urine output, and failure to respond to fluids communicated? What instructions followed?

Were they carried out? Was the patient reassessed? If the nurse remained concerned, was another level of escalation available?

The content of the communication matters as much as the fact that it occurred.

"The patient's pressure is a little low" is not the same as reporting that the pressure has fallen steadily, urine output has nearly stopped, mental status has changed, and treatment has not produced improvement.

The first report may sound routine. The second describes a deteriorating patient.

The receiving professional can respond only to the information conveyed, unless that person independently reviews the full record. The person communicating the concern may also be responsible for making its urgency clear.

These cases cannot be reduced to whether someone placed a telephone call. We need to understand what each person knew, what was communicated, and what the recipient reasonably understood. Communication also fails through fragmentation.

One person sees the abnormal laboratory trend. Another knows the patient has become confused. A third sees the falling blood pressure. Each fact may seem manageable when viewed alone. No one puts them together.

The patient's condition becomes distributed across several people rather than understood by one responsible decision-maker.

This occurs frequently in complex care. Information may be divided across shifts, departments, specialties, facilities, and electronic systems. The final chart makes the information appear unified because all the entries eventually sit in one record. At the time care was delivered, however, the professionals involved may not have seen the same information together.

A retrospective reviewer can read the nursing observation, laboratory result, imaging finding, medication record, and consultation note on the same screen. The bedside nurse may never have seen the final imaging report. The covering physician may not have received the family's repeated calls. The consultant may have assumed the primary team would act. The primary team may have believed the consultant had taken responsibility.

The chart combines the evidence after the event. Workflow reconstruction asks whether the care team combined it when it mattered. Responsibility often becomes blurred during handoffs.

A handoff is not merely the transfer of names and diagnoses. It is the transfer of clinical understanding and unfinished work. The receiving professional needs to know what has happened, what remains uncertain, what should be watched, which results are pending, and what action will be required if the patient changes.

The record may contain a formal handoff tool, a sign-out note, or a shift summary. It may contain nothing more than a later statement that the case was discussed.

Whatever form the communication took, the practical question is whether the material concern crossed the handoff.

A patient may appear stable at transfer while carrying a substantial unresolved risk. A culture is pending. A repeat blood count is due. A consultant recommended reassessment if pain worsens. The patient has not responded to treatment.

If those issues are not transferred clearly, the next team may inherit the patient without inheriting the concern.

That creates a gap in which everyone may provide ordinary care while no one follows the developing threat.

The same problem arises when responsibility moves between facilities.

A patient discharged from an emergency department may be told to see a specialist. The emergency clinician assumes the specialist will evaluate the abnormality. The specialist never receives the referral. The primary-care office does not know the study occurred. The patient does not understand the seriousness of the recommendation. The record then contains a recommendation without a completed transition.

In those cases, I want to know who was responsible for closing the loop.

Was the patient merely advised to arrange follow-up, or did the facility undertake to arrange it? Was the finding sufficiently urgent that completion needed to be confirmed? Did the institution track unresolved referrals? Could the patient realistically manage the process alone? Were language, cognition, finances, transportation, or access to care relevant?

The adequacy of the workflow may depend on the patient.

Instructions that are reasonable for one person may be unreliable for another. A medically sophisticated adult with stable housing, transportation, and portal access may be able to arrange routine follow-up. A child depends on a parent or guardian. An older adult with cognitive impairment may require direct caregiver involvement. A patient with limited English proficiency may need meaningful interpretation rather than printed instructions alone.

The communication burden changes with age, capacity, and circumstance.

This is why discharge paperwork should not be treated as proof that effective communication occurred. A form may establish that instructions were printed. It may not show that the right person received them, that the patient understood them, or that the proposed follow-up was realistic.

The question is whether the communication was adequate for the clinical risk and the patient's situation.

A patient may sign paperwork while sedated, frightened, in pain, or cognitively impaired. A parent may receive general return precautions without being told which specific change requires urgent action. A nursing-facility resident may return from the hospital with new orders that are entered incorrectly or never reconciled. A family caregiver may believe the office is arranging follow-up while the office expects the family to call.

The workflow has to be examined through what the patient's care required, not merely through what the paperwork suggests.

Medication cases often expose this issue because the medication process contains several distinct responsibilities.

A prescriber selects the drug and dose. A pharmacist reviews the order. The medication is dispensed. A nurse or patient administers it. Someone monitors therapeutic response and toxicity. Changes in renal function, weight, interactions, or other factors may require adjustment. During transitions, medication reconciliation is intended to prevent omissions, duplication, and continuation of an inappropriate regimen.

A harmful outcome may occur even when no single step appears obviously reckless.

The dose may have been reasonable when prescribed and become unsafe after renal function declined. The pharmacy may have verified the original order without seeing the later laboratory result. Nursing staff may have administered the medication exactly as written. The clinician may have assumed that monitoring would occur through another service. The patient may have been discharged with both the old prescription and its replacement.

Counsel needs to understand the full medication pathway before deciding where responsibility lies.

That may require more than the order and medication-administration record. The analysis may depend on which decision-support alerts appeared, whether they were overridden, what information the pharmacist reviewed, how laboratory abnormalities were routed, whether medication reconciliation occurred, and what the patient was told. Again, the work follows information through the process.

The same applies to consultations and referrals. A consultation request is not a completed consultation. A recommendation is not implementation.

A specialist may write, “Consider urgent MRI if symptoms persist.” The primary team may interpret that as optional. The specialist may believe the recommendation was clear. The patient may be discharged before the question is resolved. Later, each professional may describe a different understanding of who owned the decision.

The word "consider" may be relevant, but the larger issue is who was responsible for deciding, how urgent the concern was, whether the patient was reassessed, whether the consultant knew discharge was being considered, and whether the primary team understood the recommendation. The record may show overlapping professional involvement without clear ownership.

Overlap is not itself a defect. Complex care often requires shared responsibility. The problem begins when shared responsibility becomes assumed responsibility and no one confirms that the necessary action occurred.

A reliable system generally includes some form of closure. A task is assigned. Completion can be seen. An unresolved item produces follow-up. Coverage is defined when the original professional is unavailable. The patient is informed in a manner proportionate to the risk.

When those safeguards are missing, the case may involve institutional responsibility even though no individual intended to ignore the patient.

Policies and workflow materials may help explain what happened, but they are not automatic proof. A policy may describe how the institution intended a result or referral to be handled. The evidence may show that staff used a different informal process. The written process may have been sound but poorly followed. It may have been followed exactly and still contained an unsafe gap. We need to understand both the designed and operational workflow.

The designed workflow appears in policies, training materials, job descriptions, electronic settings, and official procedures. The operational workflow appears in testimony, actual message routes, staffing practices, audit trails, and the way comparable tasks were handled. The two may differ.

An institution may say that critical results are communicated directly while staff routinely rely on inbox alerts. A policy may assign follow-up to the ordering clinician while coverage arrangements route results into a pool. A referral system may contain automatic reminders that no one consistently monitors.

That discrepancy does not itself prove negligence. It identifies where the safeguard may have failed.

Workflow reconstruction should remain practical. The purpose is not to map the entire organization. It is to follow the particular clinical issue through the people and systems that touched it.

In a result-follow-up case, the pathway may begin with the order, continue through performance and interpretation, and then move through finalization, routing, receipt, patient notification, follow-up ordering, scheduling, and eventual evaluation.

In a deterioration case, it may begin with a clinical change, followed by observation, documentation, communication, instructions, implementation, reassessment, and further escalation—or the failure to escalate. Those pathways give counsel something concrete to investigate.

They also show where the evidence remains incomplete. We may know that a message was sent without knowing what it said. We may know an order was placed without knowing why it was not carried out. We may know the patient was advised to obtain follow-up without knowing whether the office undertook responsibility for arranging it.

The unresolved point should be stated directly rather than buried in a general allegation of poor communication.

Sometimes the evidence will show that communication occurred appropriately and the patient still suffered the outcome. A critical result may have been delivered promptly, understood correctly, and acted upon within a reasonable period. The disease may already have been advanced, or the treatment may not have changed the course. Communication and causation must remain separate.

A failed communication may establish a departure without establishing harm. A confusing workflow may create risk without affecting this patient. The case still requires a treatment opportunity and a probable difference in outcome.

The reverse is also possible. A communication lapse may look minor on paper but occur during a narrow and meaningful window. A short delay in conveying a stroke result, fetal concern, airway warning, or critical laboratory value may have serious consequences because the intervention was time-sensitive.

The significance of the failure depends on what the information meant and what remained possible when it should have arrived.

This is why workflow analysis follows objective-evidence review and timeline reconstruction. We first need to know what information existed, when it existed, and when it became clinically consequential. Only then can we assess whether the communication pathway functioned in time to protect the patient.

That sequence also limits hindsight. A message may look urgent after the diagnosis is known. At the time, the information may have been preliminary, nonspecific, or reasonably managed through the ordinary process. Another message may have been categorized as routine even though its content required immediate action.

The label assigned by the system does not necessarily determine the clinical urgency.

A laboratory may classify a result according to a fixed threshold even though the patient's trend makes it far more concerning. A radiology finding may not meet the institution's technical definition of critical while still requiring reliable follow-up. A bedside change may never trigger an automated alert but be obvious to someone familiar with the patient.

The workflow should fit the clinical meaning of the information, not merely its assigned category.

Age and care setting also affect the way the workflow should operate.

In neonatal and pediatric care, parents and caregivers are part of the communication system. They may be the first to notice change, the person administering medication, or the only reliable source of symptom progression after discharge. Their concerns must be interpreted in light of the child's age and ability to communicate.

A parent who reports that an infant is feeding poorly, unusually sleepy, or simply not acting normally may be describing early deterioration. The statement may remain nonspecific, but it cannot be evaluated as though the child could provide a complete independent history.

Adolescent care may involve confidentiality, emerging autonomy, parental participation, and mental-health or reproductive-health concerns. The workflow must account for who could receive information, who needed to participate in safety planning, and whether the adolescent could carry out the plan independently.

In adult care, responsibility may appear simpler until cognitive impairment, language barriers, health literacy, disability, or caregiver dependence is considered.

In nursing-facility care, information may move among aides, nurses, advanced practitioners, physicians, pharmacies, laboratories, hospitals, and family members. One person may observe a change, another document it, someone else report it through the chain of command, and an off-site professional eventually act. The record may contain several communications without showing whether anyone integrated them.

That often brings me back to one question: who had the complete picture?

When the answer is no one, the next question is whether the system should have created one.

Not every fragmented process is negligent. Healthcare necessarily divides work. The issue is whether that division preserved accountability for the patient's material risk.

A system can divide tasks without allowing responsibility to disappear.

This becomes especially important during nights, weekends, holidays, and coverage periods. A process may work during ordinary office hours and fail when the usual clinician is absent. Results may be routed differently. Messages may enter a pool. Specialists may be harder to reach. Staffing may be reduced. Temporary personnel may not know local practices.

The question is not whether fewer resources existed at night. It is whether the coverage process remained reasonable for foreseeable patient needs.

If one person must see an alert, what happens when that person is off duty? If a referral is not scheduled, who notices? If a nurse receives no response, what escalation option exists? If the patient cannot be reached, what further action is required?

A reliable process anticipates ordinary failure. It does not assume that every message will be seen and every task completed without verification.

That does not mean a system must guarantee perfect communication. Safeguards should be proportionate to the risk. The more serious and time-sensitive the information, the less reasonable it is to leave the next step unassigned.

Counsel should also be careful about treating a later process change as proof that the earlier system was negligent. An institution may revise a workflow after an adverse event for many reasons. A new process may improve safety without establishing that the prior one fell outside the reasonable range.

Its legal treatment remains counsel's decision. Clinically, the change may still help identify where the institution perceived vulnerability and should be interpreted with care.

The most useful workflow analysis is usually written as a narrative rather than assembled from policy excerpts.

It should explain how information entered the system, who could see it, who was expected to act, what happened, where the process stopped, and whether another safeguard should have detected the failure.

For example, the radiologist finalized a report recommending urgent follow-up. The report entered a shared results pool. No active clinician assumed ownership because the ordering physician had left the practice. Staff believed the result would be reassigned, but the system had no unresolved-result alert and no clear process for handling results belonging to departed clinicians. The patient was not contacted, and the finding remained unaddressed until symptoms led to diagnosis months later.

That account provides more than the statement that a result was not followed. It identifies the pathway, the failure, and the possible institutional issue.

Another case may look entirely different. The nurse documented worsening hypotension and called the covering physician. The physician ordered additional fluids and testing. Treatment was given promptly, and the patient was reassessed within thirty minutes. When the pressure did not improve, the rapid-response team was activated and the patient was transferred.

The later death may require separate treatment and causation analysis, but the evidence does not suggest that communication or escalation failed.

The same method can show that the workflow functioned.

That balance matters. Workflow analysis should not begin with the assumption that a complicated process must contain negligence. The question is whether the process handled this patient's information reasonably and in time.

Depositions in these cases should follow the pathway rather than rely on broad questions about responsibility.

In a result case, the useful inquiry concerns who received the finding, how the system identified that person, what the message displayed, what action was expected, how completion was documented, what happened if no one acted, who covered the task when the original professional was unavailable, and what the witness understood had occurred.

In bedside communication, the useful questions are what was observed, what was reported, to whom, in what terms, what response followed, whether the concern was resolved, whether the witness remained worried, and what escalation options existed.

The goal is not to obtain agreement that communication is important. Everyone will agree with that. The goal is to understand the actual path of care.

By the end of the workflow analysis, counsel should know whether the case concerns an individual act, a system process, or a combination of the two.

An individual may have failed to review a result clearly assigned to that role. A system may have routed the result without assigning ownership. A nurse may have failed to escalate a serious change. A physician may have responded reasonably to an incomplete report. A consultant and primary team may each have assumed the other was managing the issue. Responsibility should follow the evidence.

Counsel should also know which parts of the pathway remain uncertain. The content of a telephone call may not be documented. A verbal handoff may not have been recorded. A staff member may not remember who handled the task.

Those gaps should be stated plainly. The theory should not quietly fill them with the assumption most favorable to one side.

Sometimes surrounding evidence supports a reasonable inference. An immediate order may indicate that a concern was communicated. The absence of a response, combined with acknowledgment data, may support another conclusion. Counsel will determine how those facts may be argued under the applicable law. Clinical analysis gives the argument a factual structure.

Communication and workflow are sometimes treated as secondary to the medicine. In many cases, they are the mechanism through which the medical failure occurred.

The test was accurate. The recommendation was appropriate. Treatment existed. The patient remained capable of benefiting. The information simply did not become action.

When that happens, counsel needs to see more than a missing note or unanswered message. Counsel needs to understand the process through which the patient was supposed to be protected.

That is the purpose of reconstructing clinical workflow: following information from observation to decision, from decision to implementation, and from implementation to confirmation.

Only then can we determine whether a breakdown was clinically meaningful, who may bear responsibility for it, and what difference it probably made.

"Only then can we determine whether a breakdown was clinically meaningful, who may bear responsibility for it, and what difference it probably made."

"Once the patient's baseline, objective evidence, timeline, and clinical workflow are reasonably clear, the standard-of-care question becomes much easier to frame."

PART III

STANDARD OF CARE, RESPONSIBILITY, AND CAUSATION

Chapters 10–19

CHAPTER TEN

Identifying the Patient-Specific Standard of Care

Once the patient's baseline, objective evidence, timeline, and clinical workflow are reasonably clear, the standard-of-care question becomes much easier to frame.

We are no longer asking whether the care could have been better. In a complicated medical course, something more cautious, more extensive, or more aggressive can nearly always be imagined after the outcome is known. The question is what this professional was reasonably required to do for this patient, in this setting, with the information available at that point in the clinical course.

Medicine rarely offers one correct response in every circumstance. Two competent clinicians may select different tests, treatments, or periods of observation while both remain within a reasonable professional range. A poor outcome does not make the less successful choice negligent, and the existence of a more cautious alternative does not establish that it was required.

The real inquiry is narrower. What did the professional know? What should reasonably have been recognized? Which options were available? Had the patient reached a point at which reassurance, observation, or the existing treatment plan was no longer sufficient?

The answers depend on the patient and the moment. Standard of care cannot be evaluated responsibly in the abstract.

A general statement that fever may require investigation tells us very little. Fever in a healthy adult with a short viral illness presents a different problem from fever in a newborn, a patient receiving chemotherapy, a postoperative patient, or an older adult who is confused and hypotensive. The finding may be the same. Its significance is not. The professional obligation follows that significance.

When I review a possible departure with counsel, I first identify the decision actually under examination. Broad allegations such as failure to diagnose, failure to monitor, or failure to treat tend to obscure the issue. They make it sound as though the professional carried one continuous obligation from the beginning of the encounter to the final outcome. Usually, the obligation changed as the patient changed.

A patient may reasonably be discharged after an initially reassuring evaluation. If the patient returns with focal findings, persistent instability, or failure to improve, the earlier plan may no longer be acceptable. A postoperative patient may reasonably be observed during expected pain and fatigue, then require urgent escalation when the pattern begins to suggest hemorrhage, infection, or organ dysfunction.

The question is not simply whether the final diagnosis existed biologically. It is when the presentation available to the professional required another response.

That is where the clinically material timeline becomes essential. It identifies the point at which the standard-of-care question should be asked. Without that point, an expert may treat the encounter as one undifferentiated event and judge every earlier decision through what became apparent later.

A reliable opinion should be tied to a defined period.

What information was available at ten? What had changed by noon? What remained unresolved at two? At what point did the range of reasonable choices narrow?

That range is not always marked by a bright line. Early in the encounter, several approaches may be reasonable. As evidence accumulates, some become less defensible. Eventually, one course may become necessary.

An initially nonspecific presentation may permit discharge with return precautions. Persistent symptoms may justify continued observation. New objective findings may require further testing or consultation. Hemodynamic instability may require immediate intervention. The acceptable range moves with the clinical picture.

For that reason, standard-of-care analysis should not begin with a list of everything that could have been done. In almost any difficult case, counsel can identify additional testing, longer observation, broader consultation, or more aggressive treatment.

The expert needs to explain why the omitted action was required, rather than simply preferable in retrospect.

That reasoning must remain patient-specific. It should take account of the presentation, differential diagnosis, care setting, available resources, risks of action and inaction, and the information reasonably known at the time.

A conclusion that the patient should have been admitted is incomplete unless the clinical reason is clear. Was the patient unstable? Did an unresolved high-risk diagnosis remain? Had symptoms failed to respond? Was safe outpatient follow-up unrealistic? Did the patient require serial examination or monitoring that could not occur elsewhere? The recommendation should be connected to the risk.

The same is true of testing. The fact that a CT, MRI, culture, biopsy, laboratory study, or specialist consultation could have been obtained does not establish that it was required. The presentation must have created a reasonable indication for that step.

The later diagnosis can distort this analysis. Once the condition is known, the test that would have revealed it may appear obvious. At the time, the professional may have been choosing among several plausible explanations, each with different risks and investigational needs.

Reasonable care does not require every disease to be identified at its earliest biological moment. It requires a reasonable process of assessment, differential diagnosis, testing, treatment, reassessment, and follow-up.

That process may be deficient even when the final diagnosis was difficult. It may remain reasonable even though the diagnosis was missed. The distinction lies in the response to the information available at the time.

The professional's role also matters. The obligations of a radiologist, emergency physician, nurse, surgeon, pharmacist, hospitalist, specialist, and facility administrator are not interchangeable.

A radiologist may be responsible for interpreting a study and communicating a significant finding. The ordering clinician may be responsible for integrating that finding into the patient's care. Nursing staff may be responsible for monitoring, recognizing change, and escalating concern. A surgeon may be responsible for postoperative management and response to complications. A pharmacist may be responsible for reviewing dose, interaction, allergy, or organ function within the pharmacist's professional role.

The fact that several people participated does not mean they all carried the same responsibility.

The opinion should match the decision being evaluated and the professional who controlled it.

This becomes important when one expert is asked to assess an entire chain of care. A highly qualified specialist may understand the eventual injury while being poorly positioned to define the responsibilities of another profession.

A neurologist may explain the significance of stroke symptoms without being qualified to define nursing escalation requirements. A surgeon may understand a postoperative complication without being qualified to assess the radiological interpretation. A physician may explain clinical urgency without being qualified to define how an institutional result-management system should operate. The expert's qualifications must fit the question.

The care setting matters as well. A tertiary academic center may have resources very different from those available at a community hospital, rural emergency department, outpatient office, nursing facility, or home-health agency.

Reasonable care does not require every setting to have the same specialists, personnel, or technology. It does require professionals to respond appropriately within the resources and limitations of the setting.

A facility unable to provide definitive treatment may still be required to recognize the condition, stabilize the patient, obtain consultation, and arrange timely transfer. Limited resources do not remove responsibility. They shape the reasonable response.

That point can be lost when an expert describes what would have happened at the expert's own institution rather than what was required where the defendant practiced. The opinion then becomes a comparison of local custom rather than an assessment of reasonable care.

I would want the expert to explain what the defendant could and should have done in the actual setting. Was the necessary test available? Could specialist advice be obtained? Was transfer feasible? Which interim treatment could begin? What risk did delay create?

The answer may be that transfer was required precisely because definitive care was unavailable. It may also be that the evaluation remained reasonable and transfer was not yet indicated. The obligation follows the facts.

Patient choice and cooperation can affect the analysis as well. A clinician may recommend testing, admission, treatment, or transfer, and the patient may decline. That changes the inquiry, although it does not necessarily end it.

Counsel needs to know whether the patient had decision-making capacity, whether the material risk was explained, whether reasonable alternatives were discussed, and whether the refusal was documented accurately. Depending on the circumstances, another attempt at communication, family involvement, emergency authority, or a different communication method may have been necessary.

A refusal may interrupt the proposed causal pathway. It may also reveal a capacity or communication problem.

The standard of care is not necessarily satisfied by writing "patient refused." The significance of the refusal depends on what the patient understood and whether the decision was informed and competent.

The same care is needed when the record refers to noncompliance or missed follow-up. A patient may fail to take medication or attend appointments, and those facts may be important. Before assigning them causal significance, counsel should determine whether the patient received the information, whether the plan was realistic, whether care was accessible, and whether the healthcare organization had undertaken responsibility for any part of the follow-up.

That does not excuse every patient decision. It prevents a label from replacing analysis.

Reassessment is often one of the most important parts of the standard of care because an initially reasonable plan may later become inadequate.

The patient is treated according to a plausible working diagnosis. The response is less than expected. Symptoms persist. New findings appear. At that point, the original assumption may need to be reconsidered.

The failure may not lie in the first diagnosis. It may lie in continuing to rely on it after the patient's course no longer supports it.

That often produces a stronger and more accurate theory than arguing that a rare or subtle condition should have been recognized immediately. The evidence may instead show that continued reliance on the original explanation became unreasonable when the patient failed to improve. The record should show whether reassessment occurred and whether it was meaningful.

An examination that copies earlier findings without addressing the new concern may not reflect genuine reconsideration. A note describing improvement may be difficult to reconcile with persistent abnormal vital signs or continuing functional decline. Conversely, the evidence may show that the clinician reassessed carefully and reasonably concluded that no further intervention was required.

The expert should explain the clinical significance of the reassessment, rather than simply identify whether another note exists.

Documentation and care must remain separate. Poor documentation may make a case difficult to defend and may itself fall below professional expectations. It does not always establish that the underlying care was negligent. Excellent documentation does not prove that the care was reasonable. The important question is what occurred.

When the record contains no evidence of an assessment that ordinarily should have been documented, counsel may fairly ask whether it happened. The answer may come from testimony, surrounding orders, treatment response, or other contemporaneous evidence.

Absence of documentation may carry substantial weight when the event was important and charting would ordinarily be expected. It should not automatically be converted into proof that the assessment never occurred.

This is another reason the standard-of-care analysis depends on record integrity and workflow reconstruction. Counsel needs to understand where the action would usually have been recorded, who would have performed it, and which other evidence might confirm it.

Policies, protocols, and professional guidelines can help explain the expected process, but they should be used carefully.

A policy may clarify who was responsible for communicating a result, how frequently a patient should be monitored, or when the chain of command should be used. A guideline may describe accepted diagnostic or treatment approaches. A protocol may show how an institution intended to manage a particular risk.

None of those materials automatically defines the standard of care in every case.

An institutional policy may require more than ordinary professional care. A guideline may preserve substantial clinical discretion. A protocol may not apply to this patient's presentation. A deviation may be technical and unrelated to the injury.

Those materials can still be powerful when they address the precise risk that developed and the evidence shows that the intended safeguard failed.

The useful inquiry is not simply whether the document was followed. It is what obligation the document helps explain and whether the deviation affected the patient's care.

Clinical judgment also requires careful treatment because the phrase is sometimes used too broadly. Professionals are entitled to exercise judgment within a reasonable range. The phrase does not protect a decision that ignored material information, depended on an unsupported assumption, or was never reconsidered after the patient changed. The basis of the judgment should be identifiable.

Which facts supported the working diagnosis? Which findings pointed elsewhere? What risks were weighed?

What alternatives were considered? Did the decision remain consistent with the patient's response?

A judgment is easier to defend when the reasoning is coherent, even where the outcome is poor. It becomes harder to defend when the explanation first appears after the event and conflicts with the contemporaneous evidence.

The standard of care should not be transformed into a demand for perfect reasoning. Clinicians often make difficult decisions under uncertainty. The question is whether the process and conclusion remained reasonable.

The same restraint is required when a complication follows a procedure.

Many procedures carry serious risks even when performed properly. Hemorrhage, infection, nerve injury, organ damage, thrombosis, and other complications may occur without negligence.

When an injury follows a procedure, several questions need to be separated. Was the procedure indicated? Was consent adequate under the applicable law? Was the technique reasonable? Was the complication recognized? Was the response timely and appropriate?

A case may be weak on the theory that the complication should never have occurred and strong on delayed recognition. It may support negligent technique while showing prompt and appropriate rescue. It may show that both the procedure and the response remained within the reasonable range.

The fact that the injury occurred during or after a procedure establishes sequence. It does not establish departure.

The same principle applies to diagnosis. A later clinician's correct diagnosis does not prove that the earlier clinician acted unreasonably.

The later clinician may have had more information, a more developed presentation, better imaging, or the benefit of knowing the first treatment had failed.

The comparison must remain fair. What did each professional know? Which resources were available? How had the patient's presentation changed?

A specialist examining the patient after deterioration is not evaluating the same clinical picture the generalist encountered earlier. That does not excuse an earlier miss where sufficient warning signs were already present. It prevents later certainty from being projected backward without analysis.

Standard of care may also involve systems rather than individual clinical judgment. A facility may be responsible for maintaining a reasonable process for staffing, escalation, medication safety, result follow-up, or emergency response. Individual professionals may act reasonably within a process that leaves a material risk unaddressed.

A system obligation should be defined as carefully as an individual one.

What process was reasonably necessary? Which risk was foreseeable? How was responsibility assigned? What backup existed when the ordinary process failed? Did the system operate as designed?

The case should not become a general criticism of hospital administration. The system issue must remain tied to the patient's care.

The absence of an unresolved-result queue matters when it allowed this result to disappear. Staffing matters when inadequate coverage prevented required monitoring or response. A defective transfer process matters when it delayed treatment during a clinically meaningful period.

The institutional obligation becomes relevant through what happened to the patient.

At this stage, counsel should also understand what a standard-of-care opinion does not establish.

An expert may define the reasonable response and conclude that a professional departed from it. That expert may not be qualified to determine what the departure caused. The separation should remain explicit.

An opinion may establish that imaging was required, admission was necessary, escalation should have occurred, or a result should have been communicated. Causation still asks what probably would have happened if that step had occurred.

Keeping those opinions separate strengthens the analysis. It prevents the standard-of-care expert from assuming treatment benefit and the causation expert from assuming breach. Each should work from the same timeline and factual foundation while answering a different question.

There will be cases in which standard of care remains genuinely disputed. Competent experts may disagree about whether the presentation required further testing, whether discharge remained reasonable, or whether the chosen treatment fell within the accepted range.

Disagreement does not necessarily make the case unsupportable. It does affect risk.

Counsel needs to understand the source of the disagreement. Are the experts interpreting the same facts differently? Are they working from different assumptions? Does one practice in a materially different setting? Does the literature support more than one reasonable approach? Was the patient near a threshold at which professional judgment commonly varies?

A true range-of-practice dispute is different from the omission of a required step.

That distinction affects discovery, mediation, and trial. In a range-of-practice case, counsel may need to explain why this patient's particular risk moved the decision beyond the acceptable range. In a process-failure case, the issue may be whether required work occurred at all.

The stronger theory is not always the more dramatic one. It is the theory tied most closely to a defined professional obligation.

By the end of the standard-of-care analysis, counsel should be able to describe the alleged departure without relying on the final outcome.

You should be able to explain what the professional knew, what the patient's condition required, which reasonable options remained, and why the response given fell outside—or remained within—the acceptable range.

That explanation should still make sense if the eventual injury is temporarily removed from view. When it does not, the analysis may be driven by hindsight.

The question is not whether the professional failed to prevent what later happened. It is whether the care was unreasonable when it was provided.

Only after that question has been answered carefully should the case move to the separate issue that often determines its viability: what difference the disputed care probably made.

“Only after that question has been answered carefully should the case move to the separate issue that often determines its viability: what difference the disputed care probably made.”

CHAPTER ELEVEN

Distinguishing Reasonable Clinical Judgment From Departure

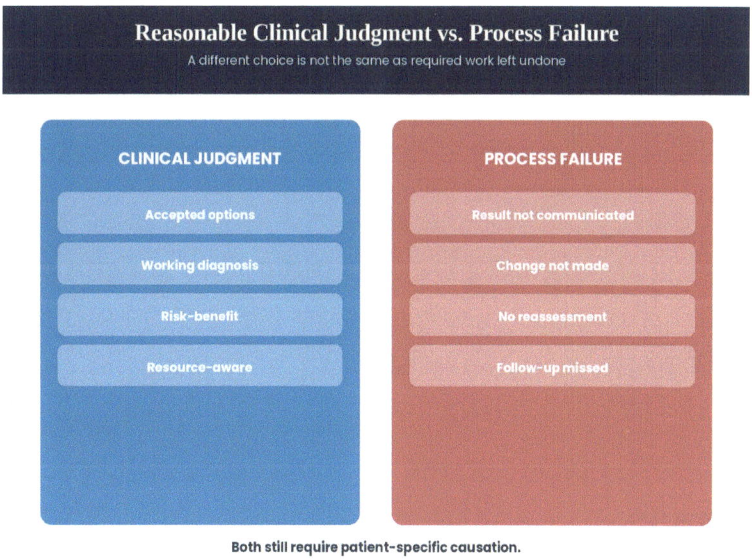

Some of the most difficult medical cases do not involve an obvious omission. They arise from a decision that was made, documented, and defensible on its face, followed later by a serious result.

A clinician selected one diagnostic path over another. A surgeon chose a recognized technique. An emergency physician discharged a patient after treatment and reassessment. A specialist recommended observation instead of intervention. A nurse interpreted a change as expected rather than urgent. The patient later deteriorated, a more serious diagnosis emerged, or the chosen treatment failed.

Once the outcome is known, the earlier decision may look plainly wrong. That does not necessarily make it negligent.

Clinical judgment is exercised under uncertainty. The professional rarely has every fact available when a decision must be made. Symptoms may be nonspecific. Test results may be equivocal. Several diagnoses may remain plausible, and each may carry different risks. Treatment for one condition may worsen another. Observation may avoid an unnecessary procedure while creating some risk of delay. Immediate intervention may reduce one danger while exposing the patient to a serious procedural or medication-related risk.

The standard of care permits judgment within a reasonable range. It does not guarantee that the course selected will produce the best result.

For counsel, the challenge is to distinguish a poor outcome following a reasonable choice from an injury associated with a decision that was no longer supportable on the information available.

That question cannot be answered simply by asking whether another competent clinician would have acted differently. In many cases, another clinician would have.

One physician may admit a patient another would discharge. One surgeon may operate while another continues observation. One specialist may obtain additional imaging while another relies on serial examination. Medicine often permits more than one acceptable approach.

The existence of a more cautious, aggressive, or ultimately successful alternative does not establish departure.

The useful inquiry is whether the decision rested on a reasonable understanding of the patient and remained within the range of acceptable responses at that point in the course.

When I examine a judgment case, I begin with the reasoning behind the decision. What information was available? Which findings supported the working diagnosis? Which findings did not fit? What risk was the clinician trying to manage? Which alternatives were available? Was the decision revisited when the patient changed or failed to improve?

A defensible decision usually has a coherent clinical basis even when the outcome is unfortunate. The clinician may have considered the serious diagnosis, found the presentation inconsistent with it, selected an appropriate evaluation, and created a plan that addressed the remaining uncertainty. Later progression does not make that earlier process negligent in retrospect.

A decision becomes harder to defend when important information was ignored, conflicting findings were never reconciled, the chosen explanation did not fit the full presentation, or the plan depended on assumptions that were never tested.

Consider a patient who presents with dizziness and nausea. The neurological examination is normal, the symptoms are positional, and the patient improves with treatment. A benign vestibular diagnosis may be reasonable even if a stroke is later identified.

Now consider a patient who cannot walk without assistance, has new speech difficulty, and reports a sudden severe headache. The chart may still use the word vertigo, but continuing to rely on that diagnosis without further neurological evaluation may fall outside reasonable judgment.

The diagnostic label does not distinguish the cases. The available evidence does.

Judgment must also be examined over time. A plan that was reasonable at the beginning of an encounter may later become inadequate.

A clinician may reasonably begin with dehydration, postoperative pain, medication effect, viral illness, or uncomplicated infection as the working diagnosis. If the patient improves as expected, the plan may remain appropriate. If the patient stays unstable, develops new findings, or repeatedly returns for care, the professional obligation changes.

The failure may not lie in the first diagnosis. It may lie in failing to reconsider it.

That is why reassessment carries so much weight in judgment cases. Uncertainty is part of medicine. Continuing the same plan after the evidence has moved away from the original explanation is a different matter. The record should show whether the professional recognized that movement.

A note stating that the patient was unchanged may support continued observation if stability was expected. The same finding may be concerning if the plan depended on improvement. A repeat examination may be meaningful when it addresses the developing risk. It adds little if it merely reproduces templated findings while ignoring what changed.

The issue is whether the judgment was renewed in light of the patient's course.

Documentation often becomes a proxy for reasoning. Sometimes that is appropriate. A clear note may show what the clinician considered, which risks were weighed, and why a particular course was chosen. Sparse documentation can make an otherwise reasonable decision difficult to understand.

Documentation and judgment, however, are not the same thing.

A well-written note does not make an unreasonable decision reasonable. A poorly written note does not prove that no clinical reasoning occurred. The analysis has to remain tied to the care itself.

When the record is thin, surrounding evidence may help. Orders, consultations, repeated testing, treatment changes, nursing communications, and later testimony may reveal what the clinician was considering. They may also show that an explanation offered after the event does not match what was done at the time.

I would be cautious when a detailed rationale first appears in deposition or expert review and has little support in the contemporaneous record. That does not make the explanation false. Clinicians do not document every thought. The later account should still fit the objective evidence and the actions taken.

A claimed concern about a diagnosis is more persuasive when the evaluation addressed it. A statement that the patient was stable should be reconciled with the vital signs and monitoring data. A claim that strict return precautions were provided should fit the discharge documentation and the patient's ability to understand and follow them.

Reasonable judgment is often visible in the consistency between the explanation and the care delivered.

Guidelines and medical literature should be used with similar restraint. A published recommendation may favor one approach without removing professional discretion.

Some guidelines are highly directive. Others are intentionally broad. Some describe population-level practice while preserving room for patient-specific variation. Others depend on thresholds that require interpretation. A particular patient may have a contraindication, atypical presentation, or competing risk that makes the usual recommendation inappropriate.

The guideline can inform the analysis. It should not replace it.

The expert should explain whether the recommendation applied to this patient, how strongly it was stated, which alternatives remained acceptable, and why the chosen course fell outside or remained within that range. Simply saying that the defendant failed to follow a guideline rarely completes the analysis.

Professional custom deserves the same treatment. What clinicians commonly do may help describe the range of practice, but custom alone does not decide what was reasonable.

A widespread practice may still be unsafe. A less common approach may be well supported and appropriate. The focus remains the patient-specific decision.

This becomes particularly important when the experts practice in different environments. A specialist at a major academic center may routinely obtain advanced imaging, immediate consultation, or intensive monitoring that is unavailable elsewhere. Another expert may practice in a setting where transfer, staged evaluation, or outpatient follow-up is more common.

The disagreement may reflect differences in resources rather than a genuine disagreement about the standard.

Counsel should determine whether the expert is describing personal preference, ordinary practice at the expert's institution, or what reasonable care required in the defendant's setting. Those are different things.

The same concern arises when a subspecialist evaluates the earlier decision of a generalist. The later specialist often has more focused training, more complete information, and a patient whose condition has become clearer. That perspective may be invaluable, but it can also make the earlier uncertainty appear smaller than it was.

A neurologist may recognize a pattern that was subtle during an emergency visit. An oncologist may understand the significance of a finding that appeared nonspecific before diagnosis. A surgeon may recognize a complication after it has progressed.

The question is not whether the specialist can now explain the case. It is whether the earlier clinician's response was reasonable when the presentation was less developed. Hindsight has to be controlled deliberately.

One practical method is to reconstruct the decision before beginning with the final diagnosis. What symptoms and findings were present? Which diagnoses would a reasonable clinician have considered? What testing and treatment followed? What did the patient's response reveal?

If the decision still appears unreasonable before the outcome is reintroduced, the departure theory is stronger. If the criticism depends mainly on knowing what happened later, it may reflect retrospective preference rather than negligence.

There are also cases in which a professional selected an accepted course but failed to carry it out safely.

Conservative management may fall within the reasonable range. It still requires appropriate monitoring, follow-up, and reassessment. Discharge may be reasonable only if the patient is stable, understands the plan, and can obtain timely follow-up. Observation may be reasonable only if the process can detect deterioration.

The judgment cannot be separated from the safeguards that make it reasonable.

Choosing observation rather than surgery may be acceptable when the patient is stable and repeat imaging is planned. If the repeat study never occurs and no meaningful reassessment follows, the departure may lie in execution rather than the original choice.

Outpatient follow-up may be reasonable for a low-risk finding when the referral process is dependable. If no one owns the referral and the system cannot identify noncompletion, the judgment may have depended on a process that did not exist in practice.

The initial decision and the workflow supporting it have to be considered together.

Complication cases present another version of the same problem. A recognized complication can occur despite reasonable care, but that proposition is often used too broadly.

Calling an injury a known complication does not answer whether the procedure was indicated, whether the technique was reasonable, whether the complication was recognized promptly, or whether the response limited additional harm.

A patient may experience bleeding, infection, thrombosis, nerve injury, organ damage, or another recognized complication without negligence. The same complication may also result from poor technique, inadequate monitoring, delayed recognition, or failure to rescue. Occurrence and management should therefore be examined separately.

Did the complication fall within the accepted risks of a properly performed procedure? Were warning signs present? Were they recognized? Was the response timely? Did delay increase the injury?

A case may be weak on the argument that the complication should never have occurred and strong on delayed recognition. It may support both theories, or neither. The evidence should not be forced into one version merely because the outcome followed a procedure.

Consent also has to be placed properly in the analysis. A signed consent form does not establish that the procedure was performed reasonably. It may show that a known risk was disclosed. The legal requirements governing informed consent vary, and counsel will apply the controlling law.

Clinically, consent may help establish that the risk was recognized as inherent and that alternatives were discussed. It does not convert negligent care into an accepted complication.

A patient may consent to a known risk. That does not mean the patient accepted care below the professional standard.

Judgment cases become especially difficult when the patient has several serious conditions and every available option carries risk. A clinician may have to choose among interventions that each create substantial danger. In retrospect, the decision may appear damaging because the selected risk materialized.

The proper analysis is whether the competing risks were understood and weighed reasonably.

Was the patient stable enough for the procedure? Would delay create a greater danger? Was a less invasive option available? Did comorbidity make the usual treatment unsafe? Was appropriate specialty input obtained?

A poor result after a high-risk decision does not establish negligence when every option was dangerous. At the same time, the severity of the situation does not eliminate the need for a coherent, informed process.

Patient preference may narrow the available choices as well. A patient may decline admission, surgery, transfusion, diagnostic testing, or another recommended intervention. The clinician may then have to choose a less effective but still acceptable alternative.

The record should show whether the patient had capacity, understood the material risk, and made the choice voluntarily. It should also show whether the remaining plan was reasonably safe.

A refusal does not excuse everything that follows. The professional still has to respond reasonably to the decision the patient actually made.

The patient's position should not be rewritten after the outcome. General reluctance is not necessarily refusal. Asking questions is not the same as declining care. Refusal of one option does not mean every alternative was rejected. The actual communication matters.

Judgment must also be distinguished from inaction. Sometimes the chart describes a choice when no meaningful decision appears to have been made.

"Continue to monitor" may reflect a reasoned plan, or it may be language used because no one reconsidered the case. "Follow up as an outpatient" may be appropriate, or it may defer a risk that required resolution before discharge. "Clinical correlation recommended" may identify a genuine need for further evaluation, or it may simply pass responsibility forward.

The language of judgment should not be accepted without examining the process beneath it.

What was being monitored, how often, and by whom? What change would trigger action? What was the proposed follow-up expected to accomplish? Was the patient stable enough to wait?

A plan becomes clinically meaningful when those questions can be answered.

This distinction sharpens both deposition and expert work. Broad questions about whether medicine involves judgment do little to advance the case. Of course it does.

The useful questions concern the basis and limits of the particular judgment. Which findings supported the diagnosis? Which findings did not fit? What change would have required reconsideration? Did that change occur? Which risk was accepted? Which safeguard supported the plan? Was the patient reassessed? Why did the chosen course remain reasonable?

Those questions allow a witness to explain the decision while also revealing whether it had a defensible foundation.

They prevent another form of overstatement. A witness may acknowledge that another option was available without conceding that the selected approach was unreasonable. The safer course is not always the required course. Ideal care is not necessarily the legal standard.

A departure theory becomes stronger when it identifies the point at which the range of reasonable judgment ended.

Discharge may have been acceptable initially and become unsafe after persistent hypoxia. Observation may have been reasonable until new neurological findings appeared. Conservative management may have remained within the range until repeat imaging showed progression. One diagnostic explanation may have been plausible until the patient failed to respond.

That account is more credible than saying the clinician chose incorrectly because the patient later worsened.

There will be cases in which qualified experts continue to disagree after the facts have been carefully reconstructed. That disagreement may reflect a genuine range of practice.

Expert disagreement does not automatically defeat a case, but counsel needs to understand its nature. Do the experts accept the same facts and differ only about the appropriate response? Does one believe a finding was present while the other does not? Are they applying different practice settings? Is one relying on later information? Does the literature support both approaches?

A genuine judgment dispute carries different litigation risk from a case involving an omitted required step or an ignored critical finding. It may still be a strong case, but it will require a clear explanation of why this patient's presentation moved the decision outside the defensible range.

For defense counsel, this analysis may show where the case should be defended firmly and where a narrower concern should be acknowledged. The initial diagnosis may have been reasonable while the reassessment was not. The complication may have been unavoidable even though the surrounding communication or documentation was poor. The care may have remained within the standard despite a catastrophic outcome.

A credible defense does not need to insist that every aspect of the care was ideal. It needs to explain why the disputed decision remained reasonable and why the alleged failure did not cause the claimed harm.

For plaintiff counsel, the stronger argument is rarely that another clinician would have done more. It is that this patient's findings required more and that continuing the selected course had fallen outside the acceptable range.

By the end of the analysis, counsel should be able to explain whether the case involves a reasonable decision followed by a bad result or a decision that became unreasonable as the evidence changed.

That explanation should come from the clinical record rather than the emotional force of the outcome. It should account for the information available, the alternatives considered, the risks being managed, the safeguards supporting the plan, and whether the judgment remained defensible as the patient's condition developed.

Only then can disagreement with the result be distinguished from a departure from reasonable care.

"Only then can disagreement with the result be distinguished from a departure from reasonable care."

CHAPTER TWELVE

Identifying Individual and Institutional Responsibility

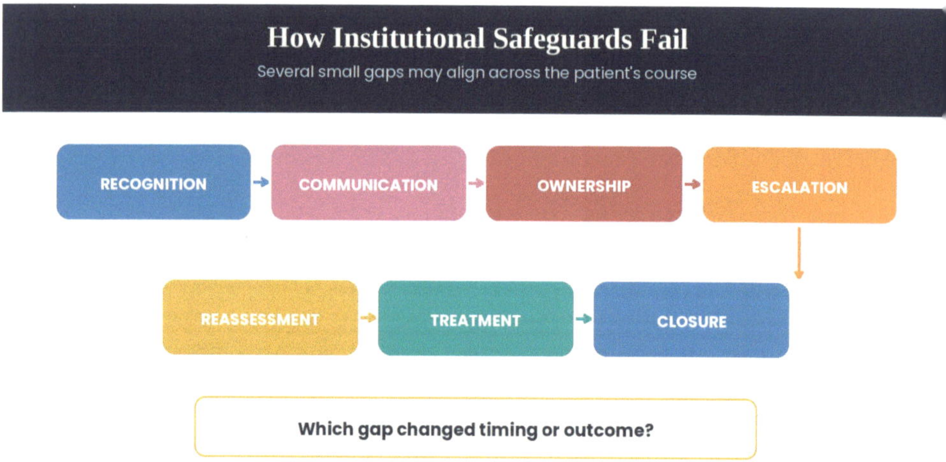

Once the standard-of-care issue is clear, the next question is often where responsibility actually belonged. That can be harder to determine than the chart suggests.

Medical records are organized around encounters and named professionals. A physician signs a note. A nurse records an observation. A radiologist issues a report. A surgeon performs a procedure. The facility's name appears at the top of every page.

That structure naturally draws attention to individual acts because individual names are visible. The clinical process is usually more distributed.

A patient may be harmed because one professional made an unreasonable decision. The injury may also result from a sequence in which several people acted within limited roles while no one assumed responsibility for the complete problem.

A result may be interpreted correctly and never reach the person who needed to act. A nurse may report deterioration and receive no meaningful response. A physician may order appropriate treatment that is not administered promptly. A referral may be entered correctly and never scheduled. An institution may have a written safeguard that does not function in practice.

Responsibility follows the work that needed to be done. It does not necessarily follow the most visible name in the record.

When I begin sorting this out with counsel, I first identify what the patient's care required at the material point. We can then ask who had the information, authority, and practical control needed to carry out that requirement.

If the patient needed an image interpreted, responsibility may rest with the radiologist. If the image was interpreted correctly but required clinical follow-up, responsibility may move to the ordering or receiving clinician. If the result entered a system that failed to assign ownership when the original clinician was unavailable, the case may involve an institutional process. If the clinician received the result and entered the correct order but the patient was never scheduled, responsibility may lie somewhere else again. One event can contain several distinct duties.

That does not mean every participant should become a defendant. It means the chain must be understood before legal responsibility is assigned.

The distinction between individual and institutional responsibility is often presented too simply. An individual case is not necessarily one involving only one person. A system case is not merely a case involving several employees. The difference lies in where the material failure occurred.

An individual departure occurs when a professional with a defined obligation fails to meet it. The relevant information was available. The role was clear. The necessary response fell within that person's authority. The process may have been sound, but the professional did not use it reasonably.

An institutional failure arises when the process through which care was supposed to occur was itself unclear, unreliable, inadequate, or unable to protect the patient from a foreseeable breakdown. Responsibility was never assigned. Coverage was undefined. A communication platform delivered information without ensuring that anyone owned it. Staffing did not permit required monitoring. A referral system recorded an order without meaningful follow-up. A medication safeguard depended on information the relevant user could not access. Many cases involve both.

A system may be poorly designed while an individual still has enough information to act. A clinician may make an unreasonable decision within an otherwise sound process. Several smaller failures may combine so that no single act fully explains the injury.

The purpose is not to force the case into one category. It is to identify the contribution made by each person and process. That requires separating role from outcome.

The person who first observed the problem may not have had authority to correct it. The person with authority may not have received the information. The person entering an order may not control when it is carried out. The professional performing the eventual intervention may enter the case only after the meaningful treatment opportunity has narrowed.

Involvement alone does not establish responsibility for the disputed failure.

Consider a postoperative patient whose blood pressure is falling. The bedside nurse notices the trend, documents it, and calls the covering physician. The physician orders fluids and laboratory testing. Fluids are started, but the specimens are not collected promptly because the unit is short staffed.

The patient continues to deteriorate. The physician, seeing no new laboratory results and receiving no further call, assumes the patient has stabilized. Several hours later, the patient is transferred in shock. That sequence does not immediately produce one clear theory.

The nurse's first escalation may have been appropriate. The physician's response may or may not have been sufficient. The delayed collection may have mattered. The absence of reassessment may have mattered. Staffing may have affected implementation. The communication process may not have required anyone to report that the ordered care remained incomplete or that the patient was still unstable.

The analysis needs to determine where the process broke down and whether each participant retained responsibility after completing the first step.

It would be easy to focus on the physician because the physician made the medical decisions. It would be equally easy to focus on nursing because the nurse remained at the bedside. Neither approach is reliable until we understand what each person knew, controlled, and was expected to do.

The role of the institution becomes clearer when the breakdown was foreseeable and no dependable safeguard existed.

Hospitals and other healthcare organizations know that results may be missed, staff may be unavailable, messages may go unanswered, patients may deteriorate between assessments, and referrals may remain incomplete. Reasonable systems do not eliminate every mistake. They reduce foreseeable failure and provide some means of identifying it when it occurs.

Depending on the risk, that may require assigned ownership, acknowledgment rules, defined coverage, escalation channels, unresolved-task monitoring, adequate staffing, medication reconciliation, or confirmation of critical follow-up.

The institutional question is not whether a perfect system could have been designed. It is whether the process was reasonably capable of managing the clinical risk presented by this patient.

A low-risk routine result may not require the same safeguard as a time-sensitive critical finding. Stable outpatient follow-up may reasonably depend more heavily on patient participation than an urgent abnormality suggesting cancer, vascular injury, or another serious condition.

The process should be proportionate to the consequences of failure.

This is why general policy language is often less useful than the actual workflow.

An institution may have a carefully written policy stating that abnormal results must be reviewed and communicated. That describes the objective. It may not explain how a result was assigned, how coverage worked, what happened when acknowledgment did not occur, or who monitored unresolved items. The operational system matters.

If a result enters a shared inbox, who opens it? If the ordering clinician leaves the practice, where does the result go? If the patient cannot be reached, what further attempts are required? If a referral remains unscheduled, who is notified? If a nurse receives no response, what escalation follows?

A process that answers those questions is materially different from one that depends on everyone assuming someone else will act.

The phrase “someone should have caught it” usually signals that the workflow has not yet been reconstructed. Who was that person? What information did the person receive? Was responsibility assigned or merely assumed? Did the person have authority and practical ability to complete the task? What backup existed?

Until those questions are answered, responsibility remains an impression.

Staffing cases require particular care because staffing is easy to allege in general terms and difficult to connect to one patient.

A unit may have been busy. A nursing assignment may have been heavy. A specialist may not have been immediately available. Those facts alone do not establish unreasonable staffing or causation.

The useful inquiry is what the patient required and what the staffing condition prevented.

Was necessary monitoring missed? Was medication delayed? Was a change not escalated? Did one nurse have more unstable patients than could reasonably be reassessed? Was transfer delayed because no qualified professional was available? Were personnel assigned to tasks for which they lacked training?

Staffing becomes clinically meaningful when it explains a material failure in care.

The schedule alone may not answer the question. The number of staff listed on paper may not reflect acuity, experience, interruptions, new admissions, or temporary coverage. Staffing numbers that look adequate may conceal a skill mix that left no one able to perform a necessary function.

The expert question is not whether additional staff would have been preferable. It is whether the resources provided were reasonable for foreseeable patient needs and whether a deficiency contributed to the event. Supervision presents a related issue.

A trainee, advanced-practice clinician, nurse, technician, or less experienced employee may provide appropriate care within a supervised structure. The existence of supervision does not make the supervisor responsible for every act. Delegation also does not remove responsibility when oversight was required.

The analysis should identify what could reasonably be delegated, what review was necessary, which information reached the supervising professional, and when direct involvement became required.

A resident may evaluate a patient and discuss the matter with an attending. The attending's obligation will depend on the setting, the severity of the patient's condition, the information communicated, and the degree of oversight reasonably required.

A nurse practitioner may manage routine care independently but require consultation once the presentation moves outside the expected range. A technician may perform a study without having authority to interpret its clinical significance.

Titles do not resolve the issue. Actual function and authority do.

That becomes important when the chart creates an inaccurate impression of responsibility. An attending physician's name may appear automatically on a note without showing meaningful involvement. A supervising clinician may have reviewed the case remotely. Another professional may have made the operative decision.

The record has to be read for what each person actually did, not merely whose name appears.

Transitions between settings frequently expose institutional responsibility because accountability can become diluted as the patient moves.

A hospital discharges a patient to a nursing facility. The discharge summary contains new medications, wound instructions, laboratory monitoring, and follow-up appointments. The nursing facility receives the patient, but some orders are missing from the transfer packet. The pharmacy has not delivered one medication. The receiving nurse believes the hospital arranged follow-up. The hospital assumes the facility will do so.

If the patient deteriorates, the transfer process must be examined as a system.

What information was required to accompany the patient? Who reconciled the medication list? Who confirmed that the receiving facility could provide the necessary care? Who owned pending results? Who arranged follow-up? What happened when the documents were incomplete?

The failure may not belong entirely to one side of the transfer. It may have occurred at the boundary.

Boundaries are clinically dangerous because each organization controls only part of the information. The sending team knows the hospital course. The receiving team controls the ongoing care. The patient and family may assume the institutions are communicating directly. No one may recognize the missing instruction until harm occurs.

The same problem appears in outpatient care. A specialist makes a recommendation. The primary physician receives the note. The patient is expected to schedule testing. The scheduling department does not complete it. Each part of the process treats the next step as belonging elsewhere.

Responsibility needs a stopping point. A clinically important task should not remain effectively ownerless.

Institutional analysis also includes the design and use of electronic systems. The issue is not that electronic records are inherently defective. They improve communication while also creating new forms of fragmentation.

Alerts may be excessive and routinely dismissed. Results may route to the wrong pool. Departments may use separate platforms. A clinician may be unable to see records from another facility. A task may appear complete when an order is entered even though the patient never receives the service.

The institution's responsibility concerns whether the system was reasonably designed, configured, supported, and monitored for the work it was intended to perform.

Were users trained? Were responsibilities clear? Did the system identify unresolved work? Were known defects addressed? Did staff rely on workarounds because the formal process did not function?

The existence of an alert does not prove that a safeguard worked. An alert buried among hundreds of low-value messages may not function as a meaningful warning. A routing rule may technically deliver information while leaving ownership uncertain.

At the same time, not every inconvenient feature creates liability. The process must be unreasonable in a way that affected this patient.

Pharmacy and medication cases often show how responsibility can be divided without being fully transferred.

The prescriber selects the medication and dose. The pharmacist reviews safety and appropriateness based on the information available. Nursing staff administer and monitor. The institution supplies the systems connecting orders, laboratory values, allergies, and alerts. After discharge, the patient may also carry some responsibility.

If toxicity occurs, counsel should not assume that the prescriber bears all responsibility because the medication originated there. Nor should pharmacy review be treated as though it displaced the prescriber's obligations. Each participant has a distinct role.

The prescriber may have selected an excessive dose for the patient's renal function. The pharmacy system may have failed to display the relevant laboratory result. The pharmacist may have overridden a clear warning without investigation. Nursing staff may have administered repeated doses despite signs of toxicity. The institution may have lacked a process for timely monitoring.

The case may contain a chain of departures, but the chain must remain clinically coherent.

Counsel should be able to explain what each participant was expected to do, what information was available to that person, and how the failure contributed to the injury.

The same discipline applies in nursing-facility and home-care matters, where responsibility may be distributed among aides, nurses, physicians, advanced-practice clinicians, pharmacies, wound specialists, therapists, and family members.

An aide may notice a skin change but lack authority to assess it. A nurse may document a wound and fail to notify the provider. The provider may issue treatment orders without examining the resident. The facility may lack the staff or equipment needed to follow the plan. A family member may raise concerns that never reach the decision-maker.

The institution may be responsible for ensuring that observation becomes assessment, assessment becomes treatment, and treatment is monitored. That does not make every employee responsible for the eventual outcome. It requires the clinical pathway to be followed through the relevant roles.

One recurring mistake is to build an institutional theory entirely around policy violations. Policies show how the organization intended care to operate. They do not automatically establish the legal duty, prove that the policy applied to the precise situation, or show that the deviation caused the injury. The stronger institutional theory begins with the patient.

What risk existed? Which process was needed to manage it? What process actually existed? Where did it fail? What effect did the failure have?

A policy may support that explanation. It should not replace it.

Another mistake is to assume that several small deviations necessarily add up to negligence. They may, but they may also be harmless administrative imperfections.

A delayed signature, incomplete form, missed checkbox, or minor policy deviation becomes clinically important only when it affects information, decision-making, treatment, monitoring, or patient protection. Counsel should distinguish documentary untidiness from operational failure.

Healthcare records are rarely perfect. A case does not become stronger by treating every imperfection as systemic negligence. It becomes stronger when the evidence shows that the system failed at the point the patient needed it to work.

Institutional responsibility may also arise from training and competency, but the analysis must remain specific.

Was someone assigned a task without the necessary training? Did the organization know that staff misunderstood the escalation process? Was a new device introduced without adequate instruction? Were similar failures occurring? Did the institution fail to address a known gap?

A general assertion that staff needed more training tells us very little. The relevant questions concern the competency required, what the person did not know, and how the deficiency affected the patient.

The same applies to credentialing, privileging, and professional competence. Counsel will determine which records are legally available and how they may be used. Clinically, the question is whether the professional had the qualifications, support, and authority required for the care provided.

A poor outcome does not prove a lack of competence. A fully qualified professional may still make an unreasonable decision. Another may practice beyond the approved scope or without the support the setting required.

Institutional concepts should not substitute for analysis of the actual care.

There are also cases in which the institution should not be blamed merely because it employed the individual involved. The process may have been reasonable. The professional may have had clear responsibility, adequate staffing, available resources, and a functioning safeguard, yet failed to act.

An institutional theory is not automatically more sophisticated than an individual one. It is supportable only when the evidence shows a system contribution.

That matters because broad institutional allegations may distract from a clear professional departure. They can expand discovery, increase complexity, and create additional expert issues without strengthening causation. Responsibility should narrow when the evidence permits it.

If the system routed the result correctly, provided coverage, generated repeated alerts, and the responsible clinician knowingly failed to act, the individual theory may be sufficient. If the clinician never received the result because the system assigned it to an inactive account, the institutional issue becomes central. The evidence should decide.

For defense counsel, this analysis may show that the professional and the institution need to be considered separately. A nurse may have escalated appropriately within a flawed chain. A physician may have responded reasonably to incomplete information produced by a system failure. An institution may have provided a sound process that one user did not follow. Those distinctions affect testimony, strategy, indemnity, settlement, and credibility.

A unified defense may become difficult when the evidence points to materially different responsibilities. Unnecessary finger-pointing can also obscure a coherent explanation that the process functioned reasonably and the outcome was not preventable.

Clinical analysis does not determine legal alignment. It makes the factual allocation visible.

For plaintiff counsel, the same work helps avoid naming everyone who appears in the chart. The stronger case may involve fewer defendants and a clearer explanation.

Party selection should follow who controlled the material decision, who possessed the necessary information, who failed to act, which institutional process contributed, and which conduct probably changed the outcome.

Those questions are more useful than the number of names in the record.

Depositions are most effective when they follow responsibility through the process.

For an individual professional, the inquiry may focus on authority, knowledge, decision-making, implementation, and reassessment. For an institutional witness, it may focus on system design, ownership, coverage, escalation, unresolved work, staffing, training, and the difference between written policy and operational reality.

The goal is not to obtain broad admissions that patient safety matters. It is to determine whether responsibility was clear and whether the process protected this patient.

By the end of the analysis, counsel should be able to describe the care without allowing responsibility to disappear into the organization.

You should know which professional decisions mattered, which roles were limited, how information moved, where authority rested, and whether the system supported or undermined the care the patient required.

You should also know whether the case involves one departure, several connected departures, an institutional failure, or a poor outcome that occurred despite a reasonable process.

Liability should not be assigned by proximity. The person nearest the patient may not have controlled the decision. The person who signed the report may not have owned follow-up. The institution is not necessarily responsible merely because the event occurred within its walls. An individual is not insulated merely because the system was imperfect.

Responsibility follows the clinical obligation, the available information, the authority to act, and the causal role of the failure.

Once those elements are clear, counsel can identify the proper defendants, expert questions, discovery, and limits of the theory without asking one person or institution to answer for a failure the evidence places elsewhere.

"Once those elements are clear, counsel can identify the proper defendants, expert questions, discovery, and limits of the theory without asking one person or institution to answer for a failure the evidence places elsewhere."

CHAPTER THIRTEEN

Using Policies, Regulations, Guidelines, and Protocols Correctly

Policies, regulations, guidelines, and protocols can be persuasive in a medical case because they seem to offer a clear answer to a difficult question.

A hospital policy may require communication of a critical result within a defined period. A protocol may call for escalation when certain vital signs are present. A professional guideline may recommend imaging, consultation, or treatment under specified circumstances. A regulation may impose requirements involving staffing, supervision, medication handling, documentation, or resident care.

When the record shows that the stated process was not followed, it is tempting to treat that deviation as the case.

Sometimes the document does identify the precise safeguard that failed and helps explain why the patient was harmed. In other matters, it provides useful context without defining what reasonable care required in the circumstances. A rule may have been technically violated even though the patient received equivalent clinical protection. The process may also have been followed exactly while failing to address the risk that caused the injury.

The document matters, but it still has to be interpreted.

When I review this material with counsel, I begin with its purpose. What risk was the document intended to manage? Which people or departments did it govern? What action did it require, and under what circumstances did the requirement apply?

Only then can we decide whether a deviation tells us something important about the patient's care.

Suppose a hospital policy requires direct physician notification whenever a laboratory result is classified as critical. The patient's result crossed the listed threshold, and the record contains no evidence of a telephone call.

That may be significant, but the absence of a call does not complete the analysis.

The result may have been routed electronically to the responsible physician and acknowledged immediately. Another qualified clinician may have received it and acted. The threshold may have been designed for general laboratory operations rather than this patient's clinical circumstances. The value may have represented a dangerous new change, or it may have been a chronic abnormality already under treatment.

Most importantly, the failure to make the call may or may not have delayed care.

The policy shows that the institution considered the result important enough to require a particular safeguard. That is useful evidence. The case still depends on whether the safeguard failed in a way that mattered clinically.

The reverse can also occur. A result may fall short of the institution's technical definition of critical even though the patient's trend and overall condition make it highly concerning. A fixed threshold cannot account for every patient-specific risk. The absence of a policy requiring direct notification does not establish that ordinary electronic routing was adequate.

Clinical significance does not always begin where the policy threshold begins.

That is why the document has to be read alongside the patient's baseline, objective evidence, timeline, and workflow. The policy shows how the organization categorized the result. Prior values and current deterioration show what the result meant for this patient. Routing information shows where it went. The timeline shows whether any delay affected treatment.

The document is one part of the analysis. It should not become the analysis itself.

Policies are often most useful when they clarify responsibility.

The chart may show that several professionals participated in the patient's care without making clear who owned a particular task. A result-follow-up policy may assign responsibility to the ordering clinician, the clinician currently managing the patient, or a designated results pool. A rapid-response policy may identify when nursing staff can escalate beyond the primary team. A medication policy may divide responsibility among the prescriber, pharmacist, and administering nurse.

That information can help counsel understand the operational structure the institution expected staff to follow.

Even then, I would want to know whether the written policy matched what happened in practice.

A policy may assign responsibility clearly on paper while the electronic system routes information differently. Staff may rely on an informal workaround because the official process is impractical. A task may technically belong to one role even though everyone expects someone else to perform it. Nights, weekends, and coverage arrangements may alter responsibility in ways the document never addresses.

The written process and the working process are not always the same.

That difference may become central in an institutional case. A hospital may have a polished policy requiring follow-up of unresolved results, but if no one monitors the unresolved queue, the policy exists without functioning as a safeguard. Another institution may use a less formal process that assigns ownership clearly, generates reminders, and reliably closes the loop.

The length or sophistication of the written policy tells us little about whether it worked.

Policy review should therefore lead naturally to practical questions. How did the task reach the people expected to perform it? What did they understand their responsibility to be? What happened when the usual person was unavailable? How was completion confirmed? What did the system do when no one acted? Those answers show whether the written process had operational meaning.

Protocols require similar care because the term covers very different kinds of documents.

Some protocols are mandatory process instructions. Others are clinical pathways that preserve substantial professional judgment. Some standardize routine care. Others identify triggers for urgent intervention.

A medication-administration protocol may leave little room for variation. A sepsis pathway may set out screening criteria and recommended responses while still requiring interpretation of the patient's condition. A postoperative pathway may describe an expected course but permit deviation based on individual risk. Not every protocol carries the same force.

The wording matters. "Must," "shall," and "required" generally convey something different from "consider," "may," or "as clinically indicated." Even directive language must be read in context. The protocol may contain exceptions, require professional judgment, or apply only after a defined threshold has been reached.

A case should not be built around one isolated sentence when the full document describes a conditional process.

Suppose a protocol states that a patient meeting certain criteria should receive a rapid-response evaluation. The chart contains two abnormal values that appear to satisfy the trigger. That may support the position that escalation was required.

Before reaching that conclusion, counsel should still determine whether the values were accurate, simultaneous, persistent, and available to staff in real time. The protocol may contain exclusions. The patient may already have received an equivalent or more immediate physician assessment. The protocol may not apply on that unit, or the care team may have acted through another accepted pathway.

The purpose is not to excuse a clear failure. It is to identify the failure that actually occurred.

The strongest protocol cases usually contain three aligned facts: the patient developed the risk the protocol was intended to detect, the required safeguard did not occur, and the absence of that safeguard contributed to delay or injury.

When those facts are present, the protocol can make the case easier to explain. The patient developed a recognizable pattern. The institution had already identified that pattern as requiring escalation. Staff did not use the process, and the treatment opportunity narrowed while no effective response occurred.

That is more persuasive than showing that someone failed to complete a form.

Professional guidelines present a different challenge. They often come from respected organizations and describe recommended practice across broad patient populations. They may be authoritative while still preserving substantial variation based on patient characteristics, available evidence, resources, and clinical judgment.

A guideline may help explain which risks were recognized, which diagnostic approaches were accepted, which treatments were available, and which factors should influence the decision. It may support an expert's description of the reasonable range of care.

It should not be treated as though it were a statute producing liability whenever a recommendation was not followed.

Guidelines are written for different purposes and with different levels of evidentiary support. Some synthesize strong research and make firm recommendations. Others address areas in which the evidence is limited and professional consensus carries more weight. Recommendations may be graded according to the strength and quality of the supporting evidence. The studied population may differ substantially from the patient in the case. The publication may postdate the event or may not yet have been generally accepted when the care occurred. Those details affect the weight the document can carry.

A strong recommendation based on substantial evidence and directed to patients closely resembling the one in the case has a different significance from a conditional recommendation based on limited evidence in another population.

Counsel does not need to become an expert in guideline methodology. The retained expert should be able to explain what the guideline says, the strength of the recommendation, and how it applies to this patient.

Was it current at the time of care? Did it address the same setting? Did the patient meet the relevant criteria? Were there exceptions or contraindications? Did the chosen alternative remain within reasonable practice? That last question often determines the document's value.

A guideline may recommend one approach while expressly recognizing another as acceptable. In that situation, failure to follow the preferred course does not necessarily establish negligence. The expert still needs to explain why the patient's presentation made the chosen alternative unreasonable.

In another case, the guideline may identify a high-risk pattern requiring prompt action, with no patient-specific reason for omission appearing anywhere in the record. That can provide substantial support for the standard-of-care opinion.

The document is most useful when it illuminates clinical reasoning rather than replacing it.

Regulations add another layer because they may impose legal requirements on facilities, professionals, and particular care settings. They can address licensing, staffing, resident rights, medication management, documentation, supervision, emergency services, infection control, and many other operational duties.

Their legal effect depends on jurisdiction, the nature of the claim, and the purpose of the regulation. Counsel will determine whether a provision creates a duty, supports a standard, permits a particular instruction, or has some other evidentiary significance.

From the clinical side, the important question is whether the regulatory requirement relates to the mechanism of harm.

A regulation may be violated without affecting the patient. An administrative deficiency may have no connection to the injury. Another violation may describe the exact safeguard that was missing when the patient deteriorated.

In a nursing-facility case, failure to satisfy a documentation requirement may affect confidence in the record without proving that the underlying care was inadequate. Failure to perform a required pressure-injury assessment, repositioning, nutritional intervention, or physician notification may have a much closer relationship to progressive tissue injury.

The regulation becomes clinically meaningful when it helps explain what protection should have existed and how the absence of that protection affected the patient. Regulatory noncompliance should not replace medical causation.

Even a clear violation leaves the practical question of what happened because of it. Did the patient miss monitoring that would have revealed deterioration? Did inadequate staffing prevent timely care? Did the absence of a qualified professional delay treatment? Did a transfer failure leave important information behind? Did the violation increase injury, prolong suffering, or accelerate death?

Without that connection, the regulation may establish a compliance problem without establishing the claimed harm.

This distinction protects both sides from overstatement. For plaintiff counsel, it prevents a technically attractive violation from carrying the case beyond what the medical evidence supports. For defense counsel, it prevents the response from ending with the assertion that the requirement was merely administrative when the safeguard was designed to prevent the event that occurred. Purpose matters.

A rule requiring prompt communication of critical findings exists because delay may harm patients. A requirement that a routine administrative field be completed may serve another purpose. Both may be mandatory, but their clinical significance is not necessarily equal.

Facility-specific policies may also cut in more than one direction. An institution may adopt an internal standard more demanding than what reasonable care generally requires. Failure to satisfy that internal rule does not automatically establish breach of the external professional standard.

At the same time, the policy may show that the institution recognized a particular risk and considered the safeguard appropriate in its own setting.

The expert should explain that relationship rather than assuming that the internal policy and the external standard are identical.

Imagine a hospital policy requiring hourly neurological checks for a certain category of patient, while professional guidance and comparable institutions permit checks every two hours depending on clinical condition. Missing one hourly check may violate the policy without proving that reasonable care required hourly assessment.

The deviation becomes more consequential if the patient developed a neurological change during that interval and timely detection probably would have affected treatment. If the patient was evaluated through another reliable method and no treatment opportunity was lost, the technical violation may carry much less weight. The clinical facts remain decisive.

The existence of an equivalent safeguard also deserves careful attention because healthcare processes can accomplish the same purpose in different ways.

A policy may require direct telephone communication, while a secure electronic system provides immediate delivery, acknowledgment, and escalation when no response occurs. A protocol may call for formal rapid-response activation while the attending physician and critical-care team are already at the bedside providing an equal or greater level of intervention.

The fact that the named process was not used does not necessarily mean the patient lacked the intended protection.

The question is whether the alternative was genuinely equivalent. Did it reach the appropriate professional? Did it communicate the urgency? Did it trigger timely assessment and treatment? Did it preserve accountability?

An informal workaround should not be called equivalent simply because someone eventually acted. It must have protected the patient in substantially the same way.

This often becomes important during deposition. A witness may say, “That is not how we usually do it,” or “We handled it another way.” The useful inquiry is what that other process involved and whether it achieved the purpose of the written safeguard.

The analysis should not become a contest between paper and practice. It should determine whether the patient received the protection reasonable care required.

There will also be cases in which strict adherence to a protocol would have been inappropriate.

Clinical pathways are intended to support judgment, not eliminate it in every circumstance. A patient may have an allergy, contraindication, unusual anatomy, advanced disease, or another condition that makes the ordinary pathway unsafe. A clinician may depart from the protocol for a sound patient-specific reason.

The record should make that reasoning understandable, particularly when the deviation concerns a material risk.

A reason may have existed even if it was not documented fully, but it should fit the surrounding evidence and the care actually provided. An explanation first offered after the adverse outcome should be tested against what was known and done at the time.

A defensible deviation usually has a clinical explanation tied to the patient.

A protocol should not be followed blindly when doing so would cause harm. It should not be ignored casually when it addresses a foreseeable danger. The central issue remains whether the professional exercised reasonable judgment under the circumstances. The date of the document matters as well.

Policies and guidelines change. A later version may contain safeguards adopted after the event. An earlier version may have been replaced before the disputed care occurred. A document found on an organization's current website may not reflect the process in effect at the relevant time. Counsel should confirm the applicable version.

The same caution applies to external guidance. A recommendation published after the care may help explain later practice, but it cannot simply be projected backward. An older guideline may remain formally current while no longer reflecting accepted practice.

The expert should place the document in the professional context of the time.

This is particularly important in rapidly changing areas of medicine, where diagnostic tools, evidence, and treatment options may evolve substantially within a few years. A test, medication, or intervention available later should not be treated as though it was reasonably accessible and accepted earlier. The analysis must remain anchored to the care as it existed then.

Age and setting also affect relevance. Pediatric protocols often use age-specific vital signs, medication doses, and escalation criteria. Obstetrical guidance may depend on gestational age, maternal condition, fetal status, and stage of labor. Nursing-facility regulations may focus heavily on assessment, care planning, skin protection, nutrition, supervision, and transfer. Emergency guidelines may assume access to resources unavailable in an outpatient office.

A document should not be carried from one setting into another without examining whether it fits.

The same symptom may create different obligations depending on where the patient is and who is providing care. An outpatient clinician may need to recognize the risk and send the patient for emergency evaluation. The emergency team may need to investigate and stabilize. A tertiary specialist may then be expected to provide definitive treatment.

The material should support role-specific analysis rather than blur it.

These documents can also identify useful discovery. A policy may refer to a form, queue, escalation log, staffing standard, training module, or electronic process that has not been produced. A regulation may identify a required assessment or record category. A protocol may show which professional should have been involved and what documentation would ordinarily accompany the process.

That can be valuable when the request remains tied to the patient's case.

The objective is not to collect every institutional rule that might be cited. It is to understand the safeguard relevant to the patient's risk.

During deposition, the document should be used to reconstruct care rather than merely obtain agreement that rules should be followed. A witness may readily admit that the policy applied and was not followed. The more useful questions concern why the policy existed, what the witness understood the patient's risk to be, what happened instead, and whether the deviation affected treatment.

Another witness may deny that the policy applied. Counsel then needs to examine its scope, definitions, exceptions, and actual use.

The document creates a line of inquiry. It does not replace clinical examination.

Experts should use these materials with the same discipline. A strong opinion does not attach several guidelines and announce that the defendant violated them. It explains how the patient met the relevant criteria, which response the material supported, what reasonable alternatives remained, and why the care provided fell outside the acceptable range.

The expert should acknowledge provisions preserving judgment or complicating the preferred interpretation. Selective quotation is easy to expose and can undermine an otherwise credible opinion.

The defense expert should be held to the same standard. It is not enough to point to language permitting discretion without explaining why discretion remained reasonable for this patient.

By the end of the analysis, counsel should be able to state the document's actual role in the case.

It may help define responsibility, identify a known risk and its intended safeguard, support an expert's description of the reasonable range of practice, reveal a system defect, or direct discovery toward evidence not yet obtained. It may also prove marginal.

What it should not do is carry conclusions it cannot support.

A violated rule does not automatically establish negligence. A departure does not establish causation. Compliance does not prove that the care was reasonable.

A guideline does not eliminate patient-specific judgment. An internal policy does not necessarily define the external legal standard.

When the document aligns with the patient's condition, the timeline, the professional role, the failed safeguard, and the resulting injury, it can become powerful evidence. It shows that the risk was known, that a process existed to address it, and that the process failed when the patient needed it.

When that alignment is absent, the document may identify an imperfection without establishing a case.

"When that alignment is absent, the document may identify an imperfection without establishing a case."

CHAPTER FOURTEEN

Separating Breach From Causation

This is the point in a medical case where disciplined analysis matters most.

A professional may have made a poor decision. A result may not have been communicated. A patient may have been discharged without adequate reassessment. A deteriorating condition may not have been escalated. A required test may not have been ordered.

Any of those facts may support a departure from reasonable care. They do not yet tell us what the departure caused.

The distinction is familiar in principle and much harder in practice because the breach and the harm often sit next to each other in the record. The failure came first. The injury followed. That sequence is emotionally persuasive and may be medically important. Sequence alone is not causation.

We still have to determine what probably would have happened if appropriate care had occurred. That counterfactual question sits at the center of the case.

It is not enough to say that earlier care might have helped, that treatment was generally available, or that the patient would have received more testing, observation, or specialist consultation. The analysis must move from the omitted step to the probable clinical consequence for this patient.

What would the test likely have shown? Which treatment would have followed? Was the patient eligible? Was the condition still reversible? What degree of benefit could reasonably have been expected? Which part of the final injury probably would have been prevented, reduced, or delayed?

Until those questions are answered, breach and causation remain separate.

This is where some otherwise compelling cases begin to weaken. The standard-of-care opinion may be strong. The expert may be clear that the patient should have been admitted, transferred, imaged, monitored, or treated sooner. When asked what probably would have been different, however, the answer becomes less precise.

"Earlier treatment would have improved the outcome" may be true. It is not yet a complete causal opinion.

Improved in what way? Would death have been prevented at that time? Would the injury have been less severe? Would function have been preserved? Would another surgery have been avoided? Would survival have been prolonged? Would some period of pain, treatment, or dependence have been prevented?

The causal claim becomes reliable when it is stated at the level the medicine can support.

Sometimes the evidence supports complete prevention. Sometimes it supports a narrower but still substantial loss. In other cases, it establishes a real departure without a supportable causal injury. The analysis has to permit each result.

Consider an abnormal imaging result that was never communicated. The failure may be clear. The report identified a suspicious mass and recommended urgent follow-up. The patient was not informed and was diagnosed with cancer months later.

It is tempting to move directly from the missed communication to the later disease stage. Before doing that, counsel must determine what the earlier abnormality represented, whether the disease had already spread, which treatment would have been available, and what that treatment probably would have accomplished.

If the disease was localized and likely curable at the earlier point, the causal theory may be broad and strong.

If the cancer was already metastatic but the patient lost access to treatment that probably would have prolonged survival, the case may remain substantial while the injury is defined differently.

If the disease was biologically aggressive and the delay probably did not change stage, treatment, or prognosis, the communication failure may be genuine without supporting the claimed wrongful death.

The breach remains the same. Its causal significance changes.

Clients can find that distinction difficult because a preventable professional failure feels as though it should lead automatically to legal responsibility. Counsel needs to explain that the inquiry does not end with whether the care was wrong. It also asks what harm the wrong caused.

That discussion should occur early, not after substantial expert expense or on the eve of mediation.

The same problem appears in failure-to-rescue cases. A patient deteriorates after surgery, and the record supports the conclusion that escalation should have occurred earlier. The next question is whether earlier rescue probably would have changed the outcome.

The length of the delay does not answer that question by itself.

We need to know which complication was developing, how far it had progressed, what intervention remained available, and what survival or functional benefit was probable during the disputed interval.

A patient with internal bleeding may still have been salvageable when hypotension first became persistent. Several hours later, irreversible shock may have developed. When the departure occurred during the earlier period, causation may be strong. When the condition was already catastrophic before the warning signs became reasonably recognizable, breach may exist while prevention remains speculative.

The clinically material window is therefore more than part of the timeline. It connects the departure with the treatment opportunity.

The same reasoning applies in stroke litigation. A patient may have presented with findings requiring neurological evaluation. Failure to obtain imaging or consultation may establish departure. Causation still depends on whether the patient had a treatable stroke, whether onset could be established, whether treatment was available and appropriate, and what neurological benefit was probable.

The patient may have lost the entire opportunity for meaningful treatment. The delay may have reduced only part of the likely benefit. The patient may have been ineligible because the injury was already complete, onset was uncertain, or the treatment carried unacceptable risk. The allegation should follow the evidence.

A phrase such as “time is brain” explains urgency. It does not prove what the delay caused in a particular patient.

Medical litigation often relies on sound general propositions. Earlier antibiotics improve outcomes in serious infection. Earlier cancer diagnosis can improve prognosis. Prompt stroke treatment may reduce disability. Recognition of fetal compromise may permit intervention. Those propositions matter, but they are not patient-specific causal opinions.

The expert still has to connect the general evidence to the patient’s condition, eligibility, timing, and probable response.

That connection is sometimes handled too casually because it feels intuitive. The patient worsened during the delay, so the delay appears to explain the worsening. Yet disease may progress despite reasonable care. A complication may become irreversible before it is reasonably detectable. The same treatment given earlier may still have produced the same outcome.

Causation requires a medically supported comparison between the course that occurred and the course likely to have occurred with appropriate care.

That comparison does not require certainty. Medicine rarely offers certainty. It does need to rise above possibility at the level required for the claim.

The language used by experts should reflect that difference. “Could have,” “might have,” and “possibly” describe a medically conceivable result. “Probably,” “more likely than not,” or the applicable jurisdictional equivalent expresses a higher degree of support.

The preferred phrase alone does not make the opinion reliable. The reasoning must explain why the evidence supports that degree of confidence.

Which facts make the alternative course more likely? What literature or clinical experience supports the expected treatment benefit? Which patient-specific factors affect the estimate? Which competing causes were considered? What evidence would materially weaken the conclusion?

The strength of the opinion lies in its reasoning, not its vocabulary.

A related problem occurs when the causation expert assumes a departure different from the one the standard-of-care evidence actually supports.

An expert may say that treatment given earlier would have improved the outcome. Earlier than what?

The standard-of-care expert may conclude that intervention became necessary at four in the afternoon. The causation expert may be assuming treatment at noon. Both opinions can sound favorable while describing different cases.

The causal analysis must begin at the point the departure occurred, not at the earliest theoretical moment when treatment could have been provided.

If the breach began at four, the expert must address the probable outcome with appropriate care beginning at four. When treatment offered substantial benefit at noon but very little by four, the case may contain a serious departure and weak causation.

The opinions have to meet at the same point in time.

The same discipline applies when the departure concerns follow-up rather than immediate treatment.

Suppose a primary-care clinician failed to arrange imaging within three months and the patient was diagnosed nine months later. The proper counterfactual is not necessarily diagnosis on the date of the original study. It may be diagnosis after the reasonable follow-up interval.

Stage, treatment, and prognosis should be assessed at the time compliant care probably would have produced evaluation.

Compressing the entire interval into one immediate missed diagnosis may overstate the causal difference. Causation should be based on the care reasonably required, not on the most favorable care imaginable.

The task is to reconstruct the probable alternative course, not an ideal one.

Patient eligibility is part of that reconstruction. A treatment may exist but not be realistically available to the patient because of contraindications, disease severity, timing, organ function, comorbidity, refusal, or another clinical limitation.

A patient with stroke symptoms may fall outside the treatment window or have a bleeding risk that makes therapy inappropriate. A patient with advanced cancer may not be able to tolerate treatment that an earlier diagnosis would theoretically permit. A patient with sepsis may require an operation that the patient is unlikely to survive.

Those facts do not automatically defeat causation. They define what appropriate care could realistically have accomplished.

Sometimes the lost opportunity lies in something other than definitive treatment. Earlier transfer, symptom control, avoidance of a more invasive procedure, preservation of stability, or retention of a treatment choice may still represent a meaningful benefit.

A case should not be abandoned merely because cure cannot be proved. It should not claim more than this patient probably could have received. That distinction is particularly important in wrongful-death cases.

The question is often framed as whether appropriate care would have prevented death. That may be the correct inquiry, but it is not always the only one.

Earlier care may have prolonged meaningful survival without preventing eventual death. It may have allowed the patient to receive treatment, spend more time at home, remain communicative, or avoid a prolonged and painful decline. It may have prevented death from occurring when it did even though the underlying disease remained serious. Those distinctions matter where the patient's prognosis was already limited.

A patient with advanced cardiac disease, cancer, or severe frailty may not have had an ordinary life expectancy. The question is not whether the defendant could have restored perfect health. It is what difference appropriate care probably would have made from the patient's actual starting point.

The additional loss may be months of survival. It may be access to a treatment carrying meaningful benefit. It may be avoidance of a more severe final course. It may be no measurable difference.

Counsel needs to know which conclusion the evidence supports.

Competing causes must also be addressed directly because medical outcomes rarely have only one cause. The patient may have had pre-existing disease, delayed presentation, biological vulnerability, or a later independent event. The alleged breach may still have contributed to the outcome.

Clinically, the expert should explain how those causes interacted.

The underlying disease may have created the original danger while delayed treatment increased the injury. A complication may have occurred despite reasonable care while delayed recognition worsened its consequences. The patient may have sustained some disability regardless, with the departure adding another level of loss.

The opinion becomes more credible when it accounts for the competing cause instead of pretending it does not exist.

Suppose a patient with severe peripheral vascular disease develops a foot infection and later undergoes an amputation. The vascular disease may have created a substantial risk of tissue loss even with appropriate treatment. That does not end the inquiry.

Earlier escalation may have prevented spread of the infection, allowed a more limited operation, or preserved part of the limb. The supportable injury may be the higher level of amputation rather than the entire loss. That is a narrower theory, but it may be a stronger one.

The same can occur in neurological cases. A patient may already have sustained some brain injury before the departure. Delayed treatment may have increased the area of damage. The causal claim should identify the additional impairment rather than attribute the entire condition to the defendant. This is where causation and damages begin to align.

If the departure caused the entire injury, damages may reflect the full resulting change. If it aggravated a pre-existing condition, damages should reflect the aggravation. If it accelerated death, the analysis should address the amount and quality of survival lost. If it caused additional treatment or suffering without changing the final prognosis, the claim should be framed at that level.

The damages theory should not extend beyond the causation opinion.

Litigation teams often begin developing damages before the causal conclusion has been controlled. A life-care planner may assume that all future care is related to the event. An economist may assume an ordinary work life. A wrongful-death presentation may assume complete prevention when the medical opinion supports only prolonged survival.

Those inconsistencies reveal that the case is not proceeding from one clinical foundation. Causation should lead damages, not follow them.

The patient's response to later treatment may provide useful evidence, but it also requires interpretation.

Improvement after delayed treatment may support the conclusion that earlier treatment would have helped. Failure to improve may suggest that the condition was already advanced or unresponsive. Neither conclusion is automatic.

Later treatment may be less effective precisely because it was given too late. A patient may improve despite a poor prognosis. The response has to be considered in relation to timing, severity, and the natural history of the condition.

Population data requires similar care. Studies may show that earlier intervention improves outcomes on average. The expert still needs to explain how closely the study population resembles the patient and what the findings can reasonably establish in an individual case.

Population evidence informs probability. It does not remove patient-specific uncertainty.

Counsel should be wary of opinions that sound more exact than the evidence permits. A statement that earlier treatment would have reduced injury by a precise percentage may appear scientific. Unless the literature and patient facts genuinely support that precision, it may create vulnerability rather than strength.

A clinically honest opinion may conclude that earlier intervention probably would have improved the neurological outcome while acknowledging that the exact degree of retained function cannot be determined.

That limitation does not necessarily make the opinion speculative. It defines the boundary of what can responsibly be said.

There is a difference between uncertainty about whether any benefit existed and uncertainty about the exact extent of that benefit. The first may undermine causation. The second may be unavoidable even in a supportable case.

Counsel needs to know which kind of uncertainty is present.

Causal mechanism should also be separated from causal attribution.

The mechanism explains how the injury occurred. Attribution explains the role the alleged departure played.

An expert may establish that the patient died from sepsis. That identifies the medical mechanism of death. The litigation still requires an opinion on whether delayed recognition or treatment materially changed the course.

An expert may establish that medication caused renal injury. The case still requires analysis of whether the dose, monitoring, or response fell below the standard and whether the injury would have occurred despite appropriate care.

The medical mechanism is necessary, but it does not complete the causal chain.

This distinction is especially important when an injury clearly follows a procedure or treatment. A nerve injury may have occurred during surgery and still fall within the recognized risks of reasonable technique. Medication may cause bleeding even when it was prescribed and monitored appropriately.

A causal connection between treatment and injury does not establish breach. Breach, in turn, does not establish that the injury resulted from it. Both directions must remain clear.

Counsel should also identify when the causal opinion depends on unresolved facts. The onset of symptoms may be uncertain. The patient's treatment preference may be disputed. Original imaging may be unavailable. Disease severity at the earlier point may have to be estimated. Those assumptions should be stated openly.

An expert opinion is only as reliable as the facts it assumes. When the conclusion remains supportable across the reasonable range of uncertainty, the case is more stable. When it depends on selecting one favorable version of a disputed fact, counsel needs to understand that risk.

Suppose treatment probably would have helped if deterioration began at two in the morning but not if it began at midnight. The patient was found unresponsive at four after an unwitnessed interval. The causation opinion cannot quietly assume two.

Monitoring data, laboratory trends, or other evidence may narrow the interval. If they do not, the uncertainty may determine the case.

This is why record integrity, baseline, objective evidence, timeline, workflow, and causation cannot be treated as separate compartments. A newly obtained image may alter the time of injury. Prior records may show that part of the impairment was pre-existing. A communication log may eliminate an alleged delay. Pathology may establish that disease was already advanced.

Causation has to be revisited when those facts change.

It is entirely possible to conclude that a professional acted unreasonably and that the patient probably suffered no additional injury as a result. That does not mean the analysis failed. It means breach and causation were answered separately.

The reverse may also occur. A departure that appears modest may have substantial consequences because the treatment window was narrow. A short communication delay may matter greatly in a time-sensitive emergency.

A missed reassessment may occur at the final point when rescue remained possible.

The apparent seriousness of the breach and the seriousness of the causal effect do not always move together.

By the end of the analysis, the case should contain a causal statement that can be understood without relying on implication.

It should identify the patient's underlying condition, the point at which the departure occurred, the treatment or response that remained available, the patient's eligibility, the probable course with appropriate care, and the additional injury, loss of function, shortened survival, or suffering attributable to the difference.

It should also identify the strongest competing explanation and address whether that explanation accounts for the entire outcome.

The conclusion may support the case, narrow it, or show that it should not proceed. What it should not be is vague.

“The conclusion may support the case, narrow it, or show that it should not proceed. What it should not be is vague.”

CHAPTER FIFTEEN

Identifying the Treatment or Rescue Opportunity

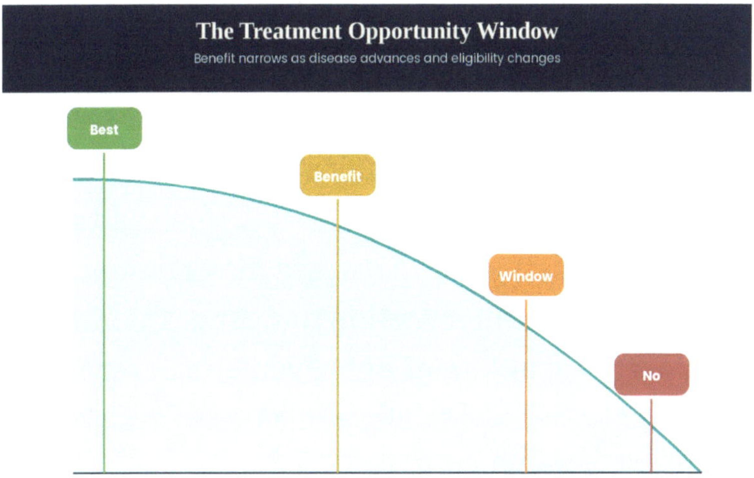

Once breach and causation have been separated, the next question is not simply whether care should have occurred earlier. It is what useful care remained available when the departure occurred. That is the treatment or rescue opportunity.

In some cases, the opportunity is relatively clear. A patient with a treatable infection needed antibiotics and source control before irreversible shock developed. A patient with an evolving stroke may have remained eligible for thrombolysis, thrombectomy, or another intervention during a defined period. A fetus showing deteriorating tolerance of labor may have been capable of benefiting from expedited delivery. A patient with internal bleeding may have remained salvageable before prolonged hypotension caused irreversible injury.

Other cases are far less straightforward. Treatment may have remained technically available while offering little realistic benefit. The patient may have had significant contraindications. The disease may already have been advanced. An intervention may have offered only a modest probability of improvement. Several treatments may have been possible, while none probably would have changed the final outcome.

That is why “earlier treatment” is too general to carry causation. Earlier than what? Which treatment? At what point in the patient’s course? Was this patient eligible? What benefit could reasonably have been expected?

Those questions have to be answered before a delay can be said to have caused harm.

When I work through this issue with counsel, I begin with what appropriate care would have looked like in practice. If the patient had been recognized correctly at the material point, what would have happened next? Would there have been further testing, admission, transfer, surgery, medication, monitoring, consultation, delivery, or another level of supportive care?

The analysis then has to move one step further. Would that action have reached the patient in time to matter?

A test is not itself a treatment opportunity unless it probably would have led to useful care. A consultation is not enough unless the consultant could have recommended or provided an intervention capable of changing the course. Transfer is not causally significant merely because another facility had greater resources. Counsel still needs to know what probably would have happened after transfer and whether the patient remained likely to benefit.

The treatment opportunity is therefore a chain rather than a label.

Recognition would have led to a response. The response would have led to an intervention. The patient would have been eligible for that intervention, and the intervention probably would have produced a defined benefit.

When one of those links is unsupported, the causal theory remains incomplete.

Consider a patient whose evolving stroke was not recognized during an emergency visit. It is easy to say that an earlier diagnosis would have permitted treatment. The actual analysis is more demanding.

When did the symptoms begin? Was onset known? What imaging would have been required? Would the vascular findings have supported intervention? Were there contraindications? How much neurological injury had already occurred? Could the treating facility provide the intervention, or would transfer have been necessary? How long would transfer realistically have taken? What degree of functional improvement was probable?

The treatment opportunity may still be strong. It simply has to be defined.

The same applies in delayed-cancer cases. Earlier recognition may have led to biopsy, staging, and treatment. The important question is what treatment probably would have been offered at the earlier stage and what difference it would have made.

Would the disease have been surgically resectable? Would chemotherapy or radiation have been more effective? Could the patient have tolerated treatment? Would earlier diagnosis probably have prolonged survival, delayed progression, preserved function, or merely changed the timing of treatment without changing the outcome?

The opinion should identify the opportunity at the level the evidence supports.

Sometimes the probable benefit is complete prevention. Sometimes it is reduced severity, additional survival, or avoidance of a more burdensome procedure. Sometimes the evidence does not support a meaningful difference. The analysis has to permit each conclusion.

One common error is treating the treatment window as a single uninterrupted period during which the probable benefit remained constant. It rarely does.

Clinical benefit usually changes over time. At one point, treatment may offer a substantial probability of recovery. Several hours later, some benefit may remain, but less. Later still, the intervention may remain technically possible while offering little chance of changing the outcome.

The window is often a slope rather than a door that simply opens and closes.

That matters because the alleged departure may occur at different points along that slope.

Suppose a postoperative patient develops sepsis. At the first appearance of fever and mild tachycardia, the presentation may remain nonspecific. Several hours later, persistent hypotension, rising lactate, falling urine output, and altered mental status may make the condition recognizable and urgent. At that point, antibiotics, fluids, source control, and critical-care intervention may still offer substantial benefit.

If treatment does not begin until profound shock develops, the opportunity may have narrowed considerably during the delay.

The expert should not stop with the statement that antibiotics work better when given earlier. The opinion should explain the patient's condition when treatment should have begun, what care would have followed, and which part of the outcome probably remained avoidable during that period.

This is where the timeline and objective evidence return to the analysis. Counsel needs to know when the patient moved from generalized risk into recognizable deterioration. Laboratory results, imaging, monitoring, examination findings, and treatment response help determine whether the condition remained reversible at that point.

A treatment opportunity cannot be placed where the evidence does not support it.

The same caution applies in birth-injury cases. A fetal tracing may progress from reassuring to concerning and then clearly abnormal. The treatment opportunity depends on when the pattern became significant enough to require intervention and whether earlier delivery probably would have reduced or prevented injury. That analysis has to account for practical time.

Recognition does not produce immediate delivery. The team may need to evaluate the tracing, mobilize the operating room, obtain anesthesia, prepare the mother, and perform the delivery. A causal opinion should reflect that sequence rather than assume intervention occurred the moment the obligation arose.

When the theory depends on delivery twenty minutes earlier, counsel needs to know whether that was realistically achievable. If injury probably occurred before that point, breach and causation may separate. If the fetus remained capable of benefiting and the delay prolonged exposure to compromise, the opportunity may be supportable.

The same issue arises whenever transfer forms part of the alternative course.

It is not enough to say that the patient should have been transferred sooner. The analysis should identify where the patient would have gone, which resources were available there, how long acceptance and transportation ordinarily required, what treatment would have occurred, and whether the patient remained stable enough to receive it.

A smaller hospital may recognize that the patient needs a higher level of care. Transfer may still require consultation, acceptance, transportation arrangements, and travel. If the intervention had to occur within a narrow period, those practical intervals matter.

A theory that ignores them may describe an opportunity that did not exist in the real world.

That does not excuse a facility that failed to begin transfer promptly. It means the expert should identify what prompt transfer probably would have accomplished.

Sometimes the meaningful opportunity lies in stabilization before transfer rather than in definitive treatment. Earlier airway management, blood-pressure support, reversal of a medication effect, hemorrhage control, antibiotics, or another interim measure may have changed the course.

The analysis should include whatever appropriate care could reasonably have occurred in the original setting. Patient eligibility is equally important.

An intervention may be standard for many patients and unsuitable for this one. The patient may have had a severe bleeding risk, renal failure, advanced frailty, late-stage disease, unstable physiology, a treatment refusal, or another condition affecting what could safely be offered.

Counsel should determine whether those limitations existed when the condition should have been recognized or developed later.

A patient may have been eligible at the material time and become ineligible by the time treatment was finally considered. In that situation, the delay itself may have removed the option.

The opposite may also be true. The patient may never have been a candidate, even with timely recognition. The failure to diagnose or communicate may be real without producing the treatment loss being claimed.

That is one reason the treatment expert needs the complete baseline rather than only the records surrounding the disputed encounter.

Organ function, performance status, comorbidities, prior treatment, medication use, and patient preference may all affect eligibility. A general statement that treatment was available cannot answer the patient-specific question. The expected benefit should also be stated honestly.

Medical treatment does not always produce cure or complete recovery. An intervention may increase the probability of survival without making survival certain. It may reduce neurological disability without restoring normal function. It may preserve a limb without guaranteeing full mobility. It may prolong life without preventing eventual death.

The opportunity should therefore be described in terms of the benefit the evidence supports. That keeps the case from becoming unnecessarily all or nothing.

A patient may have lost a meaningful benefit even when complete prevention cannot be proved. Earlier surgery may have reduced the level of an amputation. Earlier antibiotics may have prevented organ failure without eliminating the infection. Earlier cancer treatment may have prolonged survival rather than cured the disease. Earlier delivery may have reduced neurological injury without preventing every impairment. Those are substantial differences.

They should not be expanded into outcomes the medicine cannot support, and they should not be dismissed merely because the alternative outcome would not have been perfect.

The distinction between technical possibility and probable benefit becomes particularly important in catastrophic cases.

After a serious injury, it may be possible to identify an intervention that still could have been attempted. That does not mean it probably would have changed the result.

A neurosurgical procedure may remain technically possible after extensive injury is already present. A critically ill patient may be able to undergo surgery while having little realistic chance of recovery. A fetus may remain physically deliverable even though the injurious process has already occurred.

The availability of an intervention shows that treatment was not impossible. Causation asks whether meaningful benefit remained probable. The expert should explain that difference.

There are also cases in which the opportunity is diagnostic rather than immediately therapeutic. An omitted test may have allowed a condition to progress without recognition. The opportunity then depends on what the test probably would have shown and what action would have followed.

Suppose a child presents repeatedly with persistent fever, lethargy, and reduced intake. The allegation is that additional testing should have been performed. The case requires more than the statement that testing might have found an infection.

Counsel needs to know whether the proposed test probably would have identified the condition at that stage, whether treatment would then have begun, and what benefit earlier therapy likely would have provided. The test must connect to a meaningful intervention.

That analysis becomes more complicated when the result itself might have remained uncertain. Additional imaging may have been equivocal. A biopsy may not have been diagnostic. A consultant may still have recommended observation.

The alternative course should account for those possibilities rather than assume that every omitted step would have produced immediate certainty.

Appropriate care does not always lead directly to the correct diagnosis. It leads to a reasonable clinical process.

Causation depends on where that process probably would have taken the patient.

If appropriate care would have involved observation, serial examination, repeated testing, and eventual diagnosis, the expert should describe that sequence. If the risk was sufficiently high that treatment probably would have begun before diagnostic certainty, that should be explained as well.

The more closely the alternative course follows actual clinical practice, the more reliable the opinion becomes.

Patient refusal and decision-making capacity may alter the treatment opportunity substantially.

A patient may have declined admission, surgery, imaging, transfusion, or another intervention. The refusal may be clearly documented or disputed. Before concluding that the treatment opportunity remained available, counsel should consider whether the patient probably would have accepted appropriate care if the risk had been accurately explained at the relevant time.

A patient's later willingness does not prove earlier willingness. A general refusal of hospitalization does not necessarily mean the patient would have declined emergency surgery after being told that death was likely. A cognitively impaired patient may not have had capacity to refuse. A family decision-maker may never have been contacted.

The alternative course should not assume acceptance without evidence. It should not assume refusal merely because the patient expressed hesitation.

Relevant evidence may include prior treatment choices, family testimony, communications, advance directives, religious beliefs, earlier refusals, and capacity assessments. When uncertainty remains, it should be acknowledged.

A clear and informed refusal may break or substantially narrow the causal chain. When the patient knowingly declined the intervention on which the alternative course depends, that fact must be addressed directly.

The patient's delay in seeking care may also affect the opportunity.

A patient may present after symptoms have existed for hours or days. That does not eliminate every later professional obligation. It may mean that the condition had already progressed before the defendant became involved. The question is what opportunity remained when the patient arrived.

A delay by the patient may reduce the probable benefit without eliminating it. Another patient may not reach care until irreversible injury has already occurred. Delayed presentation should not be treated as either a complete defense or irrelevant background without examining its clinical effect. Competing causes also enter the analysis here.

Severe underlying disease may limit treatment benefit while leaving some opportunity intact. The expert should explain whether treatment probably would have altered the whole outcome or only part of it.

A patient with advanced vascular disease may have faced a substantial risk of limb loss even with reasonable care. Earlier recognition of infection may still have permitted a more limited amputation. The opportunity was not preservation of a perfectly healthy limb. It was preservation of the greatest amount of tissue and function realistically achievable from the patient's condition at the time.

The same reasoning applies to older and medically fragile patients.

A frail patient may not tolerate major surgery or intensive rehabilitation. The meaningful benefit may have been prevention of shock, avoidance of intubation, reduced pain, preservation of baseline function, or additional survival rather than complete recovery. The value of the opportunity is patient-specific.

The framework asks the same question across ages and care settings: what useful care remained available, and what probably would it have changed?

For a newborn, the opportunity may involve delivery, resuscitation, cooling, infection treatment, or management of metabolic injury. For a child, it may involve antibiotics, surgery, treatment of dehydration, or recognition of neurological deterioration. In adolescence, it may involve mental-health intervention, sports-injury assessment, medication monitoring, or treatment of an acute condition. For an adult, it may involve surgery, stroke intervention, cancer treatment, critical-care rescue, or medication reversal. For an older or frail patient, it may involve preserving independence, avoiding greater injury, prolonging meaningful survival, or preventing additional suffering.

The framework does not assign different value to those outcomes. It identifies what was medically achievable for the individual patient.

The treatment opportunity must also align with the defendant's role.

A nurse may have had the ability to recognize deterioration and escalate, but not to provide definitive treatment. A radiologist may have been able to identify and communicate a finding without controlling the later clinical course. A smaller facility may have had a duty to stabilize and transfer rather than provide the specialty intervention itself.

Causation may still run through those roles, but the alternative course should reflect what the professional reasonably could have caused to happen.

If the nurse had escalated, the physician probably would have assessed the patient. If the radiologist had communicated directly, the ordering clinician probably would have arranged urgent follow-up. If the facility had initiated transfer, the receiving center probably would have evaluated and treated the patient. Each step requires support.

That becomes particularly important when several decisions were required after the alleged breach. The more links between the omitted act and the proposed outcome, the more carefully the chain should be examined.

Would the next clinician have ordered the test? Would the result probably have been positive? Would the patient have accepted treatment? Would treatment have occurred within the relevant window? Would it probably have worked?

A long causal chain is not necessarily speculative. It does require evidence at each material point.

Counsel should understand where the chain is strong and where it relies on assumption.

Sometimes the treatment opportunity is lost gradually through several failures. A concerning result is not communicated. Follow-up does not occur. Symptoms develop. A later encounter also fails to recognize the condition. By the time diagnosis occurs, treatment options have narrowed.

In those cases, responsibility and causation may be distributed across the course.

The first failure may have created one opportunity. A later encounter may have created another. One defendant may argue that a later professional could have interrupted the progression. Another may contend that the disease was already too advanced. Each opportunity should be defined separately.

What could reasonably have occurred after the first result? What remained available during the later encounter? How did the probability of benefit change between those points?

The case should not collapse several opportunities into one general period of delay.

That precision may affect party selection, allocation of responsibility, settlement, and damages. It also allows counsel to identify when meaningful treatment benefit ended, which matters as much as knowing when it began.

A case may contain poor care after the condition became irreversible. Continuing to count that period as though prevention remained available can exaggerate causation. The causal interval should end when treatment no longer probably would have changed the primary outcome.

There may still be other injuries. The patient may have experienced prolonged pain, delayed palliation, deprivation of informed decision-making, or loss of dignity. Those harms should be analyzed separately rather than folded into prevention of an injury that was no longer avoidable.

This is particularly important in wrongful-death and end-of-life cases. Earlier recognition may no longer have prevented death, but it may have allowed better symptom control, family presence, informed planning, or avoidance of burdensome treatment. Those are different opportunities. They may still be medically and legally significant.

At this stage, counsel should understand the evidentiary basis of the treatment opportunity.

Direct evidence may include imaging showing limited injury at the earlier point, laboratory findings consistent with reversibility, or the patient's later response to treatment. Inferential evidence may include the natural history of the condition, its pattern of progression, and established treatment windows. Medical literature may show that earlier intervention improves outcomes in comparable patients.

A strong opinion may draw from all three, but the expert still needs to explain why they apply to this patient.

Population data can establish accepted treatment benefit and inform probability. It should not carry the conclusion by itself.

Nor should the opinion imply more precision than the evidence allows. In one case, the expert may be able to say that earlier care probably would have prevented the injury. In another, the supportable conclusion may be reduced severity. In a wrongful-death matter, the expert may identify a meaningful lost period of survival without being able to calculate its exact duration.

The conclusion should be as strong as the evidence permits and no stronger.

A useful treatment-opportunity analysis should allow counsel to say, in practical terms, that when the condition should have been recognized, a particular intervention remained available; the patient met the relevant criteria; appropriate care could have been delivered within the necessary period; and the objective evidence, disease stage, and expected response support a defined probable benefit.

The analysis may instead show that the care should have been different but that, by the time the condition became reasonably recognizable, the injury was already complete and treatment was unlikely to change the outcome. Both are legitimate conclusions.

The treatment opportunity is where the case moves from criticism to consequence. It shows whether the omitted care represented a real opportunity to change the patient's course or an action that should have occurred without probable effect.

It is the clinical bridge between what should have happened and what the patient lost.

"It is the clinical bridge between what should have happened and what the patient lost."

CHAPTER SIXTEEN

Reconstructing the Probable Alternative Course

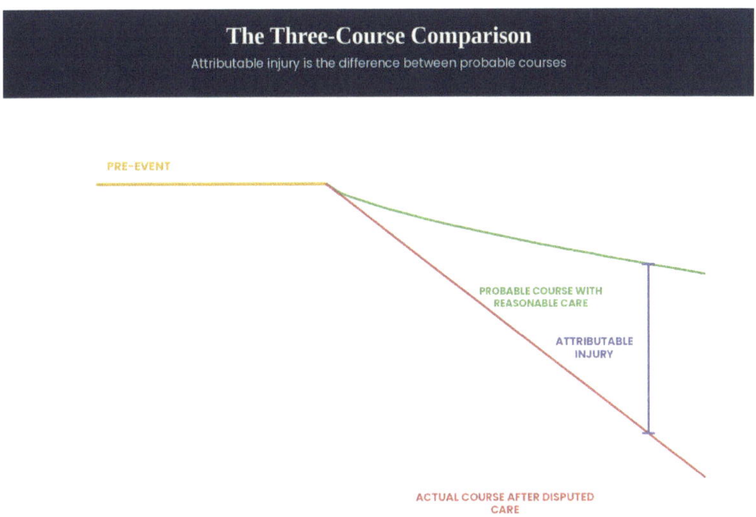

Once the treatment or rescue opportunity has been identified, the analysis has to move beyond the statement that something useful could have been done.

The next question is what probably would have happened if it had been done. That is the alternative course.

This part of the analysis is consequential because it asks us to leave the actual record briefly and reconstruct a course that never occurred. The patient was not treated at the earlier point. The transfer did not happen. The abnormal result was not followed. Surgery was not performed during the alleged window.

There is no chart showing the result. The outcome has to be inferred.

That inference must be medically grounded, clinically realistic, and tied to the patient's condition. It cannot be a best-case scenario assembled from everything that might have gone well. It also cannot assume that the actual outcome was inevitable merely because the patient was seriously ill.

The alternative course is the probable path under appropriate care.

"Probable" does a great deal of work. It requires the analysis to address what treatment would have occurred, how the patient likely would have responded, which risks would have remained, what complications might still have developed, and what degree of recovery or survival the evidence reasonably supports.

The analysis begins at the point of departure.

If reasonable care required action at two, the alternative course begins at two. It does not begin when the disease first existed biologically or when a perfect clinician with complete foresight might have acted. It begins when the available information required another response. That timing discipline matters because treatment benefit may change quickly.

A patient may have been highly salvageable several hours before the departure became recognizable. That earlier possibility is not the proper counterfactual unless the standard of care also required intervention then.

The relevant inquiry is what appropriate care at the actual breach point probably would have produced.

The alternative course must align with the breach. It must also reflect the practical sequence of care.

Recognition does not produce recovery instantly. A clinician may have to assess the patient, enter orders, obtain consultation, perform testing, mobilize a team, arrange transfer, obtain consent, prepare the patient, and deliver treatment. Each step takes time and may involve uncertainty.

Suppose a postoperative patient should have been taken back to the operating room when persistent hypotension, increasing abdominal pain, and falling hemoglobin made internal bleeding apparent.

The alternative course is not that the bleeding stopped the moment it was recognized.

Appropriate care may have involved immediate surgical consultation, resuscitation, preparation of blood products, repeat imaging or bedside assessment, operating-room mobilization, anesthesia, and exploration. The patient's condition during that sequence matters, as does the probable time to source control.

The causal opinion should address whether, through that realistic process, the patient probably would have avoided prolonged shock, organ failure, neurological injury, or death.

That is more persuasive than assuming an instantaneous rescue because it reflects how care is actually delivered. The same applies in delayed-diagnosis cases.

If an abnormal result should have prompted follow-up within thirty days, the alternative course does not usually assume diagnosis and treatment on the day of the original study. It should account for scheduling, clinical evaluation, repeat imaging, biopsy, pathology, staging, consultation, and treatment planning.

The disease should then be assessed at the probable time diagnosis would have occurred through that process.

The resulting difference may remain substantial. It may also be smaller than initially alleged. The point is to compare the actual course with the course reasonable care probably would have produced, not with a version built on perfect speed. That can materially change a cancer case.

Counsel may initially describe a nine-month diagnostic delay. If the original finding reasonably required repeat imaging after three months, followed by a reasonable period for biopsy and treatment planning, the clinically relevant difference may be closer to five or six months.

That interval may still matter greatly if the disease progressed during it. It should be described accurately.

The alternative course also begins with the patient's true baseline.

A patient with substantial pre-existing disease would not necessarily have returned to perfect health with timely care. A child with developmental delay may still have required services. A frail nursing-facility resident may have remained dependent. A patient with advanced cancer may still have had limited survival. The counterfactual should not erase those facts.

It should identify which part of the actual outcome probably would have been avoided, reduced, or delayed.

A patient with severe vascular disease may still have required an amputation, while timely treatment probably would have preserved the knee. A patient with chronic kidney disease may still have had impaired renal function but avoided permanent dialysis. A patient with prior cognitive impairment may not have returned to complete independence but may have avoided profound neurological decline.

The alternative course is measured from the patient's actual starting point, not from an imagined healthy state. This is where baseline, treatment opportunity, causation, and damages begin to converge.

The more reliable the baseline, the more accurately the alternative outcome can be described. The more precisely the treatment opportunity is defined, the less speculative the counterfactual becomes. The more candidly competing causes are addressed, the more credible the comparison will be. The analysis should move through a connected sequence.

What care would reasonably have occurred? When would it probably have occurred? Would the patient have accepted and tolerated it? Which complications would still have remained likely? What survival, function, or symptom burden probably would have followed? How does that differ from the actual course? The intermediate reasoning matters.

It is not enough to move directly from "earlier treatment was required" to "the patient would have survived."

In an infection case, the expert may need to explain that earlier recognition would have led to cultures, broad-spectrum antibiotics, fluid resuscitation, identification of the source, surgical drainage, and critical-care support before prolonged shock developed.

The opinion then has to address the probable response. Was the organism susceptible? Was source control available? Had organ dysfunction begun? Was it reversible? Which comorbidities affected prognosis? Only then can the expert responsibly address whether survival was probable. The same structure applies in neurological cases.

If a stroke should have been recognized earlier, what imaging would have been obtained? What would it probably have shown? Was the patient eligible for thrombolysis or thrombectomy? How quickly could treatment have occurred? How much tissue remained at risk rather than already infarcted? What degree of functional recovery was probable?

The alternative course may support near-complete recovery, reduced disability, or only modest improvement. The opinion should identify which conclusion the evidence supports. The same is true in obstetrical matters.

If expedited delivery was required, how long would reasonable mobilization and delivery have taken? What was the probable fetal condition at that point? Had injury already begun? Would earlier delivery probably have prevented injury, reduced its severity, or changed survival without eliminating neurological impairment?

An opinion that says only that the baby would have been delivered sooner stops before the causal issue. The question is what earlier delivery probably would have changed.

The patient's willingness to undergo treatment must also be considered when it is genuinely disputed.

A treatment opportunity may exist medically without producing an alternative course if the patient probably would have refused. That issue is often more complicated than the chart suggests.

A note may state that the patient declined admission without showing whether the risk of death, permanent injury, or lost treatment eligibility was understood. A patient may have rejected one option while remaining willing to accept another. Someone who was frightened or overwhelmed may have decided differently if the condition had been explained accurately.

The counterfactual should not assume refusal merely because the patient expressed reluctance. It should not assume acceptance merely because treatment would have been beneficial.

Relevant evidence may include prior treatment choices, family testimony, communications, advance directives, religious beliefs, earlier refusals, and capacity. When uncertainty remains, it should be acknowledged.

Appropriate care may also have produced continued diagnostic uncertainty rather than immediate treatment.

A repeat image may have remained equivocal. A biopsy may have been nondiagnostic. A consultant may have recommended continued observation. The patient may have undergone serial testing before the condition became clear. The alternative course should account for those possibilities.

Reasonable care does not always reveal the answer at the first step. It creates a process more likely to identify and manage the condition in time.

In some cases, probability lies in that process rather than in one event. An expert may conclude that appropriate admission, serial examination, repeated laboratory testing, and specialist involvement probably would have revealed deterioration before catastrophic injury. That may be a sound alternative course when the reasoning is specific.

The expert should explain which changes probably would have appeared, how frequently reassessment would have occurred, what treatment would have followed, and why meaningful rescue probably remained available. Without that detail, the counterfactual remains too general.

The natural history of the underlying condition is central.

To reconstruct what probably would have happened under appropriate care, we need to understand how the condition would have progressed without the departure.

Some diseases move rapidly. Others develop over months or years. Some injuries are complete at onset. Others expand through secondary damage. Some complications remain reversible for a period and then become permanent.

The alternative course depends on where the patient was along that biological path.

A hemorrhage may continue to expand. Infection may progress from a localized process to systemic failure. Ischemia may produce increasing tissue death. Untreated cancer may grow or spread. A pressure injury may progress from superficial damage to deep tissue destruction.

The expert should explain how intervention probably would have altered that path.

Would treatment have stopped progression, slowed it, reduced its extent, prevented a secondary complication, or preserved the patient long enough to receive another therapy? The mechanism should be understandable.

An opinion that earlier care would have produced a better result becomes more persuasive when the pathway between intervention and benefit can be explained. Earlier decompression may reduce pressure and preserve neurological tissue. Earlier antibiotics and source control may limit bacterial spread and prevent persistent shock. Earlier vascular treatment may preserve blood flow. Earlier delivery may end continued fetal exposure to a harmful environment.

The mechanism does not remove uncertainty. It makes the inference clinically coherent.

Treatment efficacy must then be considered at the level the evidence supports.

An intervention may improve outcomes in a population without guaranteeing success for one patient. The alternative course should reflect probability rather than certainty.

A treatment associated with high survival may support an opinion that this patient probably would have survived, particularly when the patient resembles the studied population and has favorable prognostic features. A treatment with modest average benefit may support a narrower conclusion. Highly variable response may make the exact outcome difficult to predict.

The expert should explain both the expected benefit and the patient-specific modifiers.

Age, organ function, disease severity, time to treatment, comorbidities, functional status, treatment tolerance, and biological characteristics may all matter.

Population data should inform the analysis without substituting for it.

This is particularly important when an expert relies on survival or staging statistics. Those figures describe groups. They do not dictate one patient's course.

A five-year survival rate may show that earlier-stage disease carries a materially better prognosis. It does not establish that this patient would have lived five years. Tumor biology, treatment eligibility, age, general health, and competing mortality risks still have to be considered.

The strongest opinion explains how the population evidence and the patient's facts fit together.

The same caution applies to percentages involving neurological recovery, limb salvage, treatment response, and procedural success.

Numbers can create an impression of certainty. They are useful when they accurately reflect relevant evidence. They become vulnerable when drawn from populations that do not resemble the patient or when they imply precision the medicine does not support.

Sometimes the probable alternative course can be stated confidently without assigning an exact percentage.

The patient probably would have survived the hospitalization. The patient probably would have avoided permanent dialysis. The patient probably would have retained independent ambulation. The patient probably would have undergone a less extensive procedure. The patient probably would have lived materially longer. Those statements may be more reliable than an unsupported numerical estimate.

The risks of the proposed treatment must also be included.

The alternative course is not automatically favorable merely because appropriate care would have involved intervention. Surgery carries risk. Anticoagulation can cause bleeding. Chemotherapy may cause toxicity. Transfer may create delay or instability. Delivery may produce maternal or neonatal complications. A realistic counterfactual considers those risks.

That does not mean assuming every conceivable complication. It means the opinion should not describe treatment as though it guaranteed benefit without burden or danger.

When the risk of treatment-related harm was low compared with the expected benefit, the alternative course may remain strong. If the patient was unusually vulnerable, the probable benefit may be lower and recovery more limited. This becomes particularly important in medically fragile patients.

A frail older adult may have survived earlier surgery but required prolonged rehabilitation. A patient with severe pulmonary disease may have avoided death while remaining at risk for ventilator dependence. A patient with advanced cancer may have gained survival while also facing substantial treatment burden.

The alternative course should describe the probable life, not merely survival as a binary outcome. That distinction becomes central during damages analysis.

Survival alone may not capture the clinical difference. Appropriate care may have preserved communication, mobility, independence, or time at home. Another patient may have survived with profound impairment even under reasonable treatment. The expected level of function matters.

The expert need not predict every detail of the patient's future. The causal opinion should provide enough information to keep the damages analysis consistent with the medical conclusion.

If the opinion supports survival with moderate disability, damages should not assume a full return to employment. If it supports reduced severity rather than complete prevention, the life-care analysis should distinguish unavoidable needs from those caused by the departure. The counterfactual and damages cannot be developed independently.

Wrongful-death cases require particularly careful reconstruction because the alternative course may involve a limited but meaningful period of survival.

A patient with advanced disease may not have had decades remaining. Appropriate care may still have provided months or years. It may have allowed treatment, family time, travel, work, or participation in medical decisions that the actual course eliminated.

The expert should identify the probable duration and nature of that survival as closely as the evidence permits.

The exact period may not be knowable. It may be possible to describe a range or a clinically meaningful interval. Counsel will determine how that opinion fits the applicable law.

Clinically, the opinion should avoid both extremes. The patient was not expected to live indefinitely. The patient was not necessarily destined to die when death occurred. The probable alternative course lies between those propositions.

There are also cases in which the main difference is not survival but the manner of decline.

Earlier recognition may not have prevented death, but it may have prevented an emergency deterioration, prolonged suffering, invasive procedures, or the loss of an opportunity for informed end-of-life planning. That is a different causal theory and should be presented as such.

The case should not claim that death was preventable when the evidence supports only a more controlled and less burdensome final course. Those harms should not be disregarded merely because additional survival was not probable.

Competing causes belong within the alternative course rather than being addressed only as objections to it.

Suppose a patient had both severe infection and advanced heart disease. Earlier treatment may have controlled the infection, but the cardiac condition still would have affected survival and recovery.

The probable alternative course might be survival of the infection and a return near baseline, with continuing risk from the heart disease. It might instead be prevention of immediate death while long-term survival remained uncertain because of the combined disease burden. Those are different conclusions.

An expert who ignores the cardiac disease may overstate recovery. An expert who attributes everything to it may understate the effect of the treatable infection. The analysis should explain how the conditions interacted.

The same applies when the patient's conduct contributed to the actual course. Delayed presentation, missed appointments, medication nonadherence, continued smoking, substance use, poor nutrition, or refusal of care may affect the probable outcome. Those factors should be evaluated clinically rather than morally.

Did they reduce eligibility? Did they accelerate the disease? Would reasonable professional care still probably have changed the outcome? Would the same conduct likely have continued during the alternative course?

The counterfactual should not assume a perfectly compliant patient unless the evidence supports that assumption.

At the same time, prior nonadherence does not establish that the patient would have rejected every serious intervention. A person may miss routine appointments and still accept surgery after a significant diagnosis. A patient may struggle with medication adherence and still comply with supervised treatment. The facts should guide the inference.

Cases involving several defendants may require more than one alternative course.

A result may have been missed initially, followed by a later failure to diagnose and then delayed treatment after admission. Each departure may have changed what remained possible.

The first counterfactual asks what probably would have occurred with timely follow-up after the original result. The second asks what remained possible at the later encounter. The third asks whether prompt treatment after admission still would have reduced the injury.

Those opportunities should not be blended into one general statement that earlier care would have helped.

Each defendant's causal role may depend on a different point in the disease process.

That precision may show that one departure caused most of the loss, another increased severity, and a third probably made no difference. It may also show that later appropriate care could not reverse harm created earlier.

Counsel needs that analysis before responsibility can be allocated coherently.

One useful test is whether the alternative course remains persuasive when the most favorable assumptions are removed.

What happens when treatment takes an ordinary amount of time rather than the fastest imaginable time? What if the patient experiences a recognized complication? What if recovery is incomplete? What if a disputed fact is resolved against the preferred theory?

When the conclusion survives those adjustments, it is more robust.

When the theory depends on immediate diagnosis, immediate treatment, perfect response, no complication, and complete recovery, it may be too fragile.

This stress test does not weaken a valid case. It identifies the version capable of withstanding serious examination.

The defense should be subjected to the same discipline.

An opinion that the outcome was inevitable should explain why appropriate care could not have changed any meaningful part of the course. It should address eligibility, timing, reversibility, and expected benefit rather than relying on the severity of the final condition.

A patient may appear unsalvageable at the end and still have been treatable earlier.

The final outcome should not be projected backward any more than an idealized alternative should be projected forward.

By the end of this stage, counsel should be able to describe two parallel courses.

The actual course begins with the patient's baseline, follows the developing condition, identifies the departure, and ends with the injury or death that occurred.

The alternative course begins at the same baseline and follows the same condition until the departure. It then proceeds through the care that should have occurred and the outcome that probably would have followed. The difference between those courses is the causally attributable injury.

That difference may be complete prevention of death, reduced neurological disability, preservation of limb length or organ function, additional survival, or avoidance of invasive treatment, prolonged pain, or catastrophic decline. There may also be no supportable difference.

A reliable alternative course does not promise perfection. It explains probability. It shows what appropriate care realistically would have set in motion, how the patient likely would have responded, which limitations would have remained, and what part of the actual outcome probably would not have occurred. That is the course against which the case must ultimately be measured.

"That is the course against which the case must ultimately be measured."

CHAPTER SEVENTEEN

Testing Competing Causes

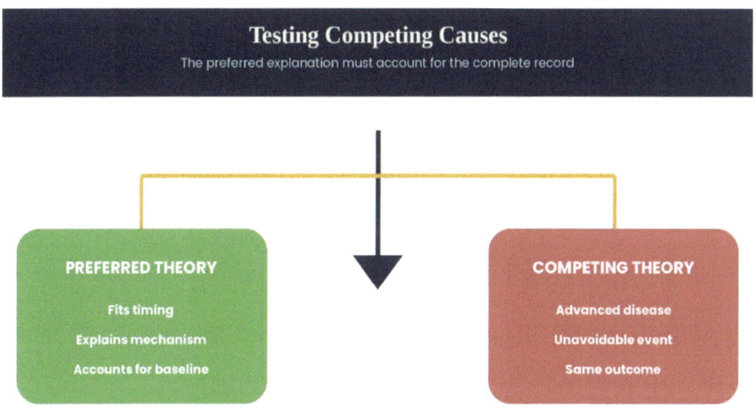

By the time a medical case reaches causation, the record usually supports more than one possible explanation for the outcome.

The patient may have had serious underlying disease. Symptoms may have begun before the defendant became involved. Treatment may have been delayed by the patient, interrupted by another provider, or limited by a condition no one caused. A recognized complication may have occurred despite appropriate care. Several physiological processes may have been operating at once. The patient may even have improved briefly and then deteriorated for reasons that appear unrelated to the original departure.

Those facts do not necessarily defeat the case. They do mean that causation cannot be developed by telling only the preferred story.

A clinically sound theory has to survive the other plausible explanations.

That does not require counsel to pursue every remote possibility that could be raised in deposition. Medicine always permits possibilities. The task is to identify the explanations that fit enough of the evidence to matter and determine whether they account for the patient's course better than the proposed causal theory. That work should occur before experts become committed to final opinions.

Once an expert has issued a report, defended the conclusion in conference, and helped shape litigation strategy, reconsidering the theory can feel like retreat. The better time to challenge causation is while the case is still being understood.

I would rather learn early that an imaging finding was chronic, that the proposed treatment was contraindicated, or that the injury probably began before the disputed interval than hear it for the first time from the opposing expert after the case has been built around a broader claim.

Competing-cause analysis is not hostile to the case. It is what allows the case to become accurate.

The starting question is straightforward: what else could reasonably explain the injury, deterioration, or death?

The answer may come from the patient's baseline. It may appear in prior imaging, pathology, laboratory trends, medication exposure, natural disease history, an intervening event, or the timing of symptoms. It may arise from the treatment itself. Sometimes it becomes visible only after the actual and alternative courses are placed side by side.

The strongest competing cause is rarely the most dramatic one. It is the explanation that accounts for the greatest amount of evidence with the fewest unsupported assumptions.

Suppose a patient dies after delayed diagnosis of an infection. The plaintiff's theory is that earlier antibiotics and source control probably would have prevented septic shock. The defense points to severe cardiac disease and argues that the patient died from heart failure.

The analysis should not stop with the labels sepsis and heart disease. We need to understand how the patient died.

Did the record show progressive infection, falling blood pressure, rising lactate, organ dysfunction, positive cultures, and a source requiring treatment? Did the cardiac condition remain stable until shock developed? Did imaging or autopsy identify another mechanism? Did the patient improve after antibiotics or drainage? Were the cardiac findings sufficient to explain the deterioration independently?

The patient may have had both sepsis and heart disease. The important question is the role each played.

The cardiac disease may have reduced physiological reserve and made the infection more difficult to survive. The infection may still have triggered the final decline. Earlier treatment may have prevented that decline even though the patient remained medically vulnerable.

In that situation, the pre-existing condition is not an alternative explanation that removes causation. It is a contributing condition that affects prognosis and expected treatment benefit. That distinction appears throughout medical litigation.

A competing cause may be independent of the departure. It may interact with the departure. It may explain part of the injury but not all of it. It may affect the degree of loss.

It may also provide a more persuasive explanation for the entire outcome. The work lies in determining which.

Underlying disease is often the first competing cause raised because it existed before the event. Its presence does not establish that it was sufficient to cause the later outcome.

Diabetes may increase infection risk and impair wound healing. It does not explain why a wound went unassessed, why infection was not treated, or why tissue damage progressed without escalation. Vascular disease may make limb loss more likely. It does not establish that the eventual level of amputation was unavoidable. Dementia may increase susceptibility to delirium. It does not explain a new hypoxic brain injury.

The underlying condition has to be connected to the outcome with the same discipline required of the affirmative theory.

How advanced was the condition? What course was expected? Which injury had it already produced? What additional injury followed? Would the same death, disability, or level of dependence probably have developed at the same time without the alleged departure?

That last question is particularly useful because it forces the competing explanation to become a counterfactual rather than remain a descriptive label.

It is not enough to say the patient was frail, elderly, or medically complex. Would those conditions probably have caused this outcome when it occurred? Sometimes the answer will be yes.

A patient may have had end-stage disease and been actively declining before the disputed event. A catastrophic hemorrhage may have been unsurvivable before anyone had a reasonable opportunity to respond. Cancer may already have been metastatic and biologically aggressive when follow-up was first required. A fetal injury may have resulted from a chronic prenatal process rather than events during labor.

When the evidence supports that conclusion, the competing cause may substantially weaken or defeat causation.

The analysis should reach that result openly rather than preserve a theory the medicine no longer supports. In other cases, the competing condition explains vulnerability without explaining timing.

A patient with severe chronic disease may have remained stable for years, then experienced an acute decline after a defined departure and never returned to baseline. The chronic illness remains relevant to treatment response, recovery, life expectancy, and future care. It may not explain the abrupt change.

Timing is often the most effective way to test competing causes.

When did the proposed cause begin? When did the patient's condition change? Do the objective findings follow that sequence? Would the competing cause ordinarily produce the same pattern?

A theory that requires the cause to operate before it existed, or after the injury was already established, is unlikely to withstand serious review.

Consider a patient who develops renal failure after receiving medication. The defense may point to pre-existing chronic kidney disease.

The important question is not whether renal impairment existed. It is whether the later failure reflects the expected progression of that disease or a new acute injury.

A stable creatinine over many months, followed by a rapid rise after medication exposure, may support a superimposed toxic or hemodynamic injury. A steady decline that began before the medication may support another conclusion. Dehydration, infection, obstruction, or contrast exposure may introduce additional causes.

The laboratory trend is more useful than the diagnostic label.

The same approach applies to neurological injury. A patient may have prior strokes, cognitive impairment, or structural brain disease. Later imaging may show a new infarct, hemorrhage, or hypoxic injury. The issue is not whether the brain was previously normal. It is which findings are old, which are new, and which explain the post-event functional change.

Original imaging may become decisive because a written report can compress several abnormalities into one conclusion. A specialist reviewing the sequence may distinguish chronic volume loss from acute injury, prior infarction from new ischemia, or a pre-existing lesion from a later complication. That distinction may narrow damages without defeating liability.

A patient may already have had some impairment and still have sustained a substantial additional injury. The case becomes stronger when it identifies that addition instead of claiming that the entire condition began with the event.

The natural progression of the disease under review is another common competing explanation.

The defense may argue that the condition would have advanced regardless of the alleged delay. That may be true. Most untreated diseases progress. The more useful question is whether appropriate care probably would have altered that progression.

In a delayed-cancer case, tumor biology matters greatly. Some cancers progress slowly and remain treatable for a considerable period. Others spread early and carry a poor prognosis even when diagnosed promptly.

Pathology, stage, growth rate, molecular characteristics, earlier imaging, and response to treatment may help determine which course is more likely.

A general statement that the cancer was aggressive does not resolve the issue. Aggressive disease may make delay more consequential because progression occurs quickly. It may also mean that earlier diagnosis would not have changed survival. The same fact can support different conclusions depending on stage, treatment options, and the length of the delay.

The biology has to be connected to the alternative course.

What stage was the disease probably in at the earlier point? What treatment would have been available? How likely was response? What progression probably occurred during the disputed interval? Could the later stage reasonably have been present already?

Those questions move the analysis beyond familiar statements about the value of early detection.

Natural history is equally important in infection cases. Some patients deteriorate rapidly despite timely antibiotics and critical care. Some infections are overwhelming. Some patients have little physiological reserve. Source control may be impossible or delayed for reasons unrelated to the alleged departure.

The existence of severe infection does not establish that earlier care would have prevented death.

The fact that some patients die despite treatment does not establish inevitability for this patient either.

We need to know the organism, source, severity, treatment susceptibility, degree of organ dysfunction, response, and timing. We need to determine whether shock had begun, whether it remained reversible, and how the patient's comorbidities affected expected survival.

The competing theory has to address the patient rather than the disease category.

A recognized complication is another explanation often used too broadly.

A complication may occur without negligence. That is clinically true. Identifying an event as a known risk does not tell us whether it arose spontaneously, resulted from technique, or became more severe because it was not recognized and treated.

A patient may experience postoperative bleeding as a recognized complication. The occurrence itself may not support departure. Failure to respond to progressive hypotension and falling hemoglobin may still support a failure-to-rescue theory.

The complication explains why the patient began to deteriorate. It may not explain why the deterioration became catastrophic.

In that setting, the complication and the negligence are not competing causes in the ordinary sense. The complication is the underlying clinical event. The departure concerns how it was managed.

Recognizing that distinction may prevent the case from becoming trapped in an unnecessary dispute about whether the complication should have occurred at all.

The more supportable theory may accept that the initial event was non-negligent and focus on the additional injury caused by delayed recognition.

The same may be true of thromboembolism, infection, arrhythmia, aspiration, or another recognized risk. The event may not have been preventable. Its consequences may have been. Intervening care also has to be examined.

A patient may experience an initial delay and later receive treatment from another professional or institution. The later care may interrupt, reduce, or increase the resulting harm. It may involve a separate departure. It may show that the injury was already irreversible.

Later negligence does not automatically eliminate the causal role of the earlier defendant. The first error also does not make every later event part of one continuous causal chain. Each interval should be reconstructed separately.

Suppose an abnormal finding was missed in an outpatient setting. Months later, the patient presents to an emergency department with symptoms that also should have led to diagnosis. The condition is finally identified after another delay.

The first failure may have eliminated an opportunity for early-stage treatment. The later failure may have eliminated a narrower rescue opportunity. The disease may already have been advanced by the second encounter, making the initial failure more significant. The analysis should identify what remained possible at each point.

That is more useful than treating the entire history as one continuous delay for which every defendant carries the same causal role. It also helps counsel determine whether later care was a competing cause, a concurrent cause, or another stage in the same progression.

Patient conduct can provide another competing explanation, but it needs careful handling.

A patient may delay seeking care, decline testing, miss appointments, stop taking medication, or fail to follow instructions. Those facts may affect causation materially. They should not be treated as moral judgments or automatic proof that the professional failure made no difference.

The clinical question is what the patient's conduct changed.

Did delayed presentation close the treatment window before the defendant became involved? Did refusal prevent the intervention on which the alternative course depends? Did failure to attend follow-up allow disease to progress after the risk had been explained adequately? Did medication nonadherence cause the deterioration independently?

Or did the patient's conduct reduce the available opportunity without eliminating it?

A patient may present late and remain treatable. Someone may miss an appointment because the urgency was not explained. A patient may stop medication because an adverse effect was not addressed. A cognitively impaired patient may be labeled noncompliant when the plan was not realistically manageable. The conduct has to be placed in context.

A chart entry stating "noncompliant" tells us very little without more detail. What was the patient asked to do? Was the patient capable of doing it? Was the risk explained? Were barriers known? What happened as a result?

The same causal discipline should apply whether the explanation favors the plaintiff or the defense. Treatment-related harm may itself become a competing cause.

A patient can deteriorate because of the disease, the treatment, or both. Medication may cause bleeding, renal injury, sedation, or arrhythmia. Surgery may produce tissue injury, infection risk, or physiological stress.

Mechanical ventilation may be lifesaving and still contribute to later complications.

The issue is whether the treatment-related event was a reasonable and unavoidable consequence, a separate negligent act, or part of the injury created by the original delay.

Suppose delayed diagnosis requires a more aggressive operation than timely care would have required. A complication arising from that operation may form part of the causal damages if the more extensive procedure resulted from the delay. If the same operation would have been necessary under appropriate care, the complication may not be attributable to the breach. The alternative course helps answer that question.

Would the patient have received the same treatment in either course? Would the risk of complication have been materially different? Did the delay convert a less invasive option into a more dangerous one?

Those questions often matter more than whether the complication is described as known.

Some competing causes are external to the medical condition itself.

A patient may suffer a fall, aspiration event, medication interruption, transportation delay, equipment failure, or another acute event after the alleged departure. The event may be related to the patient's weakened condition or entirely independent.

The analysis should ask whether the later event was foreseeable within the course created by the departure.

If a patient becomes confused and weak because of untreated infection and then falls while attempting to walk, the fall may be a consequence of the deterioration rather than an independent cause. An unrelated accident weeks later may stand differently.

The presence of another event between breach and outcome does not decide whether the causal chain remains intact. The clinical connection still has to be examined.

In some cases, the competing explanation is not one cause but a combination.

A frail older patient may die after infection, dehydration, medication toxicity, and cardiac strain develop together. No single factor may be sufficient. The question becomes whether the alleged departure materially changed the combined process. Medicine often works this way. Conditions interact.

Dehydration can worsen kidney function. Renal impairment can increase medication levels. Medication toxicity can reduce alertness and oral intake. Reduced intake can worsen dehydration. Infection can destabilize every part of the course.

The patient's decline may therefore be circular rather than linear.

A theory insisting on one exclusive cause may be less credible than one explaining the interaction and identifying where reasonable care probably could have interrupted it.

The same applies in maternal cases, where hemorrhage, coagulopathy, infection, hypertension, cardiac strain, and embolic disease may overlap. In neonatal injury, chronic placental compromise, an acute intrapartum event, infection, prematurity, and resuscitation may all require consideration.

The medicine should not be simplified beyond recognition. The task is to determine whether the departure probably made a difference within that complexity.

Objective evidence becomes especially important when the parties offer competing theories of timing.

One expert may conclude that the injury was complete before the defendant became involved. Another may say it progressed during the disputed interval. Imaging, laboratory trends, fetal monitoring, pathology, tissue findings, autopsy evidence, and treatment response may help resolve the difference. Sometimes the evidence will not permit a precise answer.

A fetal injury may have occurred within a range spanning prenatal and intrapartum periods. A stroke may have developed during an unwitnessed interval. Infection may have become irreversible at an uncertain time. The analysis should not manufacture precision. Instead, it should determine whether the opinion survives across the reasonable range.

If appropriate care probably would have helped even at the earliest plausible injury time, the theory is relatively stable. If it works only when the injury is placed at the latest possible moment, the litigation risk is substantial.

Counsel needs to understand that distinction before deciding how the case should proceed.

Treatment response may also help test the competing causes.

Rapid improvement following delayed intervention may support the conclusion that the untreated condition was driving the decline and remained reversible. Continued deterioration despite appropriate treatment may support the argument that earlier care would not have changed the outcome. Both inferences require caution.

Improvement may be temporary. Deterioration after treatment may reflect how late the intervention occurred rather than treatment futility. The therapy may not have addressed the actual cause. Several treatments may have been given together, making the effect of any one difficult to isolate.

Treatment response is evidence. It is not a verdict.

Autopsy findings can be powerful in wrongful-death cases because they may establish a mechanism not clearly recognized during life. They can also create false confidence.

An autopsy may identify pulmonary embolism, myocardial infarction, infection, hemorrhage, aspiration, or another cause of death. The finding may support the original theory, undermine it, or identify several contributing processes. The result still has to be placed in time.

When did the fatal process begin? Was it detectable? Was treatment available? Would the alleged departure have affected it?

A death certificate or autopsy diagnosis identifies the medical cause of death. It does not allocate legal causation.

The same discipline applies to pathology. Placental findings may support chronic compromise without establishing that all neonatal injury occurred before labor. Tumor pathology may show aggressive biology without proving that earlier treatment was futile. Tissue necrosis may suggest duration without fixing the exact onset.

Experts should explain the limits of what the evidence can establish.

Competing-cause analysis often exposes differences in how experts use the same fact.

One expert treats comorbidity as proof that recovery was unlikely. Another treats the same comorbidity as a risk factor that made prompt treatment more important. One interprets early abnormal imaging as proof that injury was complete. Another sees tissue that remained capable of rescue. One views poor treatment response as evidence of inevitability. Another sees the consequence of late intervention.

These are not merely different conclusions. They may reflect different assumptions about timing, mechanism, eligibility, or natural history. Counsel should identify the precise disagreement.

What fact must be true for each opinion to hold? Which evidence supports it? Which evidence conflicts with it? Is one expert using the final outcome to infer the earlier condition? Does either opinion assume a treatment course that was not realistically available?

Once the disagreement is broken down, it often becomes more manageable.

The attorney does not need to decide the medicine independently. The attorney does need to understand what is being disputed.

A useful way to test the affirmative theory is to state the strongest competing explanation in its best form, not in a weakened version designed to be dismissed.

The disease was already advanced. The treatment opportunity had narrowed. The patient had limited reserve. The proposed intervention carried substantial risk. The later course followed the natural history of the condition.

Then ask whether the preferred theory still explains the evidence more convincingly.

If it does, the case is stronger for having survived the test. If it does not, the theory should be narrowed or reconsidered.

A defense theory of inevitability should be tested the same way.

Assume the departure occurred. Assume appropriate care began when it should have. Assume treatment followed through an ordinary clinical sequence.

Can the defense still explain why no material benefit was probable?

Saying the patient was too sick is not enough. Too sick for which treatment? At what point? Based on which findings? Was the condition irreversible or simply serious?

The defense theory should withstand the same counterfactual discipline.

In many cases, competing-cause analysis does not eliminate causation. It changes the size and character of the injury.

A patient may have been likely to suffer some neurological impairment regardless, while delay increased its severity. Surgery may have been necessary in either course, but the delay led to a more extensive procedure. The patient may have had limited life expectancy, while the departure accelerated death. A resident may have been at high risk for skin breakdown, while inadequate care allowed a superficial wound to progress to infection and amputation. Those are clinically refined theories, not compromised ones. They identify what the departure actually added.

That is usually more credible than attributing the whole outcome to one defendant while ignoring significant pre-existing or concurrent causes. It also provides a more reliable foundation for damages.

Future care can be divided between needs that would have existed and needs created or increased by the event. Lost survival can be measured against the patient's actual prognosis. Functional loss can be assessed from the true baseline rather than an idealized one.

The causal opinion becomes useful rather than merely accusatory.

There will be cases in which no expert can separate the causes with confidence. The underlying disease and the alleged departure may be too intertwined. Timing may be too uncertain. The available evidence may establish several plausible mechanisms without allowing one to be preferred. That uncertainty should be stated directly.

The case may still proceed under an applicable legal theory, depending on the jurisdiction and the evidence.

Clinical review should not silently convert uncertainty into probability.

Counsel needs to know whether the medicine supports a conclusion, a range, or only a possibility.

By the end of the analysis, counsel should be able to identify the strongest competing cause without hesitation. You should know which evidence supports it, which evidence weakens it, how it interacts with the alleged departure, and whether it explains the whole outcome or only part.

You should also be able to explain why the preferred causal theory remains more probable—or why it does not.

The conclusion may be that underlying disease created vulnerability without causing the acute change. A recognized complication may have been unavoidable while delayed rescue increased the injury. Appropriate care may have improved the course despite serious comorbidity. The injury may already have been complete before any supportable breach occurred. Several causes may have combined, with the departure materially worsening the result. The conclusion will change from case to case. The method remains consistent.

We identify the plausible explanations and test each against the baseline, objective evidence, timing, natural history, treatment opportunity, and actual response. We do not dismiss inconvenient facts, and we do not allow a diagnosis or comorbidity to carry more causal weight than the evidence supports.

The final theory should not merely coexist with the competing causes. It should explain them.

"The final theory should not merely coexist with the competing causes. It should explain them."

CHAPTER EIGHTEEN

Wrongful Death, Accelerated Death, and Lost Survival

Wrongful-death cases often begin with a statement that appears straightforward: the patient died because the condition was not recognized or treated in time.

Sometimes the medicine supports that conclusion directly. The patient had a treatable condition, remained salvageable when reasonable care was required, and died after the opportunity for effective intervention was lost. Other cases are more difficult.

The patient may have had advanced disease before the disputed event. Life expectancy may already have been limited. Treatment might have prolonged survival without preventing eventual death. Earlier care may have reduced suffering, preserved function, or permitted a more controlled final course rather than producing long-term survival. Several serious conditions may have contributed to death.

In those cases, the clinical question is not simply whether death was preventable. It is what effect the departure probably had on when death occurred and on the course that led to it.

That distinction is essential because wrongful death can describe several different medical realities.

One patient may have been expected to recover and live many more years. Another may have had incurable disease but remained likely to live for months or years. A third may have been near death regardless, while negligent care added pain, emergency intervention, or the loss of meaningful time with family.

The fact of death is the same. The causally attributable loss is not.

When I review a death case with counsel, I separate three questions that are often blended together.

What caused the patient to die? When would the patient probably have died with appropriate care? What would the patient's condition and quality of life probably have been during the period between those two dates?

The first question concerns the mechanism of death. The second concerns acceleration. The third concerns the life that may have been lost between the actual and probable alternative courses.

A death certificate, autopsy, or treating physician may identify sepsis, pulmonary embolism, hemorrhage, cancer, cardiac arrest, respiratory failure, or another immediate cause. That tells us how the body failed. It does not necessarily tell us what role the disputed care played.

The patient may have died from sepsis. The case still requires a determination whether earlier recognition and treatment probably would have prevented that death. The patient may have died from cancer. The issue may be whether delayed diagnosis removed a meaningful period of survival. The patient may have died from postoperative hemorrhage. The disputed question may concern whether the bleeding was avoidable, whether rescue was delayed, or both.

Cause of death begins the causation analysis. It does not complete it.

The underlying disease must also be distinguished from the process that caused death at that time.

A patient with metastatic cancer may ultimately have been expected to die from the disease. If untreated infection caused death months earlier, the cancer remains part of the prognosis but may not explain the timing. A patient with severe heart disease may have had a shortened life expectancy and still die prematurely because a medication error caused fatal bleeding.

The chronic condition may limit the amount of survival lost. It does not establish that no survival was lost.

Descriptions such as terminal, frail, or medically complex are therefore inadequate without more.

Terminal over what period? Frail in which functional sense? Medically complex in a way that made death imminent, or in a way that increased risk while leaving meaningful survival probable? Those questions require clinical answers.

A patient can have incurable disease without being close to death. Someone receiving palliative treatment may remain active, communicative, and expected to live for a substantial period. A nursing-facility resident may require considerable assistance while remaining medically stable and under no immediate threat to life.

Baseline matters as much in death cases as it does in permanent-injury cases.

We need to understand how the patient lived before the disputed event, whether the underlying conditions were stable, which treatment was being received, and what prognosis existed at the time.

Without that foundation, the severity of the final illness can overshadow the life that preceded it.

Consider an older adult with heart failure, kidney disease, and diabetes who develops an untreated infection. By the time of death, the patient may appear profoundly ill, making the outcome seem inevitable. If the patient had been living independently, managing the chronic illnesses, and showing no terminal decline before the infection, the final condition should not be projected backward.

The patient may have had limited reserve. That affects treatment response and long-term prognosis. It does not establish that death would have occurred when it did. The same principle applies in cancer litigation.

The disease may be so advanced at final diagnosis that survival is short even with treatment. The relevant question in a delayed-diagnosis case is what the disease probably looked like when follow-up should have occurred.

Was it localized? Had it already spread? Which treatments would have been available? Was the patient eligible? What survival or disease control was probable?

The causal loss is measured from that earlier point, not solely from the condition at final diagnosis.

Death cases therefore require a disciplined reconstruction of the alternative course.

We cannot compare the actual death with an assumption of ordinary life expectancy unless the medical evidence supports that assumption. Nor should the comparison be made against the most pessimistic possible prognosis merely because serious disease existed.

The alternative course should describe what this patient probably would have experienced with appropriate care.

That may include complete recovery from the acute condition and return to baseline. It may include survival with chronic impairment. It may include successful treatment followed by later recurrence. It may involve additional months or years with progressive disease. It may involve a shorter period of survival with preserved communication, mobility, or time outside the hospital.

The description should be as specific as the evidence allows.

In some cases, the causal conclusion can be stated with substantial confidence. A healthy young adult dies from an untreated but readily reversible condition. The records show a clear treatment opportunity, and expected survival with timely care was high. The departure probably caused the death in the broadest sense. In other cases, the conclusion will be narrower.

A patient with advanced malignancy may have lost a period of survival rather than a normal lifespan. A medically fragile adult may have survived the hospitalization while remaining at increased risk from underlying disease. A newborn may have survived the acute event but faced substantial long-term disability.

The narrower conclusion is not necessarily weak. It is more accurate.

Clinical review should resist the idea that every death case must be framed as either complete prevention or no causation. Medicine rarely operates that cleanly.

A departure may accelerate death. It may reduce survival without allowing an exact duration to be calculated. It may cause one fatal process to occur before another expected process would have. It may remove access to treatment offering substantial but uncertain benefit. It may worsen the final course without changing the ultimate fact of death. Those possibilities need to be separated.

Accelerated death is often misunderstood because the patient's underlying condition remains part of the story. The defense may argue that the patient was going to die anyway. At a sufficiently broad level, that is true of every person and clinically tells us almost nothing.

The useful question is whether the patient probably died sooner because of the departure.

If the answer is yes, the next question is how much sooner and under what conditions.

Sometimes the interval can be estimated through disease stage, treatment response, survival data, prior clinical course, and expert experience. Sometimes only a range can be given. Sometimes the evidence supports material acceleration without permitting a reliable estimate of duration. The uncertainty should be stated honestly.

A precise number of months or years should not be offered simply because the damages analysis would benefit from one. False precision may weaken the opinion.

The inability to provide an exact date does not necessarily mean acceleration cannot be supported.

A physician may be able to conclude that the patient probably would have survived the acute hospitalization and returned to a stable baseline even though long-term survival cannot be predicted precisely. An oncologist may be able to say that earlier treatment probably would have provided materially longer survival without guaranteeing the duration.

The distinction between uncertainty about duration and uncertainty about whether any survival was lost is critical.

If the evidence does not support a reliable conclusion that survival would have been extended, the causal theory is weak. If extension is probable but the precise period is uncertain, the case presents a different issue. Counsel should know which uncertainty is present.

Lost-survival analysis must also address the treatment that would have occurred.

A patient may have had an earlier opportunity for surgery, chemotherapy, radiation, transplant evaluation, anticoagulation, infection treatment, or another intervention.

The expert should explain more than the existence of the treatment. The analysis should address whether the patient probably would have received it and benefited from it.

Was the patient medically eligible? Would the patient have accepted it? Was it available in the relevant setting? What risks did it carry? What outcomes were observed in patients with comparable disease and health status?

The alternative must be clinically real rather than theoretical.

This becomes especially important when a proposed treatment provides meaningful benefit to some patients but not most. The causal opinion cannot simply assume the favorable outcome.

The expert should explain why this patient's characteristics support the conclusion that benefit was probable.

Age alone should not decide that question. Diagnosis alone should not decide it either.

A vigorous seventy-five-year-old may tolerate treatment better than a much younger patient with severe organ dysfunction. Someone with several chronic diagnoses may have excellent performance status. Another person with fewer diagnoses may be too debilitated for aggressive care. The actual patient matters.

Performance status, organ function, cognition, treatment goals, available support, and prior response may all shape the alternative course.

This is where wrongful-death analysis intersects directly with baseline. Prior function helps us understand both what was lost and which treatment and recovery were realistic.

A person who was walking, working, caring for family, and managing ordinary life may have had considerable reserve despite chronic disease. A patient confined to bed with progressive multiorgan failure may have had very little.

The analysis should neither sentimentalize the first patient nor devalue the second. It should describe the probable medical difference.

A frail patient may have had less life expectancy and still lose meaningful life.

That life may have consisted of recognizing family, participating in conversation, experiencing comfort, remaining in familiar surroundings, or taking part in ordinary routines. The analysis does not require independence or employment before survival becomes significant. It asks what remained and what was lost. The manner of death deserves separate attention.

Two courses can both end in death and still differ substantially.

In one, the patient receives timely treatment, stabilizes, returns home, and later dies from underlying disease after a period of meaningful life.

In the other, the patient experiences emergency deterioration, prolonged intensive care, invasive procedures, loss of consciousness, and death before the family can understand or prepare.

The final outcome is death in both courses. The clinical experience is not equivalent.

Earlier care may also have preserved the patient's ability to make decisions that became impossible after deterioration. The patient may have had time to choose treatment, decline burdensome intervention, complete personal affairs, gather family, or arrange hospice.

Those are not substitutes for proving medical causation. They may form part of the injury when the evidence supports that timely diagnosis or communication would have preserved those opportunities. The analysis should remain specific.

Did the patient have decision-making capacity at the earlier point? Would the diagnosis have been known? Would the prognosis have been communicated? Was there a realistic period in which planning could have occurred?

A broad statement that the patient was denied dignity may be emotionally powerful and clinically vague. The record should identify the opportunity that was actually lost.

End-of-life cases require particular care because aggressive treatment is not always the proper counterfactual.

A patient with advanced disease may not have benefited from intubation, surgery, resuscitation, or intensive care. The failure may instead involve delayed recognition that the condition was terminal, inadequate symptom control, failure to communicate prognosis, or care inconsistent with the patient's wishes.

The alternative course may therefore involve better palliation rather than longer survival. That is a distinct theory.

It should not be blended with a claim that death was preventable unless both are independently supported.

A patient may have been likely to die regardless and still endure avoidable pain, agitation, repeated procedures, or separation from family because the situation was not recognized or communicated properly.

The harm in that case concerns the quality and manner of the final period, not necessarily its length.

The analysis should make room for that conclusion without expanding it into complete prevention of death.

The same discipline applies when a do-not-resuscitate order, advance directive, or other treatment limitation existed.

Those documents do not mean the patient consented to negligent care. A decision not to undergo resuscitation does not eliminate the obligation to diagnose, treat, relieve pain, or honor other treatment preferences.

The alternative course must nevertheless reflect the patient's actual choices.

If the patient would not have accepted surgery, mechanical ventilation, transfusion, or another intervention, the causal theory cannot assume that it would have occurred.

The wording and scope of the directive matter. So does the clinical context in which it operated.

A limitation on resuscitation after cardiac arrest is not necessarily a refusal of antibiotics before arrest. A preference for comfort-focused care during terminal illness may not apply to a reversible infection. Refusal of one intervention may leave several others available.

The patient's wishes should be interpreted carefully rather than treated as a broad conclusion.

Maternal-death cases may involve overlapping causation because pregnancy changes physiology and introduces several rapidly progressing risks. Hemorrhage, hypertensive crisis, embolic disease, infection, cardiac complications, and anesthesia-related events may all require consideration. The analysis still follows the same structure.

What caused the death? When did the condition become recognizable? Which intervention remained available? Would timely care probably have preserved the mother's life? Which underlying risks would have remained even with appropriate treatment?

A woman may enter pregnancy with chronic disease and still be expected to survive. A pregnancy-related complication may be serious and treatable. A high-risk pregnancy does not establish that death was unavoidable.

Conversely, a catastrophic event may have been unsurvivable despite rapid intervention. The emotional force of maternal death cannot replace the causal analysis.

The same is true in neonatal and pediatric cases. The death of a child can make every earlier uncertainty feel intolerable. The review still has to determine whether the condition was recognizable, whether treatment existed, and whether survival was probable.

A newborn may have had congenital anomalies or extreme prematurity limiting survival independently of the alleged departure. A child with serious chronic disease may still have had a stable expected course before an acute event.

The baseline and alternative course must remain specific to the child.

What developmental and medical trajectory was expected? Which treatment was realistic? Would survival have meant return to the prior course, survival with additional disability, or only a limited extension of life?

The answer should come from the medicine, not from an assumption that youth guarantees recovery.

Older adults require the opposite caution. Age should not be treated as proof that survival was short or death imminent.

An eighty-five-year-old may have substantial comorbidity and still be expected to live for years. Another may be in active terminal decline. The record should establish which patient is before us.

Life-expectancy tables may provide general context. They cannot substitute for a patient-specific prognosis.

The clinician should consider function, disease burden, recent trajectory, hospitalizations, nutrition, cognition, organ function, and treatment goals.

The question is not how long people of that age live on average. It is what survival was probable for this patient.

The opinion will often involve a range. A range can be clinically responsible when the evidence does not support one date.

An expert might conclude that the patient probably would have survived the acute event and lived at least several more months, with a reasonable possibility of longer survival depending on the underlying disease. Another patient may probably have lived for years.

The language should distinguish what is probable from what is merely possible. The same caution applies to statistical survival evidence.

Population data may show outcomes by disease stage, treatment, age, or risk group. It can help establish that earlier care materially changes prognosis. It does not determine one patient's lifespan.

A median survival figure means that half of the studied population lived longer and half lived less. It is not an individual date of death.

An expert should not treat the median as a personal expiration date.

Counsel should not disregard the data merely because it cannot produce certainty. The figures may be useful when combined with the patient's characteristics and clinical course. The issue is how closely the evidence applies.

Was the patient similar to the studied population? Would the patient have received the same treatment? Did the data concern the relevant disease stage and period? Were the comorbidities materially different? What range of outcomes did the study show?

The numbers should support clinical judgment rather than replace it.

Competing causes assume particular importance in death cases because death is often multifactorial.

A patient may have infection, respiratory failure, cardiac disease, kidney injury, and medication effects at the same time. The final collapse may not be attributable to one process alone.

The expert does not always have to identify one exclusive cause. The opinion should explain whether the alleged departure materially contributed to the fatal sequence.

Did it begin the decline? Prevent rescue? Accelerate a process already underway? Remove a treatment option? Make another condition more difficult to survive?

That explanation may be more credible than an attempt to deny every other contributing factor.

Suppose a patient with severe chronic lung disease develops an unrecognized pulmonary embolism. The lung disease may make the embolism more dangerous and reduce physiological reserve. It may not explain why death occurred at that time. Timely treatment may still have offered survival.

The causal theory should acknowledge that recovery might have been difficult and long-term prognosis limited. It should also explain why the acute death probably was not inevitable. The defense theory should receive the same scrutiny.

A conclusion that the patient would have died soon anyway should rest on more than age, diagnosis, or the severity of the final condition.

What was the course before the event? Was death expected within days, weeks, months, or years? What evidence shows that the underlying disease, rather than the untreated acute condition, probably would have caused death at substantially the same time? Would appropriate treatment have stabilized the patient?

The final critical condition cannot be used to prove that the earlier opportunity was meaningless.

A patient may appear unsalvageable at death because the rescue opportunity was lost. Timing remains decisive.

The closer the patient was to irreversible injury when the departure occurred, the more difficult it may be to establish preventable death. The earlier the patient remained stable, eligible, and likely to respond, the stronger the causal case may be.

The interval should not be measured merely in hours or days.

A brief delay can be fatal in hemorrhage, stroke, airway obstruction, or fetal compromise. A much longer delay may have limited effect in a slowly progressing condition.

Time has clinical meaning only in relation to the process underway.

Counsel should also separate the survival attributable to the departure from the survival already limited by other causes.

A patient may probably have survived the acute event while still facing death from cancer within several years. The causal loss is not necessarily a normal lifespan. It is the life between the actual death and the probable death under appropriate care.

That interval may contain substantial uncertainty. It should still be developed as carefully as possible.

What treatment probably would have followed? What response was expected? Which events were likely during the period? Would the patient have remained independent, required assistance, or undergone burdensome treatment? Would the additional survival have occurred primarily at home, in rehabilitation, or through repeated hospital care? Those facts affect how the loss is understood.

The alternative course should not portray additional survival as uniformly healthy when it probably would not have been. It also should not assume that life with illness had no value.

The task is descriptive. We are trying to identify the probable life the patient lost.

In some cases, that analysis will show that damages should be narrower than first expected. The patient may have lost months rather than decades. Employment loss may have been limited. Significant future care may have been required even under the alternative course.

In other cases, the evidence may show that the patient probably would have returned to a strong baseline and lived for many years. Damages should follow the clinical conclusion.

The same principle applies to the family's loss. Counsel will apply the governing legal categories, but the medical reconstruction defines the period and condition in which the patient probably would have remained alive.

It should not be built from a generic life-expectancy assumption when the patient's health materially affected prognosis.

There will be cases in which medicine cannot support a reliable estimate of lost-survival duration. That limitation should not be concealed.

The evidence may establish that earlier treatment probably would have improved survival without allowing a defensible estimate of how long. The legal significance of that opinion will depend on the jurisdiction and the required proof.

From the clinical perspective, the expert should distinguish what can be said from what cannot.

The patient may probably have survived the immediate hospitalization while long-term prognosis remained uncertain. Treatment may probably have delayed progression while duration varied widely. The evidence may support only a possibility of survival benefit. Those are materially different opinions.

Counsel needs to hear the distinction before the case is valued or presented.

This becomes particularly important when a lost-chance theory may arise. The availability and requirements of that theory vary by jurisdiction, and counsel will determine whether it applies.

Clinically, the expert may be able to describe how the departure reduced the probability of survival or meaningful recovery. That opinion should remain tied to the patient's condition and the relevant evidence.

A statistical reduction in survival does not automatically establish the legal claim. Population probabilities should not be converted into certainty about one person.

The medical contribution is to explain the treatment opportunity, patient eligibility, expected benefit, and change in prognosis. The legal framework comes afterward.

A useful way to test the wrongful-death theory is to state it without using the phrase wrongful death.

The patient had a defined condition. At a particular point, appropriate care required a particular response. The patient remained eligible for an identified intervention. With timely care, the patient probably would have survived the acute event and followed an expected course. Because the care did not occur, the patient instead deteriorated and died when the patient did. The patient therefore lost a defined period or quality of survival.

If that account cannot be stated clearly, the theory may remain too broad.

The same test can be applied to the defense.

At the time of the alleged departure, the patient's condition had already reached a defined stage. The proposed intervention was unavailable, contraindicated, or unlikely to provide meaningful benefit. The underlying process probably would have caused death at substantially the same time despite appropriate care. The departure therefore did not cause or materially accelerate death. That conclusion also requires a clinical foundation.

By the end of the analysis, counsel should know which death case is actually present.

Timely care may probably have prevented death and returned the patient to a meaningful baseline. The patient may probably have lived longer while still facing serious disease. Death may not have been preventable, while the final course was made more painful, invasive, or disordered. The departure may have occurred without changing death or its timing. Those distinctions determine the scope, value, and honesty of the case.

Death can make every medical failure feel absolute. The analysis has to resist that instinct and identify what the patient actually lost.

Sometimes that loss is the remainder of a long life. Sometimes it is a shorter but meaningful period of survival. Sometimes it is the opportunity to receive treatment, make decisions, or spend time with family. Sometimes it is relief from avoidable suffering during the final days.

Sometimes, despite an identifiable failure, the evidence does not support the conclusion that death or its timing was altered.

Defining the loss carefully does not diminish it. It gives the loss a form the medicine can support.

“Defining the loss carefully does not diminish it. It gives the loss a form the medicine can support.”

CHAPTER NINETEEN

Distinguishing New Injury, Aggravation, Acceleration, and Increased Severity

Once causation has been established, the next task is to define the injury precisely enough that the damages analysis rests on the medicine rather than on the emotional force of the outcome.

This is often where an otherwise sound case begins to lose stability. The patient deteriorated after the disputed care, so the entire later condition is attributed to the event. Or the patient had serious pre-existing disease, so everything that followed is treated as inevitable.

Neither position is clinically reliable unless the evidence supports it.

More often, the real issue is whether the departure caused a wholly new injury, worsened a condition that already existed, accelerated a decline that otherwise would have occurred later, or increased the severity, duration, or treatment burden of an injury that could not have been prevented completely.

Those distinctions are not merely matters of terminology. They determine what the experts can support, which future needs can fairly be attributed to the event, and what position counsel can defend without asking the evidence to carry more than it can bear.

The analysis begins, as much of this work does, with the patient's baseline.

We need to know what condition existed before the event, how it affected the patient's life, whether it was stable or progressing, what care was already required, and what course could reasonably have been expected. Only then can we compare the patient's actual post-event condition with the probable course under appropriate care.

The medically attributable injury lies in the difference between those two courses.

Sometimes that difference is obvious. A previously healthy adult sustains an anoxic brain injury after an avoidable airway failure and becomes permanently dependent. There may be little need to separate the later neurological condition from an earlier impairment because no comparable impairment existed. Other cases require far more care.

An older adult may already have had mild cognitive decline before developing severe encephalopathy and lasting neurological impairment after delayed treatment of infection. A patient with chronic kidney disease may later require permanent dialysis after medication toxicity. A nursing-facility resident with limited mobility may develop a pressure injury that progresses to infection and amputation. A child with developmental delay may sustain an additional brain injury that changes an already uncertain developmental course.

Each patient may have suffered substantial harm, but the harm is not described accurately by saying either that the patient was normal before the event or that the same outcome was inevitable. The work is to identify what changed.

That becomes difficult when the records point in different directions. Earlier diagnoses may be broad. Family members may remember the patient's function differently from the chart. Prior imaging may show abnormalities that produced little or no visible impairment. One expert may describe severe pre-existing disease even though the patient had been living independently, while another attributes every later limitation to the new injury without accounting for a decline already underway. Labels are rarely enough.

Dementia, renal disease, vascular disease, developmental delay, frailty, and chronic pain tell us that a condition existed. They do not tell us how it affected the patient. In the same way, brain injury, organ failure, amputation, and disability identify the later diagnosis without describing the degree of loss.

We need to understand the timing, severity, and functional effect of each condition.

A patient with mild dementia may still recognize family, carry on conversations, manage personal care with prompting, and participate actively in daily life. After a new hypoxic injury, that same patient may no longer communicate, eat independently, or respond meaningfully.

The earlier cognitive impairment matters, but it does not explain the entire later condition.

The injury under review is the additional loss of cognition, communication, function, and independence beyond the course that probably would have occurred without the event.

We may call that aggravation, but the word itself does not complete the analysis. The expert still has to describe the earlier impairment, the later impairment, and the difference between them. The same is true of physical function.

A patient with arthritis may have used a cane, walked slowly, and avoided stairs. After a stroke caused or worsened by delayed treatment, the patient may require a wheelchair, assistance with transfers, and help with every activity of daily living.

The arthritis was real and affected mobility before the event, but it did not produce the later level of dependence.

The useful comparison is not whether the patient had difficulty walking before. It is how the post-event limitation differs from the limitation that already existed.

That distinction becomes especially important when life-care planning begins. A future-care plan may attribute every mobility device, attendant-care hour, therapy service, and home modification to the event. If the patient already required some assistance, the plan should separate the prior need from the increase.

That does not diminish the claim. It makes the damages opinion more defensible.

The defense can make the opposite mistake by treating earlier cane use, occasional assistance, or mild memory loss as though those facts explain profound later dependence. They do not.

Needing a cane is not the same as requiring two-person transfers. Help with heavy housekeeping is not the same as continuous supervision. Mild memory impairment is not the same as losing meaningful communication. The comparison has to be made at the level of actual function.

The phrase pre-existing condition can itself create confusion because it suggests one stable entity that existed before the event and continued afterward. In practice, several things may be true at once.

The condition may have been stable. It may have been progressing slowly. It may have made the patient more vulnerable to injury or reduced the likelihood of recovery. The event may have aggravated it, accelerated it, or caused an entirely separate injury on top of it. Those possibilities should not be collapsed into one category.

Consider a patient with chronic kidney disease. Before the event, renal function may have been impaired but stable, without dialysis and without major limitation in daily life. After a medication error or prolonged hypotension, kidney function may decline sharply and never recover.

The later dialysis dependence may represent an acute kidney injury superimposed on chronic disease.

The earlier disease remains important because it made the kidneys more vulnerable and may have reduced the likelihood of recovery. It also affects damages because the patient did not begin with normal renal reserve.

But if the patient probably would not have required dialysis at that time without the event, the later dependence cannot be explained away by saying that kidney disease already existed.

The injury is the transition from stable chronic impairment to permanent dialysis dependence.

The same reasoning applies to cardiac, pulmonary, neurological, and vascular disease.

The event may not create the underlying condition. It may push the patient across a threshold that otherwise would not have been crossed at that time.

Someone with chronic lung disease may have lived independently while using oxygen intermittently, then require continuous oxygen or ventilator support after a preventable respiratory event. A patient with vascular disease may retain a limb despite poor circulation, then require amputation after delayed treatment of infection. A person with an earlier stroke may have mild weakness but remain ambulatory, then become hemiplegic after a new untreated stroke.

The earlier condition shapes the injury. It does not necessarily absorb it. Acceleration presents a related but somewhat different problem.

Aggravation usually concerns degree: the condition became worse. Acceleration concerns timing: the patient reached a condition sooner than probably would have occurred otherwise.

A patient with progressive neurological disease may eventually have required help with daily activities, but an acute injury may bring that dependence forward by years. A patient with severe vascular disease may have faced eventual amputation, but delayed wound treatment may cause the loss to occur now rather than later. A patient with advanced cancer may already have had limited survival, yet delayed diagnosis or treatment may shorten it further.

In those cases, the injury is not always the existence of the final condition. It may be the time lost before that condition probably would have occurred. That time can be medically and functionally significant.

Years of independence do not become meaningless because decline was eventually expected. Months of survival do not disappear because the disease was incurable. Earlier onset of dialysis, institutional care, or severe disability can create substantial additional treatment, expense, and loss of function.

The analysis should therefore address both the probable endpoint and the probable timing.

Would the patient eventually have reached the same condition? If so, when? What function, independence, or survival was probably lost during the interval?

Those questions require restraint because the natural course of chronic disease is rarely exact.

An expert may be able to conclude that dialysis probably would not have been required for several years without identifying a precise date. A neurologist may conclude that a prior condition was slowly progressive and unlikely to produce profound dependence in the near term. An oncologist may offer a range of expected survival under timely treatment.

That uncertainty does not necessarily defeat the opinion. It does require the expert to distinguish what is probable from what is merely possible. False precision is especially risky in acceleration cases.

If the medicine supports the conclusion that institutional care began materially earlier but does not support a precise five-year acceleration, the damages analysis should not quietly adopt five years as fact. Counsel may need to work with ranges, alternative calculations, or a more qualitative presentation, depending on the evidence.

Increased severity is another form of injury that is often overlooked because the case is framed as though the whole outcome had to be either preventable or inevitable. Many cases fit neither extreme.

The patient may have suffered some injury even with appropriate care, while the departure made that injury substantially worse.

A stroke may already have begun before the patient arrived at the hospital. Timely treatment may not have prevented every neurological deficit, but it may have reduced the area of infarction and preserved speech, mobility, or independence.

An infection may already have required surgery, while earlier care probably would have prevented organ failure or a more extensive procedure. A pressure injury may already have developed, while appropriate treatment would have prevented progression into deeper tissue, infection, or amputation. A fetal injury may have begun before intervention was required, while earlier delivery probably would have reduced its severity.

The better question is not whether the entire injury could have been prevented. It is what degree of injury probably would have remained under appropriate care.

That requires the expert to describe two outcomes: the actual injury and the probable lesser injury. The difference may be functional rather than anatomical.

A patient may have suffered a stroke in either course, but with timely treatment might have retained speech and independent walking with mild residual weakness. In the actual course, the patient may be unable to speak or walk.

The diagnosis is the same. The severity is not. The same is true in amputation cases.

One course may have required removal of a toe or forefoot, while the actual course resulted in an above-knee amputation. Both are amputations, but the consequences for mobility, rehabilitation, prosthetic use, energy expenditure, and future care are profoundly different.

Likewise, two children may both require developmental services, but the injury may increase the intensity, duration, and breadth of those services and reduce the independence the child probably would have achieved.

That type of injury can be difficult to explain because the lesser condition never appeared in the actual record. It has to be reconstructed from imaging, timing, treatment response, natural history, comparable outcomes, and expert judgment.

A general statement that the patient would have done better is not enough.

The expert should explain whether the difference involves less tissue injury, more retained function, a shorter hospitalization, greater survival, reduced attendant care, or a less extensive procedure. Duration also matters.

A departure may not change the ultimate outcome but may prolong suffering, hospitalization, disability, or treatment. A patient may have required surgery in either course, but delayed recognition may add weeks of infection, repeated procedures, and rehabilitation. A medication error may cause a serious organ injury that later resolves. A child may endure prolonged pain and immobility before the underlying condition is corrected. Temporary injury remains injury.

It should not be overstated into permanence when recovery occurred, and it should not be dismissed merely because it ended.

The medical analysis should define the period during which the patient's condition differed from the probable alternative course: what symptoms occurred, what treatment was required, what function was lost, when recovery occurred, and whether any residual limitation remained.

That distinction affects damages directly. A temporary injury may support substantial past medical expense, pain, lost income, caregiving, or educational disruption without supporting a lifetime-care claim. Treatment burden deserves similar attention.

Appropriate care may not have prevented the underlying disease but may have reduced the intensity of treatment required. A localized infection may have required oral antibiotics; delayed care may lead to hospitalization, surgery, intravenous medication, and rehabilitation. An early malignancy may have required limited surgery; later-stage disease may require chemotherapy, radiation, extensive resection, or palliative treatment. A small wound may have required routine care; progression may lead to debridement, negative-pressure therapy, prolonged hospitalization, and amputation.

The additional treatment is part of the injury even though the underlying diagnosis would have existed in both courses.

This is often missed because causation is framed only around the final endpoint.

Would the patient have died? Would the patient have lost the limb? Would surgery have been necessary? Those questions matter, but they may be too coarse.

The patient may have required some treatment in either course and still have lost substantially more time, tissue, function, and independence because of the delay.

There are also cases in which the departure causes a wholly separate injury during treatment of an existing condition.

A patient may undergo appropriate surgery for cancer and sustain a preventable nerve injury. The cancer is not the cause of the nerve damage merely because it brought the patient to surgery. A hospitalized patient may have a serious infection and then sustain an avoidable fall. The infection may affect vulnerability, but the orthopedic injury may be new. A child receiving treatment for a congenital disorder may sustain a medication-related injury unrelated to the original diagnosis.

In those cases, the baseline includes the underlying disease and the expected burden of its treatment, while the new injury is evaluated separately.

The question is whether the later condition probably would have occurred as part of the original disease or reasonable treatment even without the departure.

When the answer is no, the injury may be wholly new, although the pre-existing condition may still affect recovery and damages.

A patient with cancer is not expected to sustain every neurological, infectious, or medication-related injury that occurs during treatment. A medically fragile resident is not expected to experience every fall, wound, or infection. An infant born prematurely is not destined for every later impairment. Vulnerability does not mean inevitability.

At the same time, the alternative course must include the treatment, symptoms, limitations, and prognosis that probably would have existed even with reasonable care.

That is particularly important in cancer cases. Earlier diagnosis may have improved survival and reduced treatment burden, while the patient still would have required surgery, chemotherapy, or radiation.

Damages should not attribute all treatment to the delay when some treatment would have occurred in either course.

The additional injury may consist of more extensive treatment, greater toxicity, lost survival, reduced likelihood of remission, or loss of an organ or function that earlier treatment probably would have preserved.

Pediatric cases require special care because the baseline and alternative course are developmental rather than fixed.

A young child may already have had motor or language delay before the event. A later injury may create new deficits, broaden the developmental impairment, or reduce the level of independence the child probably would have achieved.

The child was expected to continue developing, so the analysis cannot be reduced to a fixed before-and-after comparison.

The relevant inquiry is where that development probably would have led and how the event altered the trajectory.

Would the child probably have walked independently, spoken in sentences, attended a mainstream classroom, or required only limited support? Which impairments were already present? Which became more severe? Which are new?

The evidence may come from pediatric and therapy records, school reports, developmental testing, genetics, imaging, family history, and the nature of the injury.

Some projection is unavoidable, but it should remain tied to evidence.

A child with mild delay may still have been expected to achieve substantial independence. A severe congenital disorder may already have created lifelong care needs. The event may increase those needs without creating them from nothing.

Adolescents and young adults present a related problem because much of the expected course still lies ahead.

An adolescent with a chronic condition may already have educational, social, or physical limitations while continuing to move toward independence. A new injury may interrupt schooling, prevent employment, restrict driving, or increase dependence on family.

The baseline should include both current function and emerging capacity.

A seventeen-year-old who has not yet worked full time cannot be treated as though no vocational path existed, but a hoped-for career should not be presented as certain without support.

The medical analysis should define the capacities likely to have developed, leaving vocational and economic experts to address the consequences within their own disciplines.

Older adults are often approached from the opposite direction. Pre-existing disease may be emphasized so heavily that the additional injury disappears.

A patient may have needed help with transportation or household tasks while continuing to live independently. After the event, the patient may require continuous care.

A nursing-facility resident may have depended on staff for bathing and transfers while retaining the ability to eat, communicate, participate in activities, and enjoy family visits. A later injury may eliminate those remaining abilities. A limited baseline can still contain meaningful function. The injury is the loss of what remained. That point matters in both causation and presentation.

A case should not describe the patient as fully independent when the records show otherwise, but it should not allow prior dependence to obscure a profound additional decline.

A careful description is usually more persuasive than an exaggerated one: the patient needed help with transfers but could propel a wheelchair, feed herself, recognize family, and participate in activities; after the event, she became bedbound, unable to eat safely, and minimally responsive. That tells the reader what changed.

The same method applies when the injury is acceleration of death.

A patient may already have had limited life expectancy and still lose a meaningful period of survival. The attributable injury is not the terminal disease itself. It is the earlier death and the life between the actual and probable courses.

The medical expert should define that probable survival and condition as closely as the evidence permits.

The damages analysis should not assume ordinary life expectancy when the medicine supports a shorter period, and it should not assume no loss merely because eventual death was likely.

Another difficult issue arises when the patient's post-event condition changes over time.

The initial injury may be severe, followed by partial recovery. Some limitations may resolve while others remain. A later unrelated condition may further reduce function. Aging or underlying disease may eventually become the principal source of care needs.

The damages analysis should not freeze the patient at the worst point and project that condition indefinitely unless the medicine supports it. The trajectory matters.

What recovery has occurred? What further improvement is expected? When is the condition likely to plateau? Which future needs remain attributable to the event, and which are more likely to arise from aging or earlier disease? That may require longitudinal review rather than one examination.

A patient discharged to rehabilitation in a profoundly impaired state may later regain substantial function. Another may improve briefly and then decline because the underlying injury is progressive or complications develop.

Recognizing recovery does not minimize the earlier suffering. It separates past injury from future impairment.

The same discipline is needed when a second event occurs after the first injury.

A patient may sustain another fall, stroke, infection, or accident that changes the condition further. The later event may be independent, related to the original injury, or made more likely by it.

A patient with injury-related weakness may fall because of that weakness, leaving the later injury within the causal chain. Another may experience an unrelated event that would have produced additional disability regardless.

The damages theory should not automatically attribute every later development to the first departure. It should not treat a foreseeable consequence of the original injury as wholly independent either. The mechanism matters.

For that reason, causation remains active during damages development. New records, rehabilitation outcomes, later diagnoses, and subsequent events may change the understanding of what remains attributable.

In defense work, careful separation of the injury can be one of the most effective ways to evaluate exposure without denying obvious harm.

A defense may acknowledge that the patient experienced a new complication while disputing that every later care need arose from it. It may accept that death was accelerated while disputing the claimed duration. It may recognize a temporary aggravation while showing that the patient eventually returned to baseline. That position is often more persuasive than claiming that nothing changed. The same is true for plaintiff counsel.

A narrower causal claim may support a stronger damages case because each element remains traceable to the evidence.

The patient had some impairment before, but not this impairment. The patient would have needed some care, but not this level of care. The patient faced eventual decline, but not at this time. The patient would have undergone treatment, but not this treatment burden. Those distinctions give the fact finder a reliable comparison.

The experts should be directed to make them explicit.

The causation expert should identify whether the injury is new, aggravated, accelerated, or increased in severity. The rehabilitation expert should work from the same distinction. The life-care planner should separate prior and unavoidable needs from additional needs. The economist should use the survival, employment, and care assumptions supported by the medical evidence.

If each expert relies on a different version of the injury, the damages presentation will become internally inconsistent.

One expert may say that the patient probably would have required assistance within two years, while another projects all attendant care as new for life. A life-care planner may assume permanent ventilator dependence while the treating team expects successful weaning. An economist may calculate full career earnings even though prior disease had already limited work. Those contradictions are preventable.

The litigation team needs one clinically controlled statement of injury.

That statement does not have to be written in technical legal language. It needs to explain the comparison clearly.

Before the event, the patient had a defined condition and level of function. Under appropriate care, the patient probably would have followed a particular course. After the departure, the patient instead developed additional injury, reached a condition sooner, or experienced greater severity.

Some care needs are new or increased. Other limitations probably would have existed in either course. Certain conclusions remain uncertain. That is the foundation on which damages should be built.

There will be cases in which the evidence does not permit a clean separation.

The prior condition may have been poorly documented. Its natural course may be highly variable. The new injury may overlap anatomically and functionally with the old one. Qualified experts may agree that both contributed without being able to assign a precise share. That uncertainty should be stated.

Medical evidence does not always divide injury into neat percentages. An expert may still conclude that the event materially worsened the condition without quantifying the exact proportion.

The clinical analysis should not invent an allocation merely to make damages easier to calculate.

The inability to assign a percentage is not the same as an inability to identify aggravation.

We may know that a patient moved from mild impairment to profound dependence because of a new event without being able to state that a particular percentage of the final condition belongs to one cause.

In those cases, the functional comparison may be more reliable than numerical attribution.

By the end of this stage, the injury should be described in a way that respects both the patient's prior condition and the effect of the departure.

The patient may have sustained a wholly new injury. A stable condition may have been aggravated. An expected decline may have been accelerated. An unavoidable injury may have become more severe. Treatment may have become more extensive. A temporary condition may have lasted longer. Death may have occurred sooner.

The answer will vary from case to case, but the discipline of comparison should remain the same.

We do not measure the patient against perfect health unless perfect health was the actual baseline. We do not treat pre-existing disease as though it made every later loss inevitable. We compare the actual course with the probable course under reasonable care. The difference is the injury the case can support.

"The difference is the injury the case can support."

"The injury becomes real when we describe it at the level of daily life."

“Medical records describe injury in the language of diagnosis.”

PART IV

DAMAGES, EXPERTS, AND LITIGATION STRATEGY

Chapters 20–29

CHAPTER TWENTY

Functional Damages and the Patient's Changed Life

From Diagnosis to Lived Function

Compare the patient's life across three clinical courses

BEFORE EVENT	PROBABLE WITHOUT DEPARTURE	ACTUAL AFTER DEPARTURE
Independent	Slower but manageable	Wheelchair
Independent self-care	Occasional help	Daily assistance
Working full time	Reduced work schedule	Unable to return to work
Living at home	Home with modifications	Skilled-care facility

Medical records describe injury in the language of diagnosis.

They tell us that the patient has hemiparesis, aphasia, cognitive impairment, chronic pain, renal failure, visual loss, a higher-level amputation, or a permanent airway. Those terms matter because they establish the medical condition and help define prognosis. They do not, by themselves, tell us how the patient's life changed. That is the work of functional damages.

A diagnosis tells us what happened to the body. Function tells us what the patient can no longer do, what now requires help, what takes longer, what has become unsafe, and which parts of ordinary life have been lost.

In a serious medical case, that distinction often determines whether damages remain abstract or become understandable.

A patient does not experience moderate executive dysfunction as a test result. The patient experiences an inability to manage medication, follow a recipe, organize transportation, return to work, or remain safely alone.

In the same way, a person does not live with reduced ambulatory capacity as a phrase. The person lives with the inability to reach the bathroom without help, climb the steps into the home, stand long enough to prepare a meal, or leave the house without planning around a wheelchair.

The injury becomes real when we describe it at the level of daily life. That does not mean the analysis should become sentimental or anecdotal.

Functional damages are not a collection of moving stories added after the medical work is complete. They are a clinical comparison between the life the patient probably would have lived and the life the patient now lives.

The same discipline that controlled causation must continue to control damages. We therefore begin with the comparison.

What could the patient do before the event? What probably would have remained possible under appropriate care? What can the patient do now? Which limitations are new, which became worse, which are temporary, and which are likely to remain?

We also need to identify the needs that would have existed regardless of the event.

Until that work is done, a damages presentation may describe suffering without defining the loss that is actually attributable.

When I begin this part of a case with counsel, I usually ask everyone to set the diagnostic labels aside for a moment and walk through an ordinary day.

How does the patient get out of bed? Can the patient stand, transfer, and walk safely? Can the patient bathe, dress, use the toilet, and manage personal hygiene? Can the patient prepare food, swallow safely, and eat independently? Can the patient communicate needs, remember instructions, recognize danger, and make decisions? Can the patient leave the home, drive, work, study, care for children, shop, manage money, or keep appointments?

The most useful question is often the simplest: what has to happen now that did not have to happen before?

That ordinary-day inquiry often reveals more about the injury than pages of diagnosis codes.

It also keeps the analysis from focusing only on the most visible loss.

A patient with severe mobility impairment may also have lost privacy, spontaneity, social confidence, and the ability to care for others. A patient who can still walk may have cognitive or visual limitations that make independent living unsafe. Someone who appears physically recovered may remain unable to return to complex work because attention, processing speed, judgment, or endurance has changed. Function is multidimensional.

Mobility matters, but so do cognition, communication, endurance, sensation, emotional regulation, self-direction, and participation in family and social life.

Two patients with the same diagnosis may therefore have very different functional outcomes.

A language deficit in a trial attorney, teacher, or interpreter may carry a different vocational consequence from a similar anatomical injury in work that places less demand on rapid verbal expression. A hand injury may have particular significance for a surgeon, musician, mechanic, or parent caring for an infant. Mild cognitive impairment may be manageable in a structured environment and disabling in a position requiring independent judgment.

The medical injury has to be translated into the demands of this patient's life. That translation begins with a reliable baseline.

It is not enough to know that the patient was employed or independent. We need to understand what those words meant in practice.

A patient may have worked full time while receiving help with household tasks. Another may have been retired but provided extensive unpaid care to a spouse or grandchild. A nursing-facility resident may already have needed help with bathing and transfers while remaining able to communicate, eat independently, attend activities, and direct personal decisions.

The value of function is not limited to employment or complete physical independence.

A patient can lose meaningful capacities from a baseline that was already limited.

This point is especially important in cases involving older adults and patients with disabilities.

Damages should not be built around an ideal of health the patient never had. They should not be reduced merely because illness or assistance was already part of the patient's life.

The question is what the patient retained and what the event added to the loss.

A resident who needed help with mobility may still have enjoyed meals in the dining room, regular visits, music, conversation, and control over daily routines. After a severe injury, the same resident may become bedbound, unable to communicate, and dependent for feeding.

The earlier limitations matter. They do not make the additional loss insignificant.

Pediatric cases require a more complicated comparison because the child's function was still developing.

A young child may not yet have been able to read, work, drive, or live independently, but those capacities may still have formed part of the probable future.

The analysis therefore has to consider the developmental course reasonably expected before the event.

Was the child meeting milestones? Were there existing delays? What level of communication, mobility, education, and independence was likely? How did the injury alter that course? The answer may involve a range rather than one predicted outcome.

A child may have been likely to achieve broad independence even though no one could identify a future occupation. Another child may already have required educational support while remaining likely to walk, communicate, and manage personal care.

The injury should be measured against the most supportable developmental path, not the most optimistic one.

School records, therapy notes, pediatric assessments, developmental testing, prior imaging, family history, and the nature of the injury may all help define that path.

The damages analysis should not treat every future accomplishment as certain. It should not treat the absence of an adult history as proof that no future capacity was lost.

Adolescents present a similar issue because much of their adult function is beginning to take shape but is not yet complete.

An adolescent may be attending school, playing sports, working part time, beginning to drive, and planning for college or vocational training. A new injury may affect not only current activity but movement toward adult independence.

The case may involve interruption of education, reduced employment options, inability to drive, increased dependence on family, altered social development, or the need for continuing supervision. Those losses require careful support.

A stated ambition is not the same as a probable career, but academic performance, interests, work history, and developmental course can provide a reasonable basis for understanding what was likely.

Function is not confined to earnings. It includes the ability to build an adult life.

For working adults, occupational loss should begin with the actual demands of the job rather than the title.

Manager, nurse, teacher, construction worker, and business owner can conceal very different physical and cognitive responsibilities.

What did the patient actually do during a typical day? How much standing, walking, lifting, concentration, memory, communication, or rapid decision-making did the work require? Could the patient perform part of the role with accommodation? Could the patient return in a reduced capacity? Was employment already affected by prior illness? What does the current prognosis permit? Vocational analysis should follow the functional evidence.

A person may be medically capable of sedentary work in general and still be unable to return to a former occupation requiring sustained attention, rapid processing, or public communication. Another patient may be unable to resume heavy labor while remaining capable of retraining. Those are not purely medical conclusions and usually require vocational expertise.

The medical foundation should nevertheless identify the patient's restrictions, endurance, cognitive abilities, treatment schedule, and prognosis.

The damages team should not assume total occupational disability merely because the prior job cannot be resumed. It should not assume employability merely because some physical capacity remains.

The real question is what work, if any, the patient can perform reliably and competitively.

Reliability matters because a patient may complete a task once during an evaluation and remain unable to perform it repeatedly throughout a workday.

Fatigue, pain, medication effects, slowed processing, fluctuating symptoms, dialysis, therapy, or frequent appointments may make sustained employment unrealistic.

Functional capacity is not the best performance observed under ideal conditions. It is what the patient can maintain safely and consistently.

The same principle applies to activities of daily living.

A patient may technically be able to dress while requiring forty-five minutes, adaptive equipment, rest breaks, and another person nearby. Someone may walk across a clinic with a therapist and still be unable to move safely through the home. A patient may feed himself slowly while being unable to prepare food or recognize aspiration risk.

Independence should not be reduced to whether one movement can be completed.

Safety, consistency, quality, and the time required all matter.

Therapy records are often valuable because physical, occupational, speech, cognitive, and rehabilitation notes describe performance in detail.

They may show how much cueing was required, whether the patient fatigued, what equipment was used, how far the patient could walk, and whether improvement was occurring.

Those records can also be misunderstood if a temporary rehabilitation milestone is treated as the final outcome.

One patient may improve significantly during the first months after injury. Another may plateau. Some abilities may return while others remain impaired.

The damages analysis should follow that trajectory rather than freeze the patient at the worst documented point. The opposite mistake is also common.

A brief gain in a controlled setting may not translate into independence in ordinary life. The question is what the patient can do in the environment where life is actually lived.

The home itself may matter. So may family support, transportation, community access, language, and service availability.

A patient may function reasonably in an accessible apartment with reliable caregivers and poorly in a multilevel home with narrow doors and no nearby support.

Those environmental facts do not change the medical injury. They change what the injury requires.

That is why future-care analysis should not begin with a generic list of services. It should begin with the patient's functional needs in the actual setting.

Functional damages also include the roles the patient performed for others.

A parent may no longer be able to lift a child, attend school events, supervise homework, or respond safely in an emergency. A spouse may no longer provide transportation, household management, emotional support, or physical care. An adult child may have been the principal caregiver for an aging parent. A grandparent may have provided daily childcare. Those contributions may have been unpaid and still central to the household.

The clinical reviewer should not assign an economic value to them, but should identify what the patient can no longer do and whether that limitation is attributable to the injury. The loss may run in both directions.

A patient who once cared for others may now require care from them. A spouse becomes an attendant. An adult child reduces work to provide supervision. A parent manages appointments, medication, equipment, and school services for a child whose needs have become lifelong.

Those consequences belong in the functional picture, but they should be documented rather than assumed.

Who provides the care? Which tasks are performed? How often? What happens when that person is unavailable? Is the assistance temporary, voluntary, sustainable, or medically necessary?

Informal family care can conceal the true level of need because no agency invoice exists.

A patient may appear to have modest expenses only because relatives provide extensive unpaid assistance. The absence of paid care does not establish independence.

At the same time, relatives may provide more help than is clinically necessary because of fear, habit, cultural expectation, or convenience.

A future-care opinion should identify the care reasonably required rather than automatically reproduce every current family practice.

Pain and symptom burden are functional issues as well as subjective complaints.

Pain affects sleep, concentration, movement, mood, work, relationships, and willingness to engage in activity. Fatigue may limit a patient whose measured strength appears adequate. Dizziness, urinary urgency, shortness of breath, bowel dysfunction, sensory loss, and medication side effects may shape daily life even when they are less visible than paralysis or amputation. The useful analysis describes what the symptom does. A pain score alone tells us very little.

We need to know how often the pain occurs, what triggers it, what treatment is required, whether medication helps, which activities are avoided, whether sleep is disrupted, and whether the patient can sit, stand, or concentrate long enough to function. The same is true of fatigue.

Nearly every patient reports fatigue at some point, but clinically significant fatigue may require repeated rest, shorten the usable day, interfere with employment, or make ordinary self-care exhausting. The functional consequence gives the symptom meaning.

Cognitive injury can be especially difficult to present because the patient may appear conversational and physically capable.

A person can speak fluently while being unable to plan, remember, regulate behavior, recognize risk, or manage complex tasks. Family members may describe a profound change in judgment or personality that is not apparent during a brief examination. Those cases require corroboration.

Neuropsychological testing may identify deficits in memory, attention, processing speed, executive function, or emotional control. Therapy records may show the amount of cueing required. Employment records may reveal failed return attempts. Family observations may describe unsafe decisions, repetitive behavior, or loss of initiative. No one source should carry the conclusion automatically.

Testing may be affected by effort, mood, education, language, pain, medication, and prior ability. Family members may attribute every frustration to the injury. Clinicians may underestimate impairment because the patient presents well during a structured visit.

The strongest functional picture emerges when testing, observation, history, and real-world performance point in the same direction. Communication impairment presents similar complexity.

A patient may have difficulty finding words, understanding complex language, reading, writing, or producing clear speech. The patient may answer simple questions and still be unable to participate fully in medical decisions, manage business affairs, return to work, or sustain relationships as before. Communication involves more than speech production.

It includes comprehension, expression, speed, nuance, and the ability to participate in ordinary social exchange.

For a child, communication impairment may alter education and social development. For an adult, it may affect employment, parenting, intimacy, independence, and self-advocacy. For an older person, it may remove the ability to direct care or maintain meaningful connection.

The damages presentation should explain the consequence without turning the condition into a theatrical demonstration.

The most persuasive evidence is often ordinary and specific.

The patient can no longer read a bedtime story without losing the words. The patient cannot follow a group conversation. The patient recognizes family but cannot express basic needs reliably. The patient can speak in short phrases but cannot participate in a professional discussion. Those facts allow the diagnosis to be understood. Loss of autonomy deserves the same precision.

A patient may remain physically capable of many tasks while requiring supervision because of seizure risk, confusion, poor judgment, or sudden instability. Another may make decisions independently but require physical assistance. Those are different forms of dependence.

The damages analysis should distinguish hands-on care, cueing, standby assistance, safety monitoring, and substituted decision-making. Each carries different implications for privacy, dignity, cost, and future care.

Terms such as twenty-four-hour care should therefore be used carefully.

The phrase may mean continuous hands-on assistance. It may mean that another responsible adult needs to be present in the home. It may refer to overnight monitoring because of seizure or airway risk. Those are not interchangeable needs.

A life-care plan built on an undefined phrase can become inflated or clinically incoherent.

The medical evidence should explain what may happen if the patient is left alone, how frequently assistance is required, and what level of training the caregiver needs.

Sexual function, intimacy, and reproductive capacity may also be affected materially by injury, medication, pain, neurological impairment, or psychological change.

These subjects are sometimes omitted because the records are sparse or the discussion is uncomfortable.

They should not be assumed, but they should not be ignored when the evidence supports them.

A spinal injury may affect sensation and sexual function. Pelvic injury may produce pain. Medication may reduce libido or fertility. Cognitive or behavioral changes may affect intimate relationships. Maternal injury may alter future pregnancy. The analysis should remain respectful and evidence-based.

The purpose is not to intrude into private life for dramatic effect, but to recognize that serious injury may affect areas of function that ordinary medical notes rarely explore. Emotional and psychological consequences require the same discipline.

Depression, anxiety, post-traumatic symptoms, grief, irritability, and loss of confidence may follow catastrophic injury. Some may result directly from neurological injury, while others may be understandable responses to pain, dependence, disfigurement, or changed circumstances. The causal pathway should be identified where possible.

Was there a prior mental-health condition? What changed after the event? What treatment has been required? How do the symptoms affect function? Is improvement expected?

A patient may have had depression before the event and still experience a substantial aggravation. Another may develop a new psychiatric condition.

Emotional distress does not become clinically insignificant merely because it is understandable in the circumstances.

At the same time, every expression of sadness or frustration should not be converted into a permanent diagnosis. The evidence should support the level of the claim.

Disfigurement and visible bodily change may affect function beyond appearance.

Amputation, scarring, facial injury, altered gait, a feeding tube, ostomy, or permanent airway may affect clothing, social participation, intimacy, public confidence, employment, and willingness to leave home.

The medical description should not assume the emotional consequence. It should identify the physical change and the practical effects documented for this patient.

Some patients adapt remarkably. Others struggle. Many do both at different times. Adaptation should not be used to deny loss.

A patient who learns to use a prosthesis has not restored the lost limb. A child who develops effective compensatory strategies still lives with the underlying impairment. A spouse who becomes skilled at caregiving does not make the need for care disappear. People often become capable within changed circumstances.

The damages analysis should acknowledge that capacity without treating it as erasure. This matters because improvement and resilience are easily misunderstood in litigation.

The plaintiff may fear that acknowledging progress will weaken the case. The defense may point to activity as proof that the injury is minor. Neither position captures the full picture.

A patient may regain meaningful function and still live with substantial permanent loss. Someone may return to part-time work while being unable to resume a career. A patient may walk with a prosthesis while experiencing pain, skin breakdown, limited endurance, and replacement needs. A person may communicate effectively with family while remaining unable to manage complex decisions independently. The analysis should describe both capacity and limitation. Credibility improves when the patient's achievements are acknowledged.

The same is true when surveillance, social media, photographs, or isolated observations show the patient participating in an activity.

A person may attend a wedding, travel, exercise, or complete a household task without being able to do so regularly, safely, or without significant aftereffects. Context matters.

How long did the activity last? What assistance was used? What recovery followed? Was the activity unusual? Does it contradict the claimed limitation, or only an exaggerated version of the claim?

A sound functional-damages analysis should withstand ordinary evidence that life continued.

Serious injury does not require the patient to become motionless or joyless.

The patient's own account remains central, but it should be considered with the rest of the evidence.

Patients know what they can no longer do and how their lives have changed. They may also have difficulty separating the effects of the event from aging, prior disease, later injury, or emotional response. Memory may be impaired, and expectations may change over time.

That does not make the account unreliable. It means the account should be tested clinically.

Family members, therapists, employers, teachers, caregivers, and treating professionals may each observe a different part of the patient's function.

An employer may describe reduced speed and reliability. A spouse may describe supervision and personality change. A therapist may describe performance during structured tasks. A physician may describe medical restrictions. A teacher may describe lost academic progress.

The full picture often emerges from the convergence of those accounts.

Where they conflict, the conflict should be explored rather than concealed.

A patient may report complete inability to perform a task that therapy notes show can be done with difficulty. A family member may describe constant supervision while the patient spends short periods alone. A clinician may assume independence from self-report despite substantial family assistance.

The apparent inconsistency may lie in how the task is being defined.

Can the patient do it at all? Can it be done safely? Can it be repeated? Can it be done without prompting? Does the effort consume the rest of the day? Those distinctions often resolve the conflict. Functional damages also change over time.

The first weeks after injury may involve hospitalization, intensive treatment, fear, pain, and near-total dependence. Rehabilitation may produce substantial gains. A later plateau may reveal the permanent condition.

Past and future damages should not be built from the same snapshot.

The past course should reflect the burden at each stage. The future course should reflect the best-supported prognosis.

A patient may have required continuous care for six months and now need only part-time assistance. Both facts matter.

Projecting the original level of care indefinitely would overstate future need. Describing only the current condition would erase the severity of the earlier period. The damages account should move with the patient.

Future function may remain uncertain, particularly while recovery is ongoing.

Neurological healing, childhood development, prosthetic adaptation, chronic pain, and psychological recovery may continue over years. Experts may disagree about the likely plateau.

The analysis should distinguish probable improvement from possible improvement and identify the limitations most likely to remain.

A range may be more accurate than one fixed prediction.

Counsel should know whether the patient's future is stable enough for permanent-care opinions or whether planning should account for several plausible courses.

That does not mean the case must wait indefinitely. It means the assumptions should remain visible. Age will also affect future function.

A young adult may adapt well initially but live long enough to experience cumulative joint stress, prosthetic complications, caregiver changes, or repeated equipment replacement. An older adult may have a shorter horizon and less rehabilitation reserve. A child's needs may change dramatically as the body grows and educational demands increase.

The same impairment does not create the same future burden at every age.

A wheelchair user small enough to be lifted by a parent may later require mechanical transfer equipment. A child with mild cognitive deficits may struggle more as schoolwork becomes complex. An amputee may function well in early adulthood and encounter increasing difficulty with age.

The future analysis should consider how the injury interacts with the ordinary life course.

That interaction should not become a means of attributing every future problem to the event.

Aging, unrelated illness, and pre-existing disease will continue to affect the patient. The question remains which future needs were caused, increased, or accelerated by the injury.

A patient may eventually have needed some household help because of age. The event may create that need decades earlier. Another patient may have required medical monitoring regardless but now need a much higher level of assistance.

Future-care and economic experts need a medically grounded distinction between unavoidable and additional needs. Functional damages also matter when the patient died.

The period between the departure and death may involve loss of function, awareness, communication, mobility, or independence. In an accelerated-death case, the alternative period of survival may also need to be described functionally.

Would the patient probably have returned home? Would treatment have preserved consciousness and communication? Would the patient have remained able to work, care for family, or direct personal decisions?

Would the additional survival have involved substantial treatment and dependence?

The lost life should not be described merely as a number of months or years detached from condition.

The medical reconstruction should describe the probable life within that time. It need not predict every future event, but it should provide enough detail to avoid assuming either perfect health or meaningless survival. Counsel should also be alert to double counting.

The same functional loss may appear in several damages categories, including lost earnings, household services, attendant care, loss of independence, and noneconomic harm.

Those categories may be legally distinct, but the medical foundation should make clear which actual limitation underlies them.

The inability to cook may support household assistance and illustrate loss of independence. It remains one functional consequence with several legal implications, not several separate medical injuries.

Clinical analysis does not determine how the damages categories should be presented. It prevents the medical facts from being multiplied artificially.

The same caution applies when several experts address overlapping subjects.

A treating physician may describe restrictions. A rehabilitation specialist may evaluate function. A vocational expert may address work capacity. A life-care planner may identify services. An economist may calculate expense and income loss.

Each should begin with the same underlying functional profile.

If the physician concludes that the patient can remain alone while the life-care planner assumes constant supervision, the case has a problem. If the vocational expert assumes that the patient cannot perform sedentary work while the neuropsychological evidence shows only mild deficits, the inconsistency will be exposed.

The litigation team needs one shared description of what the patient can and cannot do, and that description should remain traceable to evidence.

It is often useful to state the functional injury in plain language before assigning it to any damages category.

Before the event, the patient lived alone, drove, managed medication and finances, prepared meals, and provided regular childcare. The injury left the patient with impaired balance, slowed processing, and poor safety judgment. Personal care can be completed with additional time, but the patient cannot drive, manage complex medication, supervise children, or remain alone overnight. Some physical improvement is expected, while the cognitive-safety limitations are likely to remain. That paragraph gives every later expert a common starting point. Another case may require a different description.

Before the event, the resident needed assistance with bathing and transfers but ate independently, propelled a wheelchair, recognized family, and participated in activities. After the injury, the resident became bedbound, required feeding assistance, and lost meaningful communication. The new dependence and loss of interaction exceed the prior condition, although substantial care needs already existed.

The damages theory becomes precise because the change is visible.

By the end of the functional analysis, counsel should be able to describe the patient's changed life without relying on diagnosis alone and without overstating the baseline.

You should know what the patient could do, what now requires help, which roles have been lost, how symptoms interfere with life, what recovery has occurred, and which limitations are expected to remain.

You should also know which changes belong to the event and which probably would have existed in either course.

The strongest functional presentation is rarely the most dramatic one. It is the one that feels unmistakably true because every part of it can be traced to the patient's actual life.

Scans, laboratory values, diagnoses, and procedures establish the medical event. Function shows what the event took.

"Scans, laboratory values, diagnoses, and procedures establish the medical event. Function shows what the event took."

CHAPTER TWENTY-ONE

Future Care, Life-Care Planning, and Economic Loss

By the time we begin talking seriously about future care, most of the important medical work should already be in place.

We should know where the patient started, what changed, which part of that change can fairly be attributed to the event, and whether the patient is still improving or has reached something close to a stable condition.

When those questions remain unsettled, a life-care plan can become very detailed without becoming very reliable.

It is easy to produce a large number once therapy, equipment, medication, attendant care, transportation, home modifications, replacement schedules, and future procedures are entered into a spreadsheet. The harder question is whether the plan still describes the patient. This is where I would slow the case down.

Before anything is priced, we need to ask what this particular patient will probably need in order to live safely and as fully as the injury permits.

That may sound obvious. It is often lost once several experts become involved and each begins working within a separate discipline.

A diagnosis does not answer the question by itself.

Two patients with the same neurological injury may require very different forms of support. One may be physically dependent but cognitively able to direct care. Another may walk independently but lack the judgment to remain alone. One may live with a spouse who can provide some assistance. Another may have no reliable support. One home may already be accessible, while another makes basic transfers, bathing, and leaving the house difficult.

The plan has to follow the patient's function, environment, prognosis, and likely life course. It cannot simply be borrowed from another plan because the diagnosis looks similar.

When I work through this with counsel, I usually begin with the life the patient is expected to live rather than with a list of services.

Where is the patient likely to live? What can still be done independently? What requires hands-on assistance, and what requires supervision rather than physical help? Are there medical risks requiring trained management? What is likely to improve, what is likely to remain, and how will those needs change as the patient ages?

Once those answers are clear, the plan begins to make clinical sense.

A patient who cannot transfer safely may need physical help, equipment, and accessible space. A patient who cannot manage medication may require supervision even though mobility is good. A child with severe motor impairment may be carried by a parent now, but that arrangement will not remain possible as the child grows. A young adult with an amputation may adapt extremely well and still face decades of prosthetic maintenance, skin problems, replacement components, and secondary stress on other joints. None of those needs is established merely by naming the injury.

Each has to be connected to the way the patient actually functions. We also need to distinguish current care from future care.

The acute and rehabilitation periods often involve a level of treatment that will not continue indefinitely. A patient may attend several therapy sessions each week, see multiple specialists, take temporary medications, and require extensive help during early recovery.

That does not mean every part of the current regimen should be projected at the same frequency for life. A good plan changes as the patient changes.

There may be an intensive rehabilitation period followed by a more stable phase in which therapy becomes less frequent and focuses on maintaining function, preventing complications, or adapting to new equipment. Some specialists may remain involved. Others may discharge the patient once the condition stabilizes. Medication may be tapered, replaced, or continued. Caregiver needs may decrease if function improves or increase later when family support becomes harder to sustain.

When the same level of care is projected uniformly across decades, that usually tells me the plan was built from the present condition rather than from the probable future. Therapy is a good example.

Intensive physical, occupational, speech, or cognitive therapy may be entirely appropriate early in the course. Over time, however, the purpose often changes. Treatment may move from restoration toward maintenance. Periodic reassessment may become more appropriate than continuous weekly visits. A child may need additional therapy during growth spurts or developmental transitions. An adult may need another course after surgery, a change in equipment, or a decline in function.

The plan should explain why therapy is expected to continue and what it is expected to accomplish.

Projecting lifelong therapy simply because therapy is occurring now is not enough. Ending therapy because the patient has reached a plateau may also be wrong.

Some patients require continuing intervention to preserve range of motion, manage spasticity, prevent contracture, train caregivers, or maintain communication strategies. The future frequency should follow the future purpose. Medication needs the same attention.

A post-event chart may contain a long list of prescriptions, but not every medication belongs to the injury, and not every current drug will continue for life.

Some medications treat conditions that existed before the event. Some address temporary postoperative or rehabilitation needs. Others may remain necessary because of permanent neurological, respiratory, pain, seizure, bowel, bladder, or psychiatric consequences.

The useful question is not simply whether the patient takes the medication now. We need to know why it is being taken and how long that reason is expected to continue. That becomes especially important when medication creates additional monitoring.

A drug may require laboratory testing, specialist follow-up, or surveillance for adverse effects. Those related services may be reasonable when the medication is likely to continue, but they should not be projected separately from the treatment that creates the need.

Medical visits should be handled in much the same way.

A patient may see many specialists during the first year after a catastrophic event. That pattern usually changes. Some care becomes routine, some becomes episodic, and some is needed only if a complication develops.

A future-care plan does not have to predict every appointment. It should describe a clinical pattern that makes sense.

For a patient with brain injury, that may include rehabilitation medicine, neurology, primary care, behavioral health, and periodic reassessment of cognition or function. For an amputee, it may include prosthetic management, skin care, rehabilitation, and treatment of secondary musculoskeletal problems. For a child, the relevant specialists and therapy intensity may change as growth, education, and increasing independence create new demands.

The care plan should look like a clinical course, not a subscription schedule.

Equipment is more concrete, but it carries its own risk of overstatement.

A wheelchair, lift, hospital bed, communication device, prosthesis, brace, respiratory machine, or feeding system may be clearly necessary. Even then, the plan has to account for how the patient will use it, how long it is likely to last, when replacement may be needed, and whether the home and caregiver arrangement make the device workable.

The most advanced device is not automatically the right one.

A power wheelchair may increase independence for a patient who can operate it safely. It may be unsuitable for someone with severe visual, motor, or cognitive limitations. A communication device may be valuable only if the patient can learn to use it and has adequate support. A lift may be medically necessary for transfers, but the home needs sufficient space and the caregivers need appropriate training.

Equipment should be selected because it solves an actual problem in the patient's life, not because it appears on a standard list. Replacement schedules also need to be realistic.

A child may outgrow equipment before it wears out. A prosthetic socket may require revision as the residual limb changes. A wheelchair may need repairs, replacement parts, and eventual renewal. A communication device may become obsolete or require updating.

Those are legitimate future needs when long-term use is expected. They should be projected from ordinary clinical and functional experience, not from the shortest possible manufacturer interval.

Home modification can become one of the largest parts of a plan because serious disability often changes what the home must permit.

A patient may need an accessible entrance, wider doors, a usable bathroom, transfer space, a first-floor bedroom, or room for equipment and caregivers.

The need may be clear even when the solution is not.

The current home may be adaptable or structurally impractical. The patient may rent. Relocation may make more sense than major reconstruction. A child may require different space as equipment grows larger. A patient who needs overnight care may require a separate area for the caregiver.

The clinician's role is to identify what the patient must be able to do safely: enter the home, transfer, bathe, use the toilet, sleep, prepare food, and receive care.

An architect or accessibility specialist can determine how those needs should be met, and a cost expert can price the solution. Problems begin when those roles blur.

A physician may properly conclude that the patient needs wheelchair-accessible living space, but that does not necessarily qualify the physician to design or price a residence. A life-care planner may identify accessibility needs without treating every feature of a preferred home as medically necessary.

The analysis is stronger when each expert stays close to the work that expert actually knows.

Transportation presents a similar issue because ordinary life and medical need overlap.

A patient may be unable to drive but still be capable of riding in a standard vehicle. Another may need wheelchair-secure transportation, room for equipment, help entering and leaving, or medical support during travel. A child may need frequent transportation to school, therapy, and specialty care.

The limitation should be identified before the vehicle is selected.

Can the patient transfer into a standard seat? Must the wheelchair remain occupied? Is specialized restraint necessary? Is another driver required because the patient cannot drive? How often will medically related travel occur?

Once the need is clear, the economic analysis can price a reasonable solution.

Without that clarity, a transportation claim can quietly move from an accessibility requirement to the full cost of ordinary family vehicle ownership.

Attendant care is often the most consequential part of future damages because it may continue every day for years. It is also one of the easiest areas to describe too broadly. Twenty-four-hour care can mean several very different things.

One patient may need continuous hands-on assistance. Another may perform most activities but cannot remain alone because of seizure risk, impaired judgment, wandering, aspiration, or inability to respond in an emergency. A third may need physical help at predictable times and someone available overnight. Another may require licensed nursing for airway management, feeding, unstable medication, or complex skin care. Those levels of care are not clinically or economically equivalent.

The plan should explain what the caregiver will actually do.

Does the patient need help getting out of bed, bathing, dressing, toileting, preparing food, transferring, or repositioning? Is supervision required because the patient cannot manage medication or remember safety precautions? Are there nighttime risks? Is one caregiver enough, or do some transfers require two people? Which tasks require a nurse, and which can be performed safely by a trained attendant?

The level of care should come from the work that must be done, not from a general preference for maximum protection.

A plan that uses skilled nursing for tasks safely performed by an attendant will be vulnerable. A plan that assumes unskilled care for complex medical needs may be unsafe.

The correct level lies in the patient's actual needs.

Family care makes the analysis more difficult because the patient may already be receiving substantial support without a formal invoice.

A spouse may supervise overnight. Parents may provide tube feeding, medication management, transfers, respiratory care, and therapy exercises. Adult children may rotate transportation, meals, visits, and personal care. That arrangement can make the need appear smaller than it is.

The patient may seem to require little paid care only because the family has absorbed the work through lost income, interrupted sleep, physical strain, and personal time.

The absence of a bill does not mean the care is unnecessary.

At the same time, we should not automatically project the current family arrangement unchanged across the patient's lifetime.

Caregivers age. Parents who can lift a child may not be able to lift a full-grown adult. Spouses develop health problems. Adult children move away. Relationships change. Someone who provides care voluntarily today may not be able to continue years later.

A serious plan asks whether the arrangement is sustainable.

That does not require assuming that the family will disappear. It means medically necessary care should not depend entirely on one person remaining healthy, available, and willing for decades.

Institutional care may become relevant when the patient's needs cannot be met safely at home, but that conclusion should not be reached automatically.

Some patients with substantial disability can remain at home with appropriate support. Others may need assisted living, skilled nursing, a residential program, or specialized neurological care because of medical complexity, behavior, lack of reliable caregivers, or the intensity of supervision. The right setting depends on the patient.

A less expensive facility is not necessarily capable of providing the care. A more intensive setting is not justified merely because the diagnosis is serious. Home care may preserve family life and autonomy while requiring staffing, space, and coordination that are difficult to maintain.

The plan should compare realistic alternatives rather than assume one setting without explanation.

For children, that comparison has to extend beyond childhood.

Parents may provide extensive care while the child is small, but the physical demands may increase dramatically as the child grows. A small child can be carried and positioned manually. An adult with the same motor impairment may require mechanical lifts, larger equipment, accessible transportation, and more formal caregiving. The services also change over time.

Early therapy may focus on development. The school years bring educational support, communication access, and community mobility. Adulthood may involve vocational programming, supported living, day services, or continued family care.

A pediatric plan should move through those stages. It should not simply multiply the child's current schedule across an entire lifetime.

The same is true for an adolescent approaching adulthood.

School-based services may end. Pediatric providers may transition care. Family supervision may remain necessary after peers become independent. Employment capacity may become clearer, and the patient may need a different living arrangement. Those transitions are part of the future effect of the injury.

Adults present a different set of issues because work, retirement, ordinary aging, and pre-existing disease all intersect with the injury.

A young adult with catastrophic disability may face decades of care and repeated replacement costs. An older adult may have a shorter horizon but less rehabilitation reserve and a greater likelihood that some assistance eventually would have been required even without the event. Future-care planning should not pretend aging has stopped.

A patient may have needed household assistance at eighty even without the injury. The event may create that need at fifty. A person with diabetes may have required medical follow-up regardless but now needs someone else to manage it because of cognitive impairment. A patient with arthritis may eventually have used mobility equipment, but the event creates wheelchair dependence much earlier and at a higher level.

The attributable need may lie in timing, intensity, or type.

That is where the distinction among new injury, aggravation, acceleration, and increased severity becomes practical.

A patient who needed ten hours of help each week before the event and forty afterward has not acquired forty entirely new hours. The event may account for the increase.

A patient who probably would have entered assisted living in later life but now requires skilled care decades earlier has an accelerated and intensified need. A child who already received speech therapy but now requires several therapeutic disciplines and lifelong supervision has an increased scope of care.

The separation will not always be mathematically clean, but it still has to be attempted honestly.

Life expectancy is one of the most important assumptions in this work because every lifetime projection depends on it.

General life tables may provide context. They cannot answer the patient-specific medical question.

The injury may affect survival. So may pre-existing disease, mobility, cognition, respiratory status, feeding, infection risk, seizure control, skin integrity, and the quality of future care.

A patient with stable paraplegia and excellent preventive care may have a very different outlook from a patient with recurrent aspiration, profound cognitive impairment, immobility, and chronic respiratory complications. A child with neurological injury may face a broad range of survival depending on feeding, mobility, respiratory health, and access to skilled care.

The life-expectancy opinion should explain which factors matter for this patient. It also has to be consistent with the proposed care.

A plan that assumes comprehensive preventive care, reliable nursing, proper nutrition, skin management, and respiratory support may support a different survival estimate from one that assumes unstable or inadequate care.

The litigation team should not use one set of assumptions to calculate future care and another to calculate lifespan.

Those opinions have to describe the same future. This is where coordination among experts becomes important.

The physician defines the medical condition and prognosis. The rehabilitation specialist explains function and recovery. The life-care planner identifies reasonable services. The vocational expert evaluates work capacity. The economist calculates cost and loss. Those disciplines overlap, but they are not interchangeable.

An economist should not decide that future surgery is medically necessary. A physician should not invent construction costs. A life-care planner should not determine life expectancy from a generic table without medical support. A vocational expert should not assume cognitive incapacity that the medical evidence does not establish. The assumptions need to remain visible.

The economist's precision can be especially deceptive because the final report may contain exact present-value figures.

Those numbers are only as reliable as the medical and vocational assumptions entered into the calculation.

Therapy projected twice a week rather than once a month can change the total substantially. So can one life-expectancy assumption, one level of attendant care, or one unsupported future procedure.

Counsel should be able to trace the large numbers backward.

What service creates the cost? Why is it needed? How often will it occur? For how long? What evidence supports the frequency? Does the patient need it now? Is the future need probable? Would some of the expense have existed anyway?

Once that trail is visible, the total becomes easier to evaluate.

When the medicine supports more than one plausible future, scenario analysis may be more honest than a single figure.

The patient may require full-time care if cognitive improvement remains limited and part-time assistance if recovery continues. Life expectancy may fall within a range. A future surgery may be probable while its timing remains uncertain.

Different supported scenarios can be calculated without pretending one outcome is guaranteed.

That does not weaken the claim. It shows that uncertainty has been recognized and managed rather than hidden inside the final number.

Lost earnings should be developed with the same discipline.

The medical expert identifies restrictions and prognosis. The vocational expert determines how those restrictions affect actual employment. The economist calculates the financial consequence.

A statement that the patient is disabled usually does not tell us enough.

Disabled from the former occupation or from all competitive work? Temporarily or permanently? Because of physical limitations, cognitive impairment, pain, fatigue, treatment burden, or some combination? The answer matters.

A construction worker who cannot return to heavy labor may remain capable of other employment. A professional who appears physically well may be unable to sustain work requiring judgment, memory, speed, or complex communication. A patient may have enough capacity for part-time work but lack the endurance or reliability needed for a competitive schedule.

Work capacity is not measured by whether the patient can perform a task once. It depends on whether the task can be performed safely, consistently, and predictably over time. Treatment itself may interfere.

Dialysis, therapy, appointments, medication effects, repeated procedures, pain, and fatigue can make otherwise possible work impractical.

The vocational analysis should reflect the patient's actual week.

At the same time, the future-care plan should not create an impossible schedule.

A patient cannot be projected to attend intensive therapy several days a week, work full time, receive full-time attendant care, and undergo frequent medical treatment unless those assumptions can coexist in real life.

Reading the reports together often reveals inconsistencies that are not visible within any one of them.

The same care is required when projecting earnings for young adults, adolescents, and children.

An established work history provides one kind of evidence. A career that had not yet begun requires more judgment.

School performance, education, training, aptitude, interests, part-time work, accepted programs, and concrete plans may support a probable path. A childhood ambition alone cannot establish a specific lifetime income. The absence of an adult work history does not mean no earning capacity was lost. The projection should match the evidence.

For a child with severe injury, the medical evidence may support that independent employment was probable before the event and is now unlikely. In another case, a pre-existing condition may already have limited employment while the event removes the possibility of supported or part-time work.

The loss can be real even when it cannot be tied to one exact occupation.

Household contribution should also be considered because unpaid work often disappears from the financial picture.

A patient may have cooked, cleaned, maintained property, provided transportation, managed finances, cared for children, or assisted an older relative. Those services have value even when no wage was paid. The starting point should remain factual.

What did the patient actually do? How often? What is no longer possible? Who performs the work now?

Someone who occasionally helped around the house should not be described as providing full replacement services. A parent who managed most childcare and household activity should not have that contribution ignored simply because it was unpaid.

The medical analysis identifies the functional loss. The economic expert can value reasonable replacement services where appropriate.

Care must also be taken to avoid double counting.

The same limitation may appear in attendant care, household services, lost earnings, and noneconomic damages. Those may be separate legal categories, but the underlying functional loss should remain identifiable.

The inability to prepare meals may create a need for assistance and also illustrate lost independence. It should not become several different medical injuries merely because it supports more than one damages category.

Future procedures and complications deserve particular scrutiny because they can add very large costs to a plan.

A revision surgery, prosthetic replacement, hardware removal, joint reconstruction, scar procedure, or another intervention may be probable. It may also be only a recognized possibility.

Many things could happen over a lifetime. A future-care plan should not price all of them as though they will.

The opinion should explain what makes the procedure likely for this patient.

Is there evidence of deterioration? Is revision ordinarily required within a predictable interval? Does growth make replacement inevitable? Has a treating specialist recommended it? Do age, anatomy, or equipment use materially increase the likelihood?

When the event is only possible, that uncertainty should remain visible.

Complications should be handled in much the same way.

A patient may be at increased risk of pressure injury, aspiration, infection, contracture, falls, or hospitalization. Preventive care may clearly be necessary. It does not follow that every possible complication should be assumed to occur and fully costed.

A plan should not project the failure of the preventive care it also recommends unless the complication remains probable despite that care. Scenario analysis may be useful here.

The primary plan may include prevention and routine management, with possible complications discussed separately rather than inserted into the main total as inevitable events.

Current insurance coverage or public benefits should not determine whether care is medically necessary.

A service may be needed even when it is not covered. A service may be covered now without any assurance that coverage will continue. The clinical question is what the patient requires.

The legal treatment of collateral sources, public programs, and payment responsibility belongs to counsel. The medical plan should not be distorted to fit the current payer.

The absence of current care, however, may need explanation.

A patient may not be receiving a recommended service because of cost, access, family burden, geography, or lack of insurance. That absence does not prove the service is unnecessary.

A recommendation first made during litigation should still be examined carefully.

Treating clinicians may not have had the role or opportunity to design a comprehensive lifetime plan, so a new recommendation is not inherently suspect. It should nevertheless be grounded in the patient's condition, accepted care, and a realistic expectation that the service will actually be used.

The plan should not become a catalog of every intervention that might be beneficial. Defense review should use the same patient-centered approach.

It is not enough to say that a life-care plan is too expensive. A meaningful critique identifies where the plan no longer matches the patient.

Perhaps the attendant-care level exceeds the functional need. Perhaps services are duplicated. Perhaps current intensive therapy has been projected indefinitely. Perhaps a future procedure is possible but not probable. Perhaps the plan assigns every age-related need to the event. Perhaps the proposed living arrangement does not fit the patient's abilities or preferences.

A defense plan becomes more credible when it acknowledges genuine needs and explains where the disagreement actually lies. The same is true for plaintiff counsel.

A larger plan is not automatically a stronger one. One conspicuously unsupported item can undermine confidence in the rest.

A disciplined plan may produce a lower total and a more persuasive case because every major component can be explained in ordinary language.

The patient cannot transfer safely, so assistance and equipment are required. The patient cannot remain alone, so supervision is necessary. The child will outgrow current equipment, so replacement and renewed therapy are expected. The patient cannot return to former employment and has limited alternative capacity.

Those connections do not need dramatic presentation. They make sense because they follow the patient.

By mediation or trial, counsel should be able to explain the future without beginning with the total cost.

Where will the patient live? What help will be required? What medical care is expected? Which equipment will need replacement? What function may improve, and which limitations are likely to remain? What work is still possible? How long is the course expected to continue?

Once those questions are answered, the financial calculation has clinical meaning.

The number should follow the life being described. It should not become the organizing theory of the case.

We are not trying to imagine every service the patient might use or every expense that might arise. We are reconstructing the most probable future from the medical evidence available now.

The baseline tells us which needs likely would have existed anyway. The causation analysis tells us what the event added. The functional analysis tells us how daily life changed. Future-care planning identifies what is reasonably required to support that changed life, and economic analysis measures the financial consequence.

When those parts remain connected, the projection can tolerate uncertainty without becoming speculative.

It can acknowledge that recovery may continue, family support may change, ordinary aging will occur, and some future events cannot be predicted precisely.

What it cannot do is allow exact figures to conceal uncertain medicine.

A sound future-care analysis does more than produce a large total.

It gives counsel a coherent account of the patient's future: what care will be needed, why it will be needed, when it is likely to change, and which part of that burden belongs to the event. That is the future the case can responsibly claim.

"That is the future the case can responsibly claim."

CHAPTER TWENTY-TWO

Selecting and Directing the Correct Experts

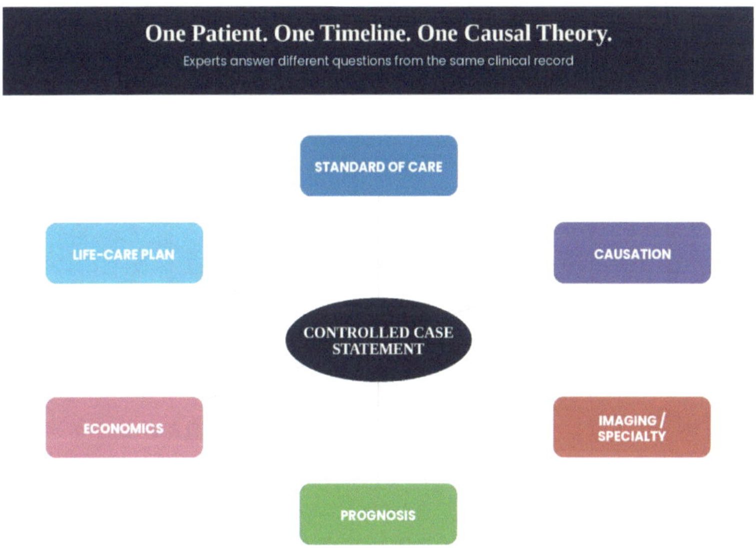

Expert selection often begins with an understandable shortcut.

Counsel sees the defendant's specialty and starts looking for a physician with the same title.

Sometimes that is exactly right. Just as often, it answers only one part of the case.

A surgeon may be the proper person to discuss whether an operation was indicated and performed reasonably while having no useful basis to reconstruct a nursing escalation failure, interpret disputed imaging, explain medication toxicity, or address whether earlier treatment probably would have preserved neurological function.

A radiologist may identify what was visible on a scan and still be the wrong person to say what an emergency physician should have done with the patient's full presentation. A treating specialist may understand the disease in great depth and have little experience with the practical decisions made in the setting under review.

Cases become unstable when one expert is asked to carry questions belonging to several disciplines, not because the expert is careless, but because the case was never divided into its actual clinical parts.

By the time we begin looking seriously for experts, we should know enough about the case to avoid that problem.

We should understand the patient's baseline, the objective evidence, the material timeline, the workflow, the professional obligation in dispute, the treatment opportunity, the probable alternative course, and the injury being claimed.

Once those pieces are visible, the expert needs usually become much easier to identify.

Without that preliminary work, selection tends to be driven by the defendant's title or the final diagnosis. Either can send counsel in the wrong direction.

A delayed-stroke case may seem to call for a neurologist, and it may. The initial evaluation may require an emergency physician. Disputed imaging may require a neuroradiologist. Treatment eligibility may call for a vascular neurologist or an interventional specialist who actually makes those decisions.

A postoperative-death case may require a surgeon to address the complication and response, a critical-care physician to explain deterioration and rescue, and perhaps a nursing expert to address bedside monitoring and escalation. That does not mean every case needs a collection of experts. The number is not the point.

The question is whether each material issue has someone genuinely qualified to answer it.

Sometimes one expert can address several related subjects without difficulty. In other cases, trying to save money by forcing one person beyond the limits of actual experience creates a much larger problem later.

The opposite can also happen. Too many experts can fragment the theory, increase expense, and leave everyone speaking about a slightly different version of the case.

I would separate the questions before searching for names.

What clinical decisions are alleged to have been unreasonable? Who made them? What specialty or role ordinarily performs that work? Is there objective evidence requiring independent interpretation? What treatment would have followed? Who can explain whether that treatment remained available and what benefit it probably offered? Are there functional or future-care questions falling outside the treating specialty?

Once those questions are written down, the expert structure often becomes fairly obvious.

Consider a patient who returns repeatedly to an emergency department with headache, dizziness, and evolving neurological symptoms and is later diagnosed with a posterior-circulation stroke.

At first glance, the case may look like a simple failure to diagnose. It rarely is.

The emergency physician may need to address the differential diagnosis, examination, disposition, and reassessment. A neuroradiologist may be required if the earlier imaging is disputed. A neurologist may explain the significance of the symptoms and the natural progression of the stroke. If causation depends on a time-sensitive intervention, someone familiar with that intervention may need to address whether the patient was eligible and what benefit probably remained.

One neurologist may be able to answer several of those questions. That does not mean the neurologist should automatically answer all of them.

Institutional cases raise the same problem in another form.

A physician may understand the consequences of a missed result but have little experience with how an organization assigns, tracks, and closes results. A nursing expert may understand bedside escalation and handoffs but know very little about the design of an electronic result-management system. An administrator may understand policy and workflow but be unable to connect a process failure to the patient's clinical decline.

The institutional theory should not be handed to the nearest clinician simply because that person is willing to discuss it. Willingness is not the same as fit.

Some physicians are comfortable offering broad opinions across specialties. Some have spent years in litigation and know how to speak confidently about almost any medical issue.

Confidence may be useful. It can also hide the fact that the opinion rests on general familiarity rather than current practice, actual training, or responsibility for the decision under review. The question is not whether the expert understands the medicine broadly.

It is whether the expert has a credible basis to define the obligation, interpret the evidence, and explain the probable outcome in the particular setting involved.

A specialist who routinely receives patients after transfer may know the definitive treatment extremely well while knowing less about the thresholds faced by the referring clinician. A physician practicing at a major academic center may have immediate access to consultants, imaging, and intervention that did not exist in the defendant's setting. A retired clinician may have extensive experience but limited familiarity with the technology, systems, or practice patterns in use at the time of the event. None of those facts automatically disqualifies the expert.

They tell counsel where the fit is strong and where explanation will be needed.

I would want to know how closely the expert's actual work resembles the decision being examined.

Does this person treat comparable patients? Practice in a similar setting? Make the disputed decision personally? Supervise the professionals whose conduct is at issue? Was the expert actively practicing during the relevant period? Can the expert explain how resources and workflow differ among institutions?

The closer the practical match, the easier it becomes for the opinion to sound like clinical judgment rather than litigation judgment.

An exact match is not always possible, and it is not always necessary.

Medicine overlaps. A well-qualified expert can understand a different environment.

What matters is knowing where the expert is speaking from direct experience and where the expert is relying on a broader understanding of the field.

Credentials need to be viewed in the same way.

An impressive title may help, but it does not answer whether the person is right for the issue.

A department chair may have exceptional academic standing and little recent hands-on practice. A nationally known researcher may understand disease biology better than almost anyone and have limited experience with ordinary bedside decisions. A community physician may have fewer publications and much more familiarity with the type of setting in which the event occurred.

The strongest expert is not always the most famous one.

It is usually the person who understands the records, remains within the discipline, explains the reasoning clearly, and can withstand serious questioning without overstating the opinion.

Litigation experience can help, although I would not make it the defining qualification.

An expert who has testified many times may understand reports, depositions, and the pressure of direct examination. That experience has value. It may also produce habits that make the testimony sound rehearsed, absolute, or more legal than clinical.

A clinician who is new to litigation may sound more natural and still have difficulty with the demands of legal proof. The person may qualify every conclusion so heavily that the opinion becomes unusable, become uncomfortable with hypothetical questions, or fail to appreciate how a disputed assumption changes the analysis. Neither profile is automatically better.

Counsel has to decide whether the expert can translate clinical judgment into reliable testimony without allowing the litigation process to reshape the medicine.

The first substantive conversation should therefore be more than an introduction and a discussion of fees. It should show us how the person thinks.

I would not begin by giving the expert the entire theory and asking whether it is correct.

I would provide the essential facts, identify the clinical issues, and listen.

What does the expert notice? What appears important? What is missing? Where does the record support a conclusion, and where does it not?

An expert who immediately adopts counsel's framing may be correct. I would still pay attention to how quickly it happened.

The most useful experts often complicate the case before they simplify it.

They notice a baseline condition that was overlooked. They question the assumed treatment window. They identify a technical limitation in the imaging. They distinguish a reasonable initial decision from a later failure to reassess. They explain that the injury being claimed is broader than the medicine supports. That can feel unhelpful when counsel is looking for confirmation.

In practice, it may be the most valuable part of the review.

An expert who narrows the theory early may keep the case from becoming indefensible later.

I would not look for a favorable opinion before looking for a sound one.

The search for support can quietly change the question from "What does the medicine show?" to "Who will say this was negligence?"

Once that happens, expert selection has become advocacy by another name.

There will be cases in which qualified professionals disagree. Consulting more than one expert may be entirely appropriate when the issue lies near the boundary of accepted judgment.

But if several well-qualified experts reject the same theory, continuing to search may not be an expert-selection problem. The medicine may simply not support the case.

Counsel needs to be able to hear that conclusion.

A good preliminary review should also be candid about the limits of the record.

The expert may need original imaging, prior records, audit data, pathology material, monitor strips, medication information, or testimony before reaching a firm view. That is different from being unable to form any opinion.

The important distinction is between evidence that is necessary and evidence that would merely be helpful.

An expert should not postpone every conclusion until discovery is complete when the available material already answers the central question. The expert should not give a definitive opinion while important source material remains missing. The level of confidence should match the record. This is where counsel's direction matters.

Experts need enough structure to review efficiently, but not so much structure that it becomes a script.

Sending an entire production with the instruction to "tell me what you think" is rarely an efficient use of anyone's time. Sending only selected records with a memorandum explaining the preferred theory is equally dangerous.

The expert should receive enough material to understand the full clinical picture, including evidence that challenges the position counsel may prefer.

That may include prior and later records, original imaging, laboratory trends, policies, deposition testimony, and competing opinions.

The expert does not need every duplicate page or administrative document at the outset. The expert does need enough to avoid building an opinion on an incomplete patient.

A focused cover letter or review memorandum can be useful when it identifies the questions rather than suggests the answers.

What did the earlier imaging show? When did the condition become clinically recognizable? What treatment remained available at that point? Was the patient eligible? What outcome was probable with appropriate care? Which later limitations are attributable to the event rather than to the patient's baseline? Those are legitimate questions.

"Please confirm that the delay caused the stroke" is not.

The difference may seem small, but it changes the relationship.

The expert should be directed toward the issue, not toward counsel's conclusion.

Chronologies and summaries can help in the same way, provided the sources remain visible.

A carefully prepared clinical timeline may save hours and allow the expert to see progression. A baseline summary may orient the review. A list of disputed facts may prevent assumptions from becoming invisible. Those materials should support the records, not replace them.

The expert should know which facts come directly from the chart, which come from testimony, which remain disputed, and which are simply working assumptions.

When counsel's summary smooths over conflict, the expert may form an opinion based on a sequence the evidence does not actually establish. That becomes especially dangerous when timing controls the case.

A chronology may state that a physician was notified at three because one note says so, while another entry places the call at 3:40. A medication may be listed as administered when it was only ordered. Symptom onset may come from a later family recollection rather than a contemporaneous note. Those differences should not disappear inside counsel's summary.

A reliable memorandum can identify the source and uncertainty without turning into a brief. Hypothetical questions are useful for the same reason.

Experts often need to address more than one factual scenario because testimony or records conflict.

If the physician was notified at three, what is the opinion? If notification occurred at 3:40, does the conclusion change? If the patient's last-known-well time was noon rather than two, what treatment remained available?

Those alternatives tell counsel whether the opinion is stable or whether it depends on one disputed fact.

A conditional opinion is not necessarily a weak opinion.

It may be more honest than a single conclusion built on an assumption no one has proved.

What counsel needs to know is which fact changes the answer.

That knowledge shapes discovery. It tells us where deposition time should be spent and which records matter most. It also protects the case from being surprised later by a factual change that quietly destroys the expert's reasoning. Expert roles should also remain clinically distinct.

The standard-of-care expert should explain the professional obligation and departure. The causation expert should explain what probably changed because of it. Damages experts should begin with the causal injury already defined.

Those roles may overlap in practice. A physician may be qualified to address both breach and causation.

There is nothing wrong with that so long as the reasoning remains separate.

The problem begins when an expert says the care was negligent because the patient had a bad outcome, or that the outcome was caused by negligence because the care was unreasonable. Those statements simply circle back to one another.

Counsel should ask the expert to walk through the steps.

What made the care unreasonable at the time? What would appropriate care have involved? What was the patient's condition then? What benefit was still probable? What injury was added?

If the expert cannot explain those steps without relying on the final outcome, the opinion may be driven by hindsight.

Defense experts should be tested in exactly the same way.

Saying the diagnosis was difficult does not answer whether the process of evaluation and reassessment was reasonable. Saying the outcome was inevitable because the patient was critically ill at the end does not answer whether the patient was treatable when the disputed conduct occurred.

A strong defense expert should be able to explain why the decision remained within the reasonable professional range and why the proposed alternative probably would not have produced a meaningful benefit.

The opinion should not rest on general uncertainty or on the severity of the final condition.

I would also pay close attention to what the expert does with inconvenient facts.

A plaintiff expert who dismisses every normal finding, period of improvement, or competing cause will be vulnerable. A defense expert who minimizes obvious deterioration or refuses to acknowledge a clear process failure will be equally vulnerable. Credible experts do not avoid the record. They explain it.

They may say a favorable fact does not change the conclusion or that an unfavorable fact narrows the opinion.

What they should not do is pretend the fact is absent. That quality often matters more than forceful language.

An expert who says the initial discharge may have been reasonable but the return visit was different may be more persuasive than someone who criticizes every encounter.

An expert who acknowledges that some injury had already occurred but explains why earlier treatment probably would have reduced its severity may give counsel a stronger case than someone promising complete prevention.

The narrower opinion is often the one that survives.

Report preparation is another point at which counsel can either sharpen the work or distort it.

The expert should understand the applicable legal standard and reporting requirements, but the report should remain the expert's reasoning.

Counsel may identify a missing issue, unclear language, unsupported assumption, or internal inconsistency. Counsel should not supply the clinical explanation.

A report that reads like a legal brief may make the expert appear less independent. A report that merely states conclusions without explaining how they were reached leaves counsel exposed in deposition.

A sound report usually identifies the important records and assumptions, explains the patient's clinical course, defines the professional obligation or causal issue, addresses the significant contrary evidence, and states the conclusion at the level the medicine supports. It does not need to reproduce the chart.

It does need to show how the expert moved from the evidence to the opinion.

That reasoning should be understandable to a lawyer who is not a physician.

When the opinion can be understood only through medical jargon, the expert may not yet have worked through the explanation clearly enough. Simplifying the language does not dilute the medicine.

A complex stroke mechanism, infection course, medication interaction, or surgical complication can be explained in ordinary language without sacrificing accuracy.

An expert who cannot do that may struggle in deposition or at trial even if the medical knowledge is exceptional.

Counsel should listen for that ability before retaining the witness.

Can the expert explain the case across a table? Answer a direct question without turning it into a lecture? Say "I do not know" without becoming defensive? Distinguish probability from possibility? Stay clear when factual assumptions are challenged? Those skills matter because litigation compresses complicated medicine into pressured exchanges.

An expert may be brilliant in conference and evasive under questioning. Another may speak plainly, remain within the discipline, and make difficult medicine understandable.

Preparation should preserve that strength rather than turn the expert into a performer.

The purpose of deposition preparation is to make the expert familiar with the record, the assumptions, the limits of the opinion, and the likely areas of challenge. It is not to teach the witness a set of phrases. Rehearsed testimony nearly always sounds rehearsed.

The expert should be able to explain the opinion in more than one way because questions will not arrive in the order counsel prefers.

The expert should also understand the weakest part of the case and be prepared to address it directly. Avoiding the weakness does not make it disappear.

If onset time is uncertain, the expert should know how the opinion changes across the plausible range. If the patient had serious comorbidity, the expert should explain its effect on prognosis. If the literature is mixed, the expert should acknowledge that and explain why the patient-specific conclusion remains supportable. That is preparation grounded in the medicine. Experts also need clear boundaries.

A radiologist should not drift into emergency-department discharge standards unless actually qualified to do so. A life-care planner should not become the principal causation witness. A treating physician should not be pushed into a legal opinion outside the treating role simply because the physician knows the patient.

Those boundaries protect credibility and reduce the risk that experts will contradict one another.

If several experts are retained, they should work from the same factual foundation.

They do not need to agree about every clinical nuance, but they should not unknowingly be describing different timelines, different injuries, or different patients.

The causation expert should know the breach point identified by the standard-of-care expert. The life-care planner should know which injuries the causation expert attributes to the event. The vocational expert should know the medical restrictions and prognosis. The economist should know which scenarios are actually supported. Coordination does not mean manufacturing agreement. It means preventing accidental inconsistency.

Suppose the standard-of-care expert says surgery should have occurred at four while the causation expert assumes it should have occurred at noon. The life-care planner then attributes all resulting impairment to the delay. Each report may appear reasonable on its own. Together, they do not describe the same case. Counsel has to find that problem before disclosure. Prognosis can create the same kind of conflict.

A rehabilitation expert may expect substantial improvement while the life-care planner projects the current care level for life and the vocational expert assumes permanent total disability. Those opinions cannot simply sit next to one another without examination. Sometimes better communication resolves the issue. Sometimes the experts genuinely disagree.

When they do, counsel needs to know whether the disagreement affects the central theory. Experts should not be pushed into artificial consensus.

A medical disagreement that is understood can be managed. One discovered for the first time in deposition can be devastating. Treating clinicians present a different set of considerations.

They may have valuable knowledge of the patient's present condition, response to treatment, prognosis, and functional needs. They may also have limited familiarity with the complete litigation record and may not see themselves as expert witnesses.

A treating physician's opinion can carry natural credibility because it arose from care rather than litigation. That does not mean the opinion answers every question.

The physician may understand the current condition but have no basis to reconstruct the earlier breach. The physician may recommend a service without considering lifetime frequency or cost. The physician may be reluctant to criticize another professional or address what might have happened at an earlier stage.

Counsel should use treating clinicians for the questions they can genuinely answer.

Trying to turn every treater into a comprehensive expert can create confusion, strain the professional relationship, and produce opinions based on incomplete facts. Clinical consultants present another distinction.

They can be extremely helpful in understanding the records, preparing discovery, selecting experts, and testing theories. Their role may not be the same as that of a testifying expert.

A consulting expert may explore possibilities more freely, identify weaknesses, and help counsel shape the case without committing to a final disclosed opinion. A testifying expert eventually has to state conclusions capable of withstanding disclosure and examination.

The same person may perform both roles in some cases. In others, keeping them separate allows the clinical discussion to remain more candid.

Counsel should decide which role is needed before the engagement begins.

Cost will always affect expert selection, but economy should be judged against the clinical question.

One broad expert may appear less expensive than two more precise experts. If that person is later excluded, impeached, or unable to support a central link, the savings disappear.

Retaining several experts without a defined need can be just as wasteful and may obscure the theory.

The most efficient structure is usually the one that answers the material questions with the fewest necessary disciplines. That requires enough preliminary clinical work before substantial expert spending begins.

Early review can show which questions do not require separate testimony, which records should be obtained first, and whether causation is strong enough to justify full development. It may also show that the case should stop.

An expert should not be retained simply because money has already been spent.

An unfavorable opinion should not automatically be treated as a problem to solve by finding another expert before counsel understands why the review was unfavorable.

Was the record incomplete? Did the expert rely on a mistaken assumption? Is there legitimate disagreement within the specialty? Or does the medicine not support the theory? Those situations call for different responses.

One may justify further review. Another may require narrowing. Another may mean the case should not continue.

The relationship between counsel and the expert should make that level of candor possible.

If the expert believes counsel wants only favorable conclusions, the expert may become less direct. If counsel treats every concern as resistance, much of the value of the review is lost. The best relationship is professional rather than promotional.

Counsel asks clear questions, provides complete material, tests the reasoning, and respects the answer. The expert remains independent, responsive, and willing to revise an opinion when the evidence changes. That last point is important.

Experts sometimes act as though changing an opinion is inherently damaging. It can be damaging when the change appears strategic or unexplained.

A medically responsible opinion should change when the factual foundation changes.

A new image may show that the injury existed earlier. A deposition may establish a different notification time. Pathology may alter staging. Additional records may reveal a contraindication or a more accurate baseline.

The expert should not preserve the original opinion merely for the appearance of consistency. The change should be explained.

What new information was received? How did it affect the reasoning? Which conclusions remain? That is intellectual honesty, not weakness.

Counsel should expect the same flexibility from the litigation team.

A theory should not become fixed simply because experts have been retained around it. New evidence may change the standard-of-care analysis, treatment opportunity, causation, injury, or damages.

The expert process has to allow the case to move when the evidence moves.

By the end of selection, counsel should be able to explain why each expert is present.

Not merely the specialty, but the question that person answers.

One expert may define the defendant's professional obligation. Another may interpret objective evidence. Another may explain treatment eligibility and probable outcome. Another may address function, future care, or economic loss.

Those opinions should connect, but they should not overlap so broadly that no one can tell where one discipline ends and another begins.

Counsel should also know the limits of each opinion.

What assumptions does it depend on? What evidence could change it? What lies outside the expert's discipline? Where is the strongest professional disagreement? Can the conclusion be explained without exaggeration?

Those questions belong to expert selection. They should not be discovered for the first time during deposition preparation.

The right expert does more than support a case. The right expert makes the case clearer.

That person tells counsel what the medicine permits, what it does not permit, and where uncertainty remains. The expert helps turn records into a clinical explanation without allowing advocacy to become medicine.

That is the person worth retaining—not simply the person most willing to testify, but the one whose reasoning allows the case to remain true when it is placed under pressure.

“That is the person worth retaining—not simply the person most willing to testify, but the one whose reasoning allows the case to remain true when it is placed under pressure.”

CHAPTER TWENTY-THREE

Using Clinical Intelligence in Discovery

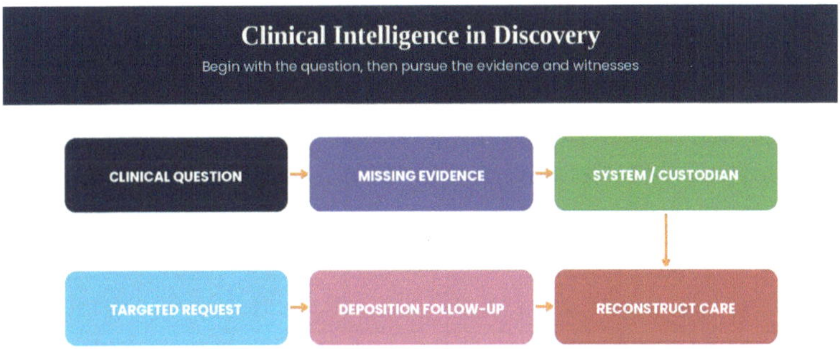

Discovery becomes expensive very quickly when the clinical theory is still unsettled.

Requests begin to expand because counsel does not yet know which records actually matter. Depositions are noticed because a person's name appears repeatedly in the chart. Interrogatories ask broad questions about staffing, supervision, training, policies, and communication without first identifying the clinical failure those subjects are supposed to explain.

By the time the case reaches expert review, the file may be much larger and the cost considerably higher, while the central question remains the same one that existed at intake: what happened to this patient, when did it become clinically consequential, and who still had a meaningful opportunity to change the course? That is where I would begin discovery.

Clinical Intelligence is not intended to turn discovery into a rigid sequence. It helps counsel decide which evidence is worth pursuing, who is likely to possess it, and whether the answer could materially change the case.

That distinction matters because medical litigation rarely suffers from a shortage of documents. More often, it suffers from a lack of clinical organization.

A hospital may produce thousands of pages and still omit the evidence needed to understand one critical hour. The chart may include the final imaging report but not the study itself. It may say that a physician was notified without telling us what was communicated. It may contain a medication order while leaving the administration time uncertain. It may show that a referral was entered without revealing whether anyone was responsible for seeing that it was completed.

A large production can look complete while leaving the clinical pathway unresolved.

Before serving another request, I would ask what the present theory still needs to know.

That requires some restraint because not every uncertainty deserves formal discovery. Some questions can be answered through prior records, objective evidence, or expert interpretation. Others may be interesting without having much effect on liability or causation.

Counsel should be able to explain why the missing evidence matters before asking someone to produce it.

Suppose the case involves postoperative deterioration. The existing record already shows persistent hypotension, falling hemoglobin, worsening pain, and eventual emergency surgery. What remains uncertain is whether the surgeon was informed when the pattern first became concerning. That uncertainty matters because it affects timing, responsibility, and breach. Discovery should follow it directly.

Who observed the change? What was reported? How was the message sent? When did it reach the surgeon or covering clinician? What instruction followed? Was the instruction carried out? When the patient remained unstable, was that reported again?

Those questions will usually tell us more than a general request for every communication policy in effect at the hospital.

The policy may matter later. The patient's actual pathway comes first.

This is one of the practical benefits of reconstructing the timeline and workflow before broad discovery begins. Once counsel understands the clinical sequence, it becomes easier to see where the evidence grows thin.

A chart entry may suggest one timeline while the medication record or audit history suggests another. A witness may resolve the discrepancy. A system record may show that a communication everyone assumed had occurred never took place at all. The unresolved clinical point should drive the request.

A baseline issue may require earlier primary-care, therapy, employment, school, or home-health records. An imaging issue may require original DICOM studies, technical data, preliminary readings, or comparison studies. A timing issue may require monitor data, audit logs, transport records, laboratory collection times, or medication-administration details. A workflow issue may require routing records, call logs, coverage schedules, inbox assignments, or referral queues. Those categories differ because the clinical questions differ.

A request for the complete chart will not necessarily reach any of them.

That phrase usually refers to the medical record maintained for patient care. It may not include device data, internal routing information, audit history, staffing assignments, pharmacy workflow, or material housed in a separate departmental system.

An institution may produce what it considers the legal health record and still omit evidence central to understanding how care was actually delivered.

Counsel therefore needs some understanding of where the relevant work was documented.

If the case concerns a critical imaging result, where did the final report go? Was there a separate alert system? Did the radiologist document direct communication in another application? Did the result route to the ordering clinician, a team inbox, or a departmental pool? Was acknowledgment required, and what happened if no one acknowledged it?

If the case concerns medication delivery, did the infusion pump preserve rate and volume data? Were there barcode scans, pharmacy-verification records, alert overrides, waste records, or a downtime process?

If the case concerns deterioration, did the bedside monitor retain waveforms or only periodic values transferred into the chart? Were rapid-response calls recorded elsewhere? Was there a paper handoff tool that never became part of the permanent record?

Discovery should follow the system that performed the work.

That may require learning something about the architecture before demanding every possible record.

A corporate witness, information-technology representative, records custodian, department leader, or knowledgeable clinician may be needed to explain where information resides and what the system captures.

Counsel does not need to become an electronic-record engineer. Counsel does need to know whether the requested evidence exists and what it can reliably prove.

Audit trails are a useful example because they can be powerful and still be overread.

An audit record may show that a user entered the chart, opened a result, placed an order, modified a note, or viewed a particular screen. It may help establish when information became available or whether documentation was entered later.

It does not always tell us what the person actually saw, understood, or decided.

A clinician may open a chart without reviewing every result. A result may appear automatically on a screen without being read. A user may remain logged in while someone else performs the work. A system may distinguish finalization, transmission, viewing, and acknowledgment in ways that are not obvious from the raw data.

For that reason, I would obtain audit evidence with a specific question in mind and have it interpreted by someone familiar with the platform.

Otherwise, the data can create more confidence than knowledge. The same caution applies to timestamps generally.

Medical systems often use several clocks, and those clocks may not be synchronized. A monitor, laboratory analyzer, medication cabinet, ambulance system, operating-room log, and electronic record may each assign time differently.

A difference of several minutes may be irrelevant in one case and decisive in another.

Before building an argument around a precise time, counsel should know what the timestamp represents.

Was it the moment the action occurred, the moment the device stored it, the moment it was transmitted, or the moment someone later finalized the entry?

Discovery can answer that, but only when the question is asked directly.

Original imaging should be pursued early whenever the dispute involves visibility, timing, progression, or mechanism.

The written report is not an adequate substitute when the real issue is what the study showed.

Even that apparently routine request can create practical problems. Only selected images may be produced. A study may be compressed or exported without all sequences. Earlier comparison studies may be missing. Images imported from another facility may not be included. A specialized reconstruction available to the treating team may never appear in the production.

The reviewing expert should be asked whether the material received is technically complete.

Counsel should not learn during deposition that the expert reviewed only screenshots or an incomplete series.

Pathology should be approached in much the same way.

When diagnosis, disease characteristics, timing, or causation depends on tissue evidence, the written report may not be enough. Slides, blocks, photographs, staining records, or outside consultation material may be necessary.

The expert should identify what is needed and why.

A broad demand for every pathology item may add little when diagnosis is uncontested. It may be indispensable when the biological process itself is disputed.

Discovery should follow the controversy rather than the category.

Laboratory cases often require less exotic evidence and more careful sequencing.

The chart may show a result time while omitting collection, receipt, processing, verification, and notification. If delay is alleged, those distinctions matter.

A test may have been ordered at ten, collected at 10:40, processed at 11:15, verified at 11:30, and reviewed at noon. Each point may involve a different part of the workflow.

Was collection late? Was processing unusually slow? Was the critical value communicated? Did the responsible clinician review it? Did action follow?

A useful request should be capable of locating the answer along that chain.

Counsel should also know when the existing record has answered enough.

It is easy to keep requesting operational information after the material point is already clear. Discovery eventually produces diminishing returns.

A new record should resolve a meaningful uncertainty, test a competing explanation, establish responsibility, or affect the probable outcome.

When it does none of those things, it may enlarge the file without improving the case. Policies are a common example.

Once a possible system failure appears, the temptation is to request every policy concerning communication, staffing, training, supervision, emergency response, medication, documentation, and quality assurance.

I would begin instead with the failed clinical pathway.

If the case involves a missed abnormal result, the relevant material may include the result-management policy, coverage process, unresolved-task procedure, role descriptions, and system configuration. A general policy on patient communication may contribute very little.

If the case involves delayed escalation from a nursing unit, the useful material may concern assessment frequency, rapid response, chain of command, physician notification, and staffing assignments during the relevant period.

The request should identify the safeguard that may have failed.

That approach controls volume, but it also helps the institutional witness understand the subject and makes it more difficult to bury the operational issue inside a broad, nonresponsive answer.

The policy should also be the version in effect at the time.

A current policy may differ substantially because of a later software change, merger, accreditation review, or adverse event. The same is true of related forms, training documents, workflow instructions, and screen prompts.

The formal policy may state the rule while the operational material shows how staff were expected to carry it out.

The written policy and the actual process should be compared rather than assumed to match.

Staffing discovery also needs to remain connected to the patient.

Raw ratios may not tell us whether this patient received reasonable monitoring and response. The relevant evidence may include assignments, patient acuity, staff qualifications, break coverage, admissions and transfers, temporary personnel, or access to specialty support.

Even then, the question is what clinical function the staffing condition allegedly prevented.

Was the patient not reassessed? Was medication delayed? Was a critical change missed? Was no qualified person available to perform the necessary task?

A general claim that a unit was understaffed is difficult to prove and easy to defend when it is never connected to an identifiable failure in care.

The medical theory should make that connection before discovery expands around it. Employment and personnel records require the same discipline.

Counsel may need information about role, training, scope, competence, or schedule, but the request should be linked to the task at issue.

When the case concerns unfamiliar equipment, training on that equipment may matter. When the issue is failure to use the chain of command, escalation training may matter. When someone acted outside an assigned role, scope and supervision may matter.

A broad demand for every prior complaint, evaluation, or disciplinary event may create proportionality and privacy disputes while adding very little to the clinical case.

The useful question is what this person needed to know or do during this event and whether the institution reasonably prepared and authorized that person to do it. Written interrogatories should follow the same logic.

Medical cases are often burdened with questions asking the defendant to identify every person involved, every communication, every policy, every fact supporting every denial, and every basis for each defense.

Some breadth is unavoidable. More focused questions are usually more revealing.

Who was responsible for reviewing this result after the ordering clinician left the practice? What process identified results that remained unacknowledged? Who was expected to reassess the patient after the intervention failed to improve blood pressure? What information was available to the covering clinician before discharge? Who had authority to initiate transfer? Those questions arise from the actual pathway of care.

They may still draw objections, but they make it harder for the responding party to conceal the operational issue inside general language.

Requests for admission can be useful when they establish undisputed clinical building blocks rather than demand a concession on the entire case.

The study was completed at a particular time. The result was available in the system. The patient met a defined criterion. No follow-up appointment was scheduled. The medication had not been administered by a particular time. The facility lacked the capability to perform the proposed intervention. Those facts may simplify later proof.

A request asking the defendant to admit negligence, causation, or institutional failure will predictably be denied and often adds little.

The more useful approach is to establish the sequence from which counsel can later argue the legal conclusion.

Discovery should also test the opposing medical theory before expert disclosures arrive.

If the defense is that the patient's underlying disease made the outcome inevitable, counsel should identify the factual basis for that position.

What condition is said to have caused the outcome? When did it become irreversible? Why would the proposed treatment not have worked? Which objective findings support that conclusion? Was the patient ineligible for the intervention?

The defense may not be required to provide a complete expert opinion through interrogatories, but the factual foundation of the position can still be explored.

That information may tell counsel whether additional records or another expert discipline will be needed. The same principle applies in the other direction.

Defense counsel should understand the plaintiff's claimed treatment opportunity at a practical level.

What treatment would have occurred? When and where? Who would have provided it? What benefit is claimed? Which part of the final condition would probably have been prevented?

Earlier treatment should not remain an undefined phrase throughout discovery.

The clearer the alternative course becomes, the more efficiently it can be tested.

Third-party discovery may also become important because some of the most useful records are often outside the defendant's chart.

Earlier clinicians may hold baseline evidence. A receiving hospital may document the patient's condition more accurately than the transferring facility. An outside radiology group may retain preliminary reports or communication records. A pharmacy may have dispensing data. Emergency medical services may document onset, observations, and treatment before arrival. Schools, employers, rehabilitation facilities, or home-health agencies may show function before and after the event. That discovery should still remain clinically directed.

A damages claim does not justify a broad examination of the patient's entire life.

The records should bear on baseline, causation, prognosis, function, or the probable alternative course. This is particularly important when the material involves mental health, reproductive care, substance use, education, or unrelated medical conditions.

A diagnosis does not make every prior record relevant.

The question is whether the material could change our understanding of the injury, treatment eligibility, life expectancy, baseline, or a competing cause.

Clinical Intelligence supports proportionate discovery because it gives counsel a reason for requesting a particular record and, just as importantly, a reason for declining to request one.

The same organization should continue after the production arrives.

A large production should not simply be read from beginning to end without a plan. Counsel or the clinical reviewer should know which unanswered questions the documents were expected to address.

Did the material clarify onset? Did it establish when a result became available? Did it identify the responsible person? Did it show that treatment was actually administered? Did it change the baseline or support a competing cause?

A production log organized around those issues may be far more useful than another general chart summary.

New evidence should then be fed back into the clinical theory.

Suppose audit data shows that the physician viewed the result earlier than the narrative record suggested. That may strengthen breach while narrowing the communication issue.

Suppose the original images show that the condition was already advanced. That may weaken the treatment opportunity.

Suppose earlier therapy notes establish substantial pre-event dependence. That may change damages without changing liability. Discovery should be allowed to change the case.

It is not simply a process for gathering support for a conclusion selected at the beginning.

Sometimes that means difficult conversations with the client or experts. A claim may become narrower after expensive discovery. One defendant may become less important. A damages assumption may no longer hold. A defense may become less credible when operational evidence contradicts the chart. Those developments do not mean discovery failed. They mean it did what it was supposed to do.

Discovery exists to reveal the case, not to preserve its first draft. Expert involvement can help considerably when used carefully.

A clinical consultant may identify which evidence is necessary before depositions and which issues can wait. The expert may know that original imaging is indispensable while a particular policy is unlikely to matter. Another may recognize a laboratory, pharmacy, or device record that counsel would not otherwise know to request.

Experts should not control discovery strategy, but they can keep counsel from asking the wrong technical question.

I would also avoid sending an expert every new document as soon as it arrives without explaining why it matters. Incremental review quickly becomes expensive and disorganized.

It is usually better to identify the new issue, provide the relevant material, and ask whether it changes a defined opinion.

Does the new onset history affect treatment eligibility? Does the audit record change the notification sequence? Do the earlier records alter baseline or prognosis? Does the policy clarify responsibility? That keeps expert work connected to the evolving case. Depositions should be sequenced for the same reason.

The order should follow what counsel needs to learn, not simply the institutional hierarchy.

A bedside witness may establish the patient's condition and the substance of a communication. A systems witness may then clarify routing and timestamps. A clinician can be examined afterward with a more accurate understanding of what information was available.

In another case, the treating decision-maker may need to be deposed first because that testimony will determine whether an institutional inquiry is necessary. There is no universal order.

The better sequence is the one that reduces uncertainty before the next witness is examined. That becomes particularly important in cases with several defendants.

Each witness may point to someone else. The nurse says the physician was called. The physician says the nurse did not convey urgency. The consultant says the primary team remained responsible. The primary team says the consultant was managing the issue. The institution says the policy assigned the task clearly.

Without prior workflow reconstruction, the depositions may become a series of vague referrals.

Responsibility should not be allowed to disappear between professional roles.

Clinical preparation also improves the selection of deposition exhibits.

Rather than moving through a thick chart page by page, counsel can use the documents marking transitions in the patient's course: the earlier baseline note, the first objective sign of deterioration, the result that changed the differential diagnosis, the communication entry, the unimplemented order, or the later study showing progression.

Those documents tell the clinical story and place the witness at the moment when the decision mattered.

The witness should not be asked to interpret evidence outside that witness's role.

A nurse should not be asked for a radiology opinion. A systems witness should not be asked to decide causation.

The exhibit should establish what the witness knew, what the witness controlled, what action followed, and whether the changing pattern affected the obligation.

A developed clinical theory also helps counsel recognize which issues not to pursue.

The chart may contain a technical documentation error that had no effect on care. A policy may have been violated in a way unrelated to the injury. A witness may have behaved poorly while contributing little to causation. A communication may be absent from the record even though later conduct shows that the information was received promptly. Not every imperfection deserves a discovery campaign.

Collateral issues can dilute the strongest theory and give the opposing side an opportunity to portray the case as an attack on every aspect of care.

Counsel should know which facts matter enough to carry into deposition and which should remain background. That judgment becomes easier when the case has a clinical center.

For plaintiff counsel, that center may be the final interval during which rescue remained probable. Discovery should establish what was known, who knew it, what action was required, and why it did not occur.

For defense counsel, the center may be that the patient's presentation remained nonspecific until the treatment opportunity had already narrowed, or that an appropriate response occurred promptly once meaningful signs appeared. Discovery should establish that progression just as honestly.

The process is the same even though the preferred conclusion differs.

By the close of fact discovery, the case should be more clinically defined than it was at the beginning.

Counsel should know which facts are established, which remain disputed, and which cannot be resolved. The material timeline should be reliable enough for expert analysis. Responsibility should be assigned to actual roles.

The treatment opportunity should be tied to a realistic sequence. The principal competing cause should be understood. Injury and damages assumptions should reflect the evidence produced.

If discovery has not improved those parts of the case, more discovery may not be the answer. The problem may be the theory.

A useful discovery record does not contain every document that could possibly have been obtained.

It contains enough reliable evidence to reconstruct the patient's course, test the important alternatives, and show where professional responsibility did or did not change the outcome. That is the practical use of Clinical Intelligence in discovery.

It turns requests into questions, productions into evidence, and depositions into a reconstruction of care rather than another recitation of the chart.

"It turns requests into questions, productions into evidence, and depositions into a reconstruction of care rather than another recitation of the chart."

CHAPTER TWENTY-FOUR

Preparing Clinically Effective Depositions

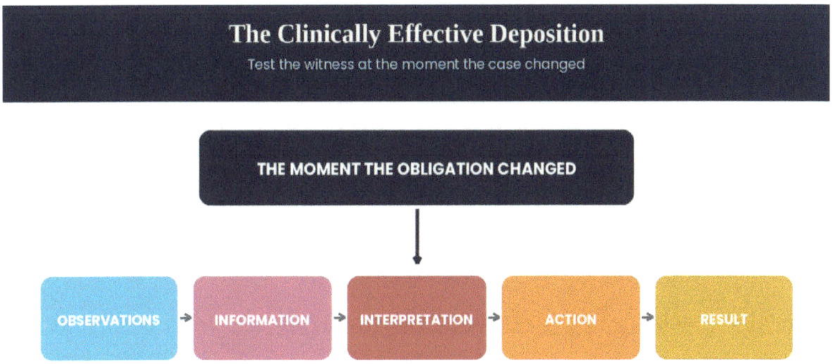

A medical deposition can look productive while yielding very little.

The witness confirms the chart. Policies are marked. Education, training, role, and routine practice are covered. Several hours pass, the transcript becomes substantial, and yet the clinical question that matters most remains unanswered:

What did this witness understand about the patient's condition at the moment the case changed? That is the question around which I would build the examination.

The purpose is not to obtain agreement that patient safety matters, communication is important, or a worsening patient requires attention. Those propositions are rarely disputed.

The useful testimony lies in how the witness perceived this patient, what information reached the witness, what meaning the witness gave it, and what action followed.

Preparation therefore begins with the clinical theory, not with a standard deposition outline.

By this point in the case, counsel should understand the patient's baseline, objective findings, material timeline, workflow, alleged departure, and treatment opportunity.

The deposition becomes a way of testing that reconstruction against the person who participated in the care.

The testimony may confirm the theory. It may also expose an assumption the record does not support.

The witness may have received less information than counsel believed, or more. A decision may have been made and never documented. The disputed delay may have occurred somewhere other than where the pleadings placed it.

A deposition is most valuable when counsel is prepared to let the case change. That requires more than familiarity with the chart.

Counsel needs to know which facts are already established, which remain disputed, and which answers would materially affect liability or causation.

If the case concerns deterioration, the key issue may be what was reported to the physician. If it concerns discharge, the issue may be whether the patient remained unstable or failed to respond as expected. If it concerns delayed diagnosis, the issue may be which diagnoses were under consideration and why further testing was not pursued. If it concerns an abnormal result, the question may be who owned follow-up and what the witness believed had already occurred.

Those are different depositions, even when the witnesses work in the same institution and appear throughout the same chart.

A bedside nurse should usually be approached through observation, monitoring, communication, implementation, and escalation.

A physician should be approached through assessment, differential diagnosis, interpretation, decision-making, reassessment, and response.

A radiologist should be examined through study quality, interpretation, communication, and the limits of what the images establish.

An institutional witness should be approached through workflow, responsibility, coverage, safeguards, and actual operation. The witness's clinical role should shape the examination.

That sounds elementary, but medical cases often blur roles because several professionals had access to portions of the same record.

A physician is asked to explain a nursing policy never used in the physician's work. A nurse is pressed to interpret imaging. A radiologist is asked what treatment should have followed. A corporate witness is asked to defend an individual practitioner's clinical judgment. Those questions may produce answers. They do not necessarily produce reliable evidence.

The better approach keeps each witness close to what that person knew, controlled, and was expected to do.

To prepare the examination, counsel should be able to tell the patient's clinical story without reading the chronology.

Who was the patient before the encounter? Why did the patient seek care? What was initially believed to be happening? What objective evidence supported or challenged that belief? When did the course change?

What treatment or rescue remained available? Where did the process fail, if it failed at all?

That internal command of the case allows counsel to recognize an important answer even when it arrives unexpectedly.

Without it, the examination becomes dependent on prepared questions.

The witness gives an answer that changes the sequence, but counsel moves to the next page because the outline says to do so.

Some of the most useful testimony appears in the space between planned questions.

A witness may say, “I was not concerned until the second blood-pressure reading.” That answer should change the examination.

Why did the second reading matter? What was different by then? Did the witness know that urine output had also fallen? Was the patient reassessed? Who was notified? What response was expected? How long did the concern continue before further escalation?

The original subject may have been one vital sign. The answer may open the real clinical interval.

A deposition needs enough structure to remain controlled and enough flexibility to follow meaning. The record remains central, but it should not dictate the examination mechanically.

Reading every entry aloud and asking whether it is accurate rarely reconstructs care. A witness may confirm dozens of pages without explaining how any decision was made.

The chart should be used at the point where it helps define a clinical issue.

A nursing note may be introduced when discussing the first observed change. A laboratory trend may be used when asking why the working diagnosis remained unchanged. An imaging report may help establish what information became available. A medication-administration record may distinguish an order from treatment actually received. The exhibit should do some work.

It should orient the witness to the moment, test memory, establish what was available, expose inconsistency, or clarify responsibility.

When it does none of those things, counsel may not need it.

This matters particularly in a long hospitalization, where the chart can overwhelm the examination.

A witness who cared for the patient during one shift does not need to be taken through every later complication. The initial focus should be the period that witness actually influenced.

What was the patient's condition when the witness assumed care? What information was handed off? Which concerns were active? What did the witness observe personally? What changed during the shift? What remained unresolved when responsibility passed to someone else?

That sequence will usually produce more useful testimony than asking the witness to endorse the final outcome.

Personal knowledge also needs to be separated from later understanding.

A clinician may now know that the patient had a stroke, infection, hemorrhage, or medication toxicity. At the time, the diagnosis may have been uncertain.

The deposition needs both perspectives, but they should not be confused.

What did the witness know then? What does the witness understand now? Does the later diagnosis change how the earlier findings are interpreted? Would the witness have acted differently with information that became available later?

That final question may be useful, but it does not establish that the information should have been known earlier.

Hindsight should be made visible rather than allowed to enter silently.

This becomes especially important when a witness uses the final diagnosis to explain earlier care.

A clinician may now say the symptoms were obviously caused by a stroke, even though the chart shows that a different diagnosis was considered at the time.

Another may insist that the symptoms were nonspecific because the diagnosis proved difficult, despite focal findings in the record that were never reconciled.

Counsel should return the witness to the contemporaneous picture.

At that time, what findings were present? Which diagnoses did they support? What did not fit? What would have caused the witness to broaden the evaluation? Did that change occur?

The point is not to insist that the clinician should have known the final answer.

It is to understand whether the clinical process remained reasonable as the evidence developed. Differential diagnosis is often explored too abstractly.

Asking a physician to list every possible cause of a symptom can produce a long and largely useless answer.

The more important question is which conditions were reasonably under consideration for this patient and how that affected care.

A broad differential is not necessarily a careful one.

The witness may say that stroke, infection, medication effect, dehydration, and anxiety were all possible. Counsel should then ask what supported each possibility, what argued against it, and what was done to distinguish among them.

Did the examination address the dangerous alternative? Was the chosen test capable of evaluating it? Was the patient observed long enough to determine whether the expected course occurred? Were the return precautions directed to the unresolved risk? That is where clinical judgment becomes examinable.

Counsel does not need to prove that the witness failed to write a complete academic differential.

The issue is whether the professional accounted reasonably for conditions that could not safely be missed.

Reassessment deserves the same attention because many cases turn not on the original decision but on what happened when the patient failed to improve.

A witness may say the patient was reassessed, and the chart may contain another note. That does not tell us what was reconsidered.

What changed after the first evaluation? What treatment had been given? What response was expected? Did the patient respond that way? Was the examination repeated? Were new findings addressed? Did the working diagnosis remain the same, and if so, why?

The examination should move beyond whether reassessment occurred and reach what the reassessment actually involved.

A second note may simply repeat the original conclusion without integrating new evidence.

Conversely, sparse documentation may accompany a meaningful bedside evaluation.

Testimony, treatment changes, orders, and the surrounding record may help distinguish the two.

That distinction is often more important than whether the note contains every phrase counsel would have preferred.

Communication testimony also requires more than establishing that a call occurred.

The entry "physician notified" can conceal almost the entire case.

The sender may have reported one isolated value, a general concern, or the full pattern of deterioration. The receiving clinician may have understood something quite different from what the sender intended. The message has to be reconstructed.

What prompted the call? What information was conveyed? Were trends discussed, or only the latest value? Was the patient's response to treatment included? Did the witness communicate urgency? What instruction followed? Was the instruction clarified or repeated back? Did the sender believe the concern had been resolved? If the patient remained unstable, what happened next?

Those questions allow communication to be evaluated clinically rather than merely documented as an event.

A nurse may have made an appropriate initial notification and still have had a further obligation to escalate when the patient continued to deteriorate.

A physician may have responded reasonably to the information received even though the patient's full condition was more serious.

A brief message may have minimized a complex pattern. An urgent call may have been misunderstood.

Responsibility cannot be assigned fairly until the content of the communication is known.

When the witness has little independent memory, routine practice may become relevant.

Medical professionals often testify that they ordinarily would have performed an assessment, conveyed a concern, or given an instruction in a particular way. That testimony may help, but it should not be confused with memory.

Do you remember this patient? Do you remember the conversation? Are you relying on the chart? Are you describing what you normally do? Is there anything in the record confirming that the usual practice occurred here?

A clinician may genuinely have no independent recollection several years later. That is entirely ordinary.

The transcript should still distinguish testimony about this event from testimony about habit. That becomes particularly important when routine practice conflicts with objective evidence.

A witness may say urgent medication is always given immediately while the administration record shows a delay. A physician may say all critical results are personally reviewed while routing data shows the result entered a shared pool. A nurse may say persistent hypotension always triggers escalation while the chart shows no escalation for hours.

Counsel does not need to argue about the routine.

Counsel needs to determine what happened in this case. Documentation gaps should also be approached carefully.

It is tempting to ask the witness to agree that if something was not charted, it did not happen.

Most clinicians will resist that proposition, often for legitimate reasons. Not every clinical act is documented perfectly.

A stronger examination asks what would ordinarily be recorded, why the documentation matters, and what other evidence would usually accompany the act.

Would a neurological examination normally be charted? Would an urgent consultation generate an order, note, or billing record? Would medication administration appear electronically? Would a direct critical-result call be documented by the radiologist? Would reassessment after a serious change ordinarily produce new findings, instructions, or orders?

The absence of documentation becomes more meaningful once the expected footprint of the action is understood.

Late entries, amendments, and copied documentation require similar care.

Those issues may affect credibility, but they should remain tied to the patient's care.

A late note is not automatically false. A copied note is not automatically worthless.

The question is whether the documentation accurately reflected the patient at the time and whether its timing or repetition concealed a material change.

When was the entry created? What source did the witness rely on? Was the witness correcting an omission? Did the copied language remain accurate? Were new findings added? Did the entry affect later care?

The clinical significance matters more than the mere existence of templating. Medical records contain repeated language everywhere.

The examination becomes more useful when it shows that the repeated language no longer matched the patient rather than simply establishing that language was copied.

Objective evidence should be used to test narrative testimony while keeping the witness within the proper role.

A physician may say the patient was stable while the vital signs show persistent hypotension and tachycardia. Counsel should ask how the physician understood those findings and why they did or did not change the plan.

A nurse may describe improving oxygenation while the monitor shows recurring desaturation. The witness can be asked whether the episodes were artifact, temporary, or clinically meaningful and what response occurred.

A radiologist may be asked what the study showed, whether it was technically limited, and whether communication was required.

The radiologist should not necessarily be asked whether surgery would have saved the patient. Each exhibit should illuminate that witness's decision.

Imaging depositions require particular preparation because attorneys can become overly dependent on the written report.

When the dispute concerns what was visible, counsel should understand enough of the expert review to ask focused questions without trying to interpret the images personally.

What clinical history was provided? Was the study technically adequate? What findings were present? Were they acute, chronic, or indeterminate? What comparison studies were available? Would additional clinical information have affected interpretation? Was the reading preliminary or final? Did the finding require direct communication?

Counsel should know exactly where the imaging disagreement lies.

Do the experts disagree about whether a finding exists, whether it was visible at the time, whether a reasonable reader should have recognized it, or what clinical significance it carried? Those are different examinations.

Showing a later, obvious image and asking why an earlier subtle finding was missed may invite hindsight rather than useful testimony.

The examination should remain anchored to the earlier study, the history available then, and the limitations of that examination. Medication cases require the same division of roles.

The prescriber, pharmacist, nurse, and institution may each control a different part of the process.

The physician may be examined about selection, dose, patient-specific risk, and monitoring. The pharmacist may be examined about verification, interaction warnings, organ function, alerts, and dispensing. The nurse may be examined about administration, observation, and escalation. The institutional witness may address system design and access to information.

An order should never be treated as proof that treatment occurred.

When did the medication become available? When was it administered? At what dose and rate? Was it interrupted? What monitoring followed? Did the patient show signs of toxicity or lack of effect? Was the medication reconciled during transition?

The answers may show that the clinically important failure occurred well after the prescription was written.

Policy testimony should remain connected to the patient in the same way.

A witness will usually agree that policies are important and should be followed. That admission rarely decides anything.

The useful testimony concerns why the policy existed, whether it applied, what risk it was designed to address, how it operated, and what occurred instead.

Was this patient within the population covered by the protocol? Did the triggering condition occur? Who was expected to respond? Was an equivalent process used? Did the departure from the policy affect the care? The policy should help reconstruct the obligation. It should not become a substitute for clinical analysis.

Institutional witnesses often arrive prepared to describe the official system.

Counsel should be ready to compare that description with the operational evidence.

The policy may assign results to the ordering clinician while audit data shows that results routed to a shared pool. The witness may describe automatic escalation while the production contains no escalation record. The institution may say every referral is tracked while the patient's referral disappeared without generating notice. The examination should move from design to operation.

How was the system configured during the relevant period? What did users actually see? Who monitored unresolved tasks? What occurred when a clinician was absent or left the practice? How was completion confirmed? What data would show that the process worked in this case?

A system should not be accepted as reliable merely because the witness can describe how it was intended to function.

The deposition should establish whether the safeguard protected this patient.

Expert depositions require a different kind of preparation because the witness has already organized the case into an opinion.

Counsel's task is to understand the reasoning well enough to test its structure rather than merely challenge its conclusion.

Which factual assumptions support the opinion? Which records matter most? What treatment opportunity is being assumed, and at what time? Which patient-specific factors affect eligibility and prognosis? What competing causes were considered? What evidence would change the opinion?

An expert can use the correct conclusion language and still rest on an unstable foundation.

The causation expert may assume a breach point earlier than the standard-of-care expert supports. The defense expert may infer inevitability from the patient's final condition. The life-care planner may assume that all present care will continue permanently. The vocational expert may rely on limitations the medical record does not establish. The deposition should make those assumptions visible.

Medical literature may help, but it should not turn the examination into a contest over isolated papers.

Counsel should understand how the expert is using the literature.

Is it offered to establish general treatment efficacy, timing, prognosis, or accepted practice? Does the studied population resemble the patient? Does the article support the precise proposition for which it is being cited? Is the expert relying on clinical experience where the literature is limited?

The objective is not to establish that one publication controls the case.

It is to determine whether population evidence has been connected responsibly to this patient.

Experts should also be required to address the strongest contrary evidence.

An opinion that survives only because inconvenient facts were ignored is not stable.

How does the expert account for pre-existing disease? What does the normal examination mean? Why does temporary improvement not change the conclusion? What effect does uncertain onset have? Would the patient have accepted the treatment? What injury probably would have remained even with appropriate care? Those questions often produce the most useful testimony. They may narrow the opinion, and that can be valuable.

An expert who acknowledges that some injury was unavoidable but explains why delay increased its severity may become more credible. A defense expert who accepts a departure while explaining why it did not change the outcome may clarify the actual dispute.

The goal is not always to make the opposing opinion collapse completely. It is to identify the precise ground on which it stands.

Preparation should also account for the language clinicians use casually.

Words such as stable, significant, acute, concerning, critical, indicated, and within normal limits often sound precise while carrying several possible meanings.

Stable may mean unchanged, not safe. Significant may refer to statistical, anatomical, or clinical importance.

Acute may mean recent without identifying an exact onset. Within normal limits may describe a population reference range while concealing a major departure from the patient's own baseline.

Counsel should ask what the word means for this patient.

When the witness says the patient was stable, stable in what respect? Was the blood pressure stable or simply persistently low? Was the neurological condition unchanged or reassuring? Was the patient clinically safe for discharge?

Precision often lies inside language the witness uses without thinking.

Counsel should also resist turning every answer into an immediate argument.

Some witnesses reveal more when they are allowed to complete the reasoning. An aggressive cross-examination style may produce denials without producing understanding. A calm sequence can expose assumptions, gaps, and role boundaries more effectively.

This is especially true with treating clinicians, who may not regard themselves as advocates. They may become defensive when every question implies wrongdoing.

The deposition should remain exacting. It does not need to become theatrical.

A witness allowed to explain may provide more valuable testimony than one forced into an artificial yes or no.

Control still matters. Counsel should know when the explanation answers the question and when it has moved away from it. That balance depends on clinical preparation.

When counsel understands the medicine, it becomes easier to distinguish a genuine explanation from evasion. The same understanding sharpens follow-up.

A witness may say further imaging was not indicated because the examination was normal. Counsel who knows the record can ask whether the examination included the specific function at issue, whether the patient could walk, whether symptoms continued, and whether the later findings were already developing. The question becomes more effective because it follows the clinical logic.

Depositions should also be planned with their eventual use in mind.

Some testimony establishes facts. Some defines the witness's reasoning. Some may support expert review, mediation, dispositive motion practice, or trial impeachment.

Not every important answer sounds dramatic in the room.

A quiet admission that no one was assigned responsibility for an unresolved result may be more valuable than an argumentative exchange about whether the institution failed the patient.

A physician's acknowledgment that the patient did not improve as expected may matter more than agreement that additional testing was technically available.

Counsel should know what proposition the testimony will later support.

That keeps the examination from becoming crowded with points that feel satisfying but do not move the case.

After the deposition, the transcript should return to the clinical model.

Did the testimony change the timeline? Clarify a communication? Identify another decision-maker? Narrow the standard-of-care issue? Alter the treatment opportunity? Support a competing cause? Change the injury or future-care assumptions?

The transcript should not merely be summarized by topic. It should be used to revise the reconstruction.

A witness may establish that the physician was notified earlier than expected, shifting the case from communication to response. Another may reveal that the patient refused treatment after a meaningful discussion, changing the alternative course. An institutional witness may show that the result-management system worked and that individual review was the real problem. Those changes should reach the experts promptly.

The deposition has done its work only when the case reflects what counsel learned.

By the end of fact depositions, counsel should be able to describe the material period through testimony as well as through records.

You should know what each participant saw, understood, communicated, decided, and controlled. You should know where memory ends and routine practice begins. You should know whether the written workflow matched the operational one. You should know which factual assumptions remain disputed and whether the expert opinions survive each plausible version. That is a clinically effective deposition record. It does more than establish that events occurred.

It explains how the patient moved through the hands of the people responsible for care, what those people understood at the time, and where the opportunity to change the outcome was preserved or lost.

"It explains how the patient moved through the hands of the people responsible for care, what those people understood at the time, and where the opportunity to change the outcome was preserved or lost."

CHAPTER TWENTY-FIVE

Evaluating the Strength of the Opposing Medical Theory

When an opposing expert report arrives, counsel naturally begins looking for weaknesses. The obvious targets are familiar: an omitted record, an unsupported assumption, an inconsistency with prior testimony, an overstatement of what the literature shows. Those points may become important later, but they are not where I would begin.

I would first ask whether the expert has actually explained the patient.

A persuasive medical opinion should account for the patient's condition before the disputed care, the information available to the treating professionals, the decisions made in response, the course that followed, and the injury ultimately sustained. It should still make sense when the inconvenient facts are included. That standard applies to both sides. A report does not become strong merely because its conclusion favors the party who retained the expert.

A defense expert may describe the presentation as nonspecific, the diagnosis as difficult, and the outcome as the product of serious underlying disease. Those may all be fair observations. They still have to explain why this patient deteriorated when and how the patient did. A plaintiff expert may say that further testing was required and that earlier treatment probably would have prevented the injury. That opinion still has to address what injury had already occurred, whether the patient was eligible for the proposed treatment, how long it would have taken to deliver, and what degree of recovery was realistically probable.

The conclusion is usually the easiest part of the report to understand. The reasoning beneath it is where the real evaluation begins.

I find it useful to restate the opinion without the expert's language. What does the expert believe was happening clinically during the disputed period? What information does the expert believe the treating team had? At what point does the expert say the professional obligation changed? What care should have followed? What does the expert believe would probably have happened if that care had been provided?

Once the theory is reduced to that sequence, the assumptions become easier to see.

A lengthy report may depend on one uncertain fact. In a stroke case, the opinion may turn on the last-known-well time. In a postoperative case, everything may depend on when the surgeon was notified. In a delayed-diagnosis matter, the theory may assume that an earlier study showed an actionable abnormality rather than an equivocal finding. In another case, the entire alternative course may depend on the patient accepting treatment that the record suggests the patient had previously resisted.

That dependency is not always announced. It may be embedded in the chronology or treated as though it were undisputed.

Counsel needs to identify it and then ask how the opinion changes when the assumption moves.

If onset occurred thirty minutes earlier, is the patient still eligible for treatment? If the physician was notified at 2:45 rather than 2:15, does the expert reach the same causation opinion? If the finding was present but subtle, would a reasonable reader still have been expected to recognize it? If some injury had already occurred, could treatment still have reduced its severity?

A theory that remains coherent across several plausible versions of the facts is usually more durable than one that survives only under the version most favorable to the party offering it.

That does not make every fact-dependent opinion unreliable. Some cases genuinely turn on a narrow factual dispute. It does mean that counsel should understand exactly how much of the case rests on that dispute.

The expert's handling of the record is often more revealing than the final opinion. Nearly every expert can identify supportive facts. The better experts also explain the facts that appear to cut the other way.

Suppose a defense expert describes the patient as stable. The report should do something with persistent tachycardia, falling blood pressure, increasing oxygen requirements, rising lactate, or repeated returns for care. Those findings may have been chronic, transient, technically unreliable, or reasonably explained at the time. Any of those may be a legitimate answer. Silence is not.

The same applies to plaintiff reports. An expert may emphasize one markedly abnormal value without acknowledging that it had been present for months. A neurological finding may be described as new even though earlier records documented something similar. A postoperative decline may be attributed entirely to delayed rescue without addressing the patient's profound instability before surgery.

An unfavorable fact does not have to defeat the opinion. It does have to be incorporated.

The opinions that hold up best are rarely the ones that insist every fact points in one direction. They are the ones capable of saying that a particular finding was reassuring but did not resolve the larger pattern, or that the patient had serious underlying disease but that the disease does not account for the timing of the acute collapse. An expert may acknowledge that some injury was unavoidable and still explain why the departure increased its severity.

That kind of qualification does not necessarily weaken the opinion. Often, it is what makes the opinion believable.

Baseline is one of the easiest places to see whether an expert is reasoning carefully.

Defense reports often describe patients as frail, chronically ill, medically complex, or high risk. Those descriptions may be accurate, but they do not tell us what the patient was capable of doing or what course was expected before the disputed event.

A patient with several chronic diagnoses may have been living independently, driving, working, managing medication, and functioning well. Another patient may have required substantial assistance despite having fewer diagnoses. The significance of the baseline lies in what the conditions were doing, not in how many appeared on the problem list.

Chronic kidney disease may make medication toxicity more likely and recovery more difficult. It may also have been stable for years and have little to do with the timing of a new neurological injury. Severe vascular disease may place a limb at risk without making amputation inevitable at that time. Metastatic cancer may limit survival without explaining death from an untreated infection months earlier.

The expert has to connect the earlier condition to the disputed outcome. "Comorbidities" is not an explanation.

Plaintiff experts can make the opposite error by minimizing the patient's earlier limitations. Living at home does not necessarily mean complete independence. Family members may already have been managing meals, transportation, medication, or personal care. A later injury may be substantial without being entirely new.

The stronger opinion defines the additional loss. The patient already had some impairment, but not this level of impairment. Some assistance was required, but not this degree of dependence. Decline may eventually have occurred, but not when it did.

That is usually more persuasive than presenting the patient as perfectly healthy before the event.

The same kind of discipline is needed when the theory reaches objective evidence.

Narrative records are important, but they reflect what clinicians observed, understood, and chose to document. Imaging, pathology, laboratory trends, monitor data, medication records, and operative findings often place firmer limits on what can reasonably be said.

Those sources are not self-explanatory. A study may be technically limited. A monitor alarm may represent artifact. A laboratory abnormality may have several possible causes. Pathology may establish the existence of disease without identifying when it became detectable. Even with those limitations, the theory has to fit the objective course.

An expert cannot describe the patient as physiologically stable while ignoring an unexplained pattern of deterioration. A report claiming rapid disease progression during a particular interval should be consistent with the imaging and clinical findings. An opinion attributing injury to medication toxicity should make sense in light of the dose, organ function, timing, and biological response.

Where the objective evidence and the narrative theory diverge, the expert should explain the divergence.

Imaging disputes are especially prone to being oversimplified. Two experts may appear to disagree about whether something was missed when their actual disagreement lies elsewhere.

One may believe the abnormality was visible. Another may agree it was present but consider it too subtle to require recognition. A third may believe it was visible and significant but not yet clinically actionable. Another may conclude that the study itself was technically unable to answer the relevant question.

Those are not variations of one dispute. They are separate issues involving existence, visibility, professional interpretation, clinical significance, and causation. Counsel should know which one is actually controlling.

A radiologist may be well qualified to explain what an image showed and whether the original reading was reasonable, yet have no reliable basis to say what treatment would have followed or whether it would have changed the outcome. A treating specialist may explain the significance of the finding without being qualified to define the radiologist's professional obligation.

Keeping those roles separate often clarifies the case considerably.

Laboratory and medication matters require the same separation. An abnormal value may be undisputed, while the real issue is whether it represented a material change for this patient, whether the information reached the person responsible for acting, and whether action at that point probably would have altered the course.

A medication error may be obvious while its relationship to a claimed permanent injury remains uncertain.

One clear error should not be allowed to carry conclusions that still require separate proof.

Professional judgment is another area where reports can sound persuasive without answering the patient-specific question.

Defense experts often say that reasonable clinicians may disagree. That is true. The important issue is what the reasonable choices were in this setting and whether the patient's course continued to support the choice that was made.

What findings supported the working diagnosis? Which dangerous alternatives remained unresolved? Was reassessment planned? Did the patient improve as expected? When new information appeared, was the original judgment reconsidered?

A decision may have been reasonable initially and become unreasonable later.

Many strong cases turn on that transition. The first encounter may have been managed reasonably. The departure may have occurred after the patient returned with a more developed presentation, after treatment failed, or after an objective result no longer fit the original explanation.

A defense opinion that treats the entire course as one continuous exercise of reasonable judgment may overlook that change.

Plaintiff opinions can make the reverse mistake by allowing the final diagnosis to turn every earlier decision into negligence. The fact that the condition later became obvious does not establish that it was reasonably diagnosable at the first encounter.

The better opinion identifies the point at which the clinical obligation changed.

That point may be the second visit, the return of a test result, the failure of treatment, or the appearance of a new finding. The persuasiveness of the theory often depends less on the diagnosis itself than on whether the expert can explain that transition.

Reassessment is particularly useful in testing this part of the opinion.

A report may criticize discharge without considering the patient's response to treatment. Another may defend discharge based on the initial presentation while ignoring that the patient did not improve as expected.

The analysis should ask what course the treating team anticipated and whether the patient followed it.

If the diagnosis was correct, what improvement should have appeared? If the treatment was working, what should have changed? When that expected response failed to occur, what did reasonable care require?

An expert who can work through those questions is explaining clinical judgment. An expert who merely repeats that the diagnosis was difficult is not doing enough.

Causation is usually where an opposing report needs the most careful review because that is where the reasoning often accelerates.

The expert identifies a departure and then states that the departure caused the injury. The missing analysis sits between those two conclusions.

What treatment remained available when the departure occurred? How long would it have taken to provide? Was the patient eligible? What benefit was probable? What injury was already present? What impairment or risk would have remained even with timely care? Those questions force the alternative course into clinical reality.

A statement that the patient needed earlier treatment does not tell us what treatment would have been delivered. A recommendation for immediate transfer does not tell us when the patient would have arrived, been reassessed, and undergone intervention. Prompt surgery does not mean surgery would have occurred the moment the obligation arose.

If transfer is part of the opinion, the expert should account for recognition, referral, acceptance, transportation, evaluation at the receiving facility, and the intervention itself. When the alleged benefit depended on a narrow period, those intervals cannot be ignored.

Plaintiff experts should not assume the fastest imaginable course. Defense experts should not build every possible delay into the alternative. The comparison is with what probably would have happened under reasonable care.

Consultation should be examined in the same way. It is not enough to say that a specialist should have been called. What would the specialist probably have recommended? Additional testing? Admission? Observation? Surgery? A change in medication?

The consultation matters because of what it was likely to produce.

Without that next step, the opinion may establish only that more care could have occurred, not that the outcome probably would have changed. Eligibility should also be addressed directly.

The patient may have had active bleeding, organ dysfunction, advanced disease, poor performance status, medication exposure, or another condition affecting the proposed treatment. Age alone rarely resolves the issue, and "too sick" is usually too imprecise to be useful.

Too sick for which intervention? Was the treatment contraindicated, unusually risky, unlikely to help, or simply less likely to produce complete recovery?

A high-risk patient may still be an appropriate candidate. Treatment may provide incomplete benefit and still materially improve the outcome. The expert should describe the actual clinical balance.

Patient choice may also affect the alternative course, but it should not be reduced to a chart entry saying the patient refused care.

A patient may decline admission for what is described as a minor problem and make a different decision when told that stroke, sepsis, or internal bleeding is a serious concern. A person may reject one procedure while accepting another. A comfort-focused plan during terminal decline may not apply to treatment of a reversible infection.

The relevant question is what decision the patient probably would have faced if the condition had been recognized and explained accurately.

Natural history is another area in which broad medical truths can sound more decisive than they are.

An expert may say the cancer was aggressive, the infection progressed rapidly, or treatment did not guarantee recovery. Those statements may be accurate and still fail to explain the case.

Aggressive cancer may make delay especially consequential or may mean that earlier diagnosis would not have changed survival. Rapid progression may explain why a short delay mattered or why the patient was already beyond rescue. Uncertain treatment response does not necessarily mean the benefit was merely possible rather than probable.

General disease behavior defines the range of possible courses. The patient's evidence determines which course is more likely.

Medical literature should support that reasoning rather than replace it.

A report with an extensive bibliography may still be weak if the studies do not address a comparable disease stage, severity, patient population, or treatment setting. Counsel should understand what each cited source is being used to establish.

A study showing that earlier treatment improves outcomes does not prove complete recovery for this patient. A study showing that some patients fail treatment does not establish futility.

Population evidence becomes useful only when the expert explains where this patient fits within the population.

The language of probability should also be read in context.

Some experts use legal terminology confidently while their reasoning supports only a possibility. Others use cautious language even when their conclusion is clinically strong. Words such as could, may, and cannot exclude are not self-interpreting.

What matters is whether the reasoning supports a probable conclusion.

A competing cause does not become persuasive merely because it can be imagined. The expert should explain why it fits the timing, mechanism, and objective evidence better than the proposed cause.

If an arrhythmia is offered as the cause of collapse, what evidence supports it? If the injury is said to have been complete before the alleged delay, what places completion at that earlier time? If the defense says infection could have progressed despite treatment, what makes that outcome probable in this patient? Possibility identifies something that might have happened. It does not tell us what probably did.

Known complications are often used in much the same way.

A postoperative bleed may occur without negligence. That does not resolve whether progressive hypotension and falling hemoglobin were recognized and managed in time. A medication reaction may be a known risk while the actual dispute concerns whether patient-specific risk was evaluated or warning signs were ignored.

Calling something a recognized complication does not explain whether the complication was unavoidable, negligently caused, or reasonably occurring but poorly managed. Mechanism matters more than the label.

Institutional opinions need to be reviewed with equal care.

A plaintiff expert may call a system unsafe because a result was missed. A defense expert may call it reliable because a policy existed.

Neither statement tells us how the work actually moved.

Who owned the result? Where was it routed? What happened if the ordering clinician was unavailable? Was acknowledgment required? Could unresolved work be identified? Did the backup process function in this case?

The answers may point toward individual conduct, institutional design, or some combination of the two. The expert structure should reflect that division.

A physician may explain why a result required urgent action but have little experience designing electronic routing systems. An operational expert may understand the workflow but be unable to determine when the patient's condition became clinically dangerous.

The stronger institutional theory connects those disciplines without asking either expert to work outside the field.

Damages opinions should be traced backward in the same way.

A life-care plan may contain detailed services and exact costs, but counsel should begin with the injury being projected. Does causation support all of it? Is the patient still improving? Which needs existed before the event? Which needs are new or increased? How long are they expected to continue?

The path should run from cost to service, from service to functional need, from need to injury, and from injury back to causation.

A precise total resting on an unsupported medical assumption is not a strong opinion.

The defense can make the opposite mistake by assuming relatives will provide care indefinitely, that public programs will satisfy every need, or that improvement will continue beyond the point supported by the medical evidence.

The number is not reliable because it is high or low. It is reliable when the future being described is probable. The expert opinions should then be read together.

A case can contain several individually credible reports that do not form one coherent theory.

The standard-of-care expert may place the departure at four in the afternoon. The causation expert may assume treatment beginning at two. The rehabilitation expert may expect substantial recovery while the life-care planner projects the current level of dependence for life. Those opinions may appear reasonable when read separately. Together, they describe different cases.

Counsel should compare the critical times, factual assumptions, injury definitions, and prognoses across disciplines. Minor differences are inevitable. One expert may use a range while another uses a representative point. One may describe injury anatomically and another functionally.

The important question is whether they are describing the same patient moving through the same alternative course.

Presentation and credentials matter, but they should not distract from the clinical reasoning.

A polished expert may defend an unstable opinion very effectively. A less experienced witness may struggle to articulate a sound one. Compensation history, testimony frequency, and prior work may affect credibility, but they rarely answer whether the opinion fits the evidence.

The more useful examination stays with the structure of the opinion.

Which assumption controls the conclusion? What fact matters most? What would change the expert's view? How does the expert account for the strongest contrary evidence? Why is one causal mechanism more probable than another?

An expert who answers those questions directly is far more formidable than one who simply repeats the conclusion with confidence.

Prior publications, lectures, protocols, and testimony may help when they show that the expert is now applying a different clinical principle. Context remains important. A statement about another population, setting, or period may not conflict with the present opinion.

The useful inconsistency is not a different phrase. It is a different rule.

The expert now says a finding required immediate intervention after previously teaching that it was nonspecific without additional features. The expert now calls a treatment contraindicated after describing the same risk elsewhere as manageable. The expert assigns responsibility to a professional role differently from the way that responsibility operates in the expert's own practice. Those differences may reveal advocacy. They may also have a legitimate explanation. Counsel should understand the difference before attempting impeachment.

There will also be times when the opposing expert is right about part of the case.

A defense radiologist may persuasively explain that the earlier image was subtle while the later encounter still presents a strong failure-to-diagnose theory. A plaintiff expert may identify a genuine workflow failure while overstating its effect on survival. A defense expert may establish that some injury was unavoidable while leaving a substantial increased-severity claim intact.

Accepting the sound portion of the opposing opinion does not require abandoning the material dispute.

The scan was subtle, but the later presentation was not.

The complication could occur without negligence, but rescue was still delayed.

The patient had limited life expectancy, but death occurred earlier.

The patient would have sustained some impairment, but not this degree.

Those positions often sound more credible because they do not ask the fact finder to reject everything the other side says.

By the end of the review, counsel should understand what the opposing theory requires the fact finder to believe.

Perhaps it depends on one disputed onset time. Perhaps it assumes the patient was already untreatable before objective evidence of irreversibility appeared. It may depend on a consultation producing an intervention no one has actually described, or on pre-existing disease explaining an acute event it had never produced before. Those dependencies form the real architecture of the opposing case.

Some will be vulnerable. Others may be difficult to disprove. Some may be stronger than counsel expected. That is not bad information.

The purpose of evaluating an opposing medical theory is not to create confidence. It is to understand the medical contest well enough to make a sound decision.

The stronger theory is not always the one stated most forcefully, supported by the longest report, or accompanied by the largest bibliography.

It is the one that explains the patient’s course with the fewest unsupported assumptions and remains coherent when the unfavorable evidence is brought back into the room. That standard should be applied to the opposing case. It should also be applied to counsel’s own.

"It should also be applied to counsel's own."

CHAPTER TWENTY-SIX

Classifying the Case After Clinical Review

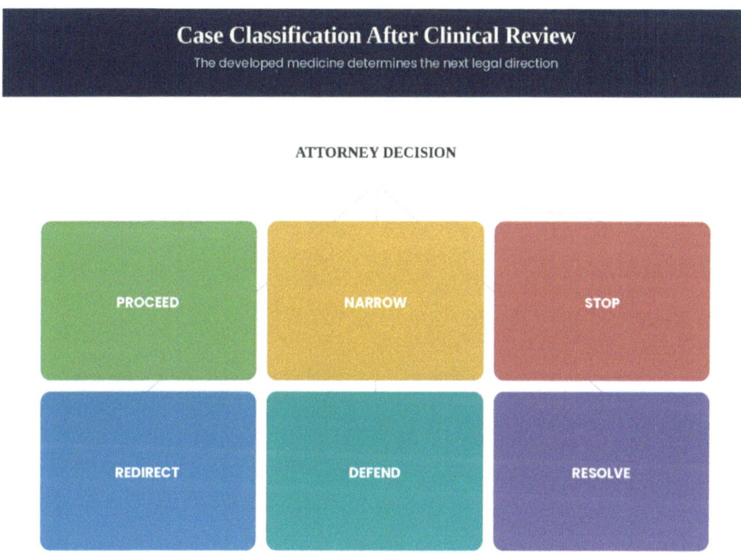

At intake, counsel usually knows the outcome before the medical event has been understood. A patient died. A child sustained permanent neurological injury. An operation ended with an unexpected complication. A diagnosis was delayed. A resident deteriorated in a facility.

Those facts explain why the matter deserves immediate attention, but they do not yet tell us what kind of case it is.

That answer comes later, after the record has been tested rather than merely collected. By then, counsel should know whether important evidence is still missing, what the patient's actual baseline was, what the objective findings showed, when the course became clinically consequential, and whether a meaningful treatment or rescue opportunity remained. The review should also have clarified which decisions fell within reasonable judgment, which did not, and whether any departure probably changed the outcome.

A case that has been worked through properly should not look exactly as it did when it arrived.

Sometimes it becomes stronger. A vague allegation of delayed care may become a precisely timed failure to respond while the patient remained salvageable. What initially appeared to be an unavoidable complication may prove to be a failure-to-rescue case. A suspected individual mistake may lead instead to a result-management system in which no one had practical ownership of the patient's follow-up.

In other matters, the case becomes narrower. Earlier treatment may probably have reduced the injury without preventing it entirely. The patient may have lost a meaningful period of survival rather than an otherwise normal lifespan. One defendant may remain central while others, although involved in the care, never had the information, authority, or remaining opportunity needed to change the course.

There are also cases that do not survive the clinical review. The care may have been imperfect without falling outside the range of reasonable practice. A departure may be supportable while causation is not. The patient may already have passed the point at which the proposed treatment was likely to help. The outcome may be tragic and still medically unavoidable.

Classification is the stage at which counsel stops asking broadly whether something went wrong and decides what the medical evidence actually permits the case to become.

That judgment should not be driven by the severity of the outcome or by whether one favorable expert can be found. It should arise from the relationship among the alleged departure, the treatment opportunity, the probable alternative course, and the injury that can fairly be attributed to the difference.

The most useful starting point is usually not a rating such as strong, moderate, or weak. It is a short, defensible clinical statement of the case.

In one matter, that statement may be broad: the patient had a treatable condition that should have been recognized, remained likely to recover when reasonable care required action, and suffered catastrophic injury because treatment was delayed.

Another matter may support less: the patient probably would have sustained some neurological injury in any event, but timely intervention would likely have preserved meaningful speech and mobility.

A wrongful-death case may be about timing rather than complete prevention. The underlying disease may ultimately have caused death, while failure to treat an acute complication probably caused death to occur materially sooner.

The conclusion may also be unfavorable to the claim. The record may show that an abnormal result was not communicated, but the patient's condition was already irreversible before communication could reasonably have changed management.

That clinical statement tells counsel far more than a general label because it defines what the case can honestly claim.

The next issue is how securely that statement rests on the evidence.

Some matters have a stable factual foundation. The original imaging is available. Laboratory progression is documented clearly. Medication timing is reliable. The patient's pre-event function is established through consistent records and testimony. Experts may disagree about the meaning of those facts, but the facts themselves are unlikely to move substantially.

Other cases turn on an uncertain symptom onset, an undocumented reassessment, a disputed telephone call, or a witness trying to recall an event years later. Under one factual version, the medical theory may be strong. Under another, it may weaken sharply. Those are different forms of risk.

A case can be medically persuasive but factually fragile. Another may have clear facts and a genuine professional disagreement about what those facts required. Counsel should not treat those cases as though they present the same problem.

Take a postoperative hemorrhage case. The decline in blood pressure, falling hemoglobin, transfusion timing, and eventual return to the operating room may all be documented. The central dispute may concern whether the surgeon responded reasonably and whether earlier intervention probably would have prevented death. The clinical judgment is contested, but the factual sequence is relatively stable.

Now consider the same type of case where the nurse says the surgeon was notified of worsening hypotension at midnight and the surgeon says the first call came at two. If the patient was probably salvageable at midnight but not at two, the causal theory may depend heavily on which witness is believed.

The second case may still be viable. It simply carries a different kind of exposure.

Counsel should know whether the central theory survives the reasonable factual range. If benefit probably remained available whether the physician was notified at midnight or 12:30, the dispute remains important without necessarily controlling the case. If the treatment opportunity closed during that interval, the timing dispute becomes much more consequential.

The same stress test should be applied to the expert opinions themselves. Does the conclusion remain supportable if the patient's baseline was somewhat worse than the family recalls? What happens if symptom onset was earlier, transfer would have taken longer, or timely treatment probably would have reduced the injury rather than prevented it entirely?

A durable case can tolerate some movement at the edges. A brittle case cannot.

That does not mean every brittle case should be rejected. It means counsel should understand that one favorable assumption is doing much of the work.

Clinical review should also identify where the case truly begins.

Medical cases are often framed too early. Counsel may initially criticize the first emergency visit because the final diagnosis was not made. After a careful review, that encounter may fall within reasonable judgment. The actionable failure may have occurred when the patient returned with new findings and the original explanation was not reconsidered.

A surgical complication may have been unavoidable. The case may begin later, when persistent deterioration was not recognized or rescue was delayed.

An abnormal study may have been interpreted correctly. The case may begin when no one assumed responsibility for follow-up.

Finding the correct beginning often makes the theory both shorter and stronger. It removes criticism of earlier care that may have been defensible and directs attention to the point at which the professional obligation changed.

The end of the causal period matters just as much.

Once the injury became irreversible, later failures may remain troubling without causing additional harm. A case that attributes the entire outcome to every subsequent delay can lose its medical center.

Counsel should be able to identify the interval during which the patient's course could still have been changed. What happened before that interval may explain the context. What happened afterward may explain the extent of the injury. The central liability and causation questions usually lie within the period when meaningful benefit remained possible.

By this stage, the nature of the alleged departure should also be clearer.

Some cases are fundamentally about professional judgment. The facts may be largely undisputed while competent experts disagree about whether the clinician's interpretation and choice remained within the reasonable range. These cases often turn on the presentation as it existed at the time, the available resources, the professional's specialty, and whether the decision continued to make sense as the patient changed.

Other cases are about process rather than judgment. The issue is whether necessary work occurred at all. Was the result reviewed? Was the medication administered? Was the patient reassessed? Was the consultant contacted? Was the referral tracked? Did information reach someone who could act?

In a process case, the clinical judgment may have been entirely sound once the information reached the correct professional. The failure lies in the pathway that never delivered the information or completed the task.

Failure-to-rescue cases have their own emphasis. The underlying complication or disease may not have been preventable. The dispute concerns whether the patient was recognized and treated while the condition remained reversible.

That distinction is important because counsel may be tempted to argue that the complication should never have occurred. The better theory may accept that bleeding, infection, obstruction, or another complication can arise during reasonable care and focus instead on why the patient was not rescued before the course became catastrophic.

Technical cases tend to be narrower. They may concern interpretation of an image, administration of a drug, performance of a procedure, protection of an anatomical structure, or execution of a defined intervention. Those matters often depend on original source evidence and an expert whose experience closely matches the act being reviewed.

Most serious cases contain elements of more than one category. The purpose of classification is not to force the matter into a rigid box. It is to identify where the real medical dispute lies.

When the case centers on judgment, discovery and expert preparation should focus on the developing presentation and the reasoning behind the choice. When the issue is process, workflow and responsibility become more important. A rescue case places the timeline and the changing probability of benefit at the center. A technical case may turn largely on source material and narrow expert fit.

Knowing where the contest lies keeps counsel from spending time and money in the wrong places. Classification should also identify who actually matters.

The medical record makes many people visible. It does not follow that everyone whose name appears had a meaningful causal role.

A patient may have been seen by nurses, residents, attending physicians, consultants, pharmacists, therapists, technicians, and administrators. Several people may have made errors. Only some may have possessed the necessary information, authority, and remaining time to change the outcome. The case should follow that opportunity.

A nurse may have documented poorly while escalating appropriately. A consultant may have given reasonable advice based on incomplete information. A physician may have made a defensible early decision and an unreasonable later one. An institution may have created a workflow in which no one understood that an abnormal result remained unresolved.

Clinical classification often narrows the defendant group because it replaces proximity with actual responsibility.

Sequential-delay cases make this especially important. A patient may experience delay at triage, during imaging, in interpretation, consultation, transfer, and treatment. Presenting all of those stages as one continuous failure may be tempting, but they may not have consumed the treatment opportunity equally.

An early delay may have had little practical effect, while a later decision caused the decisive loss. In another case, the earliest delay may have done the damage, leaving little or no meaningful opportunity by the time a later provider became involved.

Counsel should know where the actual course probably diverged from the course reasonable care would have produced.

That is the stage around which the case should be built. Other departures may remain relevant, but they should not be allowed to obscure the event that actually changed the outcome. The injury itself may also need to be reclassified.

At intake, the case may be described as causing paralysis, amputation, permanent cognitive impairment, or death. Later review may show that some portion of the outcome probably would have occurred even with appropriate care. That does not necessarily eliminate the case.

The patient may have lost a better neurological outcome rather than all neurological injury. An amputation may have become more extensive. Severe dependence may have begun years earlier than expected. Death may have been accelerated rather than completely preventable. The injury should be stated at the level the medicine supports.

The difference between complete prevention and increased severity can be substantial, but it is not always the difference between a viable case and no case. The same is true of aggravation and acceleration.

A patient who already had impairment may still have sustained a profound additional loss. A person with limited life expectancy may still have lost meaningful survival. A child with developmental limitations may still have lost the opportunity for much greater independence.

Cases generally become more credible when the earlier condition is incorporated rather than denied.

That clarification also controls damages. A life-care planner should not attribute to the event needs that would have existed in either course. A vocational expert should not assume abilities the patient probably never had. An economist should not calculate an ordinary career and lifespan from a baseline that was already materially limited.

Classification is therefore not limited to liability. It sets the medical boundary for the damages analysis that follows.

Another important distinction is between uncertainty that can still be resolved and uncertainty that belongs to the medicine.

A missing scan may still be obtained. A routing system can be explained. A witness can be deposed. Another specialist may review the evidence. Those are development issues.

The precise degree of neurological recovery that would have occurred may never be knowable. Lost survival may be expressible only as a range. The course of a rare disease may remain variable even after careful expert review. Those are residual uncertainties.

A case should not remain indefinitely unclassified simply because medicine cannot provide certainty it does not possess.

The attorney has to decide whether the evidence supports a probable conclusion despite the remaining uncertainty.

Often it does. An expert may be unable to say whether the patient would have returned to work while still concluding reliably that independent mobility probably would have been preserved. The exact period of lost survival may remain uncertain even though material acceleration of death is probable. A child's eventual occupation may be unknowable while the event's effect on lifelong dependence is clear.

In other cases, the uncertainty reaches the center of causation. If no reliable expert can say whether the proposed treatment probably would have helped at all, the matter presents a fundamentally different problem.

Uncertainty about the exact amount of benefit is not the same as uncertainty about whether any probable benefit existed. Counsel should not confuse those issues. The case must then be considered against the strongest opposing medical theory.

A favorable internal review is not enough. Counsel should ask whether the defense has a credible explanation for the timing and mechanism of injury, whether a competing cause fits the evidence well, whether the standard-of-care question falls within an area of genuine professional disagreement, and whether the plaintiff's alternative course could realistically have occurred.

A medically supportable case can still present serious trial risk. That is not a contradiction. It is part of the evaluation.

The classification should reflect both the strength of the affirmative theory and the quality of the opposing explanation.

A case in which one theory accounts for nearly all the objective evidence is different from one in which two clinical courses remain genuinely plausible. One case may involve clear breach and difficult causation. Another may involve disputed breach but strong causation if a departure is found. Those differences affect valuation and strategy, and they should be stated plainly.

Counsel should be able to describe the principal vulnerability without softening it.

The notification time is disputed, and the causation opinion depends on the earlier version. The patient had serious pre-existing neurological disease, making the additional injury difficult to separate. The evidence of departure is strong, but the proposed treatment was unlikely to prevent death. The imaging criticism is supportable, but recognition has not yet been connected to a materially better outcome. The patient probably would have survived, but future function remains uncertain.

A case that cannot tolerate an honest statement of its central weakness has not been classified carefully enough.

The same candor should identify the fact that carries the theory.

The patient returned with progression that no longer fit the original diagnosis. A critical result remained unacknowledged for days in a system without an effective backup. A previously stable patient sustained a closely timed and biologically consistent injury after a medication error. The rescue opportunity remained open while deterioration was documented repeatedly.

Those facts form the center of the case. They should shape expert preparation, discovery, mediation, and trial presentation.

Classification is useful only if it leads to a decision.

The case may be ready to proceed substantially as pleaded. It may require narrowing. A defendant may need to be dismissed or added. The theory may need to shift from complete prevention to increased severity, from individual negligence to an institutional process failure, or from negligent performance to delayed rescue.

Occasionally, one further investigation is genuinely needed before the decision can be made.

The next step should then be specific: obtain the original imaging, confirm whether the proposed treatment was available, resolve baseline through earlier therapy records, ask the causation specialist whether benefit remained probable under both onset scenarios, or determine whether the patient probably would have accepted the intervention. That is focused case development.

“Continue reviewing” is not.

Eventually, additional work stops clarifying the matter and begins postponing judgment. Clinical review should bring counsel to that point sooner.

A case should not proceed because the injury is severe, because the family deserves an explanation, because considerable resources have already been invested, or because one expert is prepared to support part of the theory. Those considerations may explain why the matter deserved careful review. They do not establish viability.

The reverse is equally important. A case should not be rejected merely because the patient had prior disease, the medicine is complicated, or the defense has retained a credible expert. Many strong cases contain real uncertainty.

The issue is whether a probable clinical conclusion remains intact after that uncertainty has been acknowledged and tested.

By the end of classification, counsel should be able to explain what happened, where the actionable failure occurred, what treatment remained available, what difference it probably would have made, and which injury can fairly be attributed to the departure.

That explanation may describe a different case from the one that first entered the office. It should describe the case the evidence can support.

"That explanation may describe a different case from the one that first entered the office. It should describe the case the evidence can support."

CHAPTER TWENTY-SEVEN

Deciding Whether to Proceed, Narrow, Redirect, Resolve, or Stop

There comes a point in every serious medical case when more investigation stops producing clarity. The records are substantially complete, the important imaging has been reviewed, the timeline is no longer changing in any material way, and the relevant experts have explained what they believe happened, what reasonable care required, and what earlier intervention probably would have changed.

Uncertainty may remain. In medicine, it usually does. By this stage, however, the uncertainty is no longer hiding inside an uncollected record or an unanswered clinical question. It has become part of the case.

That is when counsel has to decide what to do with the matter that now exists rather than the matter that first entered the office. Those two cases are often quite different.

A case that began as a catastrophic failure to diagnose may ultimately concern a much narrower failure to respond after the diagnosis became reasonably apparent. The original theory may have attributed the entire injury to delay, while the medicine supports only increased severity. A case directed initially at one physician may turn out to involve an institutional system that failed to route, track, or escalate critical information.

The reverse also happens. A matter that looked uncertain at intake may become considerably stronger once the clinical course is reconstructed. Earlier records may show that the patient's baseline was much better than the final chart suggested. The treatment opportunity may have remained open longer than anyone first understood. An imaging study accepted as negative may contain a visible abnormality. What appeared to be an unavoidable complication may have been followed by hours of deterioration that no one addressed. The decision should follow the developed case.

It should not be controlled by the emotional force of the injury, the amount of money already invested, the client's expectations, or the discomfort of changing direction after months of work. Those pressures are real, but none of them tells us what the medicine supports.

When counsel asks whether a case should proceed, I rarely begin with whether some departure can be articulated. By this stage, criticism can often be found. The harder and more important question is whether that criticism leads to an injury the medical evidence can defend under sustained challenge.

A departure without a probable causal consequence may explain why the care was troubling. It may not support the case the client believes exists.

That can be difficult to accept when the failure itself is obvious. A result was never reviewed. The patient was not reassessed. Medication was administered incorrectly. A referral disappeared. A physician failed to document a meaningful examination.

The mistake can be real and still not have caused the outcome.

When the disease was already irreversible, the treatment opportunity had closed, or the same injury probably would have occurred under reasonable care, the case may need to stop despite the quality problem that remains.

The converse is equally important. A departure that looks modest in isolation may have enormous causal consequences. A delay of less than an hour can matter profoundly in hemorrhage, airway compromise, fetal deterioration, stroke, or rapidly progressive infection. One unacknowledged result may remove the only realistic treatment opportunity.

The seriousness of a medical case does not always correspond to the visual drama of the error. It depends on where the error occurred in the patient's course and what remained possible at that time.

Proceeding is generally justified when the essential medical account remains coherent after the difficult facts are included. The patient's baseline is reasonably established. The professional obligation can be defined without hindsight. The departure occurred while an effective response remained available. The alternative course is realistic. The injury being claimed matches the probable difference between the care that occurred and the care that should have occurred. The case does not need to be perfect.

There may be legitimate disagreement about professional judgment. The precise duration of lost survival may remain uncertain. No expert may be able to say exactly how much recovery would have occurred. A witness may dispute timing, and the defense may have a credible expert with a medically respectable alternative explanation.

Those are ordinary litigation risks. They do not necessarily defeat a clinically sound case.

What matters is whether the theory can tolerate them without being rebuilt every time a fact moves. If symptom onset shifts by thirty minutes, does causation collapse? If the patient's baseline was somewhat worse than the family remembers, does the damages theory still hold? If treatment would have reduced injury rather than eliminated it, is there still a meaningful claim?

A case that remains supportable across reasonable factual variation is generally safer to pursue than one that depends on every uncertainty being resolved in the most favorable direction.

Sometimes the correct decision is not to continue with the case as originally framed, but to narrow it.

Narrowing is often treated as a concession. In medical litigation, it is frequently the result of finally understanding the case accurately.

A plaintiff may not be able to prove that timely treatment would have prevented every neurological injury. The evidence may still support that speech and mobility probably would have been preserved. A delayed cancer diagnosis may not support a normal-life-expectancy claim but may support lost survival, more extensive treatment, or loss of a less invasive option. A nursing-facility case may not sustain every allegation of institutional failure while the wound progression and delayed escalation remain compelling.

The narrower case may be more persuasive because it no longer asks the medicine to carry more than it can support.

Counsel should not assume that acknowledging unavoidable harm weakens the presentation. Jurors understand that medicine does not guarantee perfect outcomes. They are more likely to trust a case that explains what probably could have been changed and what could not.

The patient would have suffered some injury, but not injury of this severity. The patient had serious disease, but the acute failure probably caused death to occur earlier. The complication could arise without negligence, but the failure to rescue from it was avoidable.

Those are not lesser theories merely because they are less absolute. They may be considerably stronger because they fit the evidence. Narrowing may also involve defendants.

Medical cases accumulate parties easily because every person whose name appears near the critical interval begins to look involved. Once the workflow is reconstructed, however, some professionals may have had no meaningful opportunity to alter the course. Others may have acted reasonably on the information they received. The person who made the final visible decision may not be the person or institution responsible for the earlier breakdown that shaped it.

Keeping marginal defendants in the case can dilute the clinical theory. It adds expert issues, increases cost, and may allow the central failure to disappear into a crowd.

The practical inquiry is whether the person or institution had the necessary information, responsibility, authority, and remaining time to change the outcome.

When one of those elements is missing, continued pursuit may be difficult to justify.

Redirecting the case is different from narrowing it. Sometimes causation and injury remain strong, but the original theory was aimed at the wrong failure.

A missed-result case may initially appear to concern the physician who ordered the study. The evidence may later show that the physician left the practice before the result was finalized and that the organization had no reliable reassignment process. A postoperative case may begin as a technical criticism of the surgery and become a failure-to-rescue case after expert review establishes that the complication itself was recognized and accepted. A medication case may appear to concern prescribing when the actual breakdown occurred during pharmacy verification, administration, or monitoring.

Redirecting requires more than changing labels in a pleading. The expert structure, discovery, causation analysis, and damages presentation may all need to change.

That work is worthwhile when the new theory explains the patient's course more accurately. It is not worthwhile merely because the original theory is failing and another defendant remains available.

A redirected case has to possess its own clinical integrity.

The decision to resolve begins as a medical-risk decision before it becomes a negotiating one.

A case may be strong enough to proceed and still be better resolved. The treatment opportunity may be clear while damages remain uncertain. Liability may be substantial, but the opposing theory may carry enough credibility to create serious trial risk. A sympathetic injury may be offset by a poor baseline or limited survival. A defense may be strong on causation while an obvious process failure creates significant jury exposure.

Settlement is not always a compromise between confidence and fear. It may be the most rational response to a range of clinically plausible outcomes.

Counsel should understand that range before negotiations begin. What is the strongest version of the case the evidence can support? What is the strongest opposing explanation? Which facts are likely to be believed? Which injuries are secure, and which depend heavily on projection? How much of the damages model survives if the fact finder accepts only part of the causal opinion?

Those questions are more useful than assigning one percentage to the chance of winning.

A case may have a high probability of establishing some liability and a much lower probability of recovering the full damages claimed. Another may have a lower chance of establishing liability but enormous exposure if liability is found. Those matters should not be valued in the same way.

Clinical review helps counsel understand the shape of the risk rather than reducing it prematurely to one number.

The decision to stop is often the hardest one in a plaintiff matter because it affects a person or family that has already sustained serious loss. The client may have been told by another clinician that the outcome should not have happened. The record may contain obvious mistakes. The family may have spent months trying to understand what occurred.

Stopping does not mean the injury was unimportant or that the family's concerns were imagined. It means the available evidence does not support the medical and legal conclusion required to continue responsibly.

That conclusion should not be postponed merely because it is difficult to deliver.

A case generally should stop when the causal bridge remains speculative after appropriate review, when the proposed treatment was no longer likely to help, when qualified experts cannot identify a supportable departure, or when the claimed injury cannot be separated from the patient's pre-existing course.

It may also need to stop when the case depends on evidence that cannot be obtained and no other reliable source can establish the critical fact.

There is a meaningful difference between an unresolved issue and an unprovable one.

A missing record may justify further work when it probably exists and could answer the question. A conversation that no one remembers, was never documented, and is contradicted by the surrounding evidence may leave the case permanently unstable.

Counsel should know when remaining uncertainty is likely to be resolved and when uncertainty has simply become one of the facts that must be evaluated.

Stopping may also be appropriate when a matter is technically supportable but practically disproportionate. The attributable injury may be limited. The expert requirements may be unusually extensive. The jurisdiction may impose proof requirements the available medicine cannot satisfy. The client's goals may not align with the demands and duration of litigation.

Those are not purely clinical judgments, but clinical review defines what is available to weigh.

A serious departure followed by a temporary, fully resolved injury may not justify the same investment as a permanent-loss case. A highly specialized causal dispute requiring several experts may be difficult to justify when the attributable damages are modest.

That decision should be made openly rather than concealed behind another round of record requests. Defense counsel faces a parallel set of choices.

A case may be defensible in the sense that a credible expert supports the care, but that does not necessarily make trial the wisest course. The record may contain a process failure that will be difficult to explain. The defendant may be technically correct and factually unappealing. A narrow causal defense may be supportable while broad denials create unnecessary exposure.

The strongest defense may involve conceding what cannot credibly be denied.

The result was not followed. The patient should have been reassessed. The communication process failed. Treatment was delayed.

The defense can then focus on what that failure did or did not cause.

That position may be far more persuasive than defending every aspect of the care.

Conversely, a defense should not settle merely because the outcome is severe. If the patient was already beyond rescue, if the clinical decision remained within reasonable professional judgment, or if the plaintiff's alternative course is medically unrealistic, the matter may deserve a firm defense despite its emotional difficulty.

Clinical analysis does not tell counsel to avoid risk. It helps distinguish genuine medical risk from discomfort created by the optics of the case. Client communication should reflect the same honesty.

The client does not need every technical detail, but the decision should be explained in a way that preserves the real reason for it. The case is not being narrowed because the injury matters less. It is being narrowed because one part of the claimed loss is better supported than another. The case is not being stopped because no one made a mistake. It is being stopped because the mistake probably did not change the outcome. The theory is being redirected because the evidence places the meaningful failure in a different part of the care process than first believed.

Those explanations are difficult, but they are more respectful than vague references to litigation risk. They also reduce the chance that the client will hear a legal decision as a denial of what the patient or family experienced medically.

At some point, counsel should record the decision in a concise clinical form.

What was the patient's baseline? When did the material obligation arise? Did the care depart from reasonable practice? What treatment remained available? What outcome probably would have followed? Which injury can fairly be attributed? What facts or opinions create the principal risk? That statement should support the next action.

If the decision is to proceed, it becomes the foundation for discovery, expert disclosure, mediation, and trial. If the matter is narrowed, it records what has been left behind. If it is redirected, it explains why the focus changed. If the decision is to resolve, it defines the risk being negotiated. If the case stops, it demonstrates that the conclusion came from the evidence rather than fatigue or instinct.

A case should not drift from one stage to another simply because the calendar requires it.

At this point, the question is no longer whether the outcome is emotionally compelling, whether an expert can criticize some aspect of the care, or whether uncertainty remains. It is whether the medicine supports a coherent claim or defense worth carrying forward in its present form.

Sometimes the answer is yes. Sometimes it is yes after the case becomes smaller. Sometimes the evidence points toward a different defendant, a different departure, or a different injury. Sometimes resolution is the better result.

And sometimes the most responsible decision is to stop.

The value of the Clinical Intelligence Model is not that it makes those judgments easy. It makes the reason for them visible.

"The value of the Clinical Intelligence Model is not that it makes those judgments easy. It makes the reason for them visible."

CHAPTER TWENTY-EIGHT

Settlement Valuation Through Clinical Risk

Settlement valuation in a medical case is often discussed as though it were a calculation. Liability is assigned a percentage, damages are given a number, and the result is adjusted for venue, witnesses, expense, delay, and trial risk until a negotiating range appears.

That exercise may be useful, but it can also conceal the real uncertainty when the medical risk has not been understood first.

A case is not necessarily worth forty percent of full damages because counsel believes there is a forty percent chance of winning. The possible outcomes are rarely distributed that neatly.

A fact finder may accept the departure and reject causation. It may conclude that earlier care would have reduced the injury without preventing it. It may accept accelerated death while rejecting a claim based on ordinary life expectancy. It may believe one expert on liability and another on future care.

The value lies in the combinations of findings the evidence can support, not in a single abstract probability.

That is why clinical risk should be understood before it is translated into money.

I would begin by asking what the medically plausible outcomes of the case are, without regard to the negotiation position either side prefers.

At one end may be the complete plaintiff theory: the patient had a favorable baseline, the departure occurred while effective treatment remained available, and the injury probably would have been prevented or substantially reduced.

At the other end may be the full defense theory: the care was reasonable, the condition was not yet recognizable, the patient was no longer treatable, or the same outcome probably would have occurred regardless.

Between those positions, however, there are often several outcomes more realistic than either side's complete account.

The fact finder may conclude that the initial care was reasonable and the later response was not. It may find that the patient probably would have survived while remaining seriously impaired. It may decide that delay accelerated death without causing the underlying terminal condition. It may attribute some future-care needs to the event and others to the patient's baseline.

Those middle outcomes often drive actual settlement value.

They should not be treated as diluted versions of the parties' opening positions. They are distinct clinical conclusions with different financial consequences.

Consider a delayed-stroke case. The plaintiff may claim that timely treatment would have prevented severe disability, while the defense maintains that the stroke was already established and treatment would not have produced meaningful recovery.

The most realistic risk may lie between those positions. Some injury may have been unavoidable, while earlier treatment probably would have preserved speech, mobility, or a meaningful degree of independence.

That is not simply half of the plaintiff's case. It may change the entire damages structure. Lifetime attendant care, lost earnings, and noneconomic loss may remain substantial even when complete prevention cannot be established.

Wrongful-death cases present the same problem. The plaintiff may begin with a claim based on the remainder of ordinary life expectancy. The defense may argue that the patient had advanced disease and would have died soon regardless.

The medically supportable conclusion may be that death was accelerated by months or years and that the patient lost a period of meaningful function, even though the exact duration cannot be fixed.

Valuation should follow that probable loss. It should not swing between full life expectancy and no causation as though nothing exists between them.

The clinical theory should therefore be divided into the findings a fact finder could reasonably make.

Was there a departure? When did it occur? Did effective treatment remain available? What benefit was probable? What injury would have existed even with reasonable care? How much of the later condition can fairly be attributed to the event? Each answer affects value differently.

A weakness in breach does not affect valuation in the same way as a weakness in damages. A disputed departure may create largely all-or-nothing liability risk. A dispute over injury severity may preserve liability while changing the recoverable amount. A factual conflict about timing may affect both.

Counsel should know which part of the case is creating the uncertainty.

Suppose the standard-of-care theory is strong, but causation depends on a disputed symptom-onset time. Value may become highly sensitive to one factual finding. A case with less obvious breach but strong causation if breach is found will behave differently.

In the first matter, the outcomes may be polarized. In the second, several partial outcomes may be realistic. That shape matters in negotiation.

So does the ease with which the case can be understood.

A treatment delay visible on a straightforward timeline may be compelling. A subtle imaging dispute may depend heavily on expert credibility. A result left unacknowledged for several days may be easier to explain than a nuanced disagreement over whether a complicated presentation required admission.

The simpler theory is not automatically the stronger one, but it may carry less communication risk.

A medically sound case can lose practical value when the fact finder must retain too many technical steps before understanding why the outcome changed. Valuation should account for that without confusing clarity with truth.

Expert quality affects the risk in much the same way.

A sound opinion delivered poorly may carry less practical force. A polished opposing expert may increase exposure even when parts of the analysis are vulnerable.

The issue is not merely whether the witness is likable. It is whether the expert can explain the patient's course naturally, remain credible under serious challenge, and deal honestly with facts that do not favor the opinion.

An expert who acknowledges uncertainty while continuing to support a probable conclusion may increase settlement value. An expert who overstates every point may reduce it.

Opposing experts should be evaluated with equal seriousness. Counsel may disagree with an opinion and still recognize that it is likely to be persuasive.

That recognition should affect valuation. It should not produce surrender, but it should prevent the settlement range from being built on the assumption that the opposing case will collapse merely because counsel thinks it should.

Baseline is one of the largest influences on value because it affects causation, damages, and credibility at the same time.

A patient with substantial prior disease may still have a strong claim, but the attributable injury may need to be described incrementally.

The patient required some assistance before the event and now needs complete care. The patient had limited life expectancy but probably lost a meaningful period of survival. The child had developmental limitations but likely would have achieved substantially greater independence. Those claims can be powerful because they are honest.

Value becomes less stable when baseline cannot be reconstructed or the damages presentation depends on denying obvious prior impairment. A fact finder may react badly to a theory that treats a medically complex patient as previously healthy. The same fact finder may respond strongly to a careful explanation of what function remained and what the event took away.

Credibility concerning baseline affects more than the amount of damages. It affects whether the entire case is trusted.

The nature of the injury also changes the valuation.

Some losses are fixed and visible. An amputation, permanent dialysis, established paralysis, or well-documented severe brain injury may provide a relatively stable damages foundation.

Other injuries depend more heavily on prognosis. Cognitive limitations may be substantial but difficult to demonstrate in a courtroom. A child's eventual independence may remain uncertain. Chronic pain and fatigue may be real and less easily measured. Future-care needs may change as recovery continues. That uncertainty should be incorporated rather than hidden.

A damages analysis may reasonably include more than one future course. It may show care needs if the patient remains at the present level and a lower level if expected improvement occurs. It may calculate more than one plausible survival period. It may separate secure future costs from procedures that are probable but not certain.

Those alternatives help counsel see how value changes with the medical findings. They are more useful than one total that quietly assumes every disputed issue in favor of the party offering it. Economic precision can otherwise become misleading.

A life-care plan may produce an exact present value to the dollar while depending on an unsettled prognosis, disputed life expectancy, and an attendant-care assumption that no treating clinician has adopted.

The arithmetic may be precise while the future underneath it remains uncertain.

Counsel should know which parts of the total are secure and which are sensitive.

Attendant care may dominate the projection. Life expectancy may change the total substantially. Lost earnings may depend on whether the patient can return to part-time work. A proposed future procedure may add significant cost despite uncertain probability. Those assumptions should remain visible throughout valuation.

That is useful for both sides. Plaintiff counsel can distinguish core damages that survive nearly every plausible scenario from more disputed components. Defense counsel can evaluate exposure without assuming that defeating one projected item eliminates the entire claim.

The secure part of the case often creates the negotiating floor. The contested projections create much of the range.

Wrongful-death matters require particular care because the fact of death can overshadow the patient's actual prognosis.

A patient may have been elderly, frail, or seriously ill without being near death. Another may have been living independently despite carrying a diagnosis that sounds severe.

Valuation should follow the patient's probable course rather than the label attached to the disease.

How long would the patient probably have lived? In what condition? What treatment would have been required? Would that period likely have included meaningful function, communication, work, or participation in family life?

The answers may support years of loss, a shorter period of accelerated death, or no reliable causal extension at all. The number should follow that conclusion.

The nature of the final course may also matter. A patient who probably would have survived the acute event but later died from underlying disease lost more than time measured on a calendar. The probable period of survival had a condition and quality.

A case may lack a supportable extension-of-life claim while still containing strong evidence of avoidable pain, invasive treatment, or loss of capacity during the final period.

That is a different damages theory and should be valued as such. It should not be transformed into preventable death merely because death is the larger claim.

Venue, legal standards, and trial history inevitably influence settlement value, but they should be applied after the medical case has been defined.

A favorable venue cannot repair unsupported causation. A difficult venue does not erase strong medicine. Damage caps, evidentiary rules, expert requirements, and jurisdiction-specific treatment of lost chance or wrongful death may affect recoverability. They do not change what probably happened to the patient.

The clinical analysis should remain intact while counsel determines which part of it can be presented and recovered under the governing law.

That separation matters because legal limitations can quietly distort the medical theory. Counsel may feel pressure to overstate complete prevention because the jurisdiction does not recognize a narrower claim. A defense may describe probable reduction in injury as no causation because partial causation is inconvenient.

The medicine should not be reshaped to fit the preferred legal category.

Counsel needs to understand the clinical truth first. The legal consequence follows.

Settlement value should also change as the case develops.

Early valuation is often based on incomplete records, preliminary opinions, and broad assumptions about injury. Later discovery may stabilize or weaken the theory. Depositions may resolve timing. Imaging may become more or less persuasive. The patient may improve. Future-care needs may become clearer. The valuation should move with the evidence.

An early number should not become an anchor merely because it appeared in an initial memorandum or conversation. The original demand may have assumed complete prevention while later review supports increased severity. A defense reserve may have been based on inaccurate baseline information that has since been corrected. Revision should be expected.

Revaluing a case after new evidence is not inconsistency. It is responsible case management.

The same applies to negotiating posture. Counsel may begin aggressively while a central fact remains unresolved and later narrow the range after the evidence stabilizes. A case may also increase in value after a treating witness confirms that the patient remained salvageable during the disputed interval.

Negotiation should reflect what is known now, not what was believed at intake.

The strongest settlement presentation usually begins with the clinical course rather than the demand.

The patient entered with a defined baseline. These findings developed. At this point, reasonable care required action. Treatment remained available. Because the action did not occur, the patient sustained an identifiable additional injury. The future needs arise from that injury. That sequence gives the number a reason.

Beginning with the total and then listing every possible failure can make the demand feel constructed. Beginning with the patient allows value to emerge from the evidence. Defense presentations benefit from the same discipline.

The patient had serious disease before the event. The early presentation did not yet require the proposed intervention. When meaningful signs appeared, the response occurred. Even under the plaintiff's alternative course, some or all of the injury probably would have remained. The future-care model includes needs unrelated to the event. That is more useful than simply calling the demand excessive.

A credible defense identifies which part of the claim is unsupported and explains why.

Settlement often becomes easier once the parties recognize that they disagree less about the care than about the injury.

Both sides may accept that a result was missed or treatment was delayed. The real dispute may be whether the event caused death, accelerated it, or increased the severity of an already developing condition.

Once that is clear, negotiation can move toward the actual medical risk.

The reverse can also occur. The parties may agree that earlier treatment would have helped while disagreeing sharply about whether the original decision was unreasonable. That case has a different settlement structure.

Counsel should know where the agreement lies and where it does not.

A useful valuation also considers how the theory will look once compressed for trial.

Medical cases may be developed through thousands of pages and several experts, while the fact finder remembers only a few transitions. The patient was improving or was not. The symptoms changed. A result returned. Someone knew. Nothing happened. The treatment opportunity closed.

The trial presentation will eventually be built around the clinical events carrying that meaning.

When a case cannot be explained without extensive repair work, value may be affected even if the medicine remains sound. When the opposing theory requires more unsupported assumptions, that should affect the range as well.

Settlement valuation is not a prediction of certainty. It is a judgment about how the medically plausible outcomes are likely to be distributed and what each outcome means financially.

That judgment should be revisited as evidence changes. It should also be candid enough to identify the result counsel least wants to see.

For plaintiff counsel, that may be a finding of breach without causation, or increased severity rather than complete prevention. For defense counsel, it may be a finding that the initial decision was reasonable but the later failure to reassess was not, or that the patient had limited life expectancy but still lost substantial survival.

The uncomfortable middle outcome often matters more than either side's preferred extreme.

A settlement range that ignores it is rarely dependable.

By the time serious negotiations begin, the clinical risk should be capable of being stated plainly. This is the strongest plaintiff outcome. This is the strongest defense outcome. These are the most realistic intermediate findings. These facts determine which outcome is more likely. These damages remain under a narrower causal conclusion, and these disappear if the opposing view is accepted. That is the medical structure of value.

The final number will also reflect law, cost, delay, client needs, insurance, collectability, and the ordinary uncertainty of trial. Those matters belong in the decision, but they should not substitute for understanding what is actually being valued.

Value does not arise from the seriousness of the outcome alone, the existence of an error alone, or the size of an economic report. It arises from the probability that a particular departure produced a particular additional loss and from the range of losses the evidence can responsibly support.

Once that is understood, settlement becomes less about selecting a number and more about pricing the real clinical risk.

"Once that is understood, settlement becomes less about selecting a number and more about pricing the real clinical risk."

CHAPTER TWENTY-NINE

Presenting the Clinical Theory in Mediation and Trial

By the time a medical case reaches mediation or trial, everyone working on it has usually lived with it for a long time. Counsel knows the sequence almost from memory. The experts know the records. The parties have heard the central arguments repeatedly. What began as a patient becoming ill or deteriorating has become a file filled with expert reports, depositions, imaging, policies, demonstratives, economic projections, and thousands of pages of medical documentation.

At that point, the problem is rarely a lack of information. The problem is that the information has become familiar to the people presenting it and overwhelming to everyone else.

A mediator, judge, or jury does not begin where counsel begins. They do not arrive knowing which laboratory value matters, why one imaging study changed the clinical picture, or why a two-hour interval may have determined the outcome. They may not understand the difference between a recognized complication and a failure to rescue, between an abnormal result and one requiring immediate action, or between care that departed from the standard and care that actually caused harm. They have to enter the case through the patient's course.

That is the purpose of the clinical theory at mediation and trial. It is not an opportunity to display everything the litigation team has learned. It is a way to help another person follow the patient from the condition that existed before the disputed care to the injury that followed.

When that movement is clear, complicated medicine becomes manageable. When it is not, the presentation tends to fragment. One expert discusses standard of care. Another discusses causation. A third addresses damages. Counsel explains policies, timing, and communication, and the economist eventually presents the numbers. Each part may be accurate, but the listener is left to assemble the case alone. That is too much to ask.

The clinical connection should already be present in the way the case is told. The patient entered with a particular baseline. A condition developed. Findings accumulated. At some clinically meaningful point, the situation required a different response. That response did not occur, occurred too late, or proved inadequate. While the patient still had a reasonable opportunity to benefit, the opportunity narrowed and eventually closed. The actual course then produced an injury different from the one that probably would have followed with reasonable care.

That is the case. Everything else should help the audience understand it or test it.

Mediation and trial serve different purposes, but they should arise from the same clinical account. The audience changes, the available time changes, and the immediate objective changes. The medicine should not.

At mediation, counsel is generally speaking to people who understand litigation and already know the broad allegations. The task is usually to clarify risk. The mediator does not need a complete medical education. The mediator needs to understand why the case is clinically persuasive, where the uncertainty lies, and what a fact finder might reasonably conclude.

Trial carries a heavier explanatory burden. Jurors may have little medical knowledge and no familiarity with the chart. They need enough context to understand why a finding mattered when it appeared, not merely after the final diagnosis was known.

In either setting, I would begin with the patient rather than the allegation.

Who was this person before the event? Why did the patient seek care? What did the treating team reasonably understand at the beginning? How did the presentation change?

That context allows later decisions to be judged fairly. Without it, hindsight enters the case almost unnoticed. A diagnosis that now appears obvious may not have been obvious at the first encounter. A patient who was critically ill at death may have been stable and salvageable several hours earlier. A serious baseline condition may have limited prognosis without making the acute outcome inevitable.

The audience should see the patient at each meaningful stage rather than only at the end.

This is particularly important for plaintiff counsel because a catastrophic outcome naturally pulls the story backward. Once permanent injury or death is known, the uncertainty surrounding the earlier presentation begins to look smaller than it actually was. A presentation that opens with the final injury and then works backward through a list of criticisms can suggest, even unintentionally, that the outcome itself proves negligence.

The stronger approach is to allow the danger to emerge in the order the clinicians encountered it. The symptoms may have been nonspecific at first. Then a focal finding appeared. Treatment failed to produce the expected response. A test returned. The patient worsened. At that point, the clinical obligation changed.

Acknowledging the earlier uncertainty does not weaken the case. It explains why the later failure mattered.

Defense counsel benefits from the same discipline. A defense presentation should not begin and end with the propositions that the diagnosis was difficult and the patient medically complex. The audience still needs to understand why the decisions remained reasonable as the evidence developed.

What information was reassuring? Which dangerous possibilities were considered? What follow-up or reassessment occurred? When did the condition become recognizable? What treatment remained available at that point?

A defense that cannot answer those questions may sound evasive even when its general propositions are true.

Medical cases are often decided at a transition, when one clinical picture became another. The patient who had postoperative pain now had hypotension. The patient who had dizziness now had focal weakness. The child with fever now had altered responsiveness. The resident with a superficial wound now had deep tissue injury, infection, or vascular compromise.

The obligation often changes at that transition, and that is where the audience usually needs the most help.

It is not enough to show that abnormal findings accumulated. The presentation has to explain what the accumulation meant.

One elevated heart rate can have several benign explanations. Tachycardia accompanied by falling blood pressure, declining urine output, increasing pain, and a falling hemoglobin level presents a recognizable pattern. One complaint of dizziness may be benign. Persistent dizziness accompanied by gait instability, double vision, or focal neurological findings calls for a different level of concern.

The medicine becomes persuasive when the findings are connected rather than merely listed.

That is also why timelines can either clarify a case or bury it. A well-designed timeline shows when findings appeared, who received information, what response followed, and how the treatment opportunity changed. A poor timeline becomes a wall of dates, quotations, and chart entries.

The audience should not have to read twenty events before discovering why the interval matters. The critical period should be visible, and every event included should help explain baseline, recognition, responsibility, treatment, or outcome.

A complete chronology belongs in counsel's preparation. The timeline used at mediation or trial is an explanation.

Medical records used as exhibits require the same restraint. A note may be important to counsel and still be nearly unreadable to a jury. Records contain abbreviations, copied text, templates, and information unrelated to the point being made.

The relevant entry may need to be isolated, enlarged, and placed in context. When the record says "physician notified," the audience should understand what prompted the call and why the communication mattered. When a note describes the patient as stable, the surrounding vital signs may be needed to show whether stable meant reassuring or simply unchanged. When the chart describes imaging as negative, the listener may need to understand which conditions the study could and could not reliably exclude.

The document should support the clinical point rather than become the point itself.

Imaging demands even greater care. Counsel may have spent months studying the images with experts. The jury will see them for the first time.

The image has to be oriented. The audience needs to know which structure is being shown, what normal anatomy looks like, where the abnormality lies, and what the treating professional could reasonably have seen at the time. Later imaging may demonstrate progression, but it should not be used to make an earlier subtle finding look obvious.

Demonstratives can help explain anatomy or progression. They become dangerous when color, arrows, enlargement, or side-by-side comparison creates a clarity that did not exist for the original reader. The distinction between explanation and exaggeration matters.

Plaintiff counsel may lose credibility by presenting a genuinely subtle finding as glaringly apparent. Defense counsel may lose credibility by insisting that nothing was visible when every qualified reader agrees that an abnormality was present. The real disagreement may concern whether it should reasonably have been recognized or whether it was clinically actionable at that point. That is the dispute the audience should hear.

Laboratory evidence is usually easier to understand as a trend than as a series of isolated values. Most people will not remember several numbers recited in sequence. They can understand that blood pressure continued to fall while heart rate rose, kidney function worsened after medication exposure, or infection markers progressed while treatment was delayed.

A graph or simple table may help, but the visual should not imply more biological precision than the evidence supports. When the issue is whether deterioration developed over approximately three hours rather than the exact minute the condition became irreversible, the demonstrative should not invent a sharp dividing line.

Clinical change is often gradual even when the legal analysis asks for precise timing. The experts should be prepared to explain that.

The standard-of-care expert should do more than announce what should have happened. The expert should place the professional obligation inside the actual clinical environment.

What information was available? What remained uncertain? Which options were reasonable? Why did the course selected remain within, or move outside, the acceptable professional range?

The opinion becomes more credible when the expert acknowledges the choices that were genuinely available. A physician may not have been required to know the final diagnosis but may have been required to continue investigating because a dangerous condition had not been excluded. A nurse may not have been expected to diagnose hemorrhage but may have been expected to recognize a concerning pattern and escalate it. A radiologist may not have controlled treatment but may have been responsible for communicating a significant finding in a way likely to produce action. The role should remain specific.

When an expert speaks too broadly, the testimony begins to sound ideological. "Every worsening patient must be admitted" is easy to attack. "This patient remained hypotensive despite treatment, had falling hemoglobin, increasing abdominal pain, and no documented explanation before discharge" is much harder to dismiss. Clinical specificity protects the opinion.

Causation testimony needs the same concreteness. "Earlier treatment would have changed the outcome" is a conclusion. It is not yet an explanation.

The expert should walk the audience through what probably would have happened. What treatment would have been provided? How quickly could it have occurred? Was the patient eligible? What biological effect would the treatment have had? What injury had already developed, and what function or survival probably would have been preserved?

That is often the most important part of the presentation because it makes the alternative course medically real.

In a failure-to-rescue case, the expert may explain that earlier surgery probably would have controlled bleeding before prolonged shock caused organ and neurological injury. In a stroke case, timely treatment may not have eliminated every deficit but may have reduced the amount of injured brain and preserved meaningful function. In a delayed-cancer case, the difference may be earlier-stage treatment, less extensive surgery, or longer survival rather than cure. In an infection case, timely antibiotics and source control may have prevented progression to multiorgan failure even though hospitalization would still have been necessary. The alternative course should not be idealized.

Acknowledging residual injury and treatment burden generally strengthens the explanation. The patient may still have required rehabilitation. A child may still have had developmental limitations. An older adult may still have faced serious chronic disease. The issue is the difference the departure probably made.

That difference must remain consistent through the damages presentation. A life-care planner cannot project complete lifelong dependence when the causation expert expects substantial recovery. An economist cannot calculate ordinary lifetime earnings when the patient's prior condition already limited work. A wrongful-death presentation cannot assume an ordinary life expectancy when the oncology evidence supports a shorter period of survival.

The experts should be describing the same patient and the same alternative life.

This sounds obvious, but it is a common weakness in complicated medical cases. Each expert may form a reasonable opinion within a separate discipline while the assumptions beneath those opinions fail to align. The result feels inflated or disjointed even though no individual witness has necessarily done anything improper.

The solution is not to force every expert into identical language. It is to make the shared clinical foundation clear enough that each discipline begins from the same facts.

Mediation is often the best setting to show where that foundation is stable and where it remains disputed. The patient's baseline may be well documented. The critical findings may be objective. The communication time may remain contested. Treatment may have remained available under one timing scenario and become uncertain under another. The injury may be permanent while the extent of attributable future care remains disputed. That is useful risk information.

A presentation that describes every point as certain can make negotiation harder because it leaves no visible room for movement. A presentation that treats every uncertainty as fatal can undervalue a clinically sound case.

The mediator needs to understand the structure of the disagreement. Which finding could drive a plaintiff verdict? Which fact could support the defense? What intermediate causal conclusion is realistic? Which damages remain if the fact finder accepts the narrower conclusion? That allows the discussion to move beyond opening numbers.

In many cases, the most productive mediation point is not that one side is wholly wrong. It is that the matter can resolve in more than two ways. A fact finder may conclude that the initial discharge was reasonable but the return visit was not. Death may have been accelerated without being wholly preventable. A complication may have been unavoidable while rescue was delayed. Substantial future care may be recoverable even if the entire life-care plan is not accepted. Those outcomes should be visible in the negotiation.

Trial calls for a different kind of restraint because every subject competes for attention. Counsel may fear that leaving out a fact creates vulnerability. More often, trying to present every fact causes the central ones to disappear.

The case needs a clinical spine: the baseline, the transition, the obligation, the response that occurred or failed to occur, the remaining treatment opportunity, and the resulting injury.

Every witness and exhibit should connect to that spine.

Background medicine should be included only to the extent needed to understand the decision. Jurors do not need a medical-school lecture on the entire disease. They need enough medicine to understand what the clinicians knew and what timely care could have changed.

The same principle applies to anatomy. A detailed explanation of cerebral circulation may be necessary in one posterior-stroke case. It may add little in another when the central issue is whether repeated focal symptoms required further evaluation. Complexity should serve the disputed issue.

Opening statement should introduce the clinical theory without pretending to prove it. It can tell the audience what the evidence will show about the patient's condition, the developing risk, and the opportunity that was lost.

The strongest openings often avoid broad accusations. They do not begin by announcing that the defendants ignored the patient or, from the defense side, that the case is merely an unfortunate outcome. They begin with the course.

The patient entered able to walk and speak. During the next several hours, particular findings developed. The treating team received specific information. The situation required a response. By the time treatment occurred, the condition had progressed beyond the point at which the same recovery remained probable. That structure allows the criticism to emerge from the evidence.

A defense opening can do the same. The patient arrived with symptoms supporting several reasonable diagnoses. The examination contained genuinely reassuring findings. The dangerous condition did not become clinically apparent until later. When the presentation changed, the team responded. The injury had already developed or probably would not have been materially altered by the earlier intervention proposed.

The defense should explain why the care was reasonable rather than simply characterize it as reasonable.

Witness order should also follow understanding rather than convention whenever possible. The first witness does not always need to be the patient or the earliest provider. The sequence should help the jury build the clinical account without requiring unexplained details to be retained for several days.

A baseline witness may be useful early when prior function is disputed. A treating witness may introduce the presentation. An imaging expert may be easier to understand after the symptoms and clinical concerns have been explained. A causation expert should not be asked to describe an alternative course before the audience understands what actually happened. The order should feel natural.

The same principle applies within an expert examination. The expert should usually explain the patient before offering the legal conclusion. Begin with what was happening medically. Move to what the situation required. Then explain the consequence.

An expert who begins with “the defendant breached the standard of care” may sound retained before sounding clinical. An expert who first walks the audience through the developing condition is more likely to sound like a physician explaining medicine.

Cross-examination should remain clinically focused as well. Compensation, testimony history, and prior advocacy may matter, but they rarely replace an examination of the reasoning.

The most effective cross often requires the expert to live with the facts the report minimized. The patient returned with a new deficit. Blood pressure remained low despite treatment. The abnormal result had been available for two days. The proposed transfer involved several steps the expert never included. The patient already had an impairment the report described as new.

The purpose is not necessarily to make the expert adopt the opposing theory. It is to determine whether the opinion remains coherent when the difficult evidence is restored. Sometimes it will.

A strong opposing expert may explain why the abnormality remained nonspecific, why treatment was unlikely to help, or why pre-existing disease better accounts for the outcome. Counsel should know that explanation before trial.

Clinical Intelligence does not eliminate disagreement. It ensures that the disagreement occurs on the actual medicine.

Closing argument should return to the course introduced at the beginning rather than becoming a new medical presentation. By then, the audience should already understand the critical transition and the treatment opportunity. Counsel can connect the evidence to the governing legal questions.

What did reasonable care require at the point that mattered? Did the responsible person or institution provide it? What probably would have happened with appropriate care? What injury resulted from the difference?

The argument should not depend on the volume of criticism.

One clear departure with a strong causal connection is more persuasive than a list of every charting defect, policy deviation, communication problem, and discourteous interaction.

The defense should likewise resist defending everything. Conceding an immaterial documentation lapse or operational imperfection may make the central medical defense easier to hear. The patient did not receive perfect care. The issue is whether the care fell outside the reasonable professional range and caused the injury being claimed. That can be a strong position when the medicine supports it.

Plaintiff counsel can make a similar concession. The clinicians were not required to guarantee recovery or make an immediate diagnosis. They were required to respond reasonably when the patient's course changed. That keeps the case grounded.

Medical trials can become emotionally intense, particularly in wrongful-death, pediatric, maternal, and catastrophic-injury matters. Emotion is not inappropriate. The patient's loss is part of the case.

The medical theory should not depend on emotion carrying a weak causal link. Nor should the defense attempt to neutralize human loss through abstraction. A respectful acknowledgment of injury can make room for a serious causation defense.

The patient's humanity and clinical discipline can coexist. The strongest presentations usually contain both.

The patient should not be reduced to a diagnosis or a damages figure. The clinicians should not be reduced to villains or job titles. The case should be presented as a series of real decisions made under real conditions, followed by a real consequence.

By mediation or trial, the Clinical Intelligence Model should no longer be visible as a separate framework. It should have become the way the case is told.

The baseline is present because the audience understands who the patient was. Objective evidence is present because the condition can be seen developing. The timeline is present because the audience understands when the obligation changed. Workflow is present because responsibility is clear. Causation is present because the alternative course feels clinically real. Damages are present because the audience can see what the patient lost.

The framework has done its work when the case feels understandable rather than organized.

The final presentation should leave the audience with an account simple enough to carry into the decision: this patient was in this condition; at this point, the care did or did not meet what the situation required; and that difference did or did not change what followed. Everything important should fit within that explanation.

"Everything important should fit within that explanation."

PART V

APPLIED CASE ANALYSIS

Chapters 30–37

CHAPTER THIRTY

Delayed Stroke Diagnosis After Repeated Emergency Encounters

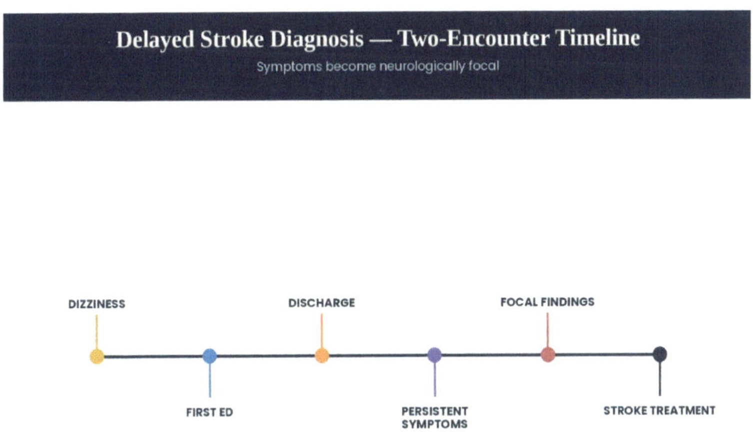

A forty-eight-year-old woman arrived at an emergency department late in the afternoon complaining of dizziness, nausea, and difficulty walking. She had awakened feeling well and developed symptoms several hours later while at work. A colleague described her as pale and unsteady and drove her to the hospital after she vomited and nearly fell while trying to stand.

Her medical history included hypertension, migraine headaches, and one remote episode of vertigo. She did not smoke. She worked full time as an office manager, drove, managed her household, and regularly helped care for her elderly mother. Nothing in the recent records suggested progressive neurological decline or any meaningful loss of function.

At triage, her blood pressure was elevated. She described a severe spinning sensation that worsened when she moved her head. The nurse recorded nausea, vomiting, and an unsteady gait. The physician documented dizziness without facial droop, speech disturbance, or focal weakness and described the general neurological examination as normal.

She received intravenous fluids, medication for nausea, and a vestibular suppressant. A noncontrast CT scan of the head was interpreted as showing no acute intracranial abnormality. After several hours, the nausea improved, although the patient continued to report dizziness. The chart stated that she could ambulate, but it did not describe her gait in any detail. She was discharged with a diagnosis of peripheral vertigo and instructed to return if her symptoms worsened.

Her husband later said that she needed help reaching the car and leaned against the wall as she walked. The discharge nurse had no independent memory of the encounter. The patient returned the following morning by ambulance.

She had remained dizzy during the night and vomited again. In the morning, her husband found that she could not stand without falling to one side. She also complained of double vision and numbness around her mouth. Emergency medical personnel documented slurred speech and severe imbalance.

At the hospital, the second physician observed horizontal nystagmus, dysarthria, and marked gait instability. A stroke alert was not activated immediately because symptom onset was recorded as the previous afternoon. The physician ordered another noncontrast CT and later a CT angiographic study. The second noncontrast scan again showed no hemorrhage. The angiographic images demonstrated a posterior-circulation abnormality that was initially described cautiously as indeterminate.

Neurology was consulted by telephone and recommended admission and magnetic resonance imaging. Several hours later, MRI demonstrated acute infarction involving the cerebellum and brainstem. While awaiting transfer to a tertiary center, the patient became less responsive and required intubation.

Further imaging showed swelling in the posterior fossa with compression of surrounding structures. She underwent emergency decompressive surgery.

She survived, but rehabilitation was prolonged. Dysarthria, impaired coordination, swallowing difficulty, and severe balance dysfunction persisted. She could walk short distances with an assistive device and another person nearby, but she could no longer drive or return to her former work. She needed help with transportation, meal preparation, medication organization, and many activities outside the home.

Her husband contacted counsel after a rehabilitation physician mentioned that posterior strokes can be missed because early CT imaging may appear normal.

The initial legal theory was broad. The first emergency physician was said to have failed to diagnose stroke, failed to order MRI, failed to obtain neurological consultation, and discharged a patient who could not walk safely. The second encounter was criticized for delayed stroke activation and delayed transfer. The resulting neurological injury was described as entirely preventable.

That theory reflected the seriousness of the outcome. It did not yet reflect the medicine.

The first task was to understand what the symptoms meant during each encounter. Dizziness is common, and most dizziness is not caused by stroke. Nausea, vomiting, and symptoms made worse by head movement can occur with peripheral vestibular disease. A history of vertigo and migraine made that explanation plausible.

The case could not responsibly be built on the premise that dizziness required an immediate stroke diagnosis.

The more useful inquiry was whether this patient's dizziness included features that should have moved the evaluation beyond a benign vestibular explanation.

The triage record described significant difficulty walking. The physician recorded a normal neurological examination but did not describe gait, limb coordination, eye movements in detail, or a structured examination intended to distinguish a central cause from a peripheral one. The discharge documentation said that the patient ambulated, but the basis for that statement was unclear. That conflict became central.

If the patient walked independently and improved substantially after treatment, the discharge decision was easier to defend. If she remained unable to stand or walk safely, the clinical picture was materially different.

Her husband's account supported continuing severe imbalance. The nursing record did not resolve the issue, and the first physician had no independent recollection. The case therefore depended partly on the weight given to the contemporaneous documentation and partly on what reasonable care required when acute persistent dizziness was accompanied by significant gait disturbance. The first CT did not answer that question.

A noncontrast CT is useful for detecting hemorrhage and several other acute conditions. It is less sensitive for early ischemic injury in the posterior circulation, particularly when the affected area is small or obscured by surrounding bone. A negative study could not, by itself, exclude the condition ultimately diagnosed.

That did not make the physician negligent for ordering or considering the CT. It meant the study had to be understood alongside the clinical presentation and its known limitations.

The original images were obtained and reviewed independently. The plaintiff's neuroradiologist found no definite acute infarction, although the expert noted a subtle asymmetry that could not reasonably be called diagnostic. The defense reviewer considered the scan appropriately negative.

The disagreement over the first CT did not become the center of the case. Neither expert could support the position that the stroke should have been diagnosed from that study alone.

The more important issue was whether continued inability to walk, if established, should have led to observation, neurological consultation, or further evaluation despite the negative scan. The standard-of-care analysis divided naturally at that point.

The emergency-medicine expert did not believe that every patient with acute dizziness required MRI or a neurological consultation. The concern arose from the combination of persistent symptoms, repeated vomiting, and severe gait disturbance.

The opinion was not that the physician should have known the final diagnosis. It was that a central cause had not been reasonably excluded before discharge if the patient remained unable to walk safely. That changed the character of the case.

The first encounter was no longer presented as an obvious stroke ignored by the emergency department. It became a difficult dizziness presentation in which the reasonableness of discharge depended heavily on whether the remaining gait abnormality had been adequately assessed and explained. The second encounter was clinically different.

By then, the patient had double vision, dysarthria, facial sensory symptoms, and profound imbalance. The presentation was no longer limited to dizziness. A posterior neurological process should have been high in the differential diagnosis.

At that stage, the principal dispute shifted from recognition to timing and treatment.

The onset history created immediate difficulty. If all symptoms were treated as one continuous event beginning the previous afternoon, some conventional time-dependent therapies may no longer have been available by the time of the second presentation. If the focal deficits reflected progression during the night, other treatment or transfer opportunities may still have remained.

The records did not establish the precise time at which the vascular event began or progressed. The patient had been dizzy for many hours before returning. No witness could say exactly when the artery became critically narrowed or occluded, when infarction began, or when the later swelling became inevitable.

That uncertainty prevented a simple conclusion that treatment during the first encounter would have produced complete recovery.

The vascular neurologist retained on causation would not give that opinion.

The expert believed that earlier recognition and advanced vascular imaging during the first encounter probably would have identified the posterior-circulation process before profound deterioration. The patient likely would have been admitted, monitored, treated medically, and evaluated at a center capable of intervention if the vascular abnormality had been confirmed.

What the expert would not say was that every area of infarction would have been prevented.

Some ischemic injury may already have been developing when the patient first arrived. Available treatment would have depended on anatomy, imaging, timing, and progression. The later swelling might still have required surgery.

The supportable causation opinion was narrower and more useful. Earlier recognition and management probably would have reduced the extent of infarction, allowed closer monitoring before neurological collapse, and improved the likelihood of preserving speech, swallowing, balance, and independent mobility. That remained a substantial claim. It was not the claim initially presented.

The second encounter required a separate analysis. The patient arrived with clearer central findings, but the duration of symptoms complicated the available treatment decisions. The emergency physician obtained imaging and contacted neurology. The concern was whether the vascular study, transfer process, reassessment, and deterioration were handled with sufficient urgency.

The initial angiographic interpretation described the posterior-circulation finding cautiously. The receiving center accepted the patient, but transfer had not occurred before she became less responsive. The record contained separate intervals for completion of imaging, communication of the report, neurological consultation, acceptance, transport arrangements, and reassessment. No single delay explained the entire outcome.

The second emergency physician had recognized the need for admission and specialty care. The radiology interpretation was disputed but did not appear plainly outside the reasonable professional range. Transfer required time, and the hospital did not have immediate neurointerventional capability.

The stronger criticism concerned the period during which the patient worsened while awaiting transfer. The chart did not show frequent, structured neurological reassessment, and escalation appeared more reactive than anticipatory.

Even there, causation remained difficult. Infarction and swelling were already progressing. Earlier transfer might have allowed intervention or decompression before profound decline, but no reliable expert could say that every later deficit would have been prevented.

The case became one of accumulated lost opportunity rather than one dramatic missed moment.

During the first encounter, the patient may have been discharged without adequate resolution of a concerning central sign. During the second, the condition was recognized, but the urgency of deterioration and transfer may not have been matched fully to the risk.

The litigation team had to decide whether to combine those stages or concentrate on one.

Combining every possible criticism created problems. It suggested that the first physician should have diagnosed an obvious stroke and that the second team did nothing for several hours. Neither proposition fairly described the record.

The stronger case began with the discharge decision at the first encounter and used the second encounter to show the progression the earlier evaluation had failed to anticipate. The conduct of the second team remained part of the clinical sequence, but every later interval was not treated as a separate cause of the entire injury. That decision affected the defendant structure.

The neuroradiology claim involving the first CT was not pursued because the original images did not support a reliable departure. The claim involving the second radiologist was narrowed because the angiographic abnormality had been identified, although cautiously. The central case remained focused on the emergency evaluation, the discharge decision, and the institution's ability to respond to a patient with a suspected posterior stroke.

Baseline was comparatively straightforward, but it remained important. Earlier records showed controlled hypertension, intermittent migraine, and one remote episode of benign positional vertigo. There was no documented gait disorder, speech impairment, swallowing difficulty, or cognitive decline.

Employment records and family testimony confirmed that the patient worked consistently, drove, managed finances, and cared for her mother.

That baseline made the later functional loss clear. It also prevented the history of vertigo from being used as though it explained the permanent neurological deficits. The prior condition mattered because it made the initial benign diagnosis more plausible. It did not account for what followed.

The injury analysis still had to separate the stroke itself from the additional severity attributed to delayed recognition.

The patient could not credibly claim that no neurological injury would have occurred. The vascular pathology was real, and symptoms had already begun. The experts could not reconstruct an alternative future of complete neurological normality.

They could identify functions that probably had a better chance of being preserved.

The later MRI showed injury in areas associated with coordination, speech, swallowing, and balance. Progression between the initial symptoms and the later collapse supported the conclusion that the injury increased over time. Earlier monitoring and treatment would not have guaranteed recovery, but the final level of disability was not considered fixed at the first presentation. The damages analysis followed that narrower conclusion.

Before the event, the patient worked full time, drove, and lived independently. After rehabilitation, she remained capable of performing much of her personal care, although it took longer and required adaptive strategies. She needed assistance with balance-dependent activities, transportation, organization, and activities outside the home.

She was not completely dependent, and the case did not present her that way.

A life-care plan assuming continuous attendant care would not have matched her actual function. The supportable needs involved periodic therapy, mobility equipment, home-safety modifications, transportation assistance, medical follow-up, and help with certain household and community activities.

Her vocational loss was nevertheless substantial. Dysarthria, impaired coordination, fatigue, and inability to drive made return to her former management position unrealistic. Whether she retained some part-time employment capacity remained a legitimate issue.

The economic analysis therefore used more than one employment scenario rather than assuming unqualified total lifetime unemployability. That strengthened the damages presentation.

The defense theory carried real weight. Acute dizziness is commonly benign. The first neurological examination was documented as normal. The CT did not show a definite acute lesion. The patient's gait at discharge was disputed. The onset and progression of the stroke could not be fixed precisely. No expert could guarantee that earlier treatment would have prevented surgery or permanent deficit. Those were not peripheral weaknesses. They were part of the case.

The plaintiff theory remained supportable because the most concerning feature was not the word dizziness. It was severe and persistent gait dysfunction in a patient whose condition may not have improved enough to make discharge safe.

The plaintiff did not need to prove that the physician should have named the stroke with certainty. The theory was that the unresolved possibility of a central neurological process required further observation or evaluation.

Causation remained the more difficult part of the matter. The opinion was based on a materially better outcome, not complete prevention. The case therefore depended on whether the fact finder would accept that earlier recognition probably would have preserved a better level of function.

That conclusion was supported by the progression of symptoms, later vascular findings, the patient's age and baseline, and the treatment opportunities available before profound deterioration. It also contained unavoidable uncertainty. The mediation presentation reflected that reality.

It did not begin with surgery or permanent disability. It began with the first emergency visit and the practical question of whether the patient could walk safely when she was discharged.

The entry stating that she had ambulated was placed alongside the triage description of marked unsteadiness and the husband's account of helping her reach the car. The medical discussion focused on why continuing severe gait instability changes the evaluation of acute dizziness.

The first CT was described accurately as nondiagnostic rather than portrayed as an obvious missed stroke.

The causation presentation then followed the progression. The patient returned with focal findings. Advanced imaging revealed the posterior-circulation process. MRI showed established infarction. She deteriorated before transfer and required decompression.

The expert explained that earlier recognition probably would not have guaranteed a normal outcome but likely would have reduced the extent and severity of injury through earlier monitoring, treatment, and specialty intervention. That was the risk presented to the defense.

The defense emphasized the documented normal examination, the common benign causes of dizziness, the negative CT, uncertainty concerning onset, and the inability to identify one intervention at the first encounter that would have prevented the entire injury. Both sides had medically coherent positions.

Settlement value did not turn on whether a jury would believe that the patient suffered a devastating stroke. That was undisputed. It turned on three narrower issues: whether the patient remained severely unable to walk at discharge, whether that condition required further central neurological evaluation despite the negative CT, and whether earlier recognition probably would have produced a materially better outcome.

The first issue depended on conflicting factual evidence. The second involved emergency-medicine judgment. The third depended on an alternative course that supported reduced severity and improved function but not complete prevention. The case resolved without trial.

The resolution reflected substantial exposure, although not the value of a case in which both liability and complete causal prevention were secure. The plaintiff's willingness to narrow the injury allowed the negotiation to focus on a defensible loss rather than an absolute theory the medicine could not carry.

The significance of the case lies less in the settlement than in the way the theory changed during review.

It began as a missed-diagnosis case and became a discharge and reassessment case. It began with the assertion that stroke should have been obvious on the first CT, but the original imaging did not support that position. It began as a claim that the entire neurological injury was preventable and became an increased-severity case based on the probable preservation of meaningful function.

The analytical work remained consistent. Baseline had to be established. Objective evidence had to be reviewed independently. The clinically material timeline had to be reconstructed. The professional obligation had to be identified at the point it arose. The treatment opportunity had to be realistic. The actual course had to be compared with the probable alternative, and the injury had to be stated at the level the medicine supported.

What changed were the facts specific to this patient and the conclusion those facts permitted.

That is the value of applying a consistent clinical method across different cases. It does not force the facts into a predetermined malpractice theory.

It allows the theory to become the case the medicine can honestly carry.

"It allows the theory to become the case the medicine can honestly carry."

CHAPTER THIRTY-ONE

Postoperative Deterioration and Failure to Rescue

Postoperative Deterioration — Failure-to-Rescue Window

Expected recovery stops fitting the data

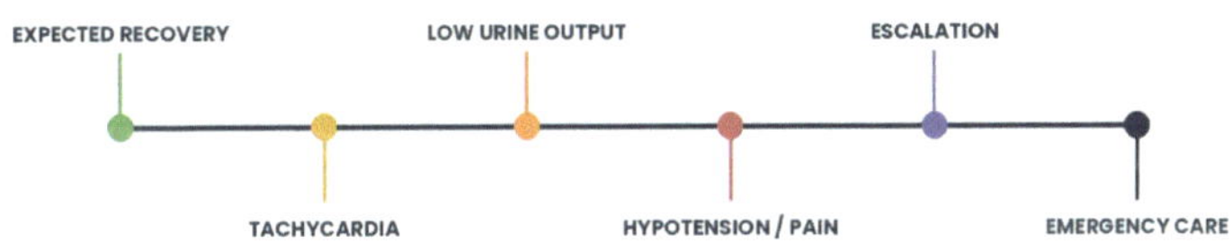

A sixty-two-year-old man underwent elective abdominal surgery for a localized malignancy. The operation was technically difficult, but the record did not identify an intraoperative complication. He arrived on the surgical floor late that afternoon awake, hemodynamically stable, and experiencing the degree of pain that would not have been unusual after a major procedure. His hemoglobin was lower than it had been before surgery, although not unexpectedly so.

Before the operation, he had been living independently with his wife and working part time in a family business. He remained physically active despite hypertension and well-controlled diabetes. His cardiac function was preserved, and he had no history of chronic kidney disease, cognitive impairment, or meaningful mobility limitation.

That baseline became important because the man who eventually returned home was not the man who entered the hospital.

For the first several hours after surgery, the team had little reason for alarm. He was awake, conversant, and able to participate in his care. During the night, however, the picture began to change. His pain increased. His heart rate rose gradually. His blood pressure moved below its usual range, and his urine output began to fall.

Shortly after midnight, the nurse called the covering surgical resident about the increasing abdominal pain and tachycardia. The resident ordered additional pain medication and intravenous fluid. For a time, the patient appeared to respond. His heart rate improved, and his blood pressure rose after the fluid bolus.

Had that improvement continued, observation might have remained a reasonable course. It did not.

Over the next several hours, the patient became pale and increasingly restless. His blood pressure fell again, urine output remained low, and the abdominal dressing showed some drainage. The abdomen was described as more distended. A repeat hemoglobin level was ordered, but the request was entered as routine rather than urgent, and the specimen was not collected promptly.

The nurse called the resident again. What she reported during that conversation became one of the factual disputes in the case. She later testified that she described the falling blood pressure, persistent tachycardia, reduced urine output, abdominal distention, and her concern that the patient might be bleeding. The resident remembered the call differently. He recalled being told that the patient remained uncomfortable and had a borderline blood pressure after receiving pain medication.

No one disputed that the attending surgeon was not called.

The resident ordered another fluid bolus and instructed the nurse to continue monitoring.

By early morning, the patient was confused and difficult to arouse. His blood pressure had fallen markedly. The repeat hemoglobin level, finally obtained more than two hours after it was ordered, showed a substantial further decline. A rapid response was activated, the attending surgeon was notified, and the patient was transferred to intensive care.

He received blood products and underwent emergency reoperation. The surgeons found a large volume of blood in the abdomen from active postoperative bleeding. The source was identified and controlled.

The patient survived, but by then he had experienced prolonged shock. He developed acute kidney injury requiring temporary dialysis, respiratory failure, and neurological impairment attributed to global hypoperfusion. He remained hospitalized for several weeks before transfer to inpatient rehabilitation.

His kidney function eventually improved enough for dialysis to be discontinued, and his respiratory condition recovered. The neurological injury did not fully resolve. When he returned home, he had impaired short-term memory, slowed processing, poor endurance, and reduced balance. He could manage most personal care, but he could no longer run the family business, drive safely, or take responsibility for complex financial decisions.

The family initially understood the matter as a surgical-error case. The patient had entered the hospital for a planned operation and emerged with permanent cognitive impairment, so counsel retained a surgical expert to determine what had gone wrong during the procedure.

The expert found no reliable evidence that the operation itself had been performed negligently.

Postoperative bleeding was a recognized complication of this surgery. The source found during reoperation could have developed despite reasonable technique. Nothing in the operative note, pathology, or later findings supported the conclusion that the surgeon had injured an unexpected structure or failed to control an obvious bleeding point before closure. That did not end the case. It changed it.

The clinically important issue was no longer why bleeding began. It was why the bleeding continued long enough to cause prolonged shock and permanent injury.

Once that distinction was made, the case moved away from technical negligence in the operating room and toward the postoperative failure to rescue.

A complication can begin without negligence and still become legally significant when deterioration is not recognized and treated while recovery remains probable. The analysis then shifts from operative technique to the course that followed.

The first task was to determine when the postoperative picture stopped looking ordinary.

Pain, tachycardia, mild hypotension, reduced urine output, and a lower hemoglobin level can all occur after major surgery. None proves active hemorrhage by itself. The question was when those findings, considered together and over time, required something more than routine monitoring and repeated fluid administration.

The answer did not lie in one number. It lay in the way the findings moved together.

The heart rate rose and remained elevated. Blood pressure improved briefly after fluid and then fell again. Urine output stayed low. Pain increased rather than stabilizing. The abdomen became more distended. Pallor and restlessness appeared, followed eventually by confusion. When the repeat hemoglobin was finally obtained, it confirmed a substantial decline.

The central issue was when those findings should have been recognized as one developing pattern rather than several unrelated postoperative problems.

The first call to the resident occurred while the patient was still awake, responsive, and physiologically recoverable. The temporary improvement after fluid gave some support to continued observation. A short-term response to treatment can reasonably influence clinical judgment.

The difficulty arose when that response did not hold.

A blood pressure that rises after fluid and then falls again does not establish stability. An improving heart rate accompanied by continued low urine output does not exclude ongoing blood loss. Once the patient failed to follow the expected course, the earlier explanation needed to be reconsidered. This marked the clinical transition.

The standard-of-care opinion did not depend on arguing that the first fluid order was negligent. It depended on what happened after deterioration continued despite the plan.

The surgical expert believed the covering resident should have returned to the bedside, treated the pattern as possible postoperative bleeding, expedited the laboratory work, and notified the attending surgeon earlier. Whether the patient should have returned immediately to the operating room at the moment of the second call was harder to determine because the examination and objective findings from that interval were incompletely documented.

What the expert could support was that the attending surgeon should have been brought into the case before the patient entered profound shock. The nursing analysis was more complicated.

The nurse had recognized deterioration and made repeated calls. The record showed frequent documentation of vital signs and eventual activation of the rapid-response process. She was not simply inattentive to the patient.

The real issue was whether she should have escalated beyond the resident when the patient continued to worsen.

The institution had a chain-of-command policy allowing nurses to contact the attending surgeon, a nursing supervisor, or the rapid-response team when an initial response failed to resolve an urgent concern. The nurse testified that she believed the resident understood the seriousness of the situation and expected him to contact the surgeon. She did not independently call the attending until the patient became confused and profoundly hypotensive. That testimony placed the issue inside the actual workflow.

The nurse had communicated. The resident had responded. Treatment had been ordered. The concern was not ignored in the ordinary sense. The failure was that the treatment did not restore stability, and the escalation pathway stopped too soon.

The plaintiff's nursing expert believed that continuing instability after repeated communication required activation of the chain of command. The defense expert emphasized that the resident was the responsible physician overnight, had issued orders, and had not instructed the nurse to contact the attending. The defense also made a fair point that nurses cannot be expected to override every physician decision merely because a postoperative patient remains uncomfortable or mildly abnormal. That argument carried weight early in the night. It became less persuasive as the clinical picture changed.

The later course involved more than persistent pain and borderline vital signs. It included recurrent hypotension, reduced urine output, progressive abdominal distention, pallor, restlessness, and altered mental status. The nursing obligation evolved with the patient.

The case did not require the nurse to diagnose internal bleeding. It required recognition that the patient remained unstable despite the resident's plan and that another level of response had become necessary.

The resident's role remained central because he received the information, interpreted the findings, and controlled physician escalation during the critical interval.

The dispute over the content of the second call mattered, but the case did not depend entirely on resolving it. The nurse described a more alarming message than the resident remembered, and the chart did not capture the full substance of either conversation. The resident nevertheless acknowledged knowing that the patient had persistent tachycardia, lower blood pressure, reduced urine output, and increasing pain. He also acknowledged that he did not return to the bedside after the second call. That narrowed the disagreement considerably.

Even under the resident's account, enough information was available to show that the patient had not responded as expected. The case did not turn on whether the nurse used the word bleeding. The physician's responsibility was to interpret the pattern rather than wait for nursing staff to provide the diagnosis.

The delayed hemoglobin result also needed to be kept in proportion.

It would have been easy to make the phlebotomy delay the center of the case because the eventual value was dramatic. The clinical evidence did not support that simplification. The patient already required reassessment and escalation before the laboratory result became available. An urgent hemoglobin would have helped confirm the problem, but the absence of that value did not justify waiting while the patient deteriorated.

The laboratory delay contributed to uncertainty. It did not create the entire failure.

That distinction affected the institutional analysis. The hospital's urgent collection procedures, escalation process, and rapid-response structure were reviewed. The order had been entered at the wrong priority. There was no evidence that the laboratory ignored an urgent request; the resident had selected routine collection.

The operational problem therefore remained linked to the clinical decision rather than becoming a separate laboratory-negligence theory.

Causation required reconstructing the patient's condition before profound shock developed.

The reoperation findings established that intra-abdominal bleeding had continued. The later organ injuries were biologically consistent with prolonged inadequate perfusion. Kidney injury, respiratory failure, metabolic disturbance, and global neurological impairment followed the period of hypotension.

The question was whether earlier recognition and control of the bleeding probably would have prevented or materially reduced those injuries.

The surgical and critical-care experts agreed that the bleeding source was treatable. The patient had no major organ failure before the deterioration. He responded temporarily to fluid, suggesting that circulation remained at least partially recoverable. The bleeding source identified during reoperation was controllable.

The experts also agreed that earlier recognition would not have produced an uncomplicated postoperative course. The patient still would have required transfusion, intensive monitoring, and probably reoperation.

The alternative course was not a smooth recovery after the original procedure.

The meaningful difference was the duration and depth of the shock.

Earlier escalation probably would have led to urgent laboratory testing, direct surgical evaluation, preparation of blood products, and reoperation before confusion and profound hypotension developed. That would not have guaranteed avoidance of every complication, but it likely would have shortened the period of inadequate organ perfusion.

The kidney injury probably would have been less severe and may not have occurred. Prolonged ventilation would have been less likely. The strongest causation opinion concerned the neurological injury, which followed sustained shock and had not existed before the event. Even there, the experts were careful.

The patient's later cognitive complaints could not simply be attributed wholesale to hypoperfusion. He had undergone prolonged hospitalization, sedation, critical illness, sleep disruption, and substantial deconditioning. Each can affect cognition, particularly during early recovery.

The persistence of deficits after rehabilitation, neuropsychological testing, and the absence of comparable preoperative impairment supported a permanent component. The damages presentation still required restraint.

The patient was not globally incapacitated. He remained communicative, lived at home, and managed most personal care. His principal losses involved executive function, short-term memory, endurance, balance, driving, and the ability to perform complex work and financial tasks.

A future-care plan based on total dependence would have overstated the injury.

The supportable needs included periodic medical follow-up, cognitive and physical rehabilitation, transportation assistance, help with financial management, home-safety measures, and assistance with selected household activities. Continuous attendant care was not justified.

The vocational loss was more significant because his work in the family business had required planning, judgment, multitasking, supervision, and financial oversight. He could no longer perform those functions reliably. Whether he retained some capacity for simple, part-time work remained open.

The economic analysis therefore reflected loss of his former role without assuming that he had no productive capacity of any kind.

The defense theory deserved serious consideration. It did not deny that the patient bled or that earlier intervention would have been preferable. It focused on the difficulty, during the early postoperative hours, of distinguishing ordinary recovery from meaningful hemorrhage. The transient response to fluid, the absence of obvious external bleeding, and the lack of an early laboratory result supported the resident's initial judgment.

The defense also disputed how much permanent neurological impairment could be attributed specifically to shock. It pointed to critical illness, medication, vascular risk, and the absence of one definitive imaging finding showing hypoxic brain injury. Those were real issues.

The early part of the night was ambiguous. The plaintiff's case became stronger only when the trajectory was considered over time. The neurological causation opinion also depended more on the clinical course and neuropsychological evidence than on one unmistakable image.

The plaintiff theory remained persuasive because it was not built around the first abnormal vital sign. It was built around what happened after the abnormalities persisted, accumulated, and stopped behaving like an ordinary postoperative course.

Temporary improvement after fluid did not end the concern. It created a reason to determine whether the improvement would last. It did not.

The mediation presentation began with the postoperative course rather than the later cognitive injury. The patient left surgery awake and stable. During the night, his heart rate rose, blood pressure fell, urine output declined, pain increased, and the abdomen became distended. Fluid produced only temporary improvement. The nurse called twice. The resident did not return to the bedside or notify the attending. The patient then became confused and profoundly hypotensive.

That sequence allowed the failure-to-rescue theory to emerge without suggesting that every earlier decision had been negligent.

The complication itself was acknowledged as a recognized surgical risk. That concession strengthened the case because it placed the criticism where the evidence supported it.

The defense could argue that the resident's initial decisions were reasonable under uncertain circumstances. The plaintiff could answer that an initially reasonable judgment did not remain reasonable after the patient failed to respond as expected. That became the center of the dispute.

Settlement discussions also reflected divided responsibility. The resident's conduct remained central. The nursing-escalation issue added exposure, but the case was not presented as though the nurse had ignored the patient. The institution's role arose from chain-of-command expectations, supervision, and the overnight response structure rather than a generalized allegation of unsafe staffing. The case resolved after the expert depositions.

The resolution reflected strong evidence of delayed rescue, a controllable bleeding source, and a coherent biological relationship between prolonged shock and later injury. It also reflected uncertainty about the precise moment at which surgery should have occurred, whether earlier intervention would have prevented every complication, and how much permanent cognitive loss could be attributed solely to the delay. The case began as an allegation that the surgeon caused the bleeding. It ended as a case about what happened after the bleeding began.

That was not a fallback theory. It was the theory the records supported.

The patient's baseline showed meaningful function and organ reserve. The objective evidence showed progressive physiological instability. The timeline revealed temporary improvement followed by continued decline. The workflow showed repeated communication that failed to produce sufficient escalation. The treatment opportunity remained open while the source was still controllable. The alternative course still included reoperation and intensive care, but probably not the same prolonged shock and permanent impairment. The injury was not the existence of postoperative bleeding.

It was what the patient lost while the bleeding continued without effective rescue.

"It was what the patient lost while the bleeding continued without effective rescue."

CHAPTER THIRTY-TWO

Missed Infection and Wrongful Death in a Medically Fragile Patient

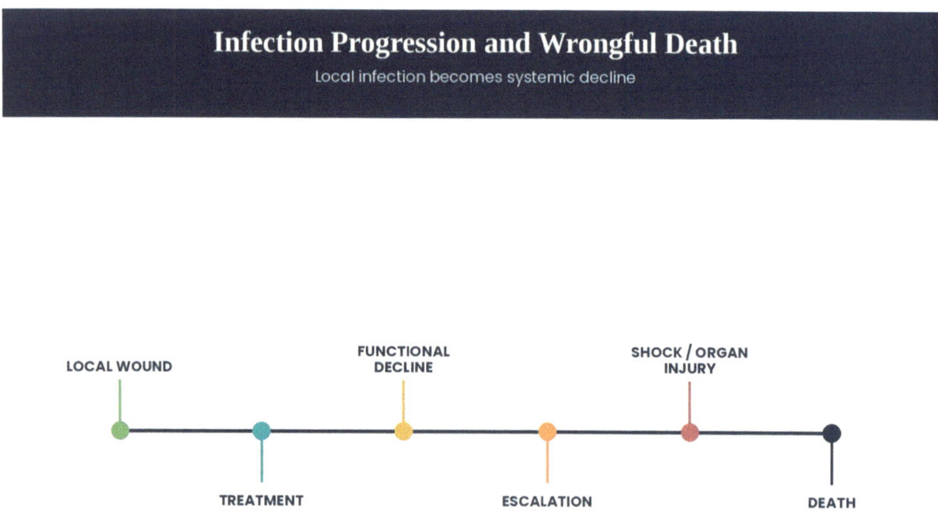

An eighty-one-year-old woman had lived in a skilled nursing facility for several years because of declining mobility. She had chronic heart failure, diabetes, kidney disease, peripheral vascular disease, and mild cognitive impairment. She needed help with bathing, dressing, and transfers. She used a wheelchair for most mobility and could walk only short distances with assistance.

Her medical history was substantial. So was the life she still had.

She recognized her children and grandchildren, participated in decisions, ate independently, attended facility activities, and spoke with family by telephone almost every day. Her chronic conditions had been stable for several months. She was not receiving hospice care, and no treating physician had documented an expectation that death was near.

That distinction became central because the facility and the family initially described the same patient in very different ways.

A staff member first noted redness and tenderness in the lower leg on a Friday morning. The skin was warm, and a small superficial wound near the ankle had begun to drain. The patient complained of more pain during transfers.

The nurse documented the finding and notified an on-call provider. Oral antibiotics were prescribed for presumed cellulitis, and the facility was instructed to monitor the area and call again if the condition worsened. At that point, the plan was not obviously unreasonable.

Over the weekend, however, the patient changed. She became less active, ate poorly, and required more assistance than usual. Her recorded temperature remained within the normal range, although she was receiving scheduled acetaminophen for chronic pain. Her blood glucose rose, and the redness extended beyond the ankle.

Weekend nursing notes referred to fatigue, poor appetite, continued drainage, and increasing sleepiness. One described her as sleepy but arousable. Another recorded a blood pressure below her usual range and a faster respiratory rate. No urgent medical evaluation occurred.

Facility staff later testified that the patient often had variable appetite, fatigue, and fluctuating blood-pressure readings. The wound was being treated, and the antibiotic had been started less than forty-eight hours earlier. Those observations were not invented after the fact. They reflected the genuine difficulty of caring for medically complex residents whose baseline is already imperfect.

By Monday morning, however, the patient was confused and difficult to wake. Her blood pressure was markedly low, and emergency medical services were called.

At the hospital, she was diagnosed with sepsis, acute kidney injury, metabolic acidosis, and an extensive soft-tissue infection involving the lower leg. Blood cultures later grew bacteria consistent with the wound as the source. She received intravenous antibiotics, fluids, vasopressor support, and surgical consultation, but her condition continued to worsen.

The surgeons believed meaningful source control would require extensive debridement and possibly amputation. By then, circulatory instability and her underlying disease made surgery extraordinarily high risk. After discussion with the family, the decision was made not to proceed once the treating team concluded that survival was unlikely even with major intervention. She died the following day.

The death certificate listed septic shock due to soft-tissue infection, with diabetes and vascular disease as contributing conditions.

The family believed the facility had allowed a minor wound to become fatal. The facility's position was that the resident had already been frail, carried several serious chronic diseases, received antibiotics promptly, and might not have survived an aggressive infection under any circumstances. Both descriptions contained part of the truth.

The case required more than deciding whether the patient was medically fragile. She clearly was. The more useful inquiry was what that fragility meant before the infection and how it affected her ability to survive after treatment was delayed.

Her baseline records showed chronic dependence but relative medical stability. She needed substantial assistance, yet she was not in active terminal decline. Her weight had been stable. Kidney function was impaired but unchanged. Heart failure had not required a recent hospitalization. She remained engaged with family and ordinary facility life.

That did not make her healthy. It showed that death was not expected when the wound first appeared.

The distinction mattered because the hospital chart described a profoundly ill woman with multiorgan dysfunction. If that final condition were projected backward, death could appear inevitable from the beginning.

The facility record from Friday and early in the weekend showed something else. She had a localized infection in a high-risk limb and enough reserve to remain awake, communicative, eating, and involved in her care.

The first clinical question was whether beginning oral antibiotics on Friday fell below reasonable practice. The review did not support that criticism.

The wound was described as superficial. Redness and warmth were consistent with cellulitis. There was no documented fever, hypotension, confusion, or systemic instability during the initial assessment. Oral treatment with close monitoring could fall within reasonable practice for a localized infection, even in a patient with diabetes and vascular disease. The case did not begin with the choice of oral medication.

It began when the patient failed to follow the expected course and the plan was not reconsidered.

An uncomplicated cellulitis responding to treatment should not ordinarily produce progressive redness, increasing pain, reduced intake, altered alertness, rising glucose, lower blood pressure, and faster breathing. Each of those findings could have had more than one explanation. Together, they showed that the patient was changing.

There was no single dramatic event in the facility record. What appeared instead was a gradual loss of baseline.

That pattern was easy to underestimate because many of its components already existed in some form. Poor appetite, fatigue, limited mobility, and variable blood pressure were not entirely new when viewed one at a time.

The clinical meaning came from the degree of departure from her usual condition.

She was eating less than usual. She needed more help than usual. She was sleepier than usual. The wound was spreading despite treatment. Her glucose and respiratory rate were rising while her blood pressure fell.

In a medically fragile patient, those changes from baseline may be more important than one normal temperature.

The absence of fever became a significant part of the defense. The patient did not mount a prominent febrile response over the weekend. That fact mattered, but it did not establish that the infection remained local. The broader pattern of systemic change carried more clinical weight.

The nursing experts agreed that the wound required serial assessment. They disagreed about when routine monitoring should have given way to urgent escalation.

The plaintiff's expert believed that by Sunday, the combination of spreading redness, poor intake, lethargy, lower blood pressure, and increased respiratory rate required prompt provider reassessment and likely hospital transfer. The defense expert regarded those findings as nonspecific in a resident with chronic illness and emphasized that the antibiotic had not yet had a full opportunity to work. That disagreement was legitimate.

Antibiotics do not produce immediate visible improvement in every infection. Redness, pain, and fatigue may persist during the first day or two. Nursing facilities also care for residents whose appetite, energy, and vital signs fluctuate. The question was whether this combination remained within this resident's ordinary range. That is where the baseline work became decisive.

Family members had spoken with her on Friday and Saturday. On Friday, she was alert and complained mainly about the leg. On Saturday evening, she ended the call early because she felt tired. By Sunday, she did not answer the telephone, which was unusual. A staff member later told the family that she had slept through much of the day.

Those details did not replace the medical record. They helped make visible a functional decline the chart described only in fragments.

The wound documentation was incomplete. Measurements varied, and no photograph from the first day had been preserved. Hospital photographs later showed extensive infection, but they could not establish exactly what facility staff had seen during the weekend. That limitation mattered.

The case could not fairly be built on the assertion that advanced tissue destruction was obvious on Friday. The more supportable theory was that systemic deterioration required escalation even if the exact depth and nature of the infection remained uncertain.

The nurse did not need to diagnose a necrotizing infection or predict that amputation might become necessary. The nurse needed to recognize that a high-risk patient was worsening despite the treatment plan.

Provider communication records were sparse. The Friday call was documented. There was no clear record establishing that the on-call provider received the Sunday changes. One nurse believed another nurse had made contact. The second nurse did not remember doing so and had not charted a call.

That gap moved part of the case away from individual judgment and toward workflow.

The facility used paper communication sheets for nonurgent provider messages. Urgent changes could be reported by telephone. The weekend system did not contain a reliable method for confirming that a message had been received, reviewed, and acted upon.

It remained unclear whether no one called, a message was left, or the information was conveyed incompletely.

From the patient's perspective, the result was the same: no prescribing clinician reassessed her before profound deterioration.

Responsibility could not be allocated fairly without preserving that uncertainty. Nursing staff had observed the changes. The organization was responsible for ensuring that those observations reached someone capable of modifying treatment. The covering provider could not reasonably be criticized for information the evidence did not show had been received.

The institutional theory therefore became stronger than a broad claim against every individual involved.

Causation was more difficult than breach because the patient's chronic disease materially affected her likelihood of survival.

Diabetes and peripheral vascular disease impaired healing and made severe limb infection more likely. Kidney and heart disease reduced her ability to tolerate sepsis, fluid resuscitation, surgery, and prolonged critical illness. By the time she reached the hospital, the chance of surviving major surgery was poor.

The defense expert argued that the infection may already have been aggressive and deep when first recognized and that earlier transfer would not necessarily have prevented septic shock or death. The expert also noted that severe vascular disease might have required amputation even with timely care. Those were medically credible possibilities.

The plaintiff could not responsibly present the patient as a healthy person with a minor infection who had been denied a guaranteed recovery.

The real issue was what treatment remained available before shock and organ failure developed.

An infectious-disease specialist and vascular surgeon reviewed the case. Both believed that transfer during the weekend probably would have led to intravenous antibiotics, laboratory testing, imaging, surgical evaluation, and closer monitoring before the patient became hemodynamically unstable.

Whether she still would have required debridement or amputation remained uncertain. The vascular surgeon considered limb loss possible even with earlier care because of the underlying circulation. The experts were more confident that treatment before shock would have given her a materially better chance of surviving the infection. That changed the wrongful-death theory.

The case was not that timely care would have preserved the leg, restored full health, and guaranteed long survival. It was that delayed escalation allowed a local or regional infection to progress into septic shock in a patient whose ability to survive became dramatically worse after organ failure developed. Her fragility mattered in two directions.

It made earlier escalation more important because she had less reserve with which to tolerate progression. It also made a favorable outcome less certain. Both had to remain visible.

The experts could not assign an exact survival percentage. They could explain why she was a much better treatment candidate before hypotension, acidosis, kidney injury, and shock. Her reserve was limited, but it had not disappeared. Once multiorgan failure developed, surgery became far more dangerous and much less likely to succeed. The treatment opportunity narrowed as the infection progressed.

By Monday, the family was being asked to choose between extraordinarily high-risk surgery and comfort-focused care. That later decision could not fairly be used to argue that the patient would have refused treatment earlier. The choices were not the same.

Earlier in the weekend, she was awake and able to participate in decisions. Treatment may have involved intravenous antibiotics, limited debridement, vascular assessment, and hospital monitoring. By Monday, the proposed intervention was major surgery during septic shock with a poor likelihood of survival.

Refusal under the later circumstances did not establish refusal under the earlier ones.

The defense also relied on age and chronic disease to argue that life expectancy was limited. That required patient-specific review rather than assumption.

Her primary-care and facility records did not show imminent death. She had several serious conditions, but no documented terminal trajectory. She was not experiencing progressive weight loss, repeated recent hospitalizations, or advanced organ failure before the infection.

No physician could say precisely how long she would have lived. The evidence supported that she probably would have survived beyond the date of death if the infection had been controlled.

The wrongful-death claim therefore concerned preventable or accelerated death in a patient with limited but meaningful life expectancy. It did not assume a normal lifespan.

The damages presentation followed the life she actually had. She was not described as independent or vigorous. She lived in a facility and required substantial care.

The loss was continuation of that existing life: recognizing her family, making decisions, attending activities, eating independently, and maintaining regular contact with her children and grandchildren.

That description avoided two distortions. It did not pretend that she had been healthy before the infection, and it did not treat a dependent life as medically negligible.

The final hospital course raised a separate issue concerning suffering. She experienced pain, confusion, invasive treatment, and critical deterioration before comfort measures were adopted. The evidence could support a claim concerning the altered manner of death, but that theory needed to remain separate from whether survival probably would have been extended.

The case did not have to choose between those injuries. It did have to distinguish them.

Earlier transfer probably would have improved her chance of survival. It also likely would have permitted treatment before severe shock, reducing the burden of the final course even if the infection ultimately proved fatal. Those conclusions were related but not identical.

The facility's defense remained substantial. The initial treatment was reasonable. The resident was medically fragile. The wound records did not establish when deeper infection developed. Some weekend findings were nonspecific. Even timely hospital care would have carried serious risk, and amputation might still have been necessary. Exact life expectancy could not be established.

The plaintiff's case remained viable because it did not depend on denying those facts.

The theory was that a high-risk patient showed a sustained departure from baseline while an infection was visibly progressing, and the facility's monitoring and communication process failed to produce timely medical reassessment.

By the time she reached the hospital, the issue was no longer whether oral antibiotics had been given enough time. She was in septic shock.

The mediation presentation began with baseline because the meaning of the weekend decline depended on it. The patient already required help, but she remained alert, engaged, and medically stable.

The first wound was not presented as proof that a catastrophic infection was already obvious. The focus remained on the weekend progression and the absence of an effective response as the patient became less like herself.

The later hospital photographs were used carefully. They showed the severity of the final infection but were not offered as proof of what facility staff necessarily saw on Friday.

The causation presentation compared the treatment opportunities at two stages. During the weekend, the patient had infection and declining function but no documented shock. By Monday, she had severe hypotension, acidosis, kidney injury, and multiorgan failure.

The experts explained why antibiotics and surgical treatment were more likely to succeed before that transition.

The defense argued that the biology of the infection, rather than facility delay, drove the outcome. The plaintiff answered that an aggressive infection makes recognition of deterioration more urgent, not less, and that continued worsening was itself evidence that the original plan was failing.

The case resolved after nursing and provider depositions clarified that no one could establish that a prescribing clinician had completed a weekend reassessment.

The settlement reflected meaningful wrongful-death exposure tempered by uncertain survival, serious baseline disease, and the possibility that earlier treatment still would have required major surgery.

The matter had begun as a simple claim that the facility ignored an infected wound. The developed case was more exact.

The initial response fell within the reasonable range. The failure occurred when the resident's condition changed and the system did not convert nursing observations into timely medical reassessment.

The death was not measured against perfect health or ordinary life expectancy. It was measured against the stable, dependent, and meaningful life the patient probably would have continued to live.

Clinical review did not remove the difficulty of the case. It made the difficulty understandable. Baseline showed both vulnerability and retained life. The timeline showed a localized infection becoming systemic illness. Workflow showed observations without reliable clinical closure. The treatment analysis explained why earlier hospital care probably offered a better chance of survival while acknowledging that better did not mean certain.

The damages analysis described the life she still had rather than the life she never had. That was the case the medicine could support.

"The damages analysis described the life she still had rather than the life she never had. That was the case the medicine could support."

CHAPTER THIRTY-THREE

Medication Error, Monitoring Failure, and Multistage Responsibility

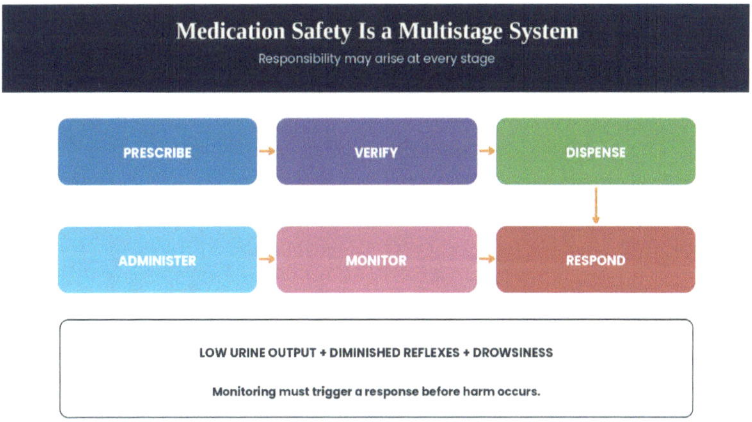

A thirty-four-year-old woman was admitted during the third trimester of pregnancy with severe hypertension, headache, visual disturbance, and increasing upper abdominal pain. She had no history of seizures, and the pregnancy had been uncomplicated until her blood pressure began rising during the previous week.

The obstetric team diagnosed severe preeclampsia and recommended delivery after stabilization. Magnesium sulfate was ordered to reduce the risk of seizure. She received a loading dose in the labor unit, followed by a continuous infusion. Antihypertensive medication was given, laboratory studies were repeated, and fetal monitoring continued while the team prepared for induction.

Her kidney function was already mildly abnormal when she arrived, and over the next several hours her urine output began to fall.

At first, she remained awake and conversational. She complained of nausea and weakness, symptoms that could reasonably have been attributed to pregnancy, preeclampsia, magnesium, or some combination of the three. Later, however, she became increasingly drowsy. Her speech slowed, and she said that she was having difficulty taking a deep breath.

The bedside nurse documented diminished reflexes but did not stop the infusion immediately. She later explained that the examination had been difficult because the patient was uncomfortable and positioned for fetal monitoring. Oxygen saturation remained within the recorded range, and no respiratory alarm sounded.

A covering resident was told that the patient was unusually sleepy and producing less urine. The resident ordered another laboratory panel but did not come to the bedside at once. No magnesium level was ordered during that call.

Less than an hour later, the patient became unresponsive and stopped breathing effectively. The fetal heart rate fell. An emergency response was activated, the magnesium infusion was stopped, calcium was administered, and the patient was intubated. An emergency cesarean delivery followed.

The infant was born severely depressed and required resuscitation. The child survived but later showed significant neurological impairment. The mother recovered respiratory function after treatment and intensive care. She did not sustain permanent cognitive injury, although the hospitalization was prolonged and she later experienced post-traumatic symptoms related to the collapse and emergency delivery.

The first explanation given to the family was that the mother had suffered a rare and sudden complication of severe preeclampsia. The discharge summary referred to respiratory arrest in the setting of magnesium therapy, renal dysfunction, and possible seizure-related disease.

Counsel initially approached the matter as an obstetrical emergency involving maternal collapse and neonatal brain injury. The chart suggested several possible failures: the infusion dose, declining urine output, delayed recognition of toxicity, inadequate laboratory monitoring, and the emergency response. What remained unclear was which of those failures actually drove the event.

Medication cases often appear simple after the outcome is known. A drug was administered, the patient deteriorated, the drug was stopped, an antidote was given, and the patient improved. That sequence may create a strong inference, but it does not show how the error occurred, who controlled each stage, or whether the entire injury came from the medication rather than from the underlying disease.

The first task was to determine whether the prescription itself had been wrong. It had not.

The written order called for a standard loading dose followed by a maintenance infusion. Pharmacy verification matched the order, and the medication-administration record showed that the correct loading dose had been given. The maintenance rate presented a different problem.

The infusion-pump history showed that the medication had been programmed at twice the ordered maintenance rate for approximately ninety minutes before the rate was changed. The electronic medication record continued to display the prescribed rate because it reflected the physician's order, not what the pump had actually delivered. That finding changed the case.

The physician had ordered an accepted regimen. Pharmacy had verified the correct prescription. The medication reached the patient at a different rate.

The delivery error was not visible in the ordinary chart. It appeared in the device data.

No one could determine with complete certainty how the programming discrepancy occurred. The nurse believed that she had selected the correct magnesium protocol from the pump library. The pump record showed that the drug library had been bypassed and the infusion entered manually. No witness remembered intentionally bypassing the safeguard, and the hospital's biomedical review found no mechanical malfunction.

Two explanations remained plausible. The nurse may have entered the wrong rate manually without realizing it, or another person may have altered the pump before the event. Assignment records and access history made the first explanation more likely, though not certain.

The case did not need to become a judgment about the nurse's character. It needed to follow the medication through the system.

The physician prescribed the drug. Pharmacy verified the order. Nursing programmed and administered the infusion. The drug library was bypassed. The actual rate exceeded the prescription. At the same time, the patient's ability to clear magnesium was declining as her urine output fell. Those developments were not independent.

An excessive infusion rate can produce toxicity even in a patient with normal renal function. Reduced renal clearance made accumulation more likely and more dangerous. The initial delivery error and the later failure to recognize changing physiology could not be separated neatly because the injury developed through both.

The excessive rate created the danger. The failure to respond to declining urine output and evolving neurological changes allowed that danger to continue. That became the central clinical account.

Magnesium is used routinely in obstetric care and is generally safe when administered and monitored appropriately. It is cleared primarily through the kidneys. When renal function worsens or urine output falls, the drug can accumulate, producing weakness, diminished reflexes, sedation, respiratory depression, and eventually cardiac instability.

The patient's progression fit that pattern. She became increasingly drowsy, her reflexes diminished, her urine output declined, and she complained of difficulty breathing before the arrest. She improved after the infusion was stopped and calcium was administered. A magnesium level obtained after the emergency was markedly elevated.

The defense correctly noted that the level had been drawn after resuscitation and could not establish the exact concentration when the earlier symptoms first appeared. The case did not require a minute-by-minute reconstruction of the blood level.

The infusion history, declining renal clearance, clinical findings, elevated later level, and response to the antidote formed a coherent picture of magnesium toxicity.

The more difficult issue was why the warning signs did not produce earlier action.

Some symptoms overlapped with pregnancy, severe preeclampsia, antihypertensive treatment, fatigue, and the expected effects of magnesium. Nausea and weakness alone would not have established toxicity. Drowsiness in a laboring patient receiving medication could also have had several explanations.

The clinical meaning changed when diminished reflexes, falling urine output, increasing sedation, and respiratory difficulty appeared together.

Those findings did not require laboratory confirmation before the infusion could be interrupted. The purpose of bedside monitoring was to identify danger before the patient reached respiratory arrest.

The hospital's nursing standards called for regular assessment of respiratory rate, reflexes, mental status, and urine output during magnesium therapy. The policy required notification and interruption of treatment when significant abnormalities developed.

The policy did not create the clinical obligation. It reflected what was already known about the drug.

The bedside record showed that urine output had been falling over several hours, but the decline was not communicated as a sustained trend until the patient was already markedly drowsy. Reflex findings were documented inconsistently. One entry described diminished reflexes, while a later templated entry appeared to mark them as normal.

The nurse explained that the later entry may have been copied forward inadvertently. That was plausible. It also showed how the documentation failed to capture the patient's changing condition.

The case was not strengthened by treating every inconsistency as falsification. The important point was that no one integrated the trend.

The patient was producing less urine, becoming more sedated, and losing reflexes while receiving a medication whose toxicity is worsened by impaired renal clearance. Those facts belonged together.

The resident's responsibility began when the nurse reported unusual drowsiness and reduced urine output. The resident knew that the patient was receiving magnesium and had abnormal renal function. Laboratory testing was ordered, but the infusion was not stopped or reduced while the patient was being evaluated.

The resident later testified that the symptoms sounded consistent with fatigue and an expected medication effect. According to the resident, the nurse did not report diminished reflexes or respiratory difficulty during the first call. That testimony narrowed the physician issue.

If the resident heard only that the patient was sleepy and producing somewhat less urine, ordering laboratory studies while continuing close observation could be defended. If the resident also heard that the reflexes were diminished and breathing had become difficult, the same response would be much harder to justify.

The chart did not establish exactly what was said. The nurse stated that she reported the reflex change. The resident denied receiving that information. No contemporaneous communication note was detailed enough to resolve the disagreement.

The case might have become dependent on choosing which witness to believe, but the broader record made the theory less fragile.

The resident had access to the urine-output trend and renal laboratory values. The resident knew that the patient was receiving a renally cleared infusion. No bedside reassessment occurred, no magnesium level was ordered, and the excessive infusion continued until the arrest.

Even under the resident's recollection, the patient required more active evaluation than she received.

The nursing and physician failures were therefore sequential rather than identical. The nurse controlled the infusion and observed the bedside changes. The resident controlled medical reassessment and the continuation of treatment after concern was reported. The institution controlled the pump library, medication safeguards, competency process, and escalation expectations.

The event could not fairly be reduced to one incorrect keystroke.

The hospital required nurses to use the drug library unless a defined exception applied. The pump was capable of issuing a high-dose warning. In this instance, the library had been bypassed, and no alert reached pharmacy or the electronic record.

The institution argued that the pump had functioned as designed and that no safety system can prevent every manual entry. That was partly true. A safeguard is not necessarily defective merely because a user can bypass it.

The more useful inquiry was whether the organization knew that bypasses occurred, monitored their frequency, trained staff effectively, and responded when manual programming became routine.

Discovery showed that bypassing the library was not unusual in the labor unit. Nurses described using manual entry when the library was slow, when a custom concentration was unavailable, or when they believed the standard protocol did not match the order. The hospital collected pump-compliance information but had not closely reviewed the labor unit's bypass rate.

That evidence did not prove that the institution itself programmed this infusion incorrectly. It showed that the safeguard existed more reliably in policy than in daily practice.

The drug library was intended to prevent precisely this kind of rate error. When staff commonly bypassed it, its effectiveness depended on training, monitoring, and corrective oversight.

The institutional theory became stronger when it remained tied to that operational fact. It would have been weaker as a general allegation that the hospital should have purchased better equipment. The equipment was capable of providing protection. The system did not consistently ensure that the protection was used. Causation for the mother was comparatively direct.

The clinical evidence supported that magnesium toxicity caused her respiratory arrest. Earlier recognition and discontinuation probably would have prevented intubation, emergency resuscitation, and at least part of the traumatic course that followed.

Her later psychological symptoms required more care. She had experienced respiratory collapse, emergency surgery, separation from her infant, and fear that she might die. Those events were real. The evidence did not permit every later emotional symptom to be attributed solely to the medication error because the infant's condition and the underlying preeclampsia also contributed.

Her injury was substantial, but it was not permanent in the same way as the child's. Causation for the child was more complicated.

The fetal heart rate deteriorated during the maternal respiratory arrest. The infant was delivered emergently and required resuscitation. Later neonatal imaging showed brain injury consistent with impaired oxygen delivery.

The plaintiff's theory was that maternal hypoventilation and arrest caused an acute reduction in fetal oxygenation that produced the child's neurological injury.

The defense argued that placental dysfunction associated with severe preeclampsia may already have compromised the fetus, that the tracing contained abnormalities before the maternal arrest, and that some injury may have begun earlier. Both theories had evidentiary support.

The fetal record showed intermittent concerning features before the arrest, but not a pattern clearly demonstrating established severe injury. The most dramatic deterioration occurred when the mother stopped breathing effectively and her blood pressure became unstable. Cord blood gases and the neonatal course supported a significant acute component.

The neonatal experts could not say that every later deficit developed during the brief maternal collapse. They could support that the collapse materially worsened fetal oxygenation and contributed to the severity of the brain injury.

That distinction mattered because the original theory assumed complete prevention. The evidence more comfortably supported increased severity.

The child may have faced some risk from preeclampsia and placental dysfunction even if the magnesium had been managed correctly. Earlier recognition of toxicity, interruption of the infusion, and a controlled delivery probably would have avoided the maternal respiratory emergency and reduced the fetal insult.

The alternative course still involved urgent or premature delivery, neonatal observation, and possible complications. It did not support a guarantee of normal development.

The child's later needs were significant. Motor control, speech, feeding, and cognition were affected, although developmental uncertainty remained because of the child's age and the evolving nature of the injury.

The life-care work therefore had to distinguish current intensive treatment from probable long-term needs. It also had to avoid assuming the most severe adult outcome before development had progressed far enough to support that conclusion.

Uncertainty did not eliminate future damages. It required more than one medically supportable projection.

The experts could identify permanent motor impairment and a likely need for continuing therapy, adaptive equipment, educational support, and caregiver assistance. The eventual degree of communication and independent function remained less certain.

The economic analysis used alternative levels of future support rather than one fixed lifelong condition.

The defense characterized that range as speculation. The plaintiff described it as the unavoidable reality of evaluating a young child. The more credible position lay between those extremes.

No one could know the child's precise adult outcome. The injury had already created permanent functional risk and substantial care needs that would not have existed in the same form without the event.

The mediation presentation did not begin with the pump-programming error. It began with why magnesium was being used and why the monitoring mattered.

The medication was intended to protect the mother from seizure. Her kidney function and urine output declined. The infusion was delivered at a higher rate than ordered. She then developed the clinical findings the monitoring process was designed to detect.

The pump history established the delivery error, but the case was not presented as though the machine itself had injured the patient. The device data formed one part of a longer medication pathway.

The nurse’s role was explained without portraying her as indifferent. She was caring for a high-risk labor patient with competing demands. She recognized some abnormalities and contacted the resident. The failure was that the findings were not understood as a connected toxicity pattern and the infusion continued.

The resident’s role was kept equally specific. The criticism was not that every sleepy patient receiving magnesium requires an emergency response. It was that this patient had declining urine output, impaired renal function, and evolving neurological signs while receiving an excessive infusion.

The institutional issue arose from the way medication safety operated in practice. A drug library intended to prevent programming errors was frequently bypassed without effective unit-level correction. The claim did not require proof that every bypass was negligent. It required showing that the safeguard failed in exactly the way it was designed to prevent.

The defense retained credible experts. The obstetric expert emphasized the complexity of severe preeclampsia, the overlap between disease and medication effects, and the absence of a magnesium level before the arrest. The nursing expert considered the bedside findings ambiguous until shortly before the collapse. The neonatal expert disputed attributing the child's entire injury to the respiratory event. Those opinions prevented the matter from becoming an oversimplified overdose case.

The plaintiff's theory remained strong because several independent forms of evidence converged. The infusion rate exceeded the order. Renal clearance declined. Recognized toxicity signs appeared. The patient improved after calcium and ventilatory support. Fetal deterioration coincided with maternal respiratory failure.

The remaining disputes concerned when toxicity should have been recognized and how much of the child's injury the event caused.

The case resolved after pump data and medication-workflow discovery made the delivery error difficult to dispute. The settlement reflected substantial exposure for the maternal respiratory arrest and fetal injury, tempered by uncertainty about the child's pre-existing fetal risk and eventual developmental course.

The matter began as an allegation that a nurse administered too much medication. That was true, but incomplete.

The developed case involved a correct prescription, a bypassed safety library, an excessive programmed rate, impaired drug clearance, fragmented monitoring, incomplete communication, delayed medical reassessment, and one maternal emergency that injured two patients. No single stage explained the event by itself.

The medication error created the danger. The monitoring failure allowed toxicity to progress. Communication and reassessment failures delayed correction. The institution weakened the safeguard that might have prevented the original error.

Causation then had to be considered separately for mother and child. The mother's respiratory injury was largely preventable. The child's neurological injury was more accurately understood as materially increased in severity.

The evidence showed where responsibility began, how it moved through the system, and what each patient lost.

"The evidence showed where responsibility began, how it moved through the system, and what each patient lost."

CHAPTER THIRTY-FOUR

Institutional Failure to Communicate or Follow Up an Abnormal Result

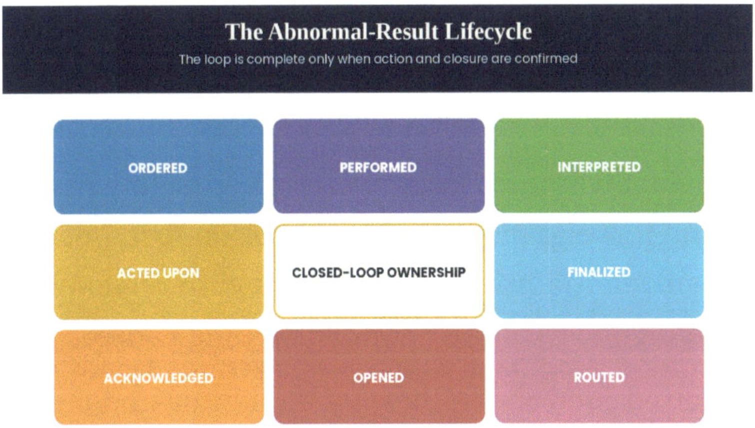

A fifty-six-year-old man underwent a chest CT after several months of cough and intermittent shortness of breath. The study was ordered by a primary-care clinician working in a large multisite medical group. The patient had smoked in the past but had stopped several years earlier. He remained employed, exercised regularly, and had no known cancer diagnosis.

The CT did not show an acute pulmonary process explaining his symptoms. It did, however, show a small but suspicious lung nodule. The radiologist recommended follow-up imaging within a defined interval and noted that further evaluation might be appropriate in light of the patient's risk factors. The final report was completed that day.

The patient was never told about the nodule, and no follow-up study was scheduled.

Eighteen months later, he returned with worsening cough, weight loss, and chest discomfort. Imaging showed a substantially larger lung mass with regional nodal involvement. Biopsy confirmed lung cancer.

He received chemotherapy, radiation, and later systemic therapy for progressive disease. He continued working for part of that period but eventually had to stop. He died a little more than three years after the delayed diagnosis was discovered.

The family's first understanding of the case was straightforward. The primary-care clinician had failed to read a radiology report, allowing an early cancer to become advanced and fatal.

The medical group responded that the clinician had never seen the final report. The study had been ordered shortly before the clinician left the practice. Results arriving after departure entered the clinician's electronic inbox. Responsibility for unresolved work had supposedly been transferred to the department, but the practice could not identify who was expected to review this report.

That explanation did not remove the problem. It moved the problem from an individual omission to an institutional failure of follow-up.

These cases can become technically dense. Counsel may spend months examining inbox design, routing rules, employment dates, coverage pools, acknowledgment settings, audit logs, and transition policies. Those details matter only because they explain why the clinical work never reached completion.

A test was ordered for a patient. It produced an abnormal result. The result required action. No one made sure that action occurred.

The importance of the system evidence lies in that unfinished pathway.

The first task was to determine what the original CT actually showed. Once the later cancer diagnosis was known, it would have been easy to describe the earlier nodule as an obvious malignancy. The imaging did not support that conclusion.

The nodule was small and not diagnostic of cancer. It could have represented a benign process. Its importance came from the patient's smoking history, its appearance, and the radiologist's recommendation for surveillance.

The radiologist had not missed the finding. The report described it and recommended follow-up.

The case was therefore not about failure to interpret the image. It was about what happened after the image had been interpreted appropriately.

The primary-care clinician ordered the study through the medical group's electronic system. Final reports were ordinarily sent to the ordering clinician's inbox. When a clinician left the practice, group policy required the department to reassign unresolved results and messages. On paper, the process sounded adequate.

The audit data showed that the report entered the former clinician's inbox and remained there. The clinician no longer had active clinical duties and never opened it. The report did not route automatically to a covering physician, and the system generated no alert when it remained unacknowledged.

The department manager believed another physician had been assigned to review the departing clinician's results. The physician identified as the successor understood the assignment differently. According to that physician, the responsibility extended only to patients with active appointments and to messages manually forwarded by staff. No written transfer list included this patient.

The electronic system also lacked a reliable method for displaying all unresolved results associated with the departing clinician.

The process depended on a series of assumptions: someone would run the correct report, the pending study would appear on it, the receiving clinician would understand the assignment, and the department would know which patients still had testing in progress. No one clearly owned those steps.

The failure was not dramatic. No one consciously chose to ignore a possible cancer. The report entered an electronic location that no active clinician was meaningfully monitoring.

That kind of institutional failure can be almost invisible in the medical chart. The record showed a final radiology report followed by silence. The operational evidence explained the silence.

The medical group attempted to place responsibility on the ordering clinician by emphasizing that physicians remain responsible for tests they order. As a general clinical principle, that argument had force. A clinician ordinarily should ensure that ordered testing is reviewed, communicated, and followed. The facts made the position more difficult.

The physician had left the organization before the report was finalized. Access to the inbox was restricted shortly afterward. The group had accepted responsibility for transferring unfinished clinical work and had instructed the departing physician not to continue managing patients through the former system.

An individual professional obligation does not simply disappear when employment ends. At the same time, an institution cannot rely on that obligation while preventing the clinician from carrying it out and failing to assign the work elsewhere.

The more practical issue was who had the authority and ability to act when the report became final.

On these facts, the answer was the medical group.

The departing clinician created the original follow-up obligation by ordering the study. Once the clinician left, the organization controlled where the result went and who could act on it. The breakdown occurred during that transition.

Front-desk and nursing staff had no independent reason to know that the CT contained an abnormal recommendation because the system generated no task for them. The radiologist had completed the reporting obligation and had not classified the nodule as requiring immediate telephone communication. That point became contested.

The plaintiff argued that a suspicious pulmonary nodule in a former smoker was important enough to require direct communication. The radiology expert disagreed. The finding required timely surveillance, but it was not an emergency or a critical result under the institution's communication policy. The report had been transmitted through the accepted channel.

The evidence did not support turning the radiologist into a backup system for failed outpatient follow-up.

Removing that theory narrowed and strengthened the case. Institutional responsibility became clearer once professionals who had completed their work reasonably were no longer treated as central defendants.

The patient's role also had to be considered. He knew that the CT had been performed and remembered being told by a staff member that there was "nothing urgent." He did not make a separate appointment specifically to review the final report.

The medical group argued that he should have sought the result himself. That position had limited clinical force.

Patients should participate in their care, but they do not ordinarily know which incidental findings require surveillance, when repeat imaging should occur, or whether silence means a study was normal. The practice ordered the test, received the final report, and was in the better position to understand and act on the recommendation.

The patient's conduct still mattered because the alternative course depended partly on whether he would have followed advice if informed.

His records showed that he generally attended appointments, completed prior testing, and followed through with referrals. There was no evidence that he had refused cancer evaluation or routinely ignored medical recommendations.

It was therefore reasonable to conclude that he probably would have undergone follow-up imaging if someone had explained the finding and recommendation. The breach issue was stronger than causation.

A result-management system should not allow a clinically significant finding to remain unattended merely because the ordering clinician leaves the organization. The medical group had difficulty disputing that proposition.

The harder question was what timely follow-up would have shown and whether earlier diagnosis probably would have changed the patient's survival.

The original nodule was small, and no biopsy had been performed at that time. Its precise biology and stage had to be reconstructed from later imaging, pathology, growth pattern, and cancer type.

The plaintiff's oncology expert believed that the earlier nodule probably represented the same cancer later diagnosed and was likely localized, or at least substantially less advanced, when first seen. Surveillance within the recommended period probably would have shown growth and led to biopsy and treatment before regional progression.

The defense expert agreed that the nodule might have represented the original cancer but disputed any certainty about stage. Microscopic nodal or distant disease could already have existed while the visible lesion remained small. Some lung cancers behave aggressively and recur despite early treatment. Both opinions were medically credible.

The case could not support a promise of cure based only on the size of the earlier nodule.

The original theory assumed that the patient would have undergone limited surgery and lived a normal lifespan. Oncology review did not support that degree of certainty.

The more reliable opinion concerned the loss of an earlier treatment opportunity and a materially worse survival course.

At the earlier point, the patient had better functional status, less visible disease, and a greater chance of receiving curative-intent local treatment. By the time of diagnosis, he required multimodality treatment for advanced disease and still faced a substantial risk of progression.

Earlier diagnosis probably would have improved prognosis and reduced treatment burden. Whether it would have produced permanent cure could not be stated reliably. That distinction became central to the wrongful-death analysis.

The patient did not lose a guaranteed normal lifespan. He lost access to earlier-stage treatment and a materially better expected course.

The legal consequence of that conclusion depended on the jurisdiction, but the clinical opinion could describe the change in treatment options and prognosis without pretending to know the individual outcome with certainty.

The recommended surveillance interval also had to be reconstructed carefully. The radiologist recommended follow-up within a range, not an immediate biopsy.

Reasonable care would not have produced treatment the day after the original scan.

The alternative course would have involved communicating the finding to the patient, assessing risk, obtaining repeat imaging within the recommended interval, and proceeding to further evaluation if the nodule persisted or enlarged.

That realistic sequence meant that several months might have passed between the first study and diagnosis.

Plaintiff counsel could not assume that treatment would have begun immediately after the report. Defense counsel could not treat the entire eighteen-month delay as unavoidable merely because appropriate surveillance itself required time.

The clinically significant delay was the period after recommended follow-up should have produced detection.

The precise point depended on the surveillance interval and likely growth of the lesion.

Original and later imaging allowed experts to estimate progression, though not with mathematical precision. Tumors do not necessarily grow at a constant rate. Apparent changes may also reflect biology, inflammation, necrosis, or differences in measurement technique.

The evidence supported substantial progression during the period without follow-up. It did not establish the date on which nodal spread occurred. That uncertainty affected valuation. It did not eliminate causation.

The damages analysis also had to account for the life the patient lived during treatment. He continued working for a period, tolerated some therapy, and remained active in many ordinary activities. Later progression brought fatigue, pain, reduced respiratory capacity, and loss of employment.

Earlier diagnosis would still have required treatment. Surgery would have carried a recovery burden, and additional therapy might have been necessary depending on stage. The alternative life was not treatment-free.

The attributable difference included more extensive therapy, greater toxicity, reduced survival, and the loss of a more favorable period before progressive disease.

The family's initial damages theory emphasized a fixed number of years of life lost. The medical evidence supported a range rather than one precise duration.

The oncology experts differed substantially. The plaintiff's expert believed earlier treatment offered a meaningful possibility of long-term survival. The defense expert believed recurrence risk would still have been high because of the tumor's biology.

Neither could identify the date on which this individual patient otherwise would have died.

The mediation presentation therefore avoided converting population statistics into a personal certainty. Stage-specific outcome data was used to show the magnitude of the lost opportunity, and the analysis then returned to the patient himself.

He was relatively young. He had good functional status. He was able to tolerate treatment. The disease was far less extensive on the earlier imaging. Those facts supported a materially better expected course with timely follow-up. They did not prove exactly how long he would have lived.

The institutional evidence was presented simply. The test was ordered and the report finalized. The ordering clinician had left. The result remained in an inactive inbox. The organization had no reliable closure process. The patient was not informed, and the nodule was not followed.

That sequence carried more force than a prolonged explanation of every technical feature of the electronic system.

Audit data and policy evidence were used to show why no one assumed responsibility. They were not presented as though the software itself had made a clinical decision.

The defense tried to describe the event as an unfortunate, isolated administrative lapse. The practice had a written transition policy and generally transferred patient work successfully.

The plaintiff did not need to prove organization-wide dysfunction.

A system may fail one patient even when it works most of the time. The issue was whether the group had a reasonable safeguard for a foreseeable clinician departure and whether that safeguard worked here.

The absence of a completed transfer, an acknowledgment process, or an unresolved-result review made that position difficult for the defense.

At the same time, the plaintiff avoided turning the case into a broad attack on corporate culture. Discovery did not show repeated identical events or deliberate disregard. The evidence supported a specific failure of ownership during a clinician transition. That was enough.

The case resolved after the institutional depositions and oncology reviews. The settlement reflected strong evidence of a follow-up failure and substantial support for the conclusion that earlier diagnosis would have improved treatment and survival. It was reduced by genuine uncertainty about microscopic stage, tumor biology, and the duration of survival timely care would have produced.

The matter began as a claim that one physician failed to read a report. The developed case was more precise.

The radiologist identified the abnormality. The ordering clinician left before the report became final. The organization accepted responsibility for transferring unfinished work. The result entered a location no active clinician reliably owned. The patient never returned to the care pathway, and the cancer progressed before diagnosis.

The objective evidence established what was visible and when. The workflow showed where responsibility disappeared. The patient's baseline established treatment capacity and meaningful life expectancy. The alternative course required realistic surveillance rather than immediate cure. The causation analysis distinguished improved prognosis from guaranteed survival, and the damages analysis followed the treatment and life the patient probably lost.

The institutional failure was not that the organization lacked a policy.

It was that the patient reached the end of the policy without reaching another clinician.

"It was that the patient reached the end of the policy without reaching another clinician."

CHAPTER THIRTY-FIVE

Nursing-Facility Decline, Wound Progression, and Amputation

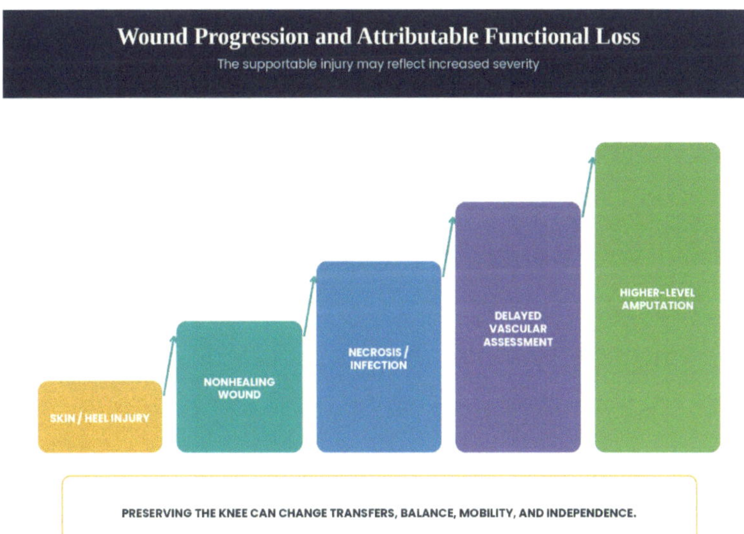

The patient was a seventy-six-year-old man who entered a nursing facility after a stroke left him weak on the right side and unable to transfer without help. He could propel his wheelchair short distances with his left arm, feed himself, carry on a conversation, and participate in decisions about his care. His speech was slow but understandable. He needed assistance with bathing, dressing, toileting, and most transfers.

His medical history also included diabetes, peripheral vascular disease, chronic kidney disease, and the prior amputation of two toes on his left foot. Those conditions placed him at substantial risk for skin breakdown and poor healing. They did not make another amputation inevitable.

For the first several months at the facility, he remained relatively stable. He attended therapy, ate in the dining room, spoke frequently with his daughter, and hoped eventually to move into an assisted-living apartment. Therapy notes showed gradual improvement in sitting balance and his ability to participate in transfers.

A nursing assistant first noticed redness over his right heel while helping him into bed one evening. The skin was intact. The following day, a nurse described a darkened area measuring less than two centimeters and noted that the heel felt soft.

A pressure-relief boot was ordered. The care plan called for elevation of the heel, regular repositioning, skin checks, nutritional monitoring, and referral to the wound-care nurse.

During the next week, however, the record became inconsistent. Some entries stated that the heel was elevated. Others said nothing about positioning. The boot was found off on several occasions. The patient sometimes removed it because it was uncomfortable, but staff also acknowledged that it was not always replaced after care.

The wound-care nurse did not assess the heel until several days after the referral. By then, the skin had opened. Dark tissue covered part of the wound, and drainage had begun.

Treatment was changed. A topical dressing was ordered, pressure relief was reinforced, and a dietary consultation was requested. The wound continued to worsen.

Over the next three weeks, it became larger and deeper. The chart repeatedly referred to diabetes and vascular disease and described the wound as difficult to heal. An outside wound-care practitioner recommended vascular evaluation because the foot was cool and the pedal pulses were difficult to detect. The referral was entered. The evaluation never occurred.

The facility later said that the vascular office had not returned the scheduling call. The referral log showed one attempt to make contact and no further escalation. No one on the clinical team appeared to have taken responsibility for confirming that the patient was actually seen.

Meanwhile, the wound-care notes began describing more drainage and odor. The patient complained of increasing pain. His appetite declined, and his blood glucose became more difficult to control.

An antibiotic was prescribed after a wound culture showed mixed bacterial growth. No physician examined him in person at that stage. The covering provider relied on photographs and nursing reports.

During a weekend visit, his daughter found him in bed rather than sitting in his wheelchair. He appeared tired and said that his foot hurt constantly. When the dressing was removed, she saw blackened tissue extending beyond the original heel area.

She asked whether he should be sent to the hospital.

A nurse told her that the wound team was already treating him and that people with diabetes often heal slowly.

Three days later, he developed fever, confusion, and low blood pressure. He was transferred to the hospital.

Imaging showed extensive soft-tissue infection with probable involvement of the bone. Vascular studies demonstrated severe arterial disease in the leg. The surgeons concluded that the limb could not be salvaged, and an above-knee amputation was performed.

He survived, but he never returned to his earlier level of function. Before the amputation, he had participated in transfers and could propel his wheelchair. Afterward, he required a mechanical lift and extensive assistance with nearly every activity. Rehabilitation was limited by the prior stroke, weakness in the remaining leg, cardiopulmonary disease, and fear of falling.

He never reached assisted living. He remained in institutional care until his death two years later from an unrelated cardiac event.

The family believed that the facility had caused the heel wound by failing to reposition him properly and then allowed it to progress until amputation became unavoidable.

The facility saw the case differently. The patient had severe diabetes, advanced vascular disease, limited mobility, prior tissue loss, and poor healing capacity. In its view, the heel injury was a foreseeable consequence of those conditions, and the eventual amputation resulted from circulation that ordinary wound care could not correct. Both sides began with medically important facts. Neither explanation was complete.

The case involved two related but distinct causal questions. Why did the heel wound develop, and why did it progress to an above-knee amputation?

A patient with stroke-related immobility, diabetes, and vascular disease may develop a pressure injury despite reasonable care. Even careful repositioning cannot eliminate every risk. The heel is particularly vulnerable because very little soft tissue lies between the skin and bone, and circulation may already be impaired.

The appearance of the initial injury could not be treated as automatic proof of negligence.

The early record showed that the facility recognized the risk and placed pressure prevention in the care plan. A boot had been ordered. Repositioning instructions were in place. The patient sometimes resisted the device.

The criticism became stronger when the review moved from what the plan said to how it actually worked.

The records did not show consistent repositioning. The boot was repeatedly absent without a reliable alternative method of relieving pressure. Staff noted that the patient removed it, but there was little evidence that anyone tried to determine whether discomfort, poor fit, cognition, or inadequate explanation was interfering with its use.

A care plan does not cease to be the facility's responsibility because a patient has difficulty following it.

That does not mean staff should simply force an uncomfortable device back onto the patient. It means the approach may need to change. Another boot might be tried. Pillows may be positioned differently. Observation may need to increase. Pain may need to be addressed. The patient and family may need a clearer explanation of the risk.

The issue was whether the plan was adapted after it became apparent that the original approach was not working.

The chart suggested that it was not adapted consistently.

Even then, the experts could not say that proper off-loading probably would have prevented the wound altogether. The patient's circulation was poor, and the tissue may already have been compromised.

The more supportable opinion was that inconsistent pressure relief contributed to the development or early progression of the wound, although its effect could not be separated cleanly from the underlying vascular disease. That was only the beginning of the case.

Once the wound opened and continued to deteriorate, the clinical situation changed. He was no longer simply a patient at risk for skin breakdown. He had an active wound in a limb affected by diabetes, poor pulses, previous tissue loss, and limited capacity to heal.

At that point, local wound treatment could not answer the most important question: did the tissue have enough blood supply to heal?

The outside wound practitioner recognized the concern and recommended vascular evaluation. That recommendation became the central event in the case.

A referral was entered, but no appointment occurred. The wound progressed while the facility continued local treatment without knowing whether healing was physiologically possible.

The institutional failure was not that one dressing was selected instead of another.

It was that the referral was treated as though the work had been completed when it had merely been sent.

In ordinary clinical practice, an order or referral can create the appearance that something has been done. From the patient's perspective, nothing has happened until the evaluation takes place or a qualified clinician determines that it is no longer necessary.

The facility documented the request. It did not reliably track the request to completion.

No one was assigned to confirm scheduling. No one escalated the matter when the vascular office failed to respond. The wound-care nurse assumed the unit clerk was handling it. The unit clerk believed nursing would say something if the appointment became urgent. The covering provider did not know the evaluation had never taken place. Responsibility disappeared between roles.

This resembled an unresolved abnormal-result case, except the failure was unfolding visibly in the patient's heel rather than sitting silently in an electronic inbox.

The wound was enlarging. Necrotic tissue appeared. Drainage increased. Pain worsened. Odor developed. His appetite declined, and glucose control became unstable.

Those changes should have increased the urgency of vascular and medical evaluation even if the original referral had been considered routine.

The facility emphasized that the patient was already receiving wound treatment and antibiotics. That was true, but it did not mean the underlying problem was being addressed.

Topical treatment cannot correct severe arterial insufficiency. Antibiotics may reduce part of the bacterial burden, but they cannot restore circulation or remove dead tissue. A wound can receive repeated treatment and still remain on a path toward limb loss when the larger physiological problem has not been addressed.

The defense experts argued that vascular intervention would not necessarily have saved the leg. Later hospital studies showed severe disease at several arterial levels. Kidney disease complicated contrast imaging and increased procedural risk. The prior stroke and general medical condition limited rehabilitation potential. Those points mattered.

The plaintiff's vascular expert could not promise that revascularization would have succeeded. Nor could the expert say that the heel would have healed completely even if circulation had been improved.

The more defensible causation opinion concerned the timing and level of the eventual amputation.

Earlier vascular assessment may have shown whether revascularization, limited debridement, partial-foot surgery, or a below-knee amputation remained possible before infection and tissue loss became extensive. By the time the patient reached the hospital in systemic decline, those options had narrowed sharply.

For this particular patient, the difference between a below-knee and an above-knee amputation was clinically and functionally substantial.

He already had right-sided weakness from the stroke. Preserving the knee would have improved positioning, sitting balance, transfers, and the possibility of limited prosthetic or assisted mobility. An above-knee amputation imposed a far greater burden. Saving the entire leg remained uncertain. Avoiding the higher amputation was more supportable. The case changed at that point.

The family initially understood the injury as the complete loss of a limb that should have been preserved. The medical evidence showed that some tissue loss, and perhaps some level of amputation, might have occurred despite timely care.

The attributable injury was better described as progression to a more extensive amputation, greater loss of transfer ability, and earlier total dependence. That did not make the damages minor.

Before the wound developed, the patient already needed assistance, but he retained meaningful function. He could sit in his wheelchair, participate in transfers, feed himself, propel himself short distances, and take part in activities outside his room.

After the above-knee amputation, he required mechanical lifting and far more assistance. He left his bed less often, participated in fewer activities, and spent increasing amounts of time isolated in his room.

The facility argued that the prior stroke and general medical decline eventually would have produced greater dependence anyway. That was possible. The records did not show that such decline was imminent before the wound. The therapy notes showed improvement, not collapse.

The proper comparison was not between this man and a healthy seventy-six-year-old. It was between the function he still possessed before the wound and the function he lost after the amputation. That incremental loss could be described clearly.

The wound documentation itself required caution. Staging changed from one note to another. Measurements were inconsistent. Photographs were missing or poorly dated. The experts disagreed about when deeper tissue injury became established.

The case did not need to depend on the precise stage assigned on a particular day.

The progression was clear regardless of terminology. A limited heel injury became a necrotic, infected wound in a poorly perfused limb, and the recommended vascular assessment did not occur while that progression was taking place.

The wound-care provider's role required close examination. The provider had recognized the need for vascular evaluation and documented the recommendation. The facility argued that this completed the provider's responsibility.

The plaintiff's expert did not place sole responsibility on the provider but disagreed that the obligation necessarily ended with the recommendation. A clinician who continues to observe deterioration may need to determine whether an important referral was completed, especially when later treatment depends on it.

The provider returned and continued documenting a nonhealing wound. Yet the later notes contained no confirmation that vascular assessment had occurred and no renewed attempt to obtain urgent evaluation. Responsibility was shared, though not equally.

The bedside staff observed the daily changes. The wound clinician recognized the circulation problem. The covering providers controlled medical escalation. The institution controlled referral tracking and coordination.

The case became more credible when those roles were described separately rather than combined into one broad institutional failure.

Antibiotic treatment also had to be evaluated carefully. A positive culture from a chronic wound does not necessarily establish invasive infection because chronic wounds are often colonized.

The initial antibiotic prescription could not be criticized merely because the wound later became infected.

The more relevant question was whether the later local and systemic changes required something beyond oral treatment.

Increasing pain, expanding necrosis, odor, drainage, lethargy, poor intake, and unstable glucose suggested that the wound was no longer a limited local problem.

By the time the daughter raised concern, hospital evaluation was reasonable even without profound hypotension or a dramatic fever.

Her testimony mattered because the chart understated how different her father appeared. She knew his usual manner of speaking, energy level, and tolerance for discomfort. Finding him in bed, unusually tired and withdrawn, helped establish a departure from baseline.

Her observations did not diagnose sepsis or vascular insufficiency. They showed that he was no longer following his ordinary course.

The defense suggested that the family's concern had been reconstructed after the amputation. Telephone records and a contemporaneous text message to the patient's son supported that the daughter had raised the concern during the visit. That made her account more durable.

The mediation presentation focused less on the original pressure injury than the family first expected.

The early redness was acknowledged as something that could occur in a high-risk patient despite preventive measures. The presentation then moved to the period when the wound failed to heal, impaired circulation was recognized, the referral remained incomplete, and the patient continued to deteriorate.

The missed appointment was not presented as an administrative mistake disconnected from the medicine.

It marked the point at which the care team recognized that local wound treatment might not be enough but failed to obtain the evaluation needed to determine whether the limb could heal.

The later hospital findings showed why that concern mattered.

The plaintiff did not claim that earlier vascular treatment certainly would have saved the entire leg. The expert explained that earlier evaluation probably would have preserved more treatment options and reduced the likelihood of an above-knee amputation.

That narrower position fit both the medical evidence and the patient's actual functional loss.

The defense still had substantial causation arguments. His circulation was severely compromised. He had diabetes, kidney disease, previous tissue loss, and limited mobility. Revascularization may have failed or may not have been advisable. Infection may have required some level of amputation even with earlier treatment. Those were legitimate reasons to discount a full limb-salvage theory.

They were less persuasive as an explanation for why no vascular evaluation occurred while the wound was visibly deteriorating.

The case resolved before trial. The settlement reflected meaningful exposure for delayed vascular and hospital evaluation, progression of infection, and the higher level of amputation. It also accounted for the likelihood that the patient would have required substantial treatment and might have lost part of the limb even with appropriate care.

The case began with the assertion that the facility caused a pressure wound by failing to turn the patient.

The developed case was more complicated, but also more defensible.

The patient was already vulnerable to skin injury. Prevention was inconsistent, but the effect of that inconsistency could not be separated fully from his underlying disease. The stronger failure occurred after the wound developed, when impaired circulation and worsening tissue loss were recognized but never brought to clinical closure.

The resulting injury was not measured against perfect mobility or perfect health.

It was measured against the function the patient still possessed and the less extensive course that earlier vascular evaluation probably would have preserved. The wound itself was visible.

The responsibility for getting it to the right level of care was not. That gap became the case.

"The responsibility for getting it to the right level of care was not. That gap became the case."

CHAPTER THIRTY-SIX

When the Model Shows the Case Should Not Proceed

A forty-one-year-old man died after two visits to urgent care and one emergency-department visit for chest discomfort, fatigue, and shortness of breath.

He had generally been healthy, worked in construction, and had no known heart disease. His death was sudden, his family was young, and the medical record contained several details that initially seemed difficult to explain.

At the first urgent-care visit, he described intermittent chest tightness and a cough that had begun after a respiratory illness. His temperature was normal. Oxygen saturation and blood pressure were within the expected range. The clinician documented clear lungs, no swelling of the legs, and no exertional pain. An electrocardiogram showed no acute ischemic change.

He was diagnosed with a likely viral or musculoskeletal condition and instructed to seek emergency care if the symptoms worsened.

Three days later, he returned because the discomfort had persisted and he felt unusually tired. He denied severe pain, fainting, or coughing blood. A second electrocardiogram was again interpreted as nonacute, and a chest radiograph was normal.

Because the symptoms were continuing, the urgent-care clinician recommended evaluation in the emergency department. The patient did not go that day.

His wife later explained that he believed the testing had been reassuring and wanted to rest at home. The written instructions, however, stated that serious causes had not been excluded and directed him to the emergency department.

Two days later, he developed more substantial shortness of breath and went to the hospital.

At triage, his heart rate was mildly elevated. His oxygen saturation was normal. He described chest discomfort that became worse when he took a deep breath. A blood test used in evaluating clot-related risk was elevated, so CT pulmonary angiography was performed. The radiologist reported no pulmonary embolism.

The emergency physician diagnosed pleuritic chest pain, discussed return precautions, and discharged him after his symptoms improved with medication.

The following evening, the patient collapsed at home and could not be resuscitated.

The autopsy identified a large pulmonary embolus obstructing the main pulmonary arteries. A clot was also found in the deep veins of one leg.

The family was told that the hospital CT must have missed the embolism.

Counsel received the case as a likely radiology and emergency-medicine failure. The patient had symptoms associated with pulmonary embolism, an elevated laboratory marker, and death from the precise condition the CT had been performed to evaluate. The timing was compelling.

The medical review did not support the expected conclusion.

The original CT images were obtained and independently reviewed by two thoracic radiologists. Neither saw an embolus. Image quality was good, contrast timing was appropriate, and the main, lobar, and segmental pulmonary arteries were clearly visualized.

There was no subtle filling defect that had been overlooked.

The autopsy finding could not simply be projected backward onto the earlier scan.

Pulmonary emboli may develop or enlarge after a negative study. A clot may be present in the leg but not yet have traveled to the lungs. A very small clot may fall below the resolution of imaging and later propagate, although the evidence did not establish that this had occurred.

The fact that the patient died from pulmonary embolism the following day did not prove that an embolus was visible during the emergency visit. That finding substantially weakened the radiology claim.

Counsel then considered whether the emergency physician should have admitted the patient or begun anticoagulation despite the negative CT.

That decision had to be evaluated from what was known at the time of discharge.

The patient had pleuritic discomfort and mild tachycardia. The elevated screening marker had appropriately led to definitive imaging. He was not hypoxic or hypotensive. There was no documented leg swelling, coughing of blood, syncope, or evidence of right-heart strain. The CT showed no pulmonary embolism or other dangerous acute process. His symptoms improved during observation.

The emergency-medicine expert concluded that discharge with clear precautions fell within reasonable care.

Empiric anticoagulation after a technically adequate negative CT would not ordinarily be required in a stable patient without another compelling indication. Anticoagulation carries a meaningful risk of bleeding and is not administered simply because pulmonary embolism remains biologically possible.

The expert also considered whether venous ultrasound of the leg should have been performed.

Ultrasound may be appropriate when clinical suspicion remains high, chest imaging is nondiagnostic, or signs of deep-vein thrombosis are present. This patient had no documented leg symptoms and a negative, high-quality pulmonary study.

The expert could not support that ultrasound was required before discharge.

The earlier urgent-care encounters were then reviewed. Persistent chest discomfort in a younger adult can justify consideration of cardiac, pulmonary, infectious, gastrointestinal, and musculoskeletal causes. The clinicians obtained electrocardiograms and later a chest radiograph. At the second visit, the patient was specifically directed to the emergency department.

The family believed a stronger warning would have caused him to go immediately.

The written instructions were direct. The patient chose not to follow them that day.

That did not make the death his fault. It affected whether the urgent-care clinicians had denied him an evaluation they had actually recommended.

The first urgent-care encounter was somewhat more debatable because pulmonary embolism had not been specifically evaluated. The presentation at that point was nonspecific, and no substantial thrombosis risk factor had been documented.

Additional records later showed that the patient had taken a long car trip the week before and had privately mentioned calf soreness to his wife. Neither fact appeared in the history he gave at urgent care or at the hospital.

The family understandably believed the clinicians should have asked more detailed questions.

The records showed that the emergency physician had asked about recent travel and leg symptoms. The patient denied both. His wife explained that he may not have considered the trip recent and thought the calf discomfort was a pulled muscle.

The case could not assign information to the clinicians that the patient did not provide and the examination did not reveal.

A failure to obtain an adequate history can be negligent. Here, the relevant questions had been asked and documented.

The death remained emotionally difficult to reconcile because the patient underwent the appropriate test for the condition that killed him and died shortly afterward.

That closeness in time created a powerful temptation to treat the outcome as proof that the evaluation must have failed. The objective evidence pointed elsewhere.

The CT was negative. The patient was clinically stable. The history contained no clear signs of thrombosis. The physician responded to the elevated screening test by obtaining the appropriate imaging. The discharge decision was medically defensible.

Counsel asked whether a smaller embolus might have been present but missed. The radiologists agreed that no clot was visible, although they could not exclude a microscopic or newly forming thrombus. That possibility did not establish breach.

Counsel then asked whether empiric anticoagulation would have prevented the later fatal embolus. It might have. That did not mean reasonable care required anticoagulation at the time. This became the central distinction in the review.

A treatment may appear beneficial in hindsight without having been indicated prospectively.

If every stable patient with persistent pleuritic discomfort and a technically adequate negative CT were anticoagulated because a clot might develop later, many patients would be exposed unnecessarily to serious bleeding risk.

The standard of care cannot be reconstructed from knowing which rare patient later experienced the feared event.

Causation presented a separate problem even if additional testing were assumed.

An ultrasound of the leg might have shown the clot found at autopsy. No leg imaging existed from the emergency encounter. The clot may have been present then, or it may have developed or propagated afterward.

The autopsy could not establish what the leg veins looked like the day before death.

Any opinion about what an unperformed ultrasound would have shown would therefore remain speculative.

It probably would have been possible to find an expert willing to support the case. The symptoms, elevated screening result, and rapid death created enough concern for someone to argue that longer observation or ultrasound would have been safer. That was not the correct inquiry.

The issue was whether such an opinion would identify a reliable professional obligation or merely describe a more cautious approach after the outcome was known.

The emergency expert consulted by counsel was clear. More testing could have been performed. Longer observation was possible. An ultrasound could have been ordered.

The expert was equally clear that reasonable care did not require those steps on the documented facts. The distinction carried practical consequences.

Medicine often permits additional testing, longer observation, or a more conservative disposition. Malpractice analysis asks whether the care provided fell outside the reasonable professional range, not whether another clinician could have done more.

The family also questioned whether the patient had been discharged too quickly. He remained in the emergency department for several hours. The CT report was final before discharge. Repeat vital signs were stable. His pain improved with medication, and no new symptom appeared during observation. The record did not support a rushed disposition.

The absence of a scheduled follow-up visit was considered as well. The physician instructed him to contact primary care and return immediately if his symptoms worsened. The fatal event occurred before an ordinary outpatient appointment probably would have taken place. That issue did not create a causal bridge. The clinical review therefore reached an uncomfortable conclusion.

The patient died from a condition that had been considered and tested for. The test was technically adequate and negative. The clinicians responded reasonably to the information available.

The embolus probably developed or became detectable after discharge, although its exact timing could not be proved. The case should not proceed.

That conclusion did not mean the healthcare system had given the family a satisfying explanation. It did not mean every question about when the clot formed could be answered. It meant the evidence did not support a professional departure that probably caused the death.

The family understandably struggled with the conclusion because the sequence appeared too close to be coincidental.

He was tested on one day and died from the condition the next.

The clinical review had to explain why timing alone was not enough.

A negative test is not protection against a disease developing later. Medical evaluation describes the patient at a particular point in time. A technically sound study may accurately show that a condition is absent and still be followed shortly afterward by development of that condition.

The closer the later event occurs, the harder that reality is to accept. The records nevertheless supported it.

The closing letter to the family did more than say that negligence had not been found. It explained the central reasoning.

The emergency physician had considered pulmonary embolism and ordered the appropriate test. Independent review found no missed clot on the scan. The patient's vital signs and examination did not require admission or anticoagulation after a negative study. The fatal embolus could not be shown to have existed or been detectable during the emergency visit.

Without that connection, the death could not reliably be attributed to the discharge decision.

The explanation also acknowledged what medicine could not determine.

No one could identify the precise moment the fatal clot formed or traveled to the lungs. It remained possible that thrombosis was beginning during the hospital visit. The evidence could not show that a required ultrasound or another reasonable intervention probably would have identified and prevented the event. That uncertainty was not converted into causation. The file was closed.

Stopping at that point avoided several predictable problems. A radiologist would have been asked to criticize a scan that contained no visible embolus. An emergency expert would have needed to argue that optional testing was mandatory. Causation would have depended on assuming that an unperformed ultrasound would have revealed a treatable clot. A jury would have been invited to reason backward from the devastating autopsy result.

The case might have survived pleading. It might even have attracted a favorable preliminary opinion. It would not have rested on stable medicine.

The same clinical method that strengthens viable cases has to be capable of ending cases the medical evidence does not support.

The patient had a favorable baseline, and the loss was catastrophic. Those facts increased the damages. They did not establish breach.

The objective evidence showed that the relevant imaging had been performed and interpreted appropriately. The timeline showed a rapid later event but did not establish that the condition existed during the earlier encounter. The professional-obligation analysis showed that additional testing was possible without being required. The alternative course depended on several unsupported assumptions. The causal bridge remained speculative.

That is the point at which clinical review must be allowed to reach an unfavorable answer.

A serious outcome does not make every earlier decision negligent. A later diagnosis does not establish that the condition was detectable sooner. A treatment that might have prevented the outcome does not prove that reasonable care required it before the outcome was known.

The responsible decision was not to continue searching until someone agreed to support the case. It was to stop when the medical evidence no longer did.

"The responsible decision was not to continue searching until someone agreed to support the case. It was to stop when the medical evidence no longer did."

CHAPTER THIRTY-SEVEN

When the Model Strengthens the Defense

The most useful defense review often begins by admitting that some part of the care could have been better.

That may feel counterintuitive, particularly when the first instinct is to defend every decision, every entry, every delay, and every person involved. Medical records rarely support such an absolute position. Documentation may be incomplete. Communication may have been awkward. A test may have been ordered later than another clinician would have ordered it. The patient may have remained in the department longer, or been discharged sooner, than someone reviewing the case years later would prefer.

None of those imperfections answers the central medical questions. Did the care fall outside the reasonable professional range, and did the disputed conduct probably change the outcome?

A defense usually becomes stronger when it stops trying to turn imperfect care into perfect care and begins separating the imperfections that mattered medically from those that did not.

This case involved a twenty-two-year-old college student who was brought to the emergency department after falling from an electric scooter. He had been drinking, struck the side of his head, and appeared dazed briefly, according to his friends. There was no prolonged loss of consciousness. He walked into the department with assistance, answered questions, and knew where he was.

At triage, he complained of headache, nausea, and pain around one shoulder. His speech was somewhat slurred, although alcohol intoxication was evident. He had a small scalp abrasion without an obvious skull deformity. Blood pressure and oxygen saturation were normal, and his heart rate was mildly elevated.

The emergency physician examined him shortly after arrival. He was sleepy but could be awakened. His pupils were equal, he moved all extremities, and no focal neurological deficit was documented. Because he had struck his head, was intoxicated, and could not provide a completely reliable account of the fall, the physician ordered a noncontrast head CT and cervical-spine imaging.

Both studies were negative. The head CT showed no acute hemorrhage, fracture, swelling, or mass effect. The patient received medication for nausea and remained under observation.

During the next several hours, he slept for long periods and became irritable when staff awakened him. His friends told staff that this was not unusual when he had been drinking heavily. He vomited once after returning from imaging.

A repeat neurological examination was documented as unchanged. Later, he stood, walked to the bathroom, drank water, and conversed with staff. He was discharged with two friends, who were instructed to return if he developed worsening headache, repeated vomiting, confusion, weakness, seizure activity, or difficulty being awakened.

The following afternoon, one of those friends found him difficult to arouse. Emergency medical services returned him to the hospital.

A second CT showed a large acute subdural hematoma with substantial mass effect. He underwent emergency surgery and survived, but he was left with permanent neurological impairment, including memory loss, reduced executive function, and weakness on one side.

At first glance, the plaintiff's theory was compelling. The patient had sustained head trauma, remained sleepy, vomited, and was discharged while still intoxicated. The following day, he returned with a large intracranial hemorrhage. The argument was that the emergency department had failed to recognize continued neurological deterioration and released him before the danger had passed.

The hospital's initial response was too broad. It asserted that the patient had been fully evaluated, that every symptom was attributable to alcohol, and that the later hemorrhage was entirely unrelated to the first visit.

The medicine did not support that degree of certainty.

He had sustained a real head injury. He had symptoms requiring evaluation. Intoxication made the examination more difficult, and the later hemorrhage arose in the same general area as the original impact. The later event could not credibly be dismissed as though something wholly unrelated had occurred after discharge.

The defense became more persuasive when the timeline and objective evidence were reviewed without trying to protect every part of the original care.

The first CT was technically adequate. Two independent neuroradiologists reviewed the images and found no acute subdural collection, subtle hyperdensity, skull fracture, or visible precursor to the large hematoma seen the following day.

The plaintiff's radiology expert initially suggested that a very thin collection might have been present. On closer review, the expert acknowledged that the perceived finding could represent normal anatomy and could not be followed reliably across adjacent images. The record did not support a missed-radiology claim.

That left the more important clinical issue. Intracranial bleeding can develop after an initially negative CT. Did the patient's condition require longer observation, repeat imaging, or admission despite the negative study?

The answer depended on what happened while he remained in the emergency department.

The plaintiff emphasized his sleepiness and the episode of vomiting. Those were relevant findings. They were also compatible with alcohol intoxication, medication, sleep deprivation, and minor head trauma. Their significance depended on whether he was deteriorating, failing to improve, or developing new neurological signs.

The contemporaneous record showed gradual improvement rather than decline.

He became easier to awaken. He walked without assistance. He drank fluids. His speech became clearer. Repeat examination showed no weakness, asymmetry, pupillary change, or increasing confusion. He vomited once, not repeatedly.

The charting was less detailed than it should have been. The repeat neurological examination did not contain every element that would have been useful later. That gave the plaintiff a legitimate area for criticism. It did not establish that the patient was clinically worsening.

The testimony of the friends also became important. The complaint described them as having warned staff that the patient was not behaving normally. During depositions, both explained that he had been heavily intoxicated before the fall and that his sleepiness in the department appeared consistent with how he usually behaved after drinking.

They were concerned about the head injury. They did not remember one-sided weakness, worsening speech, seizure activity, or an inability to awaken him before discharge.

One friend remembered the patient walking down the hallway, joking about missing class, and arguing about leaving his scooter behind.

Those details did not prove that discharge was the only reasonable choice. They made the description of obvious neurological decline much harder to sustain.

The emergency-medicine experts agreed that intoxicated patients with head trauma require particular care because alcohol can obscure neurological change. They disagreed about how long observation should have continued.

The plaintiff's expert believed the patient should have remained until he was clinically sober. The defense expert believed discharge was reasonable once the CT was negative, repeat examination remained stable, behavior was improving, ambulation was safe, and responsible adults were available to supervise him.

That was a genuine disagreement in clinical judgment. It was not a case in which one side was ignoring unmistakable danger.

The phrase clinically sober also needed explanation. It does not necessarily mean that every effect of alcohol has disappeared or that the blood-alcohol level has reached zero. In practice, it generally means that the patient can participate meaningfully in examination, walk safely, understand instructions, and leave with appropriate supervision.

According to the chart and witness testimony, he met those functional conditions before discharge.

The plaintiff also argued that continued sleepiness should have prompted another CT. The defense experts disagreed. Repeat imaging is not automatically required after a negative study merely because an intoxicated patient remains tired, particularly when the neurological examination is stable and the overall course is improving.

The threshold would have been different if the patient had developed worsening headache, repeated vomiting, focal weakness, declining consciousness, pupillary change, or another sign of neurological progression. Those findings were not documented before he left.

The later hemorrhage remained medically difficult to explain with precision. The defense could not establish the exact moment it began. It may have developed gradually after discharge. A small vessel may have started bleeding later. Another impact was theoretically possible, although there was no evidence that one occurred.

The later CT showed a large hematoma. It did not prove that a clinically significant bleed was present during the first visit. That became the center of the defense.

The hospital did not need to prove exactly why the hemorrhage developed later. It needed to show that the earlier evaluation remained reasonable on the information available at the time and that the plaintiff could not establish a probable causal benefit from a different course.

Causation was more difficult for the plaintiff than the discharge criticism itself.

Suppose the patient had been admitted overnight. Would the hemorrhage have been detected before permanent injury occurred? Possibly. Would admission probably have prevented the injury? The evidence could not answer that with the same confidence.

No one could establish when bleeding began, how quickly the hematoma enlarged, or when neurological deterioration first became clinically apparent. The friends did not wake him repeatedly during the night. He went to sleep after returning home and was found difficult to arouse the following afternoon.

Very little reliable clinical information existed during that interval.

In a hospital, he would have received periodic neurological checks. If the bleeding developed gradually and was recognized promptly, earlier imaging and surgery might have reduced the injury. If it developed rapidly later in the course, the benefit of admission would have depended on when he happened to be reassessed.

The plaintiff's neurological expert initially stated that admission probably would have prevented permanent injury. That opinion rested largely on the assumption that bleeding began soon after discharge and progressed over many hours. The imaging did not establish that assumption.

The surgeon who treated the patient described the hematoma as acute and explained that it could have accumulated over a relatively short period. The operative findings did not allow the surgeon to determine reliably when bleeding began.

The causation opinion therefore remained possible rather than probable.

That was more useful to the defense than trying to prove that the discharge decision had been unquestionably correct.

Even if a jury concluded that longer observation would have been safer, the plaintiff still had to show that longer observation probably would have led to diagnosis and treatment before irreversible injury occurred. The record did not establish that connection.

The discharge instructions created another legitimate area of concern. They were written in standard language and given to the patient and his friends. The nurse testified that she reviewed the warnings with the friends because the patient had been drinking.

One friend remembered being told to return if the patient vomited repeatedly or could not be awakened. The other remembered being told to check on him.

The instructions were not ideal. No specific waking schedule was documented, and the friends did not fully appreciate that increasing sleepiness might represent delayed bleeding rather than ordinary intoxication.

The plaintiff argued that clearer instructions would have caused them to return sooner. That argument encountered the same timing problem.

The friends did not observe a definite change during the night because they allowed him to sleep and went to their own rooms. They could not identify when he became more difficult to awaken. Even with more detailed instructions, the evidence did not establish when they would have recognized a material change or how much earlier he would have received treatment.

The failure-to-warn theory was plausible. Its causal effect could not be established reliably.

The defense review also identified a weakness that should have been conceded. The neurological reassessment was documented too briefly for an intoxicated patient with head trauma. A more complete note would have made the basis for discharge easier to understand.

That did not establish that no examination occurred. The physician and nurse gave consistent descriptions of improvement, and the patient's conduct supported them. He walked, drank, conversed, and left with friends.

The defense was better served by acknowledging the documentation weakness than by insisting the record was ideal.

The same was true of the observation period. Another physician might have kept the patient longer. Longer observation would have been more cautious.

The relevant issue was whether discharge fell outside the reasonable professional range.

The defense expert could explain why it did not.

This was not a patient with worsening mental status after a positive scan. It was an intoxicated patient with a technically adequate negative CT, stable repeat findings, improving function, and responsible supervision after discharge.

The later catastrophe did not, by itself, make the earlier judgment negligent.

The hospital also needed to resist blaming the patient or his friends. The patient had been drinking and accepted discharge. His friends did not monitor him as closely as they might have had they understood the risk more fully.

Those facts affected the timeline. They did not need to become a moral defense.

The stronger position remained clinical. The patient was evaluated for the known risk. Imaging was negative. His condition improved during observation. No new neurological finding required repeat imaging before discharge. The later hemorrhage could not be shown to have been present or detectable during the initial encounter, and the probable benefit of admission remained uncertain. That explanation did not depend on criticizing anyone's character.

The damages evidence was substantial and largely uncontested. Before the injury, the patient was academically successful, independent, socially active, and preparing for a professional career. His later cognitive and motor impairments changed almost every part of his life. Those facts created serious exposure if liability and causation were established. They did not supply the missing causal link.

That separation was essential. The magnitude of the injury made the defense emotionally difficult, but it did not change what the first CT showed or establish when the later bleeding began.

At mediation, the defense began by acknowledging the injury and the tragedy of delayed intracranial hemorrhage. It did not argue that the patient had merely been drunk or that his friends had failed him. It then returned to the first visit.

The emergency physician recognized the head injury and ordered appropriate imaging. The study showed no hemorrhage. The patient remained under observation, improved functionally, and developed no focal neurological deficit. He left with adult supervision and return instructions.

The later hematoma was real. The evidence did not show that it existed during the first visit or that admission probably would have led to treatment before permanent injury. This was the defense position.

The hospital also avoided claiming that delayed hemorrhage after a negative CT is always unforeseeable. It is a recognized risk. That is why return instructions and responsible supervision matter.

A known risk does not make every later occurrence preventable.

The case continued through expert depositions. The plaintiff's experts maintained that longer observation would have been preferable, but none could say when the bleeding probably began or when a repeat scan would have become positive. The radiology theory narrowed further when the original study was reviewed jointly.

The matter ultimately resolved for a fraction of the amount initially demanded.

The settlement reflected the severity of the injury, the sympathetic patient, the abbreviated documentation, and the possibility that a jury might conclude the discharge came too soon. It also reflected a strong defense grounded in objective imaging, clinical improvement, and the unresolved causation problem.

Clinical review strengthened the defense because it did not require anyone to describe the care as flawless.

It separated a debatable judgment issue from a weak causal conclusion. It showed why the later diagnosis could not simply be projected backward. It revealed that the plaintiff's alternative course depended on an unproved assumption about when the hemorrhage began. It allowed the hospital to acknowledge a devastating injury without allowing the injury itself to decide whether the earlier care was negligent. That is often what a strong medical defense looks like.

Not a denial that something could have been done differently.

A clear explanation of why the care remained within the reasonable range, why the later event had not been shown to be detectable earlier, and why the proposed alternative probably would not have changed the outcome.

"A clear explanation of why the care remained within the reasonable range, why the later event had not been shown to be detectable earlier, and why the proposed alternative probably would not have changed the outcome."

"Medical cases create pressure to take a position early."

PART VI

JUDGMENT, CONCLUSION, AND PRACTICE TOOLS

Chapter 38, Conclusion, and Appendices

CHAPTER THIRTY-EIGHT

Understanding Before Advocacy

Medical cases create pressure to take a position early.

A patient has died. A child has been permanently injured. A family has watched an unexplained decline. A clinician has been accused of causing a catastrophic outcome. An institution is confronting a record that looks troubling before anyone has reconstructed how the care actually worked.

The legal process asks for allegations, defenses, experts, discovery, valuation, and decisions, usually on a schedule. The medicine rarely arrives in that order. It arrives in fragments.

A note written after the event may appear clearer than the notes written while the patient was deteriorating. An imaging report may sound definitive even though the underlying study was limited. One witness remembers an urgent communication while another remembers a routine call. The final diagnosis changes the way earlier symptoms appear, sometimes fairly and sometimes only because the outcome is now known.

The work of Clinical Intelligence is to slow that process long enough to understand what actually happened.

It is not meant to make a complicated case sound simple when it is not. Its purpose is to identify what must be true before a legal position can be trusted.

The method has remained consistent across the cases in this book. Every patient had a baseline before the disputed care. That baseline may have involved excellent health, advanced disease, disability, pregnancy, infancy, aging, or years of dependence on medical support. Whatever it was, it remained the starting point.

A clinical course then unfolded. Symptoms appeared. Findings accumulated. Tests were performed or not performed. Information moved through people and systems. Decisions were made before anyone knew the outcome.

At some point, reasonable care may have required a different response. In another case, the response given may have remained within the accepted professional range.

When a departure occurred, the analysis could not stop there. What treatment or rescue remained available? How quickly could it realistically have occurred? Was the patient a candidate for it? What benefit was probable?

Only after those questions were answered could the actual course be compared with the course reasonable care probably would have produced. That comparison defined the attributable injury.

Sometimes the event caused an entirely new condition. Sometimes it aggravated disease that already existed. Sometimes it accelerated decline or death. Sometimes it increased the severity of an injury that could not have been prevented completely. In other cases, the comparison showed no probable difference at all. The method did not change when the conclusion changed.

That is why the same clinical approach could strengthen a plaintiff's case, narrow it, move responsibility to another participant, support settlement, strengthen a defense, or show that a case should not proceed.

Its value was never that it produced one preferred kind of answer.

Its value was that it prevented the outcome from becoming the analysis. That danger exists in nearly every serious medical case.

When the injury is catastrophic, the earlier care begins to look more obviously wrong. When the patient had serious pre-existing disease, the later harm can begin to look inevitable. When a complication is recognized, counsel may assume that nothing could have prevented it. When a policy was violated, the violation may be treated as though it proves causation. Clinical Intelligence interrupts those assumptions.

It asks what the professionals knew at the time, what they reasonably could have known, and what meaningful treatment opportunity the patient still had.

That does not remove clinical judgment from the case. It allows counsel to see where judgment was exercised and when the basis for that judgment changed.

A clinician may choose among several reasonable options. The fact that one option later proves unsuccessful does not make the original decision negligent. A judgment that was reasonable initially may become unreasonable when the patient fails to improve, develops a new finding, or stops following the expected course. The analysis has to move with the patient.

It cannot freeze the case at the first encounter, and it cannot judge every earlier decision through the final diagnosis.

The same movement matters in causation. A treatment opportunity is not simply open or closed as an abstract proposition. Its value changes while disease progresses, bleeding continues, tissue becomes ischemic, infection spreads, or neurological injury develops.

Earlier is not always better in a legally meaningful sense. The earlier treatment must have been indicated, realistically available, and likely to provide material benefit.

Later is not always too late. A patient may remain salvageable despite serious deterioration. The record has to show where the patient was in that course.

That is one reason objective evidence carries so much weight. Imaging, pathology, laboratory trends, medication data, device histories, and physiological monitoring can correct the story created by memory and narrative documentation.

Objective evidence still requires interpretation. It does not decide the case by itself. It establishes boundaries.

An image may show that a condition was not visible when the report was issued. A pump may show that medication was delivered differently from the physician's order. A laboratory trend may establish that deterioration began earlier than anyone recognized. Pathology may show that disease was already advanced or, in another matter, that a meaningful treatment opportunity remained.

Objective evidence keeps the theory from resting entirely on retrospective confidence.

Workflow reconstruction serves a similar purpose because many injuries do not arise from one dramatic clinical decision. They develop when information, responsibility, or follow-up disappears between roles.

A result may be interpreted correctly and never reach an active clinician. A nurse may recognize deterioration but communicate only part of the pattern. A referral may be entered without anyone confirming that the evaluation occurs. A medication may be prescribed correctly, verified correctly, and programmed incorrectly.

The chart may show that everyone completed some portion of the work.

The patient may still reach no one capable of bringing that work to completion.

Institutional responsibility becomes understandable only when the clinical task is followed from beginning to end.

A written policy does not establish that the task was completed. The absence of a perfect policy does not prove that care failed. The useful inquiry is whether the system assigned real ownership to work that mattered and whether that ownership functioned for this patient.

That is usually more revealing than a broad argument about culture or safety. The same precision belongs in expert selection.

The right expert is not simply someone who shares the defendant's specialty or someone willing to support the theory counsel prefers. It is the professional whose knowledge and experience match the question the case actually requires.

One expert may address whether the original clinical decision was reasonable. Another may interpret imaging. Another may reconstruct treatment eligibility and probable outcome. A rehabilitation professional may explain function, and a life-care planner may identify future needs.

Experts do not strengthen a case by repeating one another. They strengthen it by carrying separate parts of the same clinical account.

That account becomes unreliable when the assumptions begin to drift. The causation expert may assume treatment at a time the standard-of-care expert does not support. The life-care planner may project permanent total dependence while the rehabilitation expert predicts meaningful recovery. The economist may calculate ordinary lifetime earnings for a patient whose prior disease had already limited work. Those are not merely drafting inconsistencies. They are different cases occupying the same file.

Clinical review has to identify that before the opposing side does. It also requires counsel to tolerate narrower answers.

Litigation creates pressure to describe injury in absolute terms. The death was preventable. The leg would have been saved. The child would have developed normally. The patient would have returned to work. Sometimes the evidence supports those conclusions. Often it supports something more exact.

Death probably occurred sooner. A lower level of amputation might have been avoided. Neurological injury probably would have been less severe. The patient would have needed assistance, but not this degree of assistance.

A narrower conclusion is not a lesser form of truth. It may be the only version that remains reliable under serious examination.

The willingness to narrow can strengthen the defense as well.

A defendant does not need to prove that every part of the care was ideal. A documentation lapse may be acknowledged. A process failure may be conceded. A delay may be accepted while its effect on the outcome remains disputed.

The stronger defense often begins where reflexive denial ends.

Yes, the result should have been followed, but the available treatment probably would not have changed the outcome.

Yes, reassessment should have occurred sooner, but the evidence does not show that the injury remained preventable at that time.

Those positions are usually more credible than insisting nothing went wrong simply because the eventual injury may have been unavoidable. The model is not aligned with plaintiffs or defendants. It is aligned with clinical coherence.

That coherence matters because medical litigation eventually compresses complexity. At mediation or trial, thousands of pages become a small number of questions.

Who was this patient before the event? What was happening medically? When did the obligation change? What response remained available? What difference did the disputed conduct probably cause?

A case that cannot answer those questions may still contain suffering, error, anger, and poor care. It may not yet contain a reliable legal and medical theory.

A case that can answer them becomes understandable without becoming simplistic. That is the point at which the framework should disappear.

The mediator should not hear a model being recited. A jury should not see a checklist. They should understand what happened to the patient.

The patient was stable and then changed. A finding appeared and carried a particular meaning. Someone responded or failed to respond while treatment remained useful. The actual course then separated from the course reasonable care probably would have produced. The loss lies in that difference.

When the explanation is clear, advocacy becomes more disciplined. Counsel does not need to attack every note or defend every action. The strongest evidence can carry the case because everyone understands why it matters.

When the explanation remains unclear, advocacy often becomes louder. More criticisms are added. More experts are retained. More events are placed on the timeline. The file grows in volume because the theory has not become coherent.

Clinical Intelligence is intended to prevent that growth from being mistaken for development.

The framework remains relatively constant because the underlying questions do not change. The answers change with every patient.

A newborn has a different baseline from a frail nursing-facility resident. A young adult with stroke has a different treatment opportunity from a patient with metastatic disease. Maternal medication toxicity may affect both mother and fetus. A missed radiology result may involve months of lost surveillance rather than hours of failed rescue.

The same relationships still have to be understood: baseline, objective evidence, timeline, workflow, professional obligation, treatment opportunity, alternative course, and attributable injury.

Those are not headings that must be imposed mechanically on every file. They are the clinical relationships that must be understood whether anyone names them or not. The attorney's decision comes afterward.

The case may proceed. It may need to be narrowed, redirected, resolved, stopped, or defended.

Each can be the proper result of serious review.

The quality of the work should not be measured by the number of cases that survive. It should be measured by whether the decision reflects the medicine honestly.

That honesty matters to everyone involved. A family deserves to know when the evidence supports its concerns and when it does not. A defendant deserves a defense based on the actual clinical course rather than automatic denial. Experts deserve questions that remain within their disciplines. Judges and juries deserve a theory that does not ask them to confuse tragedy with causation or imperfection with negligence.

Most of all, the patient's life should not be simplified merely to fit an argument.

The patient may have been healthy or chronically ill, independent or dependent, young or approaching the end of life. The loss has to be measured against the life that actually existed and the course that probably remained.

That is why baseline appears at the beginning of the analysis and returns at the end.

Without baseline, damages become abstract. Without causation, injury becomes detached from the departure. Without a realistic alternative course, the case becomes a description of what happened rather than an explanation of what reasonable care would have changed.

Understanding has to come before advocacy because advocacy magnifies whatever understanding already exists.

When the clinical theory is sound, advocacy can make it accessible.

When the theory is incomplete, advocacy may conceal the incompleteness for a time. It cannot make the medicine support what it does not support.

The durable case is the one that remains coherent after the unfavorable facts are included, after its assumptions are exposed, and after the opposing experts have given their strongest explanation. That is the case worth carrying forward.

It may be broader or narrower than the one first imagined. It may belong against a different participant. It may support a different injury. It may ultimately belong to the defense. The framework does not promise the answer counsel hoped to find. It provides a way to understand why the answer should be trusted.

"It provides a way to understand why the answer should be trusted."

Conclusion

The Case the Medicine Can Support

Medical-malpractice litigation begins with an outcome that demands explanation. A patient died. A condition progressed. A treatment opportunity was lost. Someone who entered care with meaningful independence returned home dependent on others. A family was left trying to understand whether the harm was unavoidable, whether something important was missed, or whether the system failed at the point when intervention still mattered.

The seriousness of that outcome justifies investigation. It does not determine what the investigation will show.

The work begins by returning to the patient before the disputed event. Counsel must understand the patient's actual baseline, not simply the diagnoses listed in the record. That means knowing how the person lived, what function remained, what treatment burden already existed, what prognosis was reasonably expected, and what changed after the care at issue.

From there, the record must be treated as evidence rather than as a complete narrative. The ordinary chart may not contain the original imaging, device history, routing data, secure communications, medication-delivery information, referral records, or operational evidence that explains how care actually moved. A large production can still be clinically incomplete.

The timeline must then be reconstructed around the patient's condition rather than around document timestamps. The important interval is not necessarily the entire hospitalization, every emergency visit, or every hour before diagnosis. It is the period during which the clinical picture changed, the significance of that change became reasonably apparent, the professional obligation evolved, and meaningful treatment remained available.

That is where standard of care and causation begin to separate.

A decision may have been reasonable when first made and become unreasonable when the patient failed to improve. A process may have been imperfect without affecting the outcome. A complication may have occurred despite appropriate care and still have required earlier rescue. A result may have been missed without changing prognosis. The analysis must identify not only what should have happened, but what difference that alternative course probably would have made.

The treatment opportunity has to be real. It must account for consultation, transfer, eligibility, contraindications, treatment time, patient choice, and the injury already present. "Earlier care" is not enough. The alternative course should be reconstructed with the same discipline applied to the course that occurred.

The resulting injury may be broader or narrower than the one first alleged. Appropriate care may have prevented the entire outcome. It may instead have preserved function, reduced severity, avoided a higher level of amputation, prolonged survival, reduced treatment burden, or prevented a more difficult final course.

That narrower conclusion is not a compromise when it reflects the medicine accurately. It is often what makes the case credible.

The same discipline strengthens the defense. A defendant need not prove that every aspect of care was ideal. Documentation may have been incomplete. A communication process may have failed. Another clinician may have chosen a more cautious course. Those facts can be acknowledged while counsel still asks whether the conduct fell outside the reasonable professional range and whether it caused the injury being claimed.

Clinical Intelligence is therefore not a plaintiff framework or a defense framework. It is a method for determining which account of the patient's course remains coherent when the entire record, including the difficult facts, is considered.

That method should affect every later decision.

It should guide which records are pursued, which defendants remain in the case, which experts are needed, how depositions are prepared, how damages are framed, how settlement risk is valued, and how the case is eventually presented. It should also tell counsel when the matter needs to be narrowed, redirected, resolved, defended, or stopped.

The framework has succeeded when it is no longer visible as a framework.

By mediation or trial, the audience should not hear a checklist. It should understand the patient. It should see when the condition changed, what information became available, who had responsibility, what response remained possible, and what difference the disputed care did or did not make.

That understanding is the foundation of effective advocacy.

The final legal strategy may be aggressive, restrained, narrow, or comprehensive. It may support a substantial plaintiff claim, a focused causation defense, an institutional theory, or a conclusion that litigation should not continue. Whatever the result, the strategy should arise from the same disciplined inquiry.

What happened to this patient?

When did the professional obligation change?

What treatment or rescue remained available?

What probably would have occurred under reasonable care?

What part of the final harm belongs to the difference?

Those questions do not make medical litigation simple. They make it honest.

The strongest case is not the one with the most criticism, the largest record, or the most forceful expert. It is the one that explains the patient's course without asking the evidence to support more than it can carry.

That is the case worth advancing.

That is also the case worth defending.

Appendix A

The Clinical Intelligence Case-Review Framework

The following framework is intended to help counsel organize medical evidence before committing the case to a final theory. It is not a substitute for legal analysis, expert opinion, or jurisdiction-specific requirements.

Record Integrity

Determine whether the available production contains the evidence needed to answer the disputed clinical questions.

Consider:

- original imaging and underlying diagnostic material;
- laboratory trends rather than isolated values;
- medication orders, administration records, pharmacy data, and infusion information;
- audit trails, routing histories, inbox activity, and acknowledgment records;
- nursing flowsheets, monitoring data, device downloads, and alarm histories;
- telephone records, secure messages, referral systems, and transfer communications;

- records from earlier and subsequent facilities;
- operative, pathology, autopsy, rehabilitation, and home-health records;
- policies, protocols, staffing information, and chain-of-command documents.

The practical inquiry is not whether the file is large. It is whether the file is clinically complete for the issue being evaluated.

Baseline Profiling

Establish who the patient was before the disputed event.

Review:

- diagnoses and prognosis;
- mobility, cognition, communication, and self-care;
- employment, education, parenting, caregiving, and household responsibilities;
- prior symptoms or limitations related to the claimed injury;
- treatment burden and existing care needs;
- recent trajectory, including stability, improvement, or decline;
- patient goals, directives, and treatment preferences.

Baseline should describe the patient's life, not merely the problem list.

Objective Evidence Analysis

Identify the evidence that anchors the medical course.

Evaluate:

- imaging;
- laboratory trends;
- pathology and autopsy findings;
- vital signs and monitoring;
- medication delivery;
- operative findings;
- physical measurements;
- response to treatment;
- rehabilitation and functional assessments.

For each item, determine what it establishes, what it suggests, and what it cannot reliably prove.

Clinical Timeline Reconstruction

Reconstruct the patient's course according to clinical change rather than note order alone.

Identify:

- symptom onset;
- symptom reporting;
- examination time;
- order time;

- test performance;
- interpretation and finalization;
- communication and acknowledgment;
- reassessment;
- treatment initiation;
- treatment response;
- deterioration;
- transfer or escalation;
- closure of the meaningful treatment opportunity.

The timeline should show when the patient's condition changed, when that change became reasonably recognizable, and when the existing plan no longer fit.

Standard-of-Care Analysis

Define the patient-specific professional obligation.

Ask:

- What information was available at the time?
- What did that information reasonably mean?
- Which professional or institution had responsibility?
- What options remained within the accepted range?
- Was a particular response required?
- What occurred instead?

- Was the issue one of reasonable judgment, incomplete work, or process failure?

Avoid evaluating the care through the final diagnosis alone.

Institutional and System Analysis

Determine how information, responsibility, and work moved through the organization.

Examine:

- ownership of results and follow-up;
- handoffs and coverage;
- escalation pathways;
- referral tracking;
- medication safeguards;
- staffing and supervision;
- transfer processes;
- backup systems;
- closure mechanisms;
- what occurred when the ordinary process failed.

A written policy matters only when connected to the patient, the intended safeguard, and the actual operational failure.

Causation Mapping

Place the alleged departure within the biological course.

Define:

- the disease or injury mechanism;
- the point at which the alleged departure occurred;
- the treatment or rescue that remained available;
- the patient's eligibility;
- realistic timing of consultation, transfer, testing, or intervention;
- contraindications and competing risks;
- the probable alternative course;
- the injury already present;
- the additional harm attributable to the disputed difference.

Causation should identify what probably changed, not merely what might have changed.

Damages Analysis

Compare the course that probably would have occurred with the course that did occur.

Determine:

- what injury was new;
- what prior condition was aggravated;
- what decline was accelerated;
- what function was lost;
- what care needs increased;

- what treatment became necessary;
- whether survival was shortened;
- what additional suffering or burden occurred.

Damages should remain aligned with baseline and the causal opinion.

Attorney Decision

At the end of the clinical review, counsel should be able to determine whether the case should:

- proceed as originally alleged;
- proceed under a narrower theory;
- focus on another encounter or defendant;
- shift from individual to institutional responsibility;
- pursue aggravation, acceleration, or increased severity rather than complete prevention;
- obtain additional records or expert review;
- be positioned for resolution;
- be defended;
- or be discontinued.

Appendix B

Preliminary Medical-Malpractice Case Assessment

This abbreviated assessment may be used at intake or during early case development.

The Patient

Who was the patient before the event?

What was the patient able to do independently?

What chronic conditions, symptoms, or limitations already existed?

What prognosis or treatment course was reasonably expected?

The Disputed Event

What event does the patient or family believe caused the harm?

Are there multiple encounters or decision points that need to be separated?

Was the alleged problem one of diagnosis, treatment, monitoring, communication, follow-up, medication, surgery, transfer, or rescue?

The Outcome

What condition was ultimately diagnosed?

What treatment followed?

What permanent impairment, additional treatment, loss of function, increased care need, death, or lost survival is alleged?

How much of the outcome may have existed before the disputed event?

The Available Evidence

Which records are present?

Which records are missing?

Are original images available?

Do the records show what was ordered, what was administered, what was communicated, and what was acknowledged?

Is the production clinically sufficient to evaluate the claim?

The Preliminary Standard-of-Care Question

What professional decision or process appears to matter?

What information was available at that time?

What response may have been required?

Was there a judgment call, an incomplete task, or a breakdown in workflow?

The Preliminary Causation Question

What treatment or rescue would appropriate care have produced?

Was the patient eligible?

How quickly could the intervention realistically have occurred?

What benefit remained probable?

What harm had already occurred?

The Strongest Contrary Explanation

Was the disease already too advanced?

Were the symptoms too nonspecific?

Was the complication unavoidable?

Was treatment contraindicated?

Did the patient decline care?

Would the same outcome probably have occurred despite timely intervention?

The Initial Decision

Does the matter justify additional investigation?

Which records or experts are needed next?

Is preservation action necessary?

Should the theory remain provisional?

Appendix C

Questions for Expert Review

Expert review should be directed toward the actual dispute rather than a broad request for an opinion on the entire record.

Foundation

What materials did you review?

What additional evidence would materially affect your opinion?

Which facts are assumed, disputed, or incomplete?

Clinical Course

What was happening medically?

When did the condition become clinically significant?

When did it become reasonably recognizable?

What findings changed the meaning of the presentation?

Standard of Care

What did reasonable care require at the relevant time?

Was more than one approach reasonable?

What professional role or institutional process controlled the response?

Was the alleged failure one of judgment, execution, monitoring, communication, or follow-up?

Treatment Opportunity

What intervention would have followed appropriate care?

Was the patient eligible?

What timing would have been realistic?

What risks, contraindications, or limitations applied?

Causation

What probably would have happened under appropriate care?

What injury had already occurred?

What injury remained preventable?

Did the alleged departure cause complete injury, increased severity, accelerated decline, lost survival, or additional suffering?

Competing Causes

What other conditions or events materially contributed?

Do those causes defeat the preferred theory, narrow it, or coexist with it?

Which explanation best accounts for the full clinical course?

Opinion Boundaries

Which conclusions fall outside your specialty?

What can the evidence establish with reasonable medical probability?

What remains possible but not probable?

Appendix D

Clinical Intelligence in Relation to Established Patient-Safety and Diagnostic Frameworks

The Clinical Intelligence Model was developed for a purpose different from most established patient-safety and diagnostic frameworks. Those frameworks are generally designed to improve healthcare delivery, classify adverse events, strengthen teamwork, identify system contributors, or support organizational learning. Clinical Intelligence applies many of the same underlying principles to the evaluation of medical-malpractice, wrongful-death, and healthcare-negligence litigation.

Its distinctive function is not merely to identify error or explain how harm occurred. It connects the patient's baseline, available evidence, clinical progression, professional and institutional responsibility, treatment opportunity, probable alternative course, and attributable injury to the decisions counsel must make.

The model should therefore be understood as complementary to established diagnostic-safety, systems-engineering, communication, and incident-analysis frameworks rather than as a substitute for them.

Glossary

Acceleration

A shortening of the time before a decline, complication, or death that probably would have occurred later from an underlying condition.

Additional Injury

The portion of the patient's final harm that is reasonably attributable to the disputed care rather than to the underlying disease or pre-existing condition alone.

Aggravation

A worsening of a condition that existed before the disputed event.

Baseline

The patient's medical condition, function, prognosis, treatment burden, and care needs before the event at issue.

Breach

A failure to meet the applicable standard of care. In this book, breach is analyzed separately from causation.

Causation Mapping

The process of placing the alleged departure within the biological course and identifying what difference appropriate care probably would have made.

Clinical Detectability

The point at which a disease or abnormality could be identified through available testing or evaluation.

Clinical Intelligence

The disciplined interpretation of medical evidence, patient course, professional responsibility, treatment opportunity, causation, and loss for litigation decision-making.

Clinical Timeline

A reconstruction of how the patient's condition evolved, when its significance changed, and when professional obligations and treatment opportunities changed.

Competing Cause

A disease, condition, event, or mechanism that may independently or jointly explain the outcome.

Disease Time

The biological period during which a disease or injury process existed, which may begin before it was clinically recognizable.

Failure to Rescue

A failure to identify and respond adequately to deterioration or complication while meaningful treatment remained available.

Functional Damages

The effect of injury on mobility, cognition, communication, self-care, work, education, relationships, caregiving, independence, and participation in ordinary life.

Increased Severity

Additional harm caused when an injury could not be completely prevented but probably could have been less serious.

Institutional Responsibility

Responsibility arising from organizational systems, staffing, supervision, communication, referral, result management, medication processes, or other operational functions.

Lost Survival

A loss of additional life expectancy or survival opportunity caused by delayed diagnosis, treatment, or rescue.

Material Clinical Interval

The period during which the patient's condition became significant, professional obligations changed, and intervention still offered meaningful benefit.

Objective Evidence

Imaging, laboratory data, pathology, monitoring, medication records, operative findings, device information, physical measurements, and other evidence that anchors the clinical course.

Patient-Specific Standard of Care

The reasonable professional obligation arising from the patient's presentation, risks, setting, available information, professional role, and available resources.

Professional Recognizability

The point at which the available information reasonably required a professional to identify, investigate, or respond to a clinical concern.

Record Integrity

The completeness, reliability, timing, source, and meaning of the evidence used to evaluate the case.

Treatment Opportunity

The realistic intervention, rescue, or clinical response that remained available at the time of the alleged departure.

Wrongful Death

A legal claim arising from a death alleged to have been caused by wrongful conduct. The medical analysis may involve complete prevention, accelerated death, or lost survival, depending on the evidence and applicable law.

About the Author

Michelle Carroll

Michelle Carroll is the founder of Lexcura Summit and the developer of a clinically disciplined approach to evaluating medical-malpractice, wrongful-death, and healthcare-negligence matters.

Her work focuses on helping attorneys understand complex medical records, reconstruct the patient's clinical course, identify meaningful treatment opportunities, distinguish professional departure from causal injury, and align damages with the medical evidence.

Through Lexcura Summit, she works at the intersection of medicine, litigation strategy, and case development. Her approach emphasizes patient-specific analysis, objective evidence, realistic alternative courses, and balanced consideration of both supporting and competing medical explanations.

Clinical Intelligence in Medical Malpractice reflects that work. It is designed to help counsel move beyond record volume and retrospective criticism toward a clearer understanding of what happened, what reasonable care required, and what difference another course probably would have made.

About Lexcura Summit

Lexcura Summit is a clinical strategy and medical-legal consulting firm based in Gainesville, Florida.

The firm supports attorneys handling medical-malpractice, wrongful-death, healthcare-negligence, and complex injury matters by helping them interpret medical evidence, reconstruct clinically meaningful timelines, examine professional and institutional responsibility, evaluate causation, and define the injury the evidence can support.

Lexcura Summit's work is grounded in a central principle: effective advocacy begins with an accurate understanding of the medicine.

The firm's clinical intelligence approach is designed to assist counsel with case assessment, record analysis, expert strategy, discovery preparation, deposition planning, damages alignment, mediation, trial preparation, and defense evaluation.

For professional inquiries:

Lexcura Summit
Gainesville, Florida
Website: www.lexcurasummit.com
Email: contact@lexcurasummit.com
Telephone: 352-703-0703

Professional Use and Training

The Clinical Intelligence framework may also be used in law-firm training, case-review conferences, litigation-team development, expert preparation, and continuing professional education.

For information regarding consulting, speaking, workshops, or training programs, contact:

Lexcura Summit
Website: www.lexcurasummit.com
Email: contact@lexcurasummit.com

References

Diagnostic reasoning and diagnostic error

National Academies of Sciences, Engineering, and Medicine. *Improving Diagnosis in Health Care*. Washington, DC: National Academies Press; 2015.

Singh H, Graber ML. Improving diagnosis in health care—the next imperative for patient safety. *New England Journal of Medicine*. 2015;373:2493–2495.

Systems analysis and institutional responsibility:

Carayon P, Schoofs Hundt A, Karsh BT, et al. Work system design for patient safety: the SEIPS model. *Quality and Safety in Health Care*. 2006;15(suppl 1):i50–i58.

Carayon P, Wooldridge AR, Hoonakker P, et al. SEIPS 3.0: human-centered design of the patient journey for patient safety. *Applied Ergonomics*. 2020;84:103033.

Patient-safety incident analysis

World Health Organization. *The Conceptual Framework for the International Classification for Patient Safety*. Geneva: WHO; 2010.

World Health Organization. *Patient Safety Incident Reporting and Learning Systems: Technical Report and Guidance*. Geneva: WHO; 2020.

Communication, teamwork, and escalation

Agency for Healthcare Research and Quality. *TeamSTEPPS 3.0*. Rockville, MD: AHRQ.

Post-event investigation and resolution

Agency for Healthcare Research and Quality. *Communication and Optimal Resolution—CANDOR Toolkit*. Rockville, MD: AHRQ; 2016.

Patient and family evidence

Epstein HM, Haskell H, Hemmelgarn C, et al. *The Patient's Role in Diagnostic Safety and Excellence: From Passive Reception Toward Co-Design*. Rockville, MD: Agency for Healthcare Research and Quality; 2024.

How the Clinical Intelligence Model Compares

A comparison of established patient-safety and diagnostic frameworks with the Clinical Intelligence Model

Framework	Primary purpose	Main unit of analysis	Where it overlaps with Clinical Intelligence	What Clinical Intelligence adds
National Academies diagnostic-process framework	Improve diagnosis and reduce diagnostic error	Diagnostic team and diagnostic process	Patient participation, information flow, recognizability, diagnostic timing, system conditions	Converts those concepts into litigation questions involving breach, causation, treatment opportunity, and attributable injury
SEIPS	Understand and improve healthcare work systems	People, tasks, technology, organization, environment	Workflow, staffing, supervision, communication, institutional responsibility	Connects system design to a specific disputed case, defendant roles, discovery, causation, and damages
WHO patient-safety framework	Classify and learn from patient-safety incidents	Incident, contributing factors, outcomes, and corrective action	Event reconstruction, contributing causes, patient outcome, system factors	Adds counterfactual analysis: what reasonable care probably would have changed

Framework	Primary purpose	Main unit of analysis	Where it overlaps with Clinical Intelligence	What Clinical Intelligence adds
TeamSTEPPS	Improve teamwork and communication during care	Healthcare team performance	Escalation, handoffs, role clarity, closed-loop communication, situational awareness	Evaluates whether communication failure became a legally and medically material cause of harm
CANDOR	Respond to unexpected harm and resolve events fairly	Organizational post-event response	Investigation, transparency, patient harm, institutional learning	Focuses on independent litigation evaluation rather than organizational disclosure and resolution
Clinical Intelligence Model	**Evaluate medical-malpractice, wrongful-death, and negligence cases**	**The patient's entire clinical and litigation course**	**Incorporates diagnostic, system, communication, and patient-safety principles**	**Integrates record integrity, baseline, timeline, standard of care, institutional responsibility, alternative treatment course, causation, damages, expert strategy, and attorney decision-making**

www.ingramcontent.com/pod-product-compliance
Lightning Source LLC
LaVergne TN
LVHW072348011026
849160LV00021B/19
* 9 7 9 8 9 5 2 0 9 4 0 6 2 *